Naḥal Mishmar (Wadi Mahras), near the Dead Sea.

THE ISRAEL EXPLORATION SOCIETY

THE INSTITUTE OF ARCHAEOLOGY, THE HEBREW UNIVERSITY OF JERUSALEM

THE DEPARTMENT OF ANTIQUITIES AND MUSEUMS,
MINISTRY OF EDUCATION AND CULTURE

JUDEAN DESERT STUDIES

THE CAVE OF THE TREASURE

THE FINDS FROM THE CAVES IN NAHAL MISHMAR

To Dorothy,
in loving memory

The Cave of the
Treasure in the
cliff-face of Naḥal
Mishmar.

Pessaḥ Bar-Adon

THE CAVE OF THE TREASURE

The Finds from the Caves
in Naḥal Mishmar

The Israel Exploration Society · Jerusalem 1980

THIS VOLUME IS PUBLISHED WITH THE ASSISTANCE OF
RICHARD J. SCHEUER
NEW-YORK, USA

Translated from the Hebrew
by Inna Pommerantz

Printed in Israel

Typesetting by Isratypeset Ltd., Jerusalem

Printed by Central Press, Jerusalem

CONTENTS

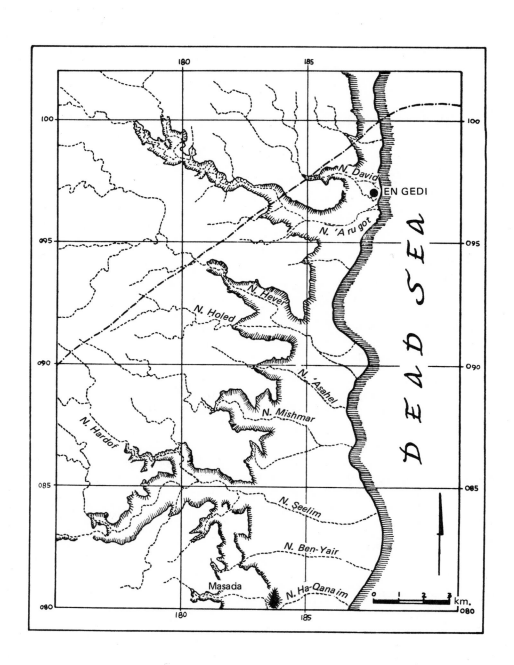

PREFACE

This book deals with the artifacts discovered in the course of the excavations in the caves of Naḥal Mishmar (Wadi Mahras), and particularly with the astonishing finds in one of the caves, which since then has been named after this discovery "The Cave of the Treasure". 429 splendid objects of copper, ivory and haematite, most of them of unique type and of beautiful design and workmanship, were found below the sparse stratum of Bar-Kokhba's time in a natural crevice of the cave wall, wrapped in a reed mat. We had been within inches of missing the treasure, and its discovery was only due to the spirit of co-operation, the devotion and the enthusiasm of all members of the expedition.

The discoveries in the Cave of the Treasure have made an important, even revolutionary contribution to our knowledge of the Chalcolithic period and its civilization. In the fourth millennium B.C.E., man, who had used only stone and flint in prehistoric times, and pottery vessels in the late Neolithic period, first learnt to smelt copper ores, and to make copper objects for his use.

This period is considered to be the dawn of history, when the foundation was laid for the development and rapid progress of civilization from those ancient times until the present day. Since the discovery in the early thirties of Teleilat Ghassul, near the north end of the Dead Sea, archaeological excavations have revealed numerous Chalcolithic sites in many parts of this country and further east. The wealth of interesting finds reflects the high standard of development of this civilization in many fields, such as housing and agriculture, technology and art, religious and ritual symbols, as well as evidence of relations with foreign countries. However, the scarcity of copper objects found on these sites indicates that their manufacture was still in its first stages. No wonder, therefore, that the discovery of our Treasure, with its hundreds of copper artifacts of such an unexpectedly high artistic standard, aroused great surprise. Suddenly, new light was thrown on this period and new horizons were opened for research into the interpretation of this civilization, its ramifications and its influence on the culture of later generations.

Due to the arid climate of the Judean desert, the finds that were preserved in the caves of this region, such as those in Wadi Murabba'at and its vicinity, included, in addition to the usual stone and clay objects, remains of organic materials of the Chalcolithic period. Here, too, a surprise awaited us. The Cave of the Treasure, as well as the neighbouring caves, contained uncarbonized food remains, including some which have not been found before, a straw sieve, straw mats and trays, textiles, some of them coloured, leather objects, wooden tools and a loom with accessories that are unique and have never before been found in archaeological excavations in Israel. The burials found in the caves are of great help in determining the ethnic make-up of the inhabitants, their origin and their affinity with contemporary inhabitants of other countries. In view of the wealth and variety of the finds, it has not been found possible to include them all in this book, and we had to limit ourselves to selected and representative examples. Detailed discussions of several problems which are beyond the scope of an archaeological report, will be published separately. Here they have only been given in a condensed form, in the text, the notes and the summaries.

Special praise and thanks are due to the volunteers from kibbutzim and other settlements in Israel, and to the students, both from Israel and from abroad, whose names are given below, Their work during the three seasons of excavation and the subsequent survey of the caves was characterized by a team-spirit and enthusiasm that greatly contributed to the success of the enterprise. The work was indeed difficult and dangerous: climbing with the aid of ropes and ladders, walking along goat-paths on the edge of sheer precipices, back-breaking excavation in thick clouds of dust and constant danger from falling rock. The soldiers and their officers, in spite of their arduous tasks in connection with security and the camp arrangements, helped us with unflagging enthusiasm, and devoted every spare hour of their time to reconnaissance surveys and work inside the caves.

The success of the enterprise was greatly furthered by the assistance of the late Mr. David Ben-Gurion, at that time Prime Minister and Minister of Defence, General Haim Laskov, then Chief of Staff and General Abraham Yaffe, then O.C. Southern Area, who infected all his subordinates with his enthusiasm. I also wish to thank Mr. H.E. Sossnow and Mr. M. Goldberg (Great Britain), Prof. Mandelbaum, former President of the Jewish Theological Seminary of New York and Mr. M. Marcus (U.S.A.), whose assistance made it possible to continue the surveys and soundings in the Judean Desert caves. I am deeply greateful to Mr. Richard J. Scheuer, whose generous gift made possible the publication of the English version of this book.

The memory of those days in the Judean desert will never fade for those who took part in our excavations, who looked upon the awe-inspiring desert landscape and the magnificent sunrises and sunsets; who saw the streams that gushed forth suddenly from the hills and roared down into the ravine, dozens or hundreds of metres below; who were partners to the excitement gripping us all with every new discovery that lay bare a hidden chapter of our country's history, which had suddenly become tangible; certainly all those who were privileged to be present at that breath-taking moment when we saw the first of the objects in the cache of the treasure, and took part in the outburst of rejoicing when the full measure of the find was revealed.

I am also grateful to all those who helped in preparing this book for publication and especially to Inna Pommerantz, who translated the book from Hebrew into English and who made many valuable editorial suggestions; to J. Aviram, Honorary Secretary of the Israel Exploration Society and Director of the Institute of Archaeology in the Hebrew University, Jerusalem, whose initiative and efforts contributed greatly to the publication of this book; to my friend, S.J. Schweig, for the artistic photographs of the treasure and of other finds; to Ernst Jacob, who prepared the ms. for the press and who is responsible for the attractive appearance of the book; to Hanna Katzenstein, who read some of the proofs; to the photographers who took part in the enterprise at various times: R. Kneller, P. Hirschbein, D. Harris, W. Braun, D. Rubinger, M. Baram, M. Piletzky-Pan, R. Erde, who photographed the caves and their surroundings, Mrs. Helen and Prof. Bieberkraut, Hava Salomon, Tamar Vardi and Y. Nataf, who photographed the finds; to Jean Liger for his drawings of the elaborate artifacts of the treasure and the reconstruction of the loom, and to Doron Bar-Adon for his drawings and cross-sections of the rest of the artifacts; to engineer Y. Bernstein of the "Ort" Vocational School, Jerusalem, who designed an instrument for measuring the thickness of the walls in the hollow standards; to the draughtswomen Piri Yarden, Margalit Eichelberg and Judith Arnold for their excellent drawings of the pottery, the straw and leather objects and other finds; to B. Engelhard, for the drawing of the straw sieve, for the plans and also for his helpfulness; to the geologist C. Key, for surveying the caves and drawing up their plans; to the sculptress Jane Schacherl-Hillman and to Shoshana Yisraeli, who restored the pottery; to D. Shenhav, who was responsible for the conservation treatment; to Antonina Fried and R. Braun and the staff of the Israel Museum Laboratories, for the conservation of the organic materials; to all the scholars whose names are mentioned in the text of the book and to all the scientists who were always ready to help, each one in his field.

I should also like to thank the Ben-Zevi family, the owners of the Central Press and their staff, for their devoted work in printing the book.

THE EXCAVATIONS

The Judean Desert, with its hidden caves and crevices, has always served as a refuge for fugitives, such as David when fleeing from Saul (1 Sam. 24:1 ff.). As the region was of strategic, political and economic significance and was traversed by important roads, many forts and towers were built there during the Judean Monarchy (2 Chron. 26:10; 27:4) and remains of some of these were discovered in the course of archaeological surveys.[1] Later, during the periods of the Second Temple and of Bar-Kokhba, the desert served as hiding place and rallying ground for rebels against Roman rule. It was also a retreat for Essenes and members of similar sects, who sought the silence and the solitude of the desert to commune with their souls and their Maker. Some of the caves contained traces of brief occupation in the Middle Bronze Age II (18th–17th centuries B.C.E.),[2] and again in the Iron Age (Israelite period; ca. 10th and 8th–7th centuries B.C.E.).[3] These must have been left by transient shepherds or wayfarers. Signs of longer occupation have remained only from the late Chalcolithic period.

The proposal to undertake a full-scale exploration of the Judean Desert caves was put forward after the remarkable discoveries made by the late Prof. Y. Aharoni and his expedition in the Naḥal Ṣe'elim caves in January 1960, and his earlier explorations in 1953, 1955 and 1956.[4] The expedition was undertaken jointly by the Hebrew University, Jerusalem, the Israel Exploration Society and the Department of Antiquities and Museums in the Ministry of Education and Culture. At a meeting held under the chairmanship of Prof. Binyamin Mazar, it was decided to explore all the valleys between Masada and 'En-gedi. The whole area was divided into four operational sectors, and each sector was allocated to an independent group. The division was as follows: Sector A – south bank of Naḥal Ṣe'elim and its southern ramifications – group headed by Prof. N. Avigad; Sector B – north bank of Naḥal Ṣe'elim and Naḥal Hardof – Prof. Y. Aharoni; Sector C – Naḥal Mishmar, Naḥal 'Asahel, Naḥal Ḥoled and the south bank of Naḥal Ḥever – the author, P. Bar-Adon; Sector D – north bank of Naḥal Ḥever and Naḥal 'Arugot – Prof. Y. Yadin. The organization of the entire expedition and the co-ordination between the four groups was entrusted to J. Aviram.[5]

Camp C. Living quarters of the expedition.

THE FIRST SEASON

The first season lasted from 23rd March to 6th April, 1960.[6]

At the outset, the group was divided into five reconnaissance parties, and a week was spent in examining dozens of caves, some of which were inaccessible except with the aid of ropes and a paratrooper's harness. In Naḥal 'Asahel and in Naḥal Ḥoled large, deep caves were located, whose floors were covered with blocks of rock-fall. Almost everywhere, we found evidence that the Beduin had already visited and searched the caves. Soundings were carried out in many caves, which revealed sherds of the Roman or Chalcolithic periods, and in some places, sherds of both periods. In some caves were found other traces of human occupation, such as fireplaces, soot-marks on the ceilings, remains of wood, textiles and basketware.

Cave 1. The Cave of the Treasure

After careful consideration we chose for thorough excavation the "Scouts Cave", situated at the first bend of the north bank of Naḥal Mishmar. This cave was later renamed "The Cave of the Treasure" (Cave 1). The choice of this cave was based on a number of reasons: a first check revealed that the cave had not been visited by Beduin, apparently because of the dangerous access. The ceiling was heavily coated with soot, and on the floor, in a layer of bird droppings which had accumulated over many generations, were discovered a fair number of varied finds, including Chalcolithic and Roman potsherds, fragments of glass vessels, bits of textiles, mats, pieces of wood, some of them charred, worked stones, animal bones and a human skull.

Naḥal Mishmar originates in the west, in the wadis of the Hebron hills, and it winds its way to the Dead Sea. The western part of the valley is shallow, while further east there is a sudden drop of about three hundred metres into a steep gorge. The top of the canyon cliff is 270 m above, and its bottom 30 m below sea level.

In the steep cliff face, about 50 m below the top, with a sheer drop of about 250 m below it, lies the opening of a large cave – the Cave of the Treasure. Today it can only be reached with the aid of ropes and a paratrooper's harness, but there is no doubt that in ancient times the approach was easier. A trail still visible on the cliff face, north of the cave, indicates that in the past there had been some kind of narrow track along which a man could pass, but which was partly obliterated in the course of time. Nevertheless, access to the cave must have been difficult even in ancient times, and this increased its value as a place of refuge, since an enemy could not take the cave dwellers by surprise and could only besiege them.[7]

Two springs rise from the rocky cliff face, about 200 m below the cave. Their water collects in a small cistern and in a number of hollows in the wadi bed. However, if these springs indeed flowed during the periods under consideration, they could only have been used when conditions were normal, since many parts of the path were exposed to view. In winter time, as we noticed during our stay, it was possible to draw water from rock-pools in the vicinity, which were filled by rains or by flood waters coming from the west.

The Cave of the Treasure is a natural cave, with a wide entrance, and comprises two halls (A and B), several deep crevices, two low tunnels under the occupation level (3 and 5) and small natural niches (1, 2, 4, 6). The cave measures 14 × 12 m. The aggregate length of the crevices and the low tunnels is 5–6 m, their width varying between 0.5 and 2.0 m, and their height between 0.4 and 2.5 m. The small natural niches measure 1.0–2.0 × 0.5–1.0 m. The height of the cave before excavation was 1.0–3.5 m, and we could only move about by crawling. When we left, the average height was 3–4 m, and we could walk upright almost everywhere. In some parts of the cave the roof was in danger of collapse, and we had to support it with wooden beams. Large fallen rocks, that could not be dynamited inside the cave for fear of causing a further roof collapse, were rolled out over the edge of the sheer cliff into the ravine below by an almost superhuman effort, in order to clear the area for further excavation.

As already mentioned, the whole area, including the crevices, was filled with masses of fallen rock and bird droppings. Extensive lighter patches in the blackened ceiling of Hall A indicate that part of the ceiling had collapsed after the inhabitants had left the cave. On the other hand, the ceiling in the north-west corner of Hall B was intact and sooty all over. In this corner we found a heap of medium-sized rocks, which the cave dwellers had for some reason not thrown out of the cave.

Excavating inside a cave is quite unlike excavating a tell or an open-air site. The excavator's task is hampered by the topographical conditions and by the fallen rock. The work must proceed with utmost caution, and attention must be paid to every change, whether natural or otherwise.

After clearing Hall A from the fallen rocks, some of which still showed traces of the soot which blackened the ceiling, a 5–15 cm thick occupation layer was revealed. Here we found, in addition to vessels dated by comparative material from other sites, fragments of characteristic papyri and ostraca, indicating the identity of the cave dwellers and their time — the period of Bar-Kokhba. Some vessels belong to first century C.E. types and may perhaps be considered as a continuation of this tradition into the second century. This layer also contained glass vessels, metal objects, basketware, remains of clothing and a lock.

Below this layer (I in section) were found portions of a floor of beaten earth mixed with straw (II in section). In Hall B, below a fragmentary upper layer, at a depth of 12–20 cm, parts of a similar floor also came to light. This floor contained a few remains of the Chalcolithic period.

Two hearths were found in the upper layer of Hall A. One, in the northern part, is square (40 × 40 cm), and is enclosed by flat, upright stones (see photo). The other, in the southern part, on the same level as the first, is circular (ca. 1 m in diameter), and made of rough stones, with a partition of smaller stones down the middle (see photo). Both hearths contained ashes, charcoal, cinders, broken cooking-pots of the Bar-Kokhba period, animal bones and charred food remains. Scattered around them were ashes, roots and partially burnt pieces of wood. Traces of fire were found in pits of the upper layer, particularly in Hall B. There were also indications of hearths and fires on the second floor of Hall B.

It was not possible to determine with any degree of certainty which finds belong to the lower floor and which to the upper layer. Apart from the confusion caused by the pits which had been dug for the hearths, the finds could not be related stratigraphically, and we had thus to rely mainly on typology. The same problem also arose when it came to determining the attribution of the finds which came from the layer extending between the lower floor of the Bar-Kokhba period and the Chalcolithic stratum (III in section). This layer, which varies in depth from a few centimeters to 10–15 cm, contained, apart from leather and textile objects, also Roman and Chalcolithic potsherds. Wherever there was the slightest doubt, we preferred to attribute finds to this intermediate layer or to mark them with a question-mark. This explains the relatively large number of finds attributed to this layer.

Three large fallen rocks in Hall A were made use of by later inhabitants of the cave: in one, two hollows were carved — one served as a mortar (diam – 20 cm) and the other for grinding. The other two rocks had only grinding hollows. A small stone mortar and pestle were also found on the upper floor.

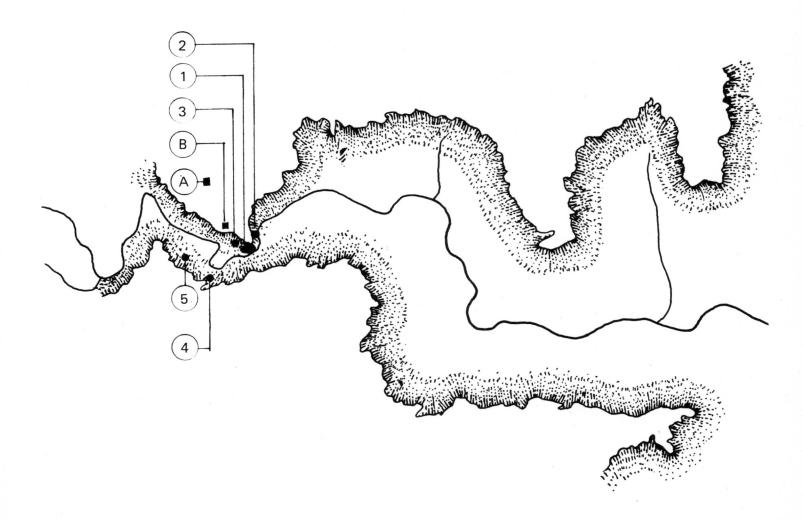

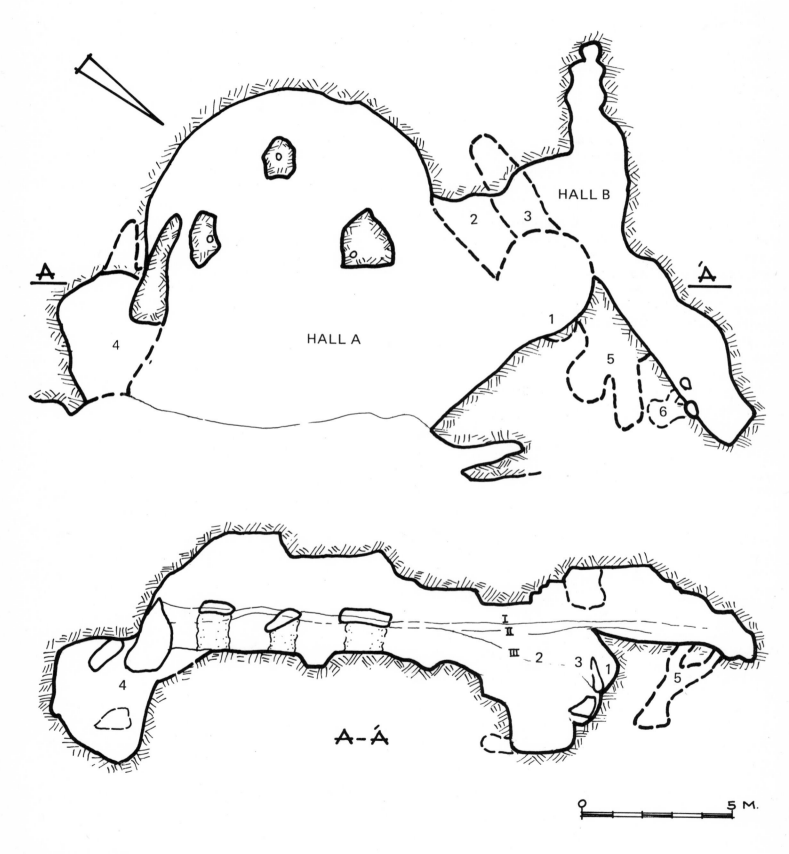

HALL B

HALL A

A–Á

I – Bar-Kokhba
II
III

0   5 M.

Plan and section of Cave 1.
The Strata: I – Bar-Kokhba; II – Intermediate; III – Chalcolithic.

Rectangular and round hearths in Bar-Kokhba stratum.

During the gap of several thousands of years between the Chalcolithic and the Bar-Kokhba periods, an uneven layer of bird droppings of varying thickness accumulated in the cave and protected the lowest stratum (III), with the exception of the places where pits had been dug for the fireplaces, which contained mixed material from both periods.

The lowest stratum was composed of layers of ashes and debris. Hearths and fireplaces were uncovered in this stratum. Some were partly covered with stones, apparently placed there in order to provide reasonably flat surfaces for everyday purposes. This stratum yielded rich finds of the Chalcolithic period, which included a variety of objects made of clay, stone, straw, leather, metal and bone, ornaments, pieces of wood, worked wooden sticks, fragments of fabric, animal bones and various food remains. Particular mention should be made of the hearth uncovered near the south wall of Hall A, ca. 30 cm below the top of stratum III, which contained pottery typical of the Chalcolithic period. Near the hearth were found a straw sieve, a large quantity of grain, a leather sandal and various straw objects. Five human burials were discovered in crevice No. 5 and in Hall B.

Straw sieve and half of pottery jar *in situ* in the Chalcolithic stratum.

Mortar hollowed out in one of the fallen rocks in Cave 1 by inhabitants of the Bar-Kokhba period.

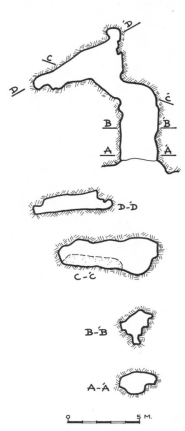

Plan and sections of Cave 2.

Cave 2

Cave 2 is situated in the same cliff face as Cave 1, ca. 15 m to the north-east and on a slightly higher level. The cave is relatively small and has two chambers. The first is 6.5 m long, 1.5–2.5 m wide and 1.5–2.5 m high. The inner chamber, oriented north-south, is 6.5 m long, 3.2–8.8 m wide and 1.6 m high.

Beduin had excavated over the whole area of the cave, and mixed up the pottery sherds. Fortunately they did not dig deep, and six human skeletons were found undisturbed. On some of these were remains of linen or leather clothing, as well as mats. In the southern corner of Room B was found a skeleton with remains of hair on its skull, dessicated skin and tendons on its legs, as well as dessicated portions of internal organs.

Carbon 14 analysis of about 20 gr. of the cloth in which skeleton No. 2 had been wrapped (see p.198), proved conclusively that the people were buried here in the Chalcolithic period. This cave must have served as a place of burial for the inhabitants of the Cave of the Treasure.

Contracted burial of child in Cave 2.

Human skull in Cave 1.

THE SECOND SEASON

The interesting finds discovered in the course of the first season led us to continue the excavation next year, from the 14th to the 29th March, 1961,[8] with the same organizational setup as in the first season.[9] This season, too, we were fortunate in finding a wealth of unique objects, both from the Bar-Kokhba and the Chalcolithic periods. We continued the excavation of the Cave of the Treasure, and we cleared, among others, Cave 3.

Discovery of the Treasure

During the first season and part of the second season, relatively modest finds were discovered in Cave 1. The excavation of the shallow Bar-Kokhba stratum was completed, and work was started in the deep Chalcolithic stratum, which did not at first hold a promise of any exciting discoveries. Nevertheless, I decided to continue the excavation. I had a glimmer of hope that we would be able to find a solution to the enigma — what made Chalcolithic man choose to live in the Judean Desert caves, what was the character of the settlement, when did it begin and what caused its abrupt end.

The evening before the discovery, I had reviewed with the members of the expedition the results of the excavation in our cave so far and the prospects of continuing the work, and they unanimously agreed to carry on. Most of the volunteers, who had originally signed up for half the season only, decided to remain and to work until the end. This proved to be an important decision, as the new batch of volunteers who were supposed to relieve them did not arrive – they had been directed to the other sectors, which offered greater promise of success. Only three turned up to join our group.

The great surprise came on the 21st of March, 1961, at 2 p.m. It was our custom to relieve from time to time those who worked in a cloud of dust inside the cave, by others who were working near its mouth. On that day it fell to the lot of one of the students, Ruth Pecherski, and one of the soldiers, Freddy Halperin, to relieve those working inside. After a short while they came upon a sloping stone covering a crevice (4 on plan). With hands trembling with excitement they started to take out, through a crack, a number of copper objects, all the while muttering breathlessly "there are more"!

In spite of our excitement and curiosity, we had to curb our impatience and to proceed with caution, since before moving the stone we had to widen the excavation carefully and to photograph and register every detail. It was difficult to tear ourselves away from the site. We worked until nightfall, when we were forced to leave and to postpone the removal of the objects until next morning, as it was dangerous to undertake the difficult climb out of the cave in complete darkness. This was a sleepless night for us all. We waited, drawn and tense, for the morning, and the break of dawn found us back in the cave.

It took us three hours to remove all the articles from their hiding place. We stood thrilled and excited at the sight of the growing heap of objects, whose number and quality, strangeness and beauty of design aroused our wonder and admiration.

The manner in which the articles had been wrapped in a mat and hidden, gave the impression that the whole cache constituted a homogeneous collection of articles belonging to one and the same period.

Some of the artifacts could be identified on the evidence of their similarity to objects found in other sites dating from the end of the Chalcolithic and the beginning of the Early Bronze periods. Most of the artifacts, however, were of completely unknown types, which had never been found before, either in this country or elsewhere.

The depth of the Chalcolithic stratum varied in most places between 40 and 110 cm, according to the folds of the natural rock floor and the amount of fallen rock. Only in the western part of the cave, in Hall B, did the thickness of the stratum reach ca. 1.30 m, and next to the north wall it was as much as 2 m, probably as a result of digging the pit in front of the crevice where the treasure was hidden.

There is no doubt that the treasure was hidden towards the end of the occupation of the cave in the Chalcolithic period. At that time, in order to gain access to the crevice, a pit was dug in front of it, starting from the top of the Chalcolithic deposits. Thus a section through these deposits was formed opposite the crevice opening. After carefully clearing the loose stones and debris in the vicinity of the treasure, we found a cooking-stove and a worked stick, both broken in half (Ill. 54:2). One half of the stick was found in the loose debris at the top of the layer, and the other ca. 20 cm below the treasure. The stick must have been broken during the excavation of the pit. The upper part of the cooking-stove was found ca. 40 cm below the surface of the layer, while the lower portion was ca. 30 cm lower, lying on a 20 cm thick layer of earth and twigs.

Near the hearths and at several other spots in the Chalcolithic level, various food remains were found, among them uncarbonized spikelets and grains of wheat and barley, which had been preserved owing to the aridity of this region. This is the first time that uncarbonized ancient cereal remains have been found in this country.

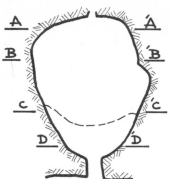

Plan and sections of Cave 3.

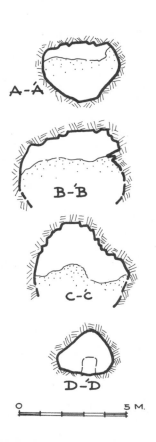

Cave 3

Cave 3 lies about 20 m west of the Cave of the Treasure, in the shallow part of the valley. Its orientation is north–south, and it is entered from the south. The low and narrow entrance measures 1.00 × 0.80 m. The single chamber of the cave measures 6.80 × 5.00 m. In the north wall there is a niche, which has not yet been excavated.

The cave is in a very dangerous condition. The walls and ceiling are full of cracks, and many rocks are poised precariously. Large boulders fallen on the floor have filled the cave almost to the ceiling. After clearing the first stones, we uncovered debris mingled with bird droppings, in which were found a human skull, scattered bones, fragments of a pottery churn (see below, p. 143) and many Chalcolithic sherds. More burials were found under the heaps of rubble in the course of the third excavation season. In all, ten burials were discovered, some in contracted position. Next to skeletons Nos. 6 and 7 were found a characteristic Chalcolithic jar and bowl, indicating a date in the Chalcolithic period for the burials. This dating has been confirmed by Carbon 14 analysis.

Contracted burial of male in Cave 3. Next to the skull, a jar of the Chalcolithic period.

Entrance to Cave 3.

THE THIRD SEASON

About a year later, from the 5th to the 27th March 1962, the author's group continued the work alone,[10] in order to finish the excavation of the caves that we had not been able to clear completely. This season yielded new finds, including additional fragments of objects that had been found during the previous seasons, and remains of organic matter, which enabled us to date the burials in Caves 2 and 3, and to relate them to the Chalcolithic occupation levels of the Cave of the Treasure.

Two more caves, Nos. 4 and 5, were investigated and two structures on the cliff-top were excavated. One belongs to the Roman period (see below, p. 211) and the other to the Chalcolithic period.

Cave 4

Cave 4 is in the nature of a fault in the rock. It measures 3.8 × 2.5–4.0 × 1.3 m. The entrance is fenced with stones, and it was probably used by Beduin shepherds.

In the thin burnt layer were a few sherds of the Iron Age I and II, this being the first time that Iron I remains were found in this region. Up to the present no archaeological evidence of the early Israelite period (Iron I) has been found, either in the vicinity of 'En-gedi or in the other towns of the Judean Desert mentioned in the territory of the tribe of Judah (Joshua 15:61–62). All archaeological excavations carried out so far in the Judean Desert have yielded material from a late stage of the Israelite period (Iron II) only. Special interest attaches, therefore, to the pottery fragments found in Cave 4, which include a bowl with irregular burnish and a cooking-pot with a concave collar rim (see photo p. 10). This easily accessible cave is situated at the bottom of the valley, and probably served as a transient shelter for shepherds.

Some iron objects as well as a few Chalcolithic and Roman sherds were also found. The position of the iron knife and forked object gives no indication of their stratigraphical context with any degree of certainty.

Iron fork.

Iron knife

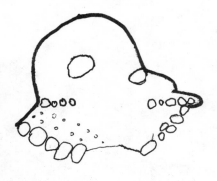

PLAN

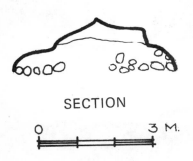

SECTION

0   3 M.

Plan and section of Cave 4.

Entrance to Cave 4.

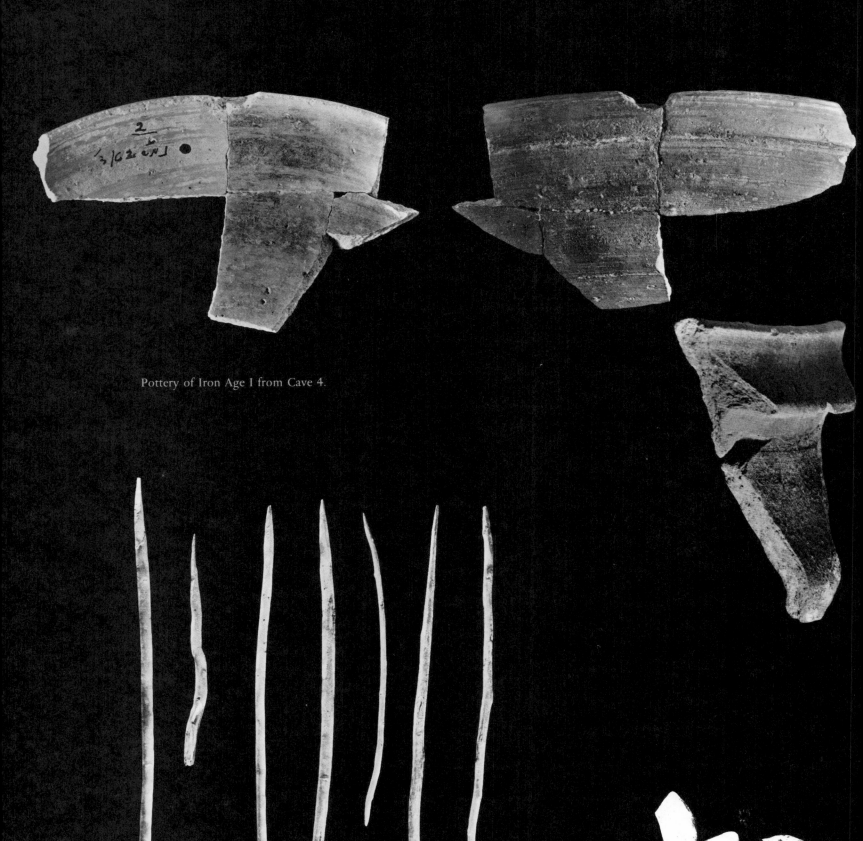

Pottery of Iron Age I from Cave 4.

Pointed sticks from Cave 5.

Bundle of thongs from Cave 5.

Cave 5

Cave 5 is the largest of the Naḥal Mishmar caves. It is 76 m long, and is composed of a narrow passage and four halls, whose height reaches 8–10 m. The halls are connected by passages and tunnels. Each hall has a great number of upper and lower niches and crevices. In Hall I were discovered wooden sticks sharpened at both ends, charred sticks, ashes, charcoal, a rope made of thongs and bound with a leather band, and many animal bones. A roof, or platform, made of wooden beams, was found in the entrance to Hall I.

The blocked entrance and passage indicate that the cave was inhabited in ancient times, but the period could not be established, and further excavation and thorough examination are required.

Entrance to Cave 5.

Platform of wooden beams above the entrance to Hall I in Cave 5.

The Chalcolithic Enclosure

An oval enclosure, oriented north-south, was discovered in 1955 by Aharoni on the cliff-top above Caves 1 and 2, ca. 150 m north-west of the edge of the cliff. The enclosure is 37 m long and 27 m wide at its centre. Our trial excavations yielded Chalcolithic sherds only.

The enclosure wall consists of one row of unhewn stones, some upright and others lying flat. Many stones are scattered on both sides of the wall, and it is difficult to know if they originally formed part of the wall (in the plan the wall is represented schematically as a single row of stones). A small circular enclosure, 1.80 m in diameter, is attached to the outside of the north wall. Another enclosure, semi-circular in shape and measuring 3 × 2.5 m is attached to the east wall. A third enclosure, which, too, is circular and 1.80 m in diameter, is attached to the southern end of the eastern entrance. Opposite this, in the western wall, is another entrance. Both entrances are ca. 4.5 m wide. Two sections of wall cut across the southern end of the enclosure, running in a straight line between the southern side of the two entrances. The east section is 9 m long, and is built of one row of stones, while the west section is 3 m long, about 40–50 cm wide and is built of two rows of stones. Between both wall sections, about 2.5 m from their ends, is a roughly rectangular structure, measuring 4 × 5 m, whose eastern corners are rounded. The walls, which are built of unhewn stones, are ca. 60 cm thick and 80–100 cm high (4–5 courses). The floor, made of beaten earth, is ca. 40 cm below the top of the walls. On the floor were found irregularly placed stones, a row of stones oriented south to north, loose earth and a small quantity of Chalcolithic potsherds. All the sherds are fragments of large vessels made of coarse gritty clay, and similar sherds were found all over the enclosure. In the south-west corner of the building is an opening 80 cm wide. South-east of the building is a row of a few stones. About 4.5 m north of the building was an oval structure, measuring 1.5 × 1.2 m, and in the western and the northern parts of the enclosure were another five small structures, some rectangular and some rounded. In the absence of any other indications, it is difficult to decide whether these were hearths. Five short parallel walls extend into the enclosure from the north wall. The

Chalcolithic enclosure, plan and section.

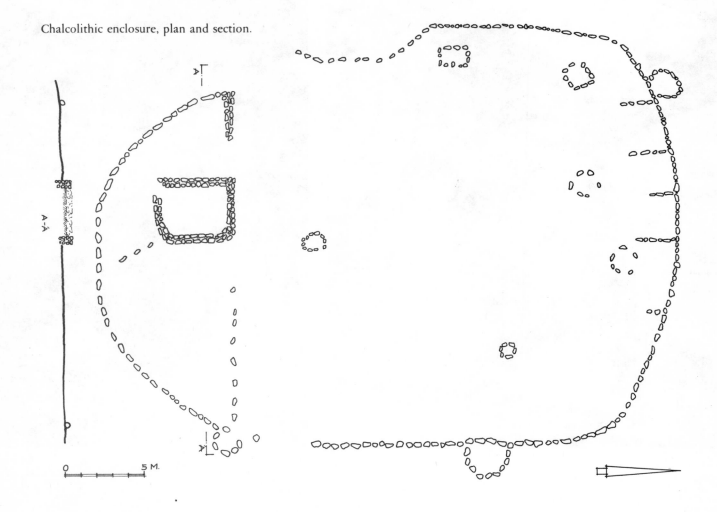

Aerial view of Chalcolithic enclosure.

distance between them is 3–4.5 m, and they may have been partitions forming rooms.

In view of the wide openings of the enclosure, and the structure within it, it cannot have served as a livestock enclosure. I suggest that it was an open-air cult place, which was used by the cave dwellers of this region. This assumption is supported by discoveries made at other sites.

In 1941 Stekelis discovered twelve oval and circular enclosures at Ala-Safat, near Wadi Zerka in Transjordan.[11] This followed the discovery of a similar enclosure at Teleilat Ghassul. All these enclosures, including the one at Ghassul, were located in dolmen fields. The Ghassul enclosure measured 15 × 20 m, while the others ranged between 20 × 30 and 40 × 45 m. The entrances were either single or double and were 4 m wide. Attached to the outer walls were structures, some rounded (2–4 m), others recangular (2 × 3 m) and one trapezoidal. Parallel partitions extended inwards from the walls at intervals of 5–7 m (in one enclosure 12–15 m). Within one of the enclosures was a rectangular structure, measuring 4 × 5 m, similar to that in our enclosure. All the walls were built of unhewn stones, with dry joints. Tumuli in one of the enclosures contained human burials in contracted position. In one of the tombs only a human skull was found. The other enclosures contained only sherds, or sherds and charred bones. Stekelis dates these enclosures to 3200–2850 B.C.E., and suggests that as they were found in dolmen fields, they must be connected with a cult of the dead. No dolmen tombs were discovered in the vicinity of our enclosure, but the caves on the slopes of the valley and in the cliff were used for burial.

THE CHALCOLITHIC PERIOD

THE TREASURE

The top of the stone covering the cache was found at a depth of 1.70 m below the surface of the upper level. The stone was leaning at an angle against the wall, resting on a thin layer of debris which had accumulated above the opening of the niche. The flat, unhewn stone-slab measures 0.90×1.20 m, and is similar to others found in the cave. The niche (No. 4), which is a natural rock-crevice, is situated in the northern wall of Hall B. Deeper near the middle, and narrowing towards the east, it is 1.50–1.80 m long (inside length: 0.70–0.90 m) and 0.70–0.80 m high. The stone which covered the cavity protected the hoard and only a little debris penetrated into the cache.

At the bottom of the niche was a 10–20 cm thick layer of earth and ashes mingled with Chalcolithic sherds and organic matter, including a 1.10 m long wooden stick. It may well be that the niche was deepened at this point to make room for the hoard.

Part of the artifacts were wrapped in a reed mat, measuring 0.80×1.20 m. Those found outside the mat probably fell out when the hoard was placed in the crevice. The artifacts were packed without any order, showing that they were hidden in a hurry. Uppermost in the hoard lay copper standards, plain, grooved and otherwise decorated, basket-shaped vessels and a few mace-heads. Between them the tip of a perforated ivory object was just visible. Below them were a copper pot, sickle-shaped perforated ivory objects, plain and decorated copper "crowns" — and more standards. At the bottom lay an ivory box, mace-heads and standards. Some of the knobs or bosses on the standards and "crowns" were broken, probably before the hoard was hidden. A number of copper tools and the figurine of a human head were also found.

The artifacts of the treasure as found inside a crevice in the north wall of Cave 1. Some are still wrapped in a straw mat.

Ivory Objects

Five sickle-shaped objects were found in the hoard. They are perforated all over, and have a central perforation surrounded by a raised rim. According to Prof. G. Haas, all five are made of hippopotamus ivory. A fragment of a similar object, also of hippopotamus ivory, was found at Beersheba. It measures 5 × 6 cm, and is also perforated (five complete and four broken-off holes), with a central perforation.[1] So far, no other excavations have yielded complete or fragmentary objects of this kind.

The perforations do not follow a definite pattern, but seem to have been made in accordance with the length of the tusks (45.5–57.5 cm). The number of holes is different in each object: No. 1–55 holes; No. 2–47 holes; No. 3–67 holes; No. 4–66 holes; No. 5–73 holes. At the wide end of No. 2 is a small hole, in which a piece of linen thread has been preserved. No. 3 has two small holes near the wide end.

These objects were probably standards, which were carried on wooden poles inserted into the central perforations. The superb quality of these objects surely reflects their importance, but we have no means of knowing their real purpose. Can we infer from their shape that they were ceremonial agricultural implements? Clay sickle-shaped objects have been found in Mesopotamia,[2] and a polished ivory sickle was discovered at Beersheba,[3] but without flint sickle-blades, such as were common in ancient sickles. Were the holes perhaps intended to hold plants or ears of grain? We have no explanation regarding the function of the thread preserved on object No. 2, or the two holes in one of the others. Were they used to attach something, or did the thread serve for suspension? In any case, they were evidently not musical instruments, such as the Mesopotamian harp, since the holes show no sign of wear from strings.

An elongated box of elephant ivory was found together with these five objects.

No. 1 (Reg. No. 61–160)

Object made of hippopotamus tusk. Curved, convex in cross-section, perforated over its entire area. One end is wide (7.3 cm, width at middle – 7.5 cm), with a triangular cavity in cross-section. The other end is pointed. The perforations (1–1.8 cm diam), are arranged in three rows. The central perforation is larger (2 cm diam) and has a rim projecting 0.6 cm from the surface. Near the wide end, and in line with the central row, is a 0.5 cm diam hole.
L (along outer curve) – 55 cm; Th – 2.9 cm; Wt – 800 gr; No. of holes – 55.

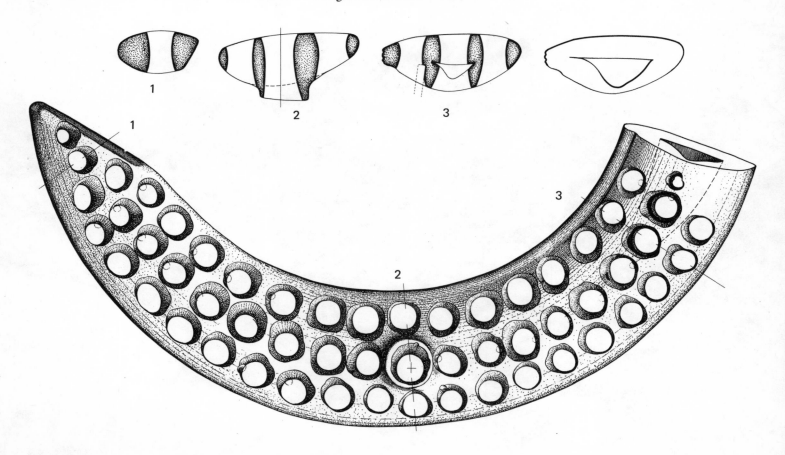

0 |_|_|_|_|_| 5 CM

No. 2 (Reg. No. 61–157)

Object made of hippopotamus tusk. Curved, flat, perforated over its entire area. One end is wide (7.3 cm, width at middle – 7.8 cm). The other end is narrow and truncated (1.8 cm). The perforations (1.6 –1.8 cm diam) are arranged in three rows. The central perforation is larger and has a rim projecting 1.3 cm from the surface. Near the wide end, in line with the outer row of perforations, is a 0.4 cm diam hole, with remains of a twisted linen thread. For about a quarter of its length from the wide end, the tusk has split, damaging its upper face. Traces of drilling and incisions with a sharp instrument are visible in the holes.

l. (along outer curve) – 45.5 cm; Th – 1.8 cm; Wt – 567 gr; No. of holes –47.

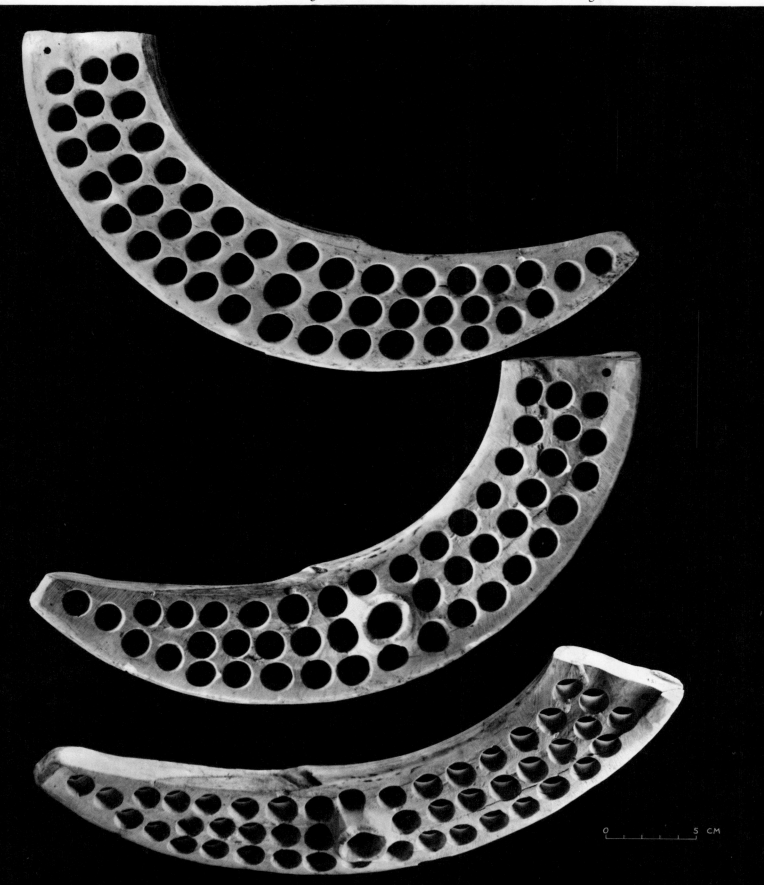

0   5 CM

18

No. 3 (Reg. No. 61–158)

Object made of hippopotamus tusk. Curved, flat, perforated over its entire area. One end is wide (6.8 cm, width at middle – 5.7 cm), the other pointed. The perforations (1.3–1.5 cm diam) are arranged in three rows. The central perforation is larger (1.7 cm diam) and has a rim projecting 0.9 cm from the surface. Near the wide end, above the outer row of perforations, are two holes, 0.4 and 0.5 cm in diameter. For about half of its length from the wide end, the tusk has split, damaging its upper face.

L. (along outer curve) – 57.5 cm; Th – 2.1 cm; Wt – 484 gr; No. of holes – 67.

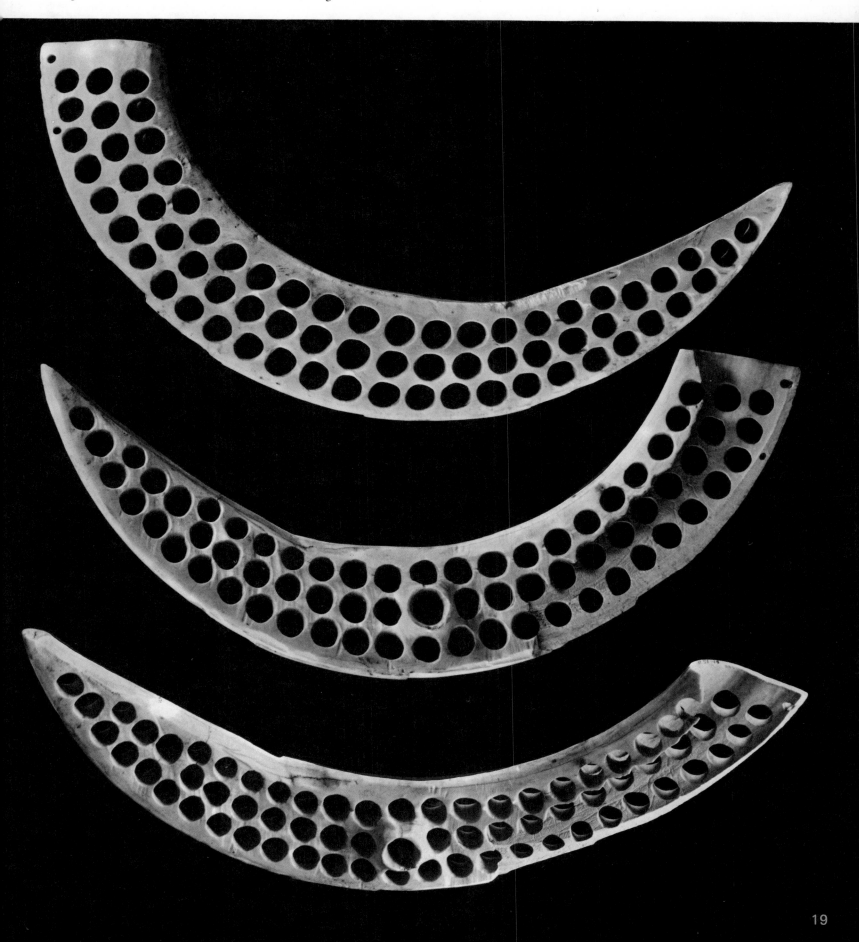

No. 4 (Reg. No. 61–159)

Object made of hippopotamus tusk. Curved, flat, perforated over its entire area. One end is wide (7.5 cm, width at middle – 7.2 cm), the other pointed. The perforations (0.9–1.5 cm diam) are arranged in three rows. The central perforation is larger (1.9 cm) and has a rim projecting 1 cm from the surface. For half of its length from the wide end, the tusk has split, damaging its upper face.

L (along outer curve) – 55 cm; Th – 2.1 cm; Wt – 563 gr; No. of holes – 66.

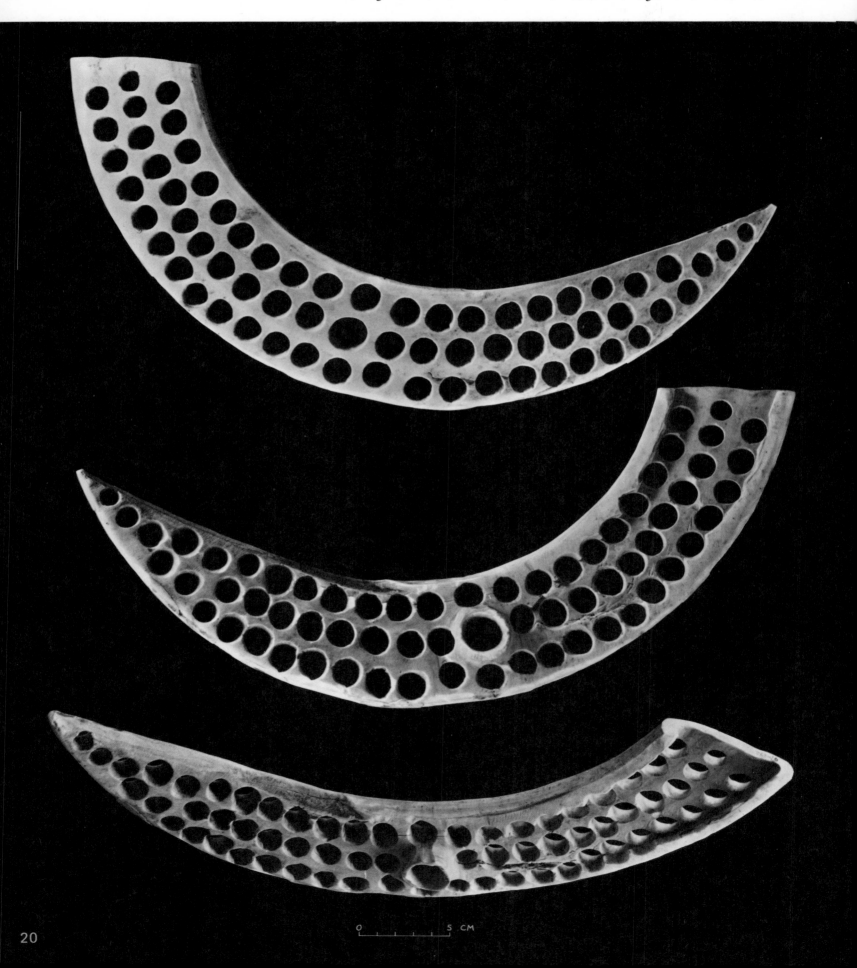

No. 5 (Reg. No. 61–161)
Object made of hippopotamus tusk. Curved, flat, perforated over its entire area. One end is wide (8.2 cm, width at middle – 7.8 cm) and damaged. The other end is narrow and truncated (2.4 cm). The perforations (1.2–1.8 cm diam) are arranged in three rows. The central perforation is larger (2 cm) and has a rim projecting 1.3 cm from the surface. For about a quarter of its length from the wide end, the tusk has split, damaging its upper face. L (along outer curve) – 54 cm; Th – 2.2 cm; Wt – 590 gr; No. of holes – 73.

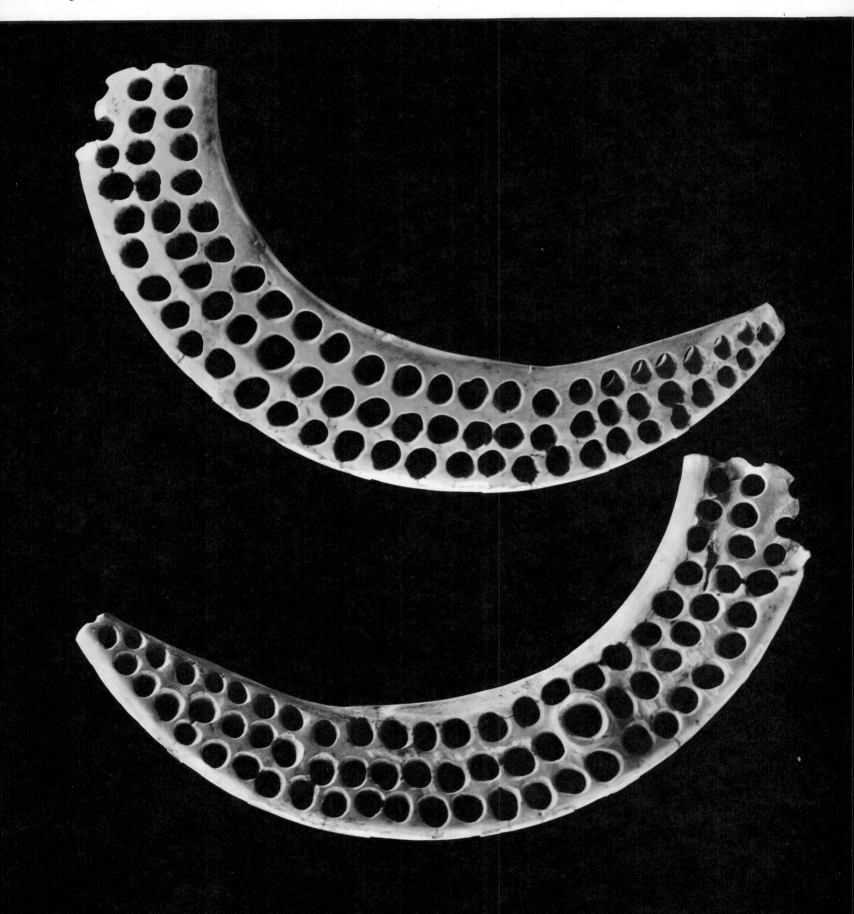

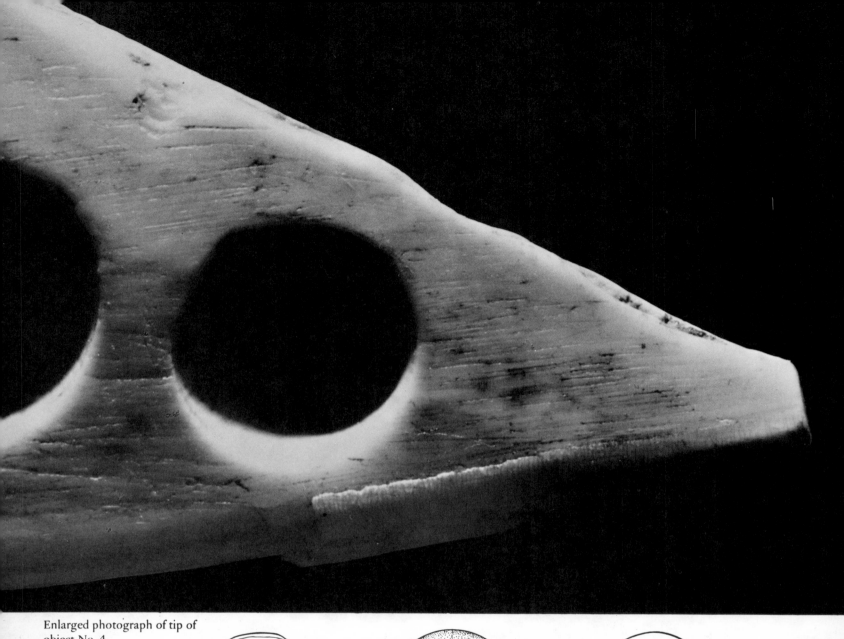

Enlarged photograph of tip of object No. 4.

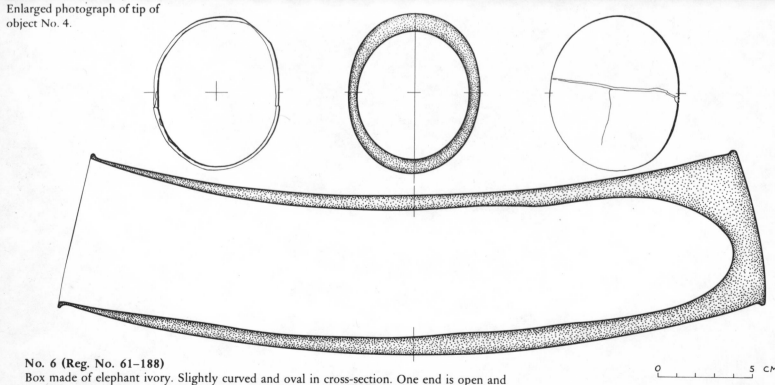

No. 6 (Reg. No. 61–188)
Box made of elephant ivory. Slightly curved and oval in cross-section. One end is open and the other (the base) is solid. The wall thickens gradually from the opening to the base. At both ends the objects terminates in a slight ring-shaped projection.
L – 38.3 cm; axes of oval cross-section – 6.6 and 8.5 cm; Wt – 1150 gr.

0   5 CM

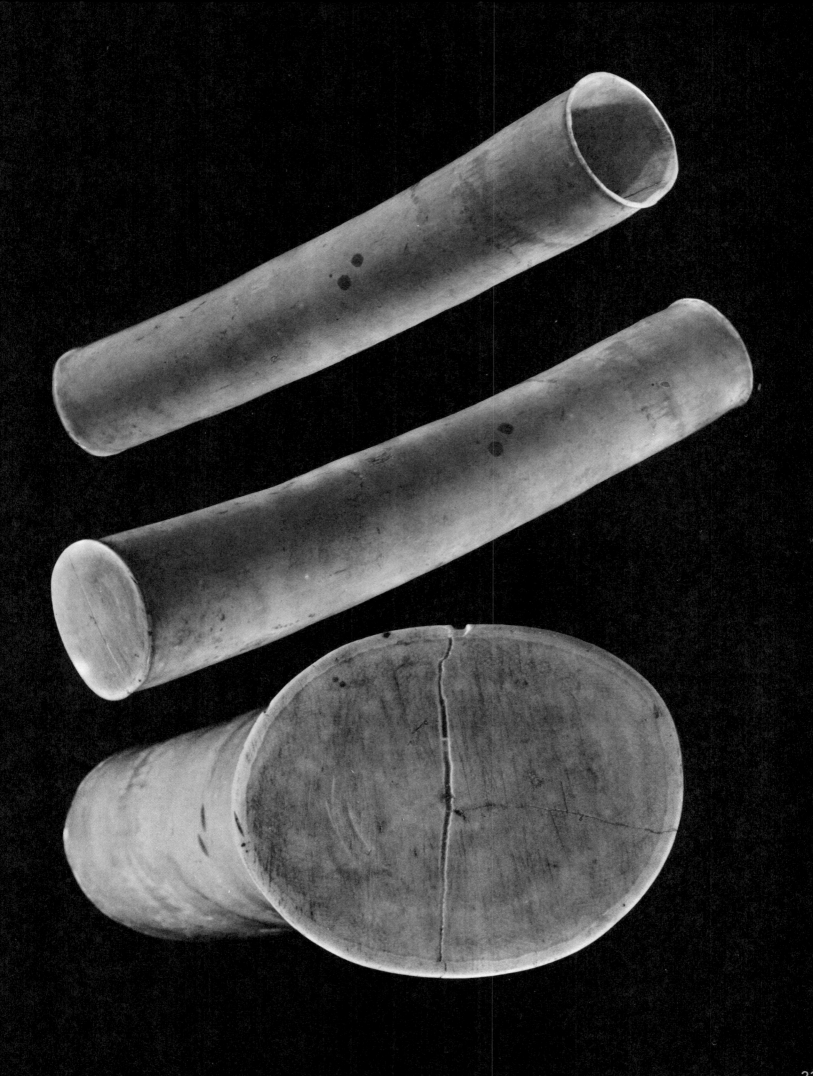

Copper "Crowns"

Ten copper "crowns" were found in the treasure, all generally similar in shape, though differing in decoration, ranging from plain to highly elaborate. We have called them "crowns" for want of a better word, but their purpose remains an enigma.

Almost all the decorative elements on the "crowns" – knobs, bosses, grooves, zigzag lines, stars, animal heads or horns, birds and a schematic human face – appear on the standards and on the other objects forming part of this treasure.

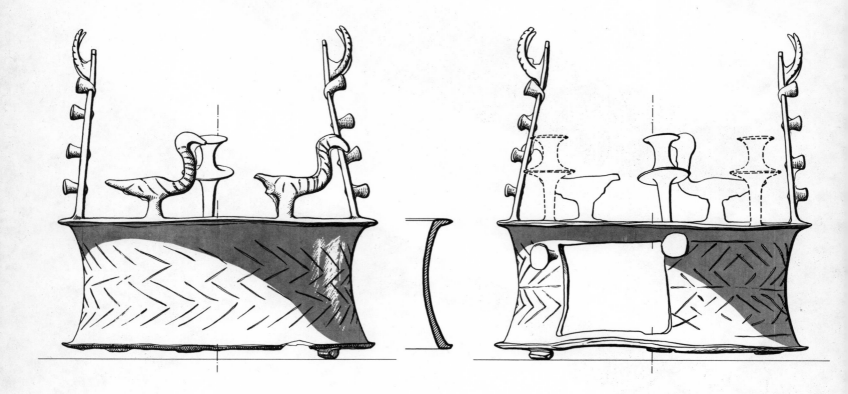

No. 7 (Reg. No. 61–177)

"Crown". Cylindrical. Projecting flattened rims. Standing on the upper rim are plastic decorations. A boss-shaped foot (0.6 cm) is soldered to the lower rim and two perforations in this rim were no doubt intended for attaching similar bosses. The remains of small projections on the lower rim may have been left from the casting process. The walls are slightly concave and contain a square opening (5.5×5.2 cm). Flanking the top corners of this opening are cylindrical bosses with disk-shaped heads. The outer wall of the "crown" is decorated with three discontinuous faint horizontal grooves, and between them are herring-bone designs. To the right of the opening, where the herring-bone patterns meet, the design forms rhombuses. On the upper rim, above the right-hand jamb of the opening and the boss, stands a pillar-shaped object, 5.1 cm high, ending in a small disk, with a larger disk below it. To the right and left of this "pillar" are two broken projections. There was apparently at least one more "pillar" over the left jamb of the opening. Also rising from the upper rim are two 10.5 cm high "gates" placed opposite each other on either side and facing outwards. The "gates" consist of rectangles 7 cm high, which are topped by elongated frontons. The "gate" openings are 5.7 cm high and 2 cm wide. Each of the "gate" uprights is decorated with four small bosses, up to the shoulder of the "gate" frame. From each fronton protrudes a pair of grooved horns. On the upper rim of the "crown" are also two schematically represented birds (4.7 cm high) with elongated necks. The bodies and the necks are decorated with grooves. H (overall) – 17.5 cm; cylindrical body – 7 cm; Diam – 16.8 cm; Th – 0.4–0.5 cm; Wt – 1374 gr.

Details of decoration of crown No. 7.

No. 8 (Reg. No. 61–176)

"Crown". Cylindrical. Flat everted rims. Three horns, which are bent inwards, project from the upper rim. Three small projections (2.3 cm high) are probably the remains of other horns. The side of the "crown" is decorated with two groups of horizontal grooves, one group above the lower rim, and the other below the upper rim. Between them is a grooved herringbone design. There are some holes, apparently due to faults during casting, and four soldered patches.

H – 10.5 cm; Diam – 15.6 cm; Th – 0.4 cm; Wt – 941 gr.

No. 9 (Reg. No. 61–178)

"Crown". Cylindrical. Slightly concave walls. Sharp everted rims. Above the rim rises a bent hook, with a broadened top, and remains of six other projections, whose nature is not clear. On the lower rim are seven small projections, which may be feet or remains of the casting process. The upper and lower parts of the walls are decorated with zigzag grooves. Between them is a band formed by two parallel grooves, which do not quite meet. In the gap thus formed is a seven-pointed star. The band is decorated with six groups of herring-bone designs. Near the upper rim is a representation of a human face, with a prominent nose (7 mm), round eyes and emphasized pupils. On the upper rim, above the face, are the remains of two soldered projections, one of them cylindrical, whose nature is not clear (horns?). H – 9–9.7 cm; Diam – 18 cm; Th – 0.4 cm; Wt – 1295 gr.

No. 10 (Reg. No. 61–175)
"Crown". Cylindrical. Plain, concave walls. Narrow ledge-rims. Projecting from the top rim are two 2.5 cm high schematic horned animal heads (ibexes?). Three holes (casting defects?) and soldered patches on the inside.
H – 9 cm; Diam – 17.3 cm; Th – 0.5 cm; Wt – 1285 gr.

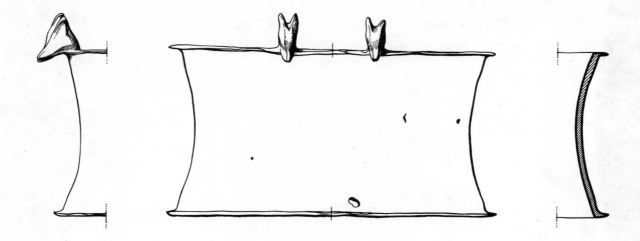

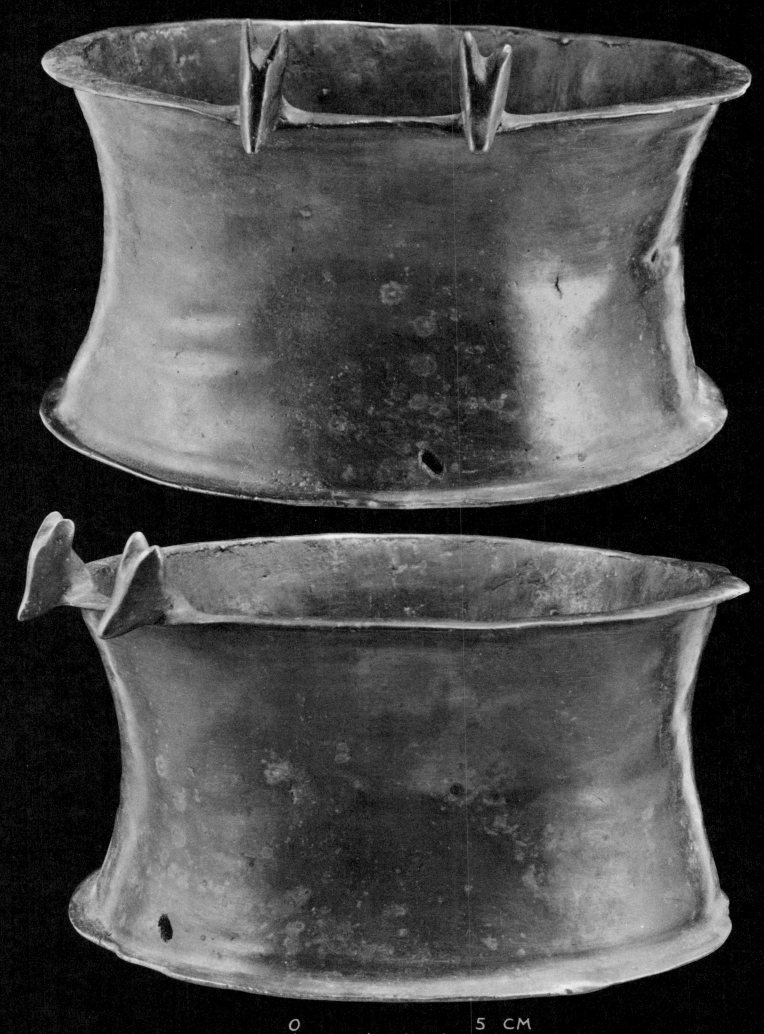

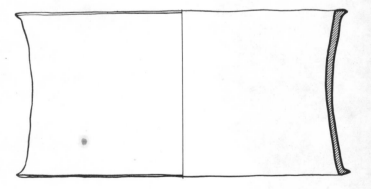

No. 11 (Reg. No. 61–171)
"Crown". Cylindrical. Plain, slightly concave walls. Everted rims. Seven holes in the side,
probably casting defects. Another hole may have been made intentionally.
H – 9.1 cm; Diam – 17.2–17.7 cm; Th – 0.4 cm; Wt – 1312 gr.

No. 12 (Reg. No. 61–174)
"Crown". Cylindrical. Slightly concave walls. Flattened everted rims. The side is decorated
with seven horizontal rows of herring-bone patterns. Soldered repairs.
H – 10.8–11.7 cm; Diam – 19 cm; Th – 0.4 cm; Wt – 1971 gr.

No. 13 (Reg. No. 61–172)

"Crown". Cylindrical. Plain, concave walls. Sharp rims. On the inside of one of the rims are four equally spaced projections, which may have been left from the casting process. The copper has a reddish tint.

H – 8.5 cm; Diam – 15.7 cm; Th – 0.3–0.4 cm; Wt – 928 gr.

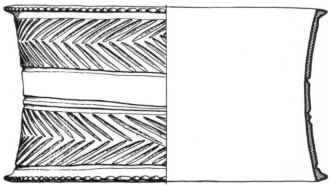

No. 14 (Reg. No. 61–173)
"Crown". Cylindrical. Slightly concave walls. Flattened scalloped rims. The side is decorated
with two horizontal bands of herring-bone pattern between horizontal grooves, separated by
a plain 2 cm wide horizontal band. Holes, probably due to casting defects.
H – 9.1 cm; Diam – 17.3 cm; Th – 0.4 cm; Wt – 1112 gr.

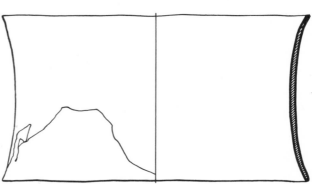

No. 15 (Reg. No. 61–170)
"Crown". Cylindrical. Plain, slightly concave walls. Sharp rims. Two soldered repair patches
in one rim.
H – 9 cm; Diam – 16.3 cm; Th – 0.3–0.4 cm; Wt – 997 gr.

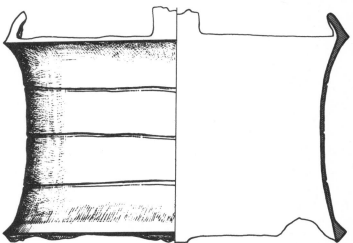

No. 16 (Reg. No. 61–179)

"Crown". Cylindrical. Slightly concave walls. Flattened everted rims. On the upper rim there are remains of four strap-like projections bent inwards (height – 1.5–2.0 cm, width – 2.2, 2.6, 2.5, 2.9 cm). On the lower rim are four knobs, which may be feet or remains of the casting process. A flaw in the edge of the lower rim may be a casting defect. The walls are ringed by three horizontal grooves.

H – 11 cm; Diam – 18.4–19.1 cm; Th – 0.4–0.5 cm; Wt – 1556 gr.

Copper Standards

Of the numerous copper standards found in the treasure, no two are equal in size or identical in decoration. Most of them are hollow, some are partly solid, and only a few are solid throughout, probably due to a fault in the casting process. Though the standards are similar in general appearance, they differ in decoration and in other particulars. The designs – herringbone, zigzag, diagonal, interlacing and crisscross ridges and grooves, knobs, bosses, spiralling or horizontal ridges, appear in almost endless combinations, without ever repeating exactly the same composition. Most of the standards consist of a shaft and a bulbous, globular or piriform part, resembling a mace-head and usually placed near the top of the shaft. In the following catalogue this part of the standard is termed the "head". Unless otherwise indicated, the scale of the objects in the illustrations is 3:5.

Remains of wood were found inside some of the standards. In one of these (No. 115), most of the inner space is filled with what appear to be the remains of a wooden staff. It seems therefore likely that the standards were carried on such staffs, perhaps in processions.

A thin pointed stick was found inside another of the standards (No. 107). A third standard (No. 62) contained a twisted linen thread, which had apparently served to attach a light object. Patches of black incrustation are found on some of the standards, both inside and outside.

The upper portion of a hollow copper standard, similar to our No. 107, was found in the excavations of Beersheba.[4] A copper standard similar to our No. 115 was found in stratum IX at Tepe Gawra.[5]

Enlarged photographs of standards containing remains of wood (Nos. 107, 115), a thread (No. 62) and a copper plug (No. 71).

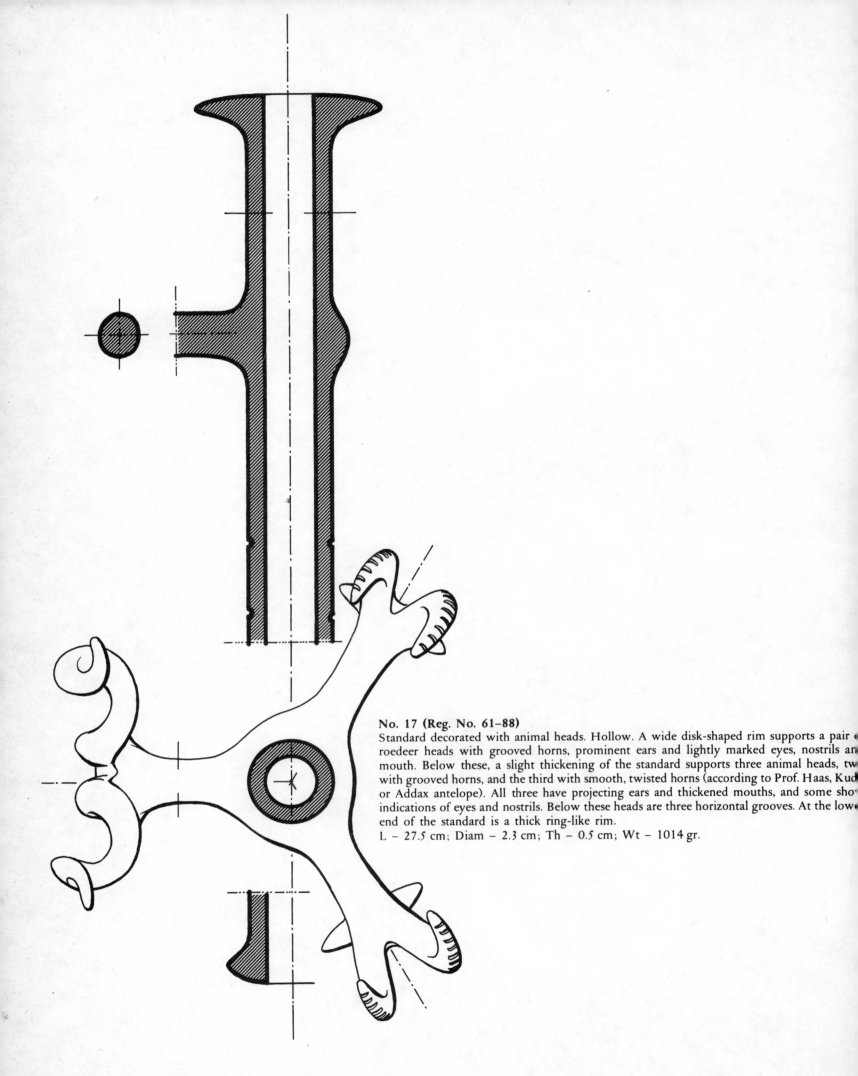

No. 17 (Reg. No. 61–88)
Standard decorated with animal heads. Hollow. A wide disk-shaped rim supports a pair of roedeer heads with grooved horns, prominent ears and lightly marked eyes, nostrils and mouth. Below these, a slight thickening of the standard supports three animal heads, two with grooved horns, and the third with smooth, twisted horns (according to Prof. Haas, Kudu or Addax antelope). All three have projecting ears and thickened mouths, and some show indications of eyes and nostrils. Below these heads are three horizontal grooves. At the lower end of the standard is a thick ring-like rim.
L – 27.5 cm; Diam – 2.3 cm; Th – 0.5 cm; Wt – 1014 gr.

Four views of standard No. 17.

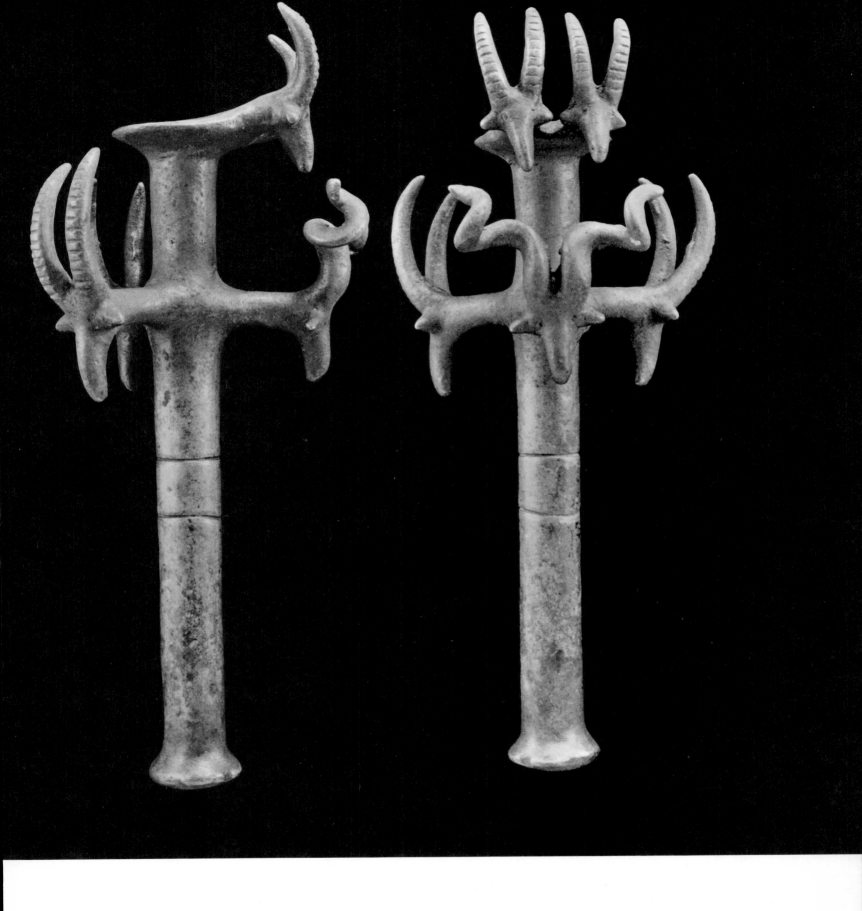

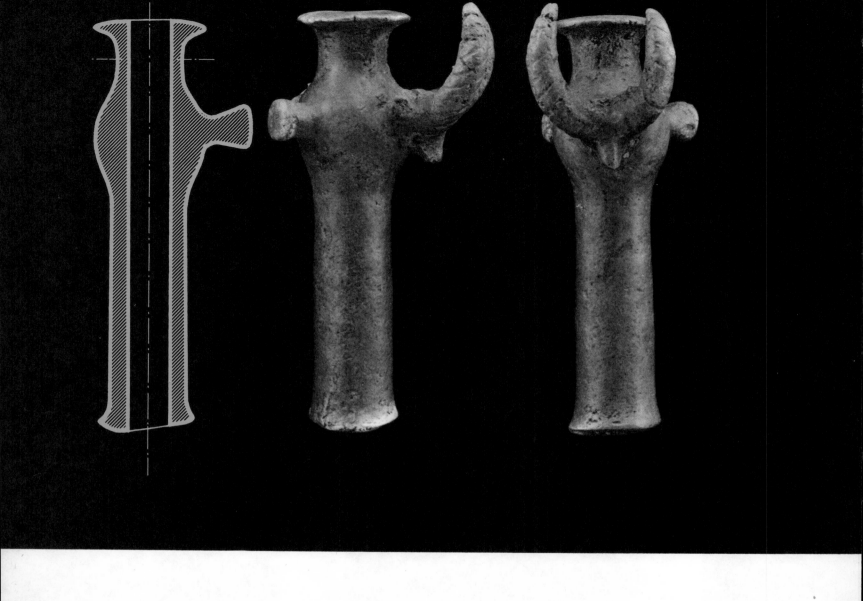

No. 18 (Reg. No. 61-85)
Standard decorated with animal head. Hollow. Disk-shaped upper rim. The horned animal head projects from one side of a slight thickening of the shaft. It has spirally grooved horns, a small head, and some indications of eyes and mouth. Opposite the animal head are two cylindrical bosses widening towards the end.
L – 11 cm; Diam – 2 cm; Th – 0.5 cm; Wt – 225 gr.

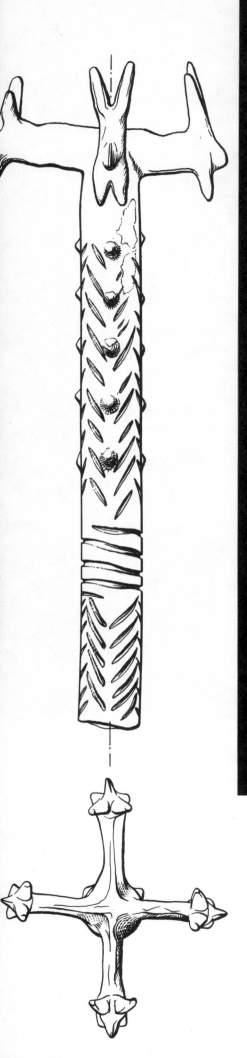

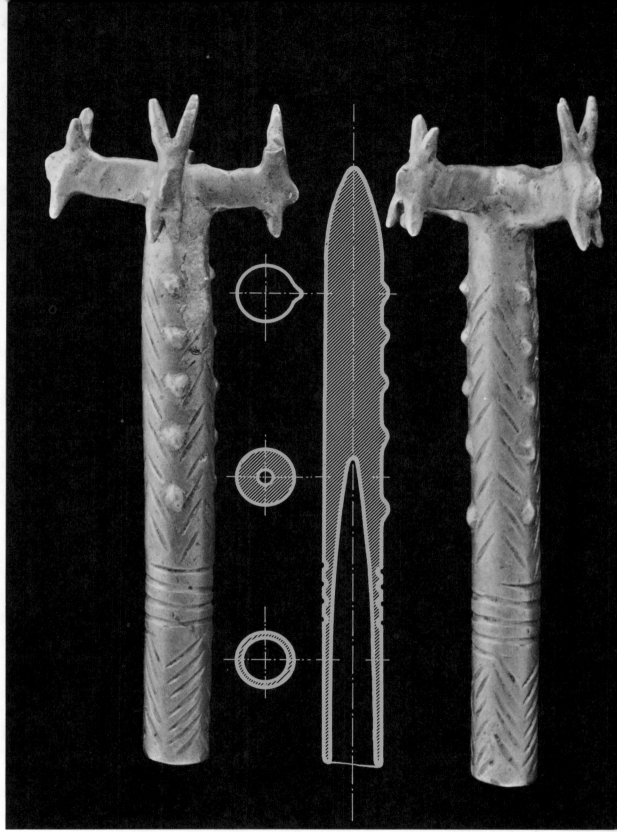

No. 19 (Reg. No. 61–86)
Standard decorated with animal heads. The upper part is solid, with a conical top. The lower part is hollow. The standard terminates in four intersecting animal heads with straight horns (some of which are broken), prominent noses and forked beards. The shaft is ornamented with grooved herring-bone designs, interrupted by horizontal grooves. Above them, between the herring-bone patterns, are three vertical rows of knobs, five in each row.
L – 18.2 cm; Diam – 1.8 cm; Th – 0.3 cm; Wt – 249 gr.

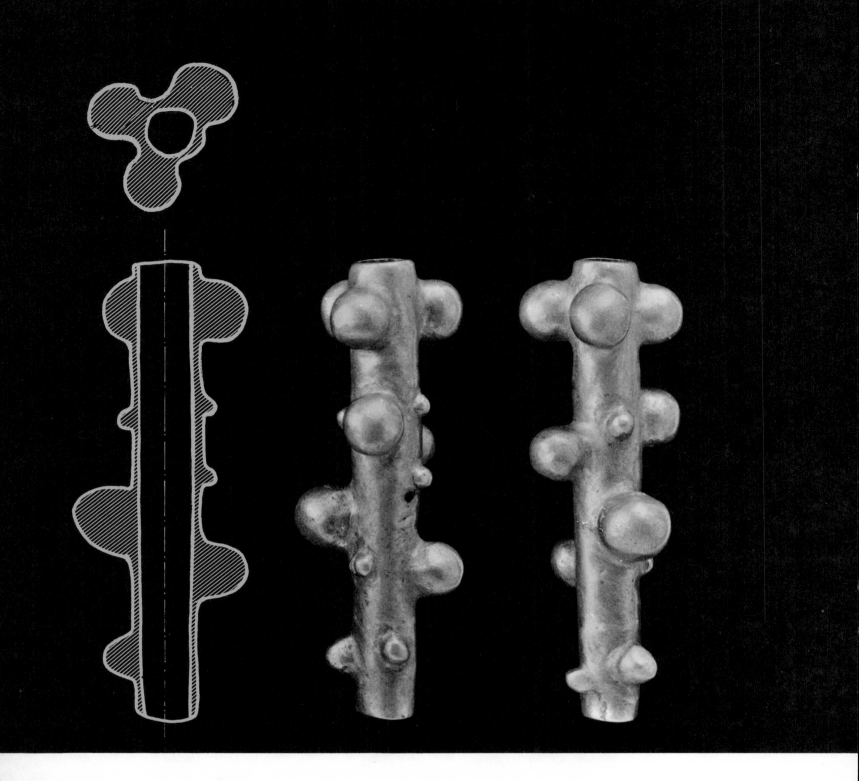

No. 20 (Reg. No. 61–89)
Figurine-standard. Hollow. Decorated with asymetrically placed bubble-shaped projections of various sizes.
L – 12.1 cm; Diam – 1.7 cm; Th – 0.2–0.3 cm; W – 237 gr.

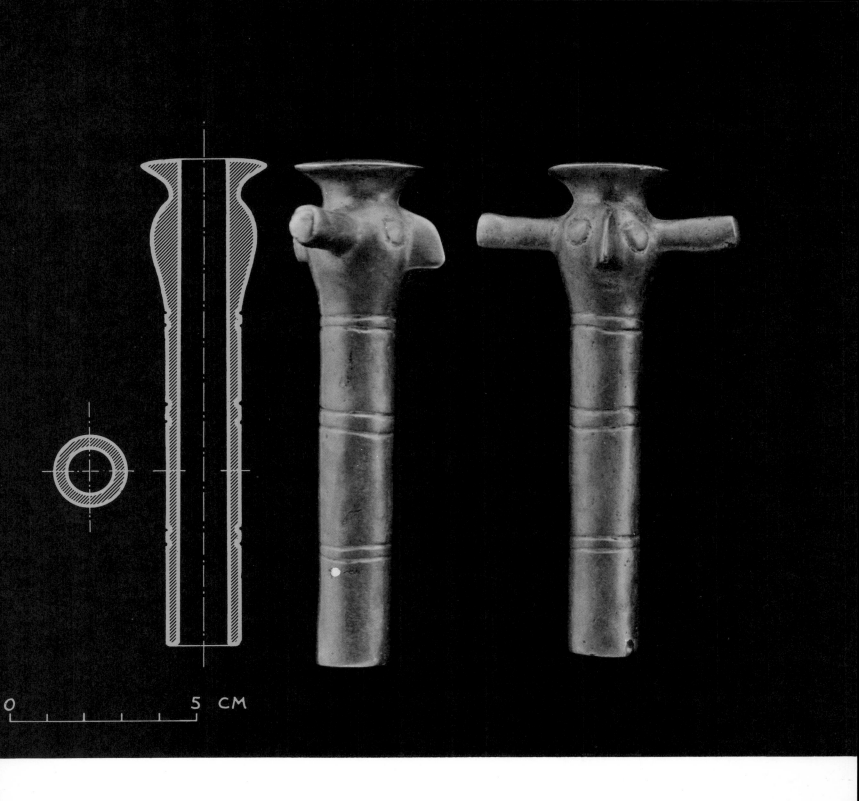

No. 21 (Reg. No. 61–84)
Figurine-standard. Hollow. Below the disk-shaped rim the shaft swells into a bulbous human
head, with large round eyes, prominent aquiline nose and a suggestion of a mouth. On both
sides of the head project two elongated bosses (2.3 cm), and remains of a third project from
the back of the head. The shaft has three pairs of horizontal grooves.
L – 13.2 cm; Diam – 1.9 cm; Th – 0.3 cm; Wt – 268 gr.

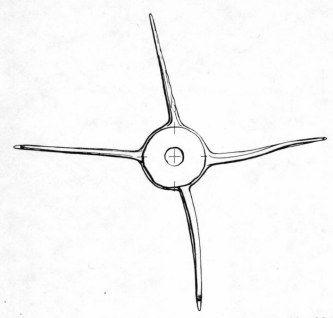

No. 22 (Reg. No. 61–87) Decorated standard. Flattened upper rim and ring-like lower rim. Four flat hooked arms with splayed ends project from the globular part of the standard. L – 22.5 cm; Diam – 1.9 cm; Th – 0.4 cm; Wt – 476 gr.

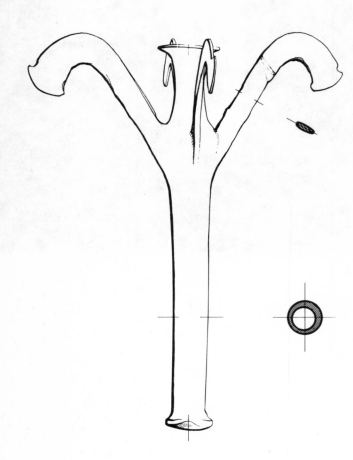

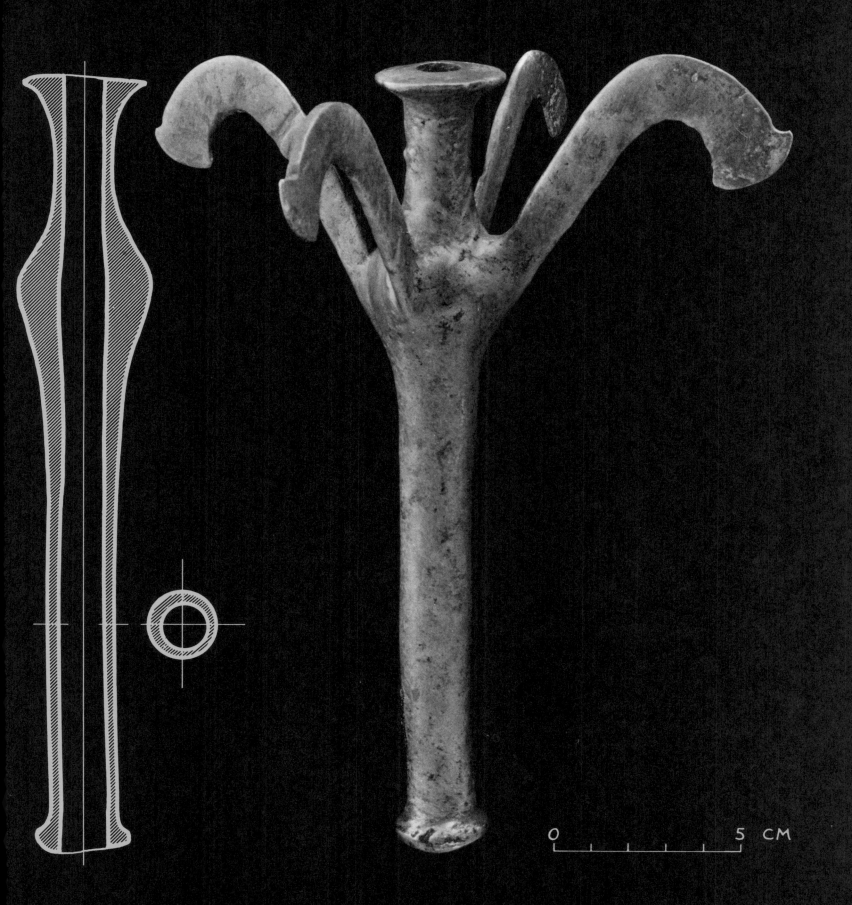

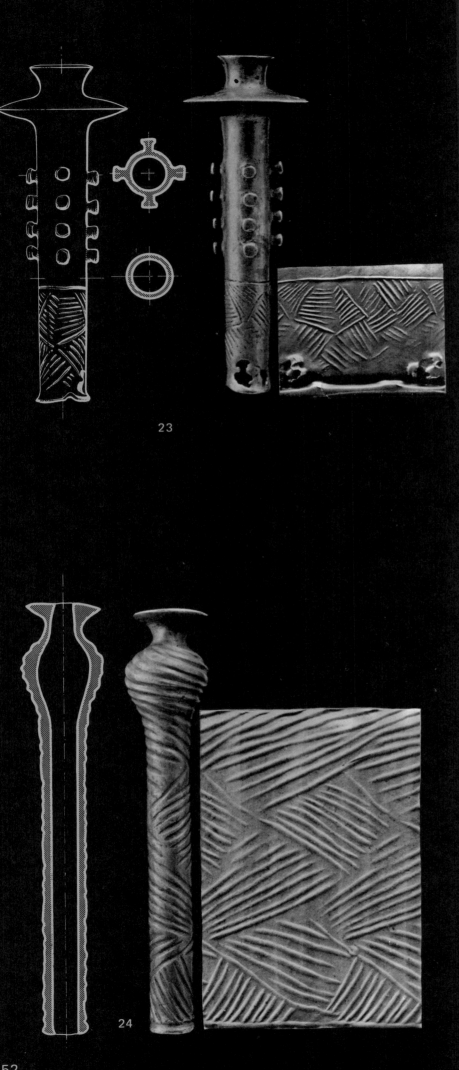

23

24

No. 23 (Reg. No. 61–103)
Standard. Hollow. Disk-shaped upper rim and below it a larger disk-shaped projection. Ring-shaped lower rim (damaged), and above it, some holes. The shaft is decorated with four vertical rows of cylindrical knobs, a horizontal groove and an irregular grooved weave-design.
L – 15.2 cm; Diam – 2.2 cm; Th – 0.2 cm; Wt – 350 gr.

No. 24 (Reg. No. 61–54)
Standard. Hollow. Disk-shaped upper rim and ring-shaped lower rim. Spherical, spirally grooved head. The shaft is grooved in an irregular weave-design.
L – 19.2 cm; Diam – 2 cm; Th – 0.4 cm; Wt – 389 gr.

No. 25 (Reg. No. 61–78)
Standard. Hollow. Disk-shaped upper rim and small dis[k]-shaped lower rim. Spherical head, from which spring eig[ht] bosses, four above and four below. The bosses end [in] double disks, the outer disk being smaller than the inn[er]. Some of the bosses are damaged. The shaft is decorat[ed] with an irregular grooved weave-design.
L – 26.1 cm; Diam – 1.7 cm; Th – 0.3 cm; Wt – 325 g[r]

No. 26 (Reg. No. 61–91)
Standard. Hollow. Slightly tapering. Ring-shaped rim. [Ir]regular spiral grooves, and near the top, two intersectin[g] grooves. Large hole in lower part. Black incrustation.
L – 15.5 cm; Diam – 3.4 cm; Th – 0.3 cm; Wt – 379 g[r]

No. 27 (Reg. No. 61–9)
Standard. Hollow. Disk-shaped upper rim and ring-shap[ed] lower rim. Plain spherical head. On the shaft, three pairs [of] horizontal grooves. Between the upper two pairs, [a] grooved irregular weave-design.
L – 13.3 cm; Diam – 2 cm; Th – 0.4 cm; Wt – 350 g[r]

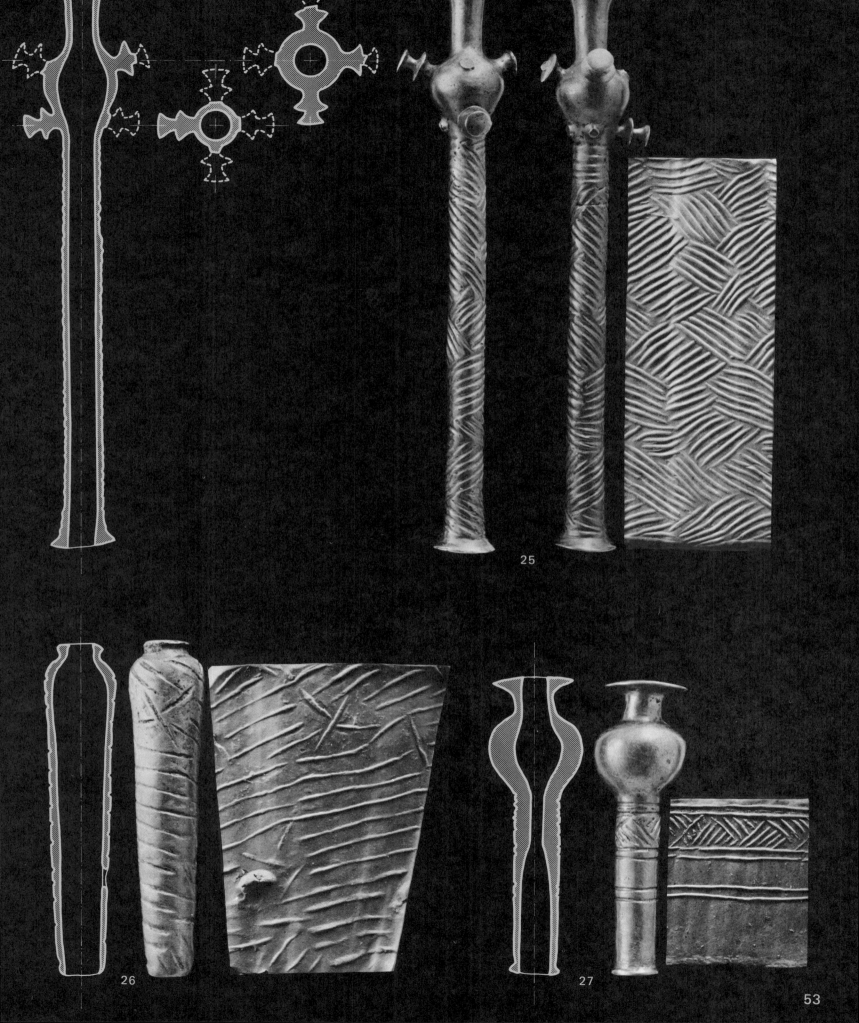

25

26

27

53

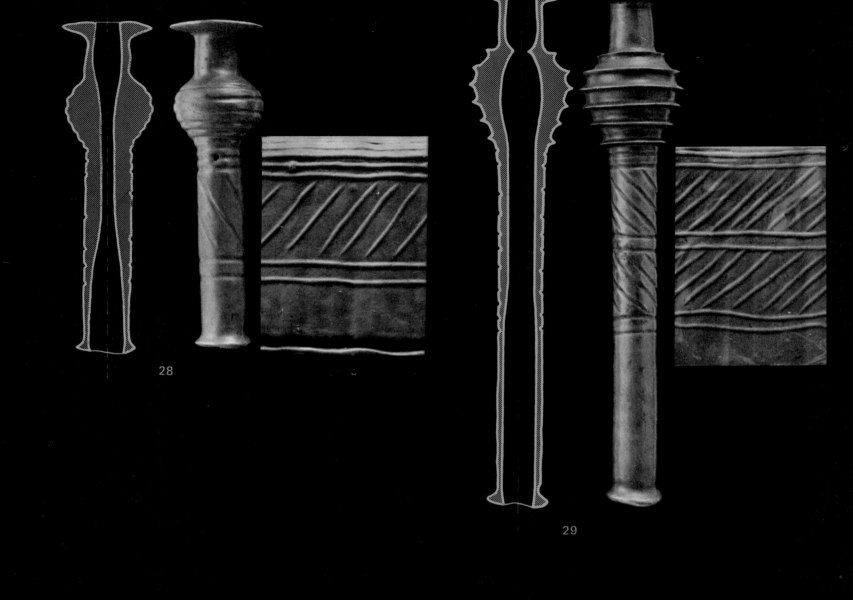

No. 28 (Reg. No. 61–58)
Standard. Hollow. Disk-shaped upper rim and ring-shaped lower rim. Spherical, horizontally grooved head. On the shaft, diagonal grooves between horizontal grooves. Hole in wall of shaft.
L – 14.9 cm; Diam – 2.1 cm; Th – 0.4 cm; Wt – 303 gr.

No. 29 (Reg. No. 61–31)
Standard. Hollow. Disk-shaped upper rim and ring-shaped lower rim. Piriform head ringed with sharp parallel ridges. On the shaft, three pairs of horizontal grooves, with diagonal grooves between them.
L – 23.2 cm; Diam – 2 cm; Th – 0.3 cm; Wt – 476 gr.

No. 30 (Reg. No. 61–71)
Standard. Hollow. Disk-shaped upper rim and ring-shaped lower rim. Upper half of shaft has a raised spiral decoration between disk-shaped projections. The lower half has three groups of horizontal grooves, and between them, two herring-bone designs – one horizontal, the other vertical.
L – 21.3 cm; Diam – 2.4 cm; Th – 0.4 cm; Wt – 518 gr.

No. 31 (Reg. No. 61–42)
Standard. Hollow. Disk-shaped upper rim and ring-shaped lower rim. Piriform head ringed with sharp parallel ridges. On the shaft, three pairs of horizontal grooves. Between them, diagonal grooves in the upper register, and vertical grooved herring-bone patterns in the lower register.
L – 24 cm; Diam – 2.5 cm; Th – 0.4 cm; Wt – 370 gr.

No. 32 (Reg. No. 61–76)

Standard. Hollow. Disk-shaped upper rim and ring-shaped lower rim. Spherical head, from which spring four small cylindrical bosses with disk-shaped heads. The shaft is ringed by two ridges and four grooves, and between them are three vertical grooved herring-bone designs.
L – 17.5 cm; Diam – 1.9 cm; Th – 0.3 cm; Wt – 295 gr.

No. 33 (Reg. No. 61–8)

Standard. Hollow. Disk-shaped upper rim and ring-shaped lower rim. Plain spherical head and below it, two horizontal grooves. On the shaft, three vertical grooved herring-bone designs.
l – 11.2 cm; Diam – 2.3 cm; Th – 0.4 cm; Wt – 252 gr.

No. 34 (Reg. No. 61–55)

Standard. Hollow. Disk-shaped upper rim and ring-shaped lower rim. Sharp ridge below upper rim. Piriform head with diagonal ridges. The shaft is ringed by two grooves, and below them is a vertical herring-bone design.
L – 20.5 cm; Diam – 2 cm; Th – 0.3 cm; Wt – 334 gr.

No. 35 (Reg. No. 61–74)

Standard. Hollow. Disk-shaped upper rim and ring-shaped lower rim. Flattened spherical head, from which spring four cylindrical bosses with disk-shaped heads. The shaft is ringed by five pairs of grooves. In the top and the bottom registers, grooved herring-bone design.
L – 18.5 cm; Diam – 2.1 cm; Th – 0.3 cm; Wt – 473 gr.

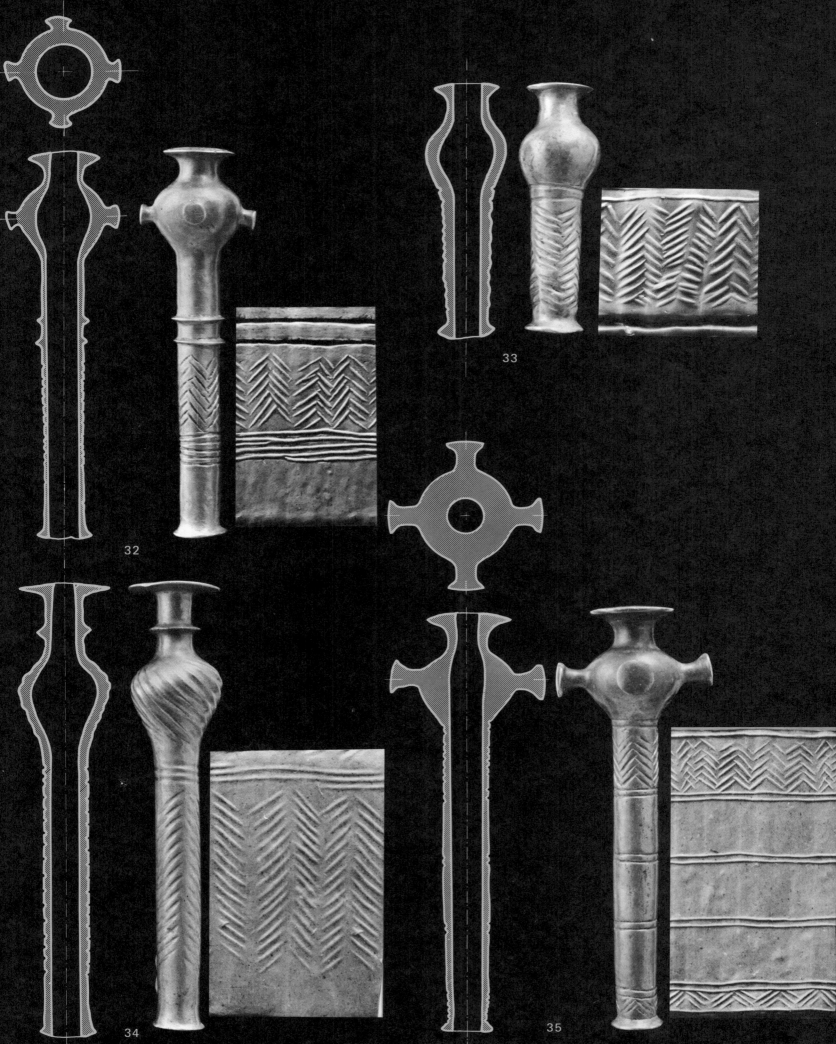

32

33

34

35

No. 36 (Reg. No. 61–7)
Standard. Hollow. Disk-shaped upper rim and ring-shaped lower rim. Plain piriform head and above it, two faint horizontal grooves. The lower part of the shaft has grooved zigzag lines between groups of horizontal grooves.
L – 18.1 cm; Diam – 2.4; Th – 0.3 cm; Wt – 406 gr.

No. 37 (Reg. No. 61–38)
Standard. Hollow. Disk-shaped upper rim and ring-shaped lower rim. Below the upper rim, three grooves and a barrel-shaped head ringed with sharp parallel ridges. On the shaft, two groups of three and two pairs of horizontal grooves. In the upper register, zigzag grooves. Three holes in wall of shaft. Black incrustation inside the shaft.
L – 33.7 cm; Diam – 2.2 cm; Th – 0.4–0.6; Wt – 598 gr.

No. 38 (Reg. No. 61–62)
Standard. Hollow. Disk-shaped upper rim and ring-shaped lower rim. Barrel-shaped head with spiral grooves. The entire shaft is covered with a horizontal grooved zigzag pattern.
L – 18 cm; Diam – 2.7 cm; Th – 0.3 cm; Wt – 318 gr.

37

38

No. 39 (Reg. No. 61–67)
Standard. Hollow. Disk-shaped upper rim and ring-shaped lower rim. Spherical head ringed with parallel ridges. Near the centre of the shaft, biconical swelling with nipple-like knobs. Above and below it, diagonal grooves, and a horizontal groove near lower rim.
L – 20.8 cm; Diam – 1.6 cm; Th – 0.3 cm; Wt – 230 gr.

No. 40 (Reg. No. 61–12)
Standard. Hollow. Disk-shaped upper rim and ring-shaped lower rim. Plain piriform head and below it, three horizontal grooves and a disk-shaped projection. The shaft is ringed by four pairs of grooves, with irregular grooves between them.
L – 20.8 cm; Diam – 1.9 cm; Th – 0.4 cm; Wt – 360 gr.

No. 41 (Reg. No. 61–72)
Standard. Hollow. Disk-shaped upper rim and ring-shaped lower rim. The tubular standard is ringed with horizontal and vertical grooved herring-bone patterns between horizontal grooves.
L – 18.8 cm; Diam – 2 cm; Th – 0.3 cm; Wt – 287 gr.

No. 42 (Reg. No. 61–104)
Standard. Hollow. Small disk-shaped rims at both ends. Flattened spherical head, from which spring six cylindrical bosses with disk-shaped heads. On the shaft, grooved vertical herring-bone designs and two horizontal grooves.
L – 10 cm; Diam – 2.2 cm; Th – 0.4 cm; Wt – 239 gr.

39

40

41

42

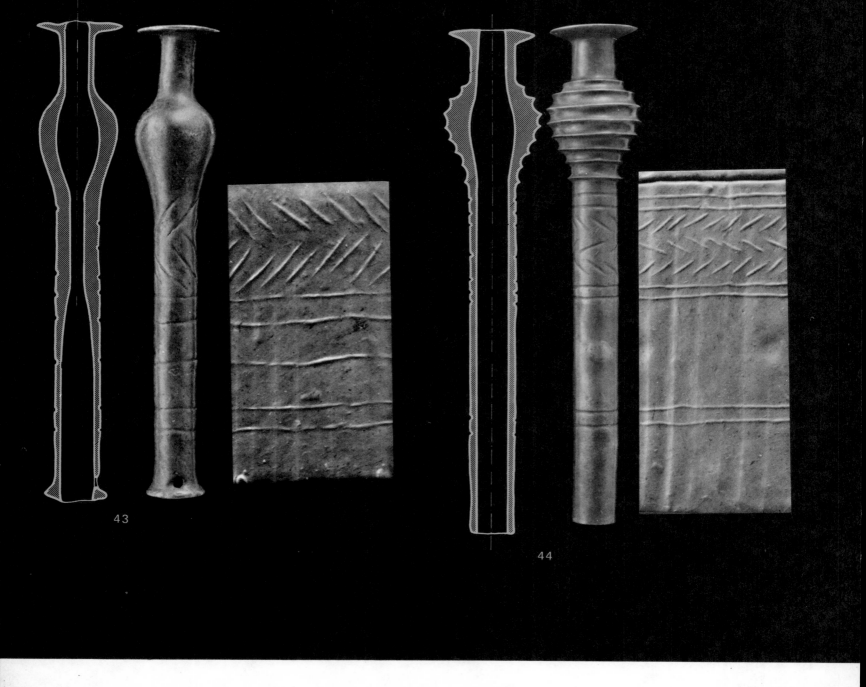

No. 43 (Reg. No. 61–10)
Standard. Hollow. Disk-shaped upper rim and ring-shaped lower rim. Plain, piriform head.
Upper part of shaft has diagonal grooves and below them, five horizontal grooves.
L – 21.8 cm; Diam – 2 cm; Th – 0.2 cm; Wt – 407 gr.

No. 44 (Reg. No. 61–32)
Standard. Hollow. Disk-shaped upper rim. Piriform head ringed with sharp parallel ridges.
On the shaft, three pairs of horizontal grooves. In the upper register, irregular grooved
herring-bone designs. Soldered patch.
L – 22.9 cm; Diam – 2 cm; Th – 0.3 cm; Wt – 375 gr.

No. 45 (Reg. No. 61–49)
Standard. Hollow. Disk-shaped rim. Barrel-shaped head with diagonal ridges. On the shaft, three horizontal grooves, and between them grooved zigzag lines. The lower end is damaged.
L – 27.3 cm; Diam – 2.4 cm; Th – 0.3 cm; Wt – 565 gr.

No. 46 (Reg. No. 61–27)
Standard. Hollow. Disk-shaped upper rim and ring-shaped lower rim. Piriform, spirally ridged head between two disk-shaped projections, the upper larger than the lower. The shaft has two grooves, and below them, a vertical zigzag pattern of short double grooves. Hole in wall of shaft.
L – 17.7 cm; Diam – 1.8 cm; Th – 0.3 cm; Wt – 258 gr.

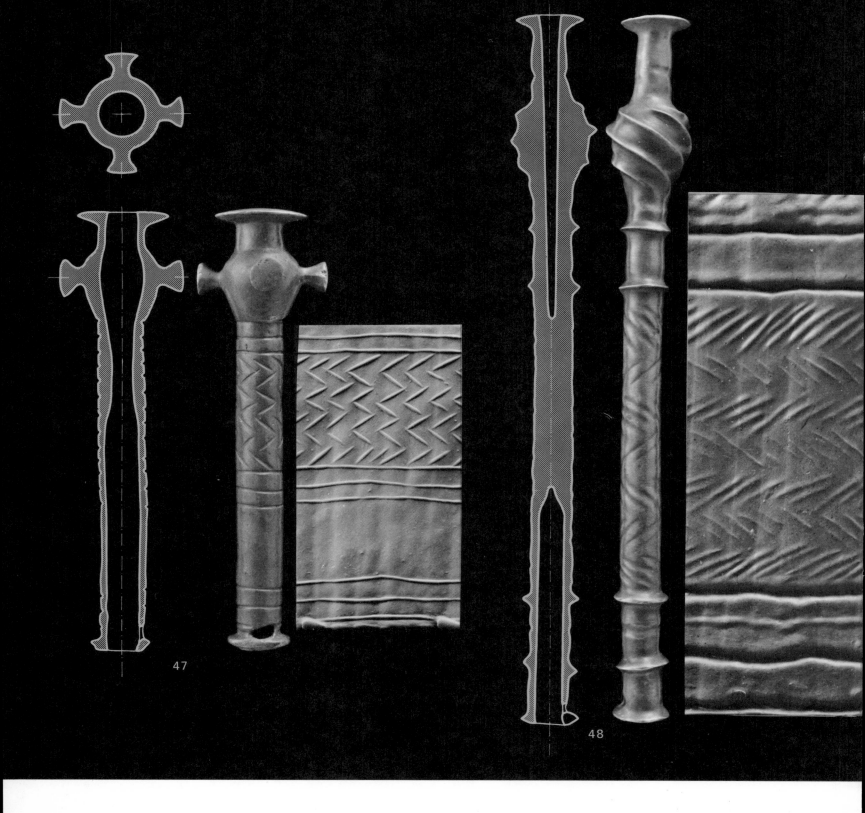

No. 47 (Reg. No. 61–75)
Standard. Hollow. Disk-shaped upper rim and ring-shaped lower rim. Piriform head, from which spring four bosses with disk-shaped heads. On the shaft, three groups of three horizontal grooves. In the upper register, design of zigzag grooves. Hole near lower rim.
L – 20 cm; Diam – 2.1 cm; Th – 0.3 cm; Wt – 393 gr.

No. 48 (Reg. No. 61–40)
Standard. Partly solid. Disk-shaped upper rim and ring-shaped lower rim. Piriform head with spiral ridges and a horizontal groove above it. The shaft has two pairs of disk-shaped projections with zigzag grooves between them and one horizontal groove between the bottom pair.
L – 24 cm; Diam – 2.5 cm; Th – 0.4 cm; Wt – 493 gr.

No. 49 (Reg. No. 61–3)
Standard. Hollow. Plain. Damaged disk-shaped upper rim and ring-shaped lower rim.
Piriform head.
L – 18.8 cm; Diam – 2 cm; Th – 0.3 cm; Wt – 285 gr.

No. 50 (Reg. No. 61–2)
Standard. Hollow. Plain. Disk-shaped upper rim and ring-shaped lower rim. Spherical head.
L – 14.8 cm; Diam – 2.1 cm; Th – 0.4 cm; Wt – 417 gr.

No. 51 (Reg. No. 61–1)
Standard. Hollow. Plain. Disk-shaped rims, the upper larger than the lower, which is
damaged. Piriform head.
L – 18.9 cm; Diam – 1.9 cm; Th – 0.4 cm; Wt – 383 gr.

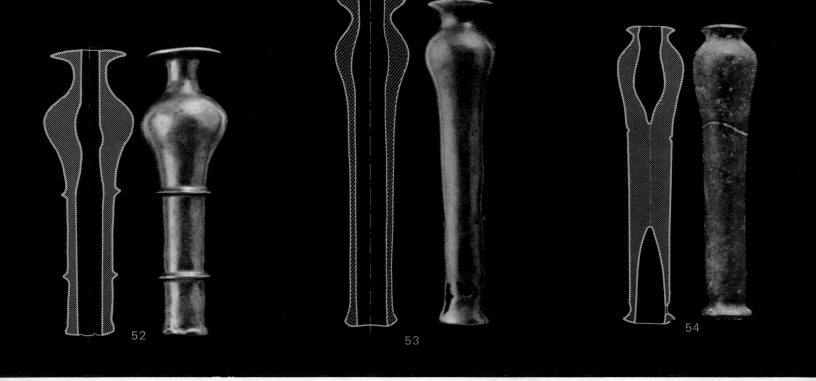

No. 52 (Reg. No. 61–6)
Standard. Hollow. Disk-shaped upper rim. Plain. Piriform head. Two horizontal ridges on shaft.
L – 12.7 cm; Diam – 2 cm; Th – 0.4 cm; Wt – 262 gr.

No. 53 (Reg. No. 61–21)
Standard. Hollow. Plain. Disk-shaped upper rim and ring-shaped lower rim, which is damaged. Piriform head.
L – 15 cm; Diam – 2 cm; Th – 0.2 cm; Wt – 268 gr.

No. 54 (Reg. No. 61–4)
Standard. Partly solid. Plain. Ring-shaped rims at both ends. Slight thickening at top, and below it, a groove. Hole near the lower end. Remains of wood inside the shaft (C-14 analysis carried out).
L – 13.3 cm; Diam – 2 cm; Th – 0.3 cm; Wt – 222 gr.

No. 55 (Reg. No. 61–65)
Standard. Hollow. Disk-shaped upper rim and ring-shaped lower rim. Piriform head with one zigzag groove. On the shaft, grooved vertical herring-bone design, and a horizontal groove below.
L – 18.3 cm; Diam – 1.8 cm; Th – 0.2 cm; Wt – 250 gr.

No. 56 (Reg. No. 61–11)
Standard. Hollow. Disk-shaped upper rim and ring-shaped lower rim. Plain piriform head. On the shaft, zigzag grooves between horizontal grooves.
L – 22 cm; Diam – 2.1 cm; Th – 0.3 cm; Wt – 408 gr.

No. 57 (Reg. No. 61–5)
Standard. Hollow. Disk-shaped rim. Barrel-shaped head. On shaft, three groups of three horizontal grooves. Four holes near lower end. Black incrustation inside and outside.
L – 27.9 cm; Diam – 2.1 cm; Th – 0.3 cm; Wt – 515 gr.

No. 58 (Reg. No. 61–57)
Standard. Hollow. Disk-shaped upper rim and ring-shaped lower rim. Piriform head with horizontal grooves. On the shaft, two pairs of horizontal grooves. The lower end is damaged and has a hole.
L – 18.1 cm; Diam – 2.7 cm; Th – 0.2 cm; Wt – 254 gr.

No. 59 (Reg. No. 61–63)
Standard. Hollow. Disk-shaped rim. Piriform head with horizontal grooves. The lower end is compressed.
L – 14.3 cm; Diam – 2.2 cm; Th – 0.4 cm; Wt – 270 gr.

No. 60 (Reg. No. 61–90)
Standard. Hollow. Spherical head and ring-shaped lower rim. On the shaft, vertical grooved herring-bone patterns between two horizontal grooves.
L – 8.5 cm; Diam – 2.4 cm; Th – 0.3 cm; Wt – 203 gr.

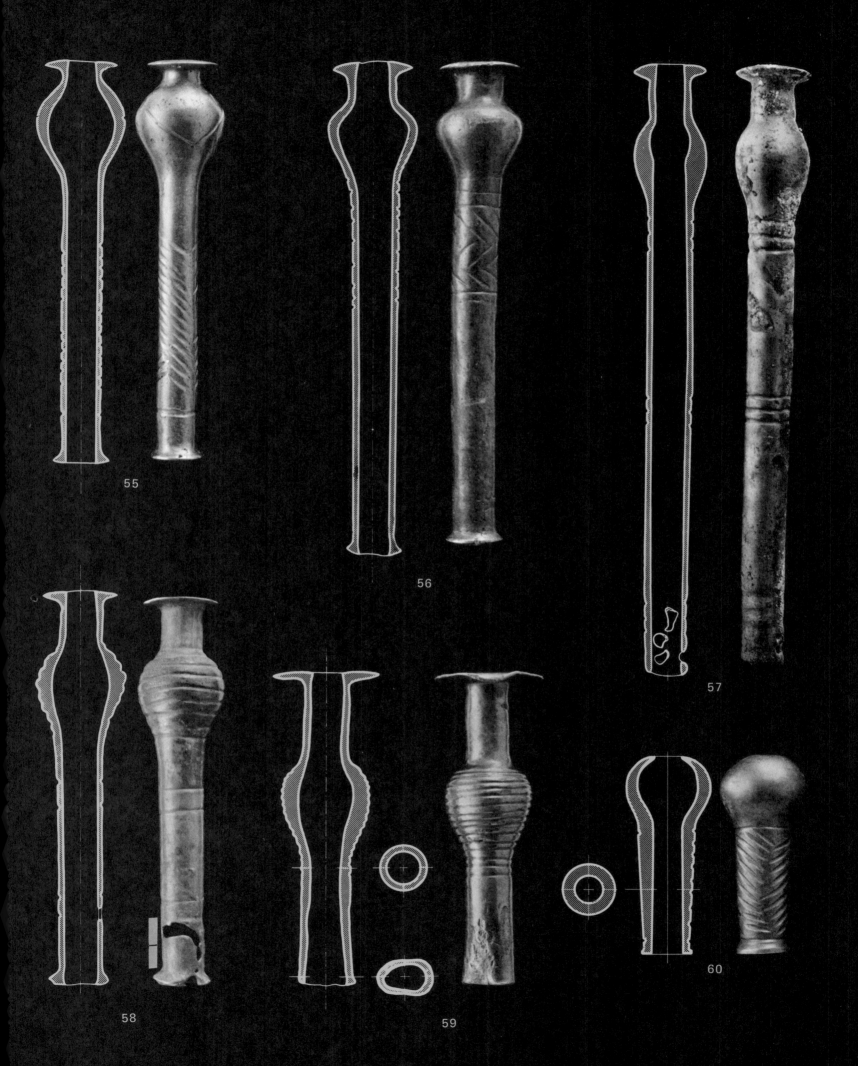

55

56

57

58

59

60

67

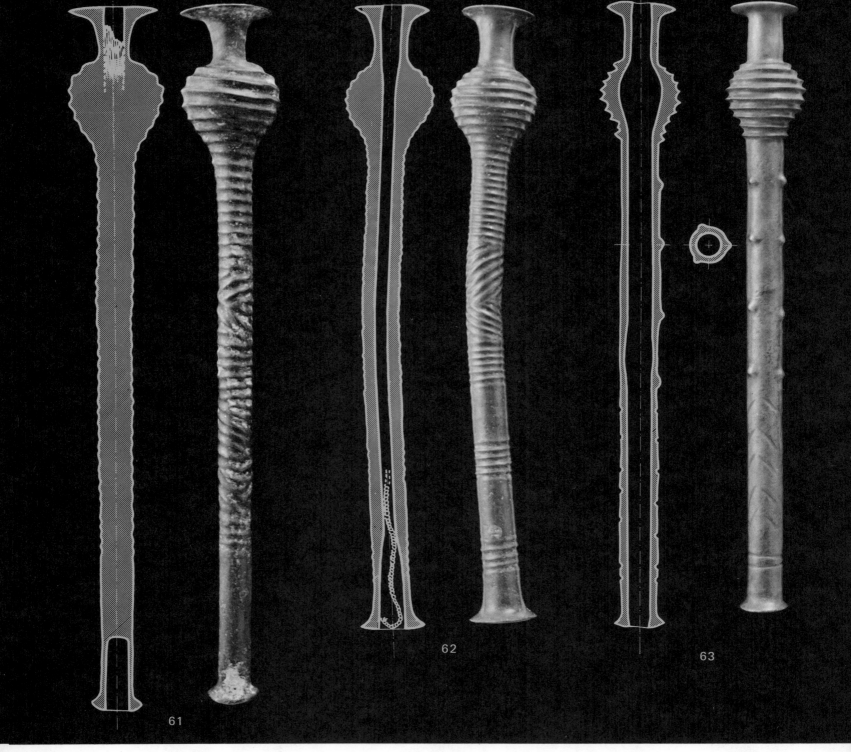

No. 61 (Reg. No. 61–46)
Standard. Almost entirely solid. Disk-shaped upper rim and ring- shaped lower rim. Spherical head with closely spaced spiral ridges, which continue down the shaft, where they combine with a zigzag pattern. Black incrustation.
L – 32.3 cm; Diam – 1.4 cm; Th – 0.2 cm; Wt – 366 gr.

No. 62 (Reg. No. 61–45)
Standard. Hollow. Disk-shaped rims. Piriform head ringed with parallel ridges, which continue for some distance down the shaft. Below them, decoration of zigzag lines and two groups of six and one of four horizontal ridges. Inside the shaft, a twisted thread.
L – 28.4 cm; Diam – 1.6 cm; Th – 0.3 cm; Wt – 349 gr.

No. 63 (Reg. No. 61–43)
Standard. Hollow. Disk-shaped upper rim and ring-shaped lower rim. Spherical head ringed with parallel ridges. On the shaft, three vertical rows of small knobs, herring-bone patterns and two horizontal grooves.
L – 28.7 cm; Diam – 1.6 cm; Th – 0.3 cm; Wt – 367 gr.

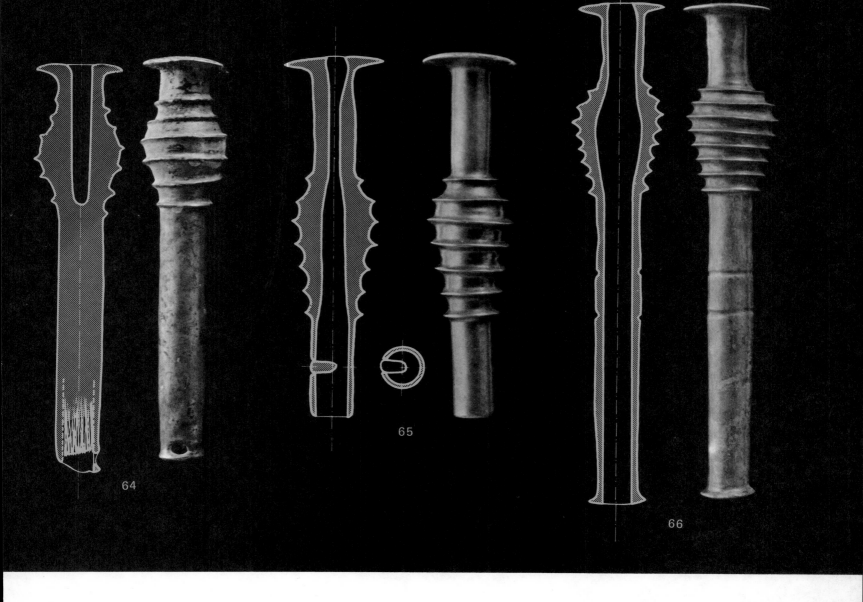

No. 64 (Reg. No. 61–82)
Standard. Partly solid. Damaged disk-like rim. Barrel-shaped head with spiral ridges. Hole at lower end. Black incrustation. Inside the shaft, remains of wood.
L – 18.6 cm; Diam – 2.1 cm; Th – 0.3 cm; Wt – 420 gr.

No. 65 (Reg. No. 61–22)
Standard. Hollow. Disk-shaped upper rim. Near the middle of the shaft, elongated head ringed with sharp parallel ridges. Plugged hole near lower end.
L – 16.4 cm; Diam – 1.9 cm; Th – 0.3 cm; Wt – 302 gr.

No. 66 (Reg. No. 61–30)
Standard. Hollow. Disk-shaped upper rim and ring-shaped lower rim. Piriform head ringed with sharp parallel ridges. On the shaft, two horizontal grooves.
L – 22.7 cm; Diam – 1.9 cm; Th – 0.3 cm; Wt – 393 gr.

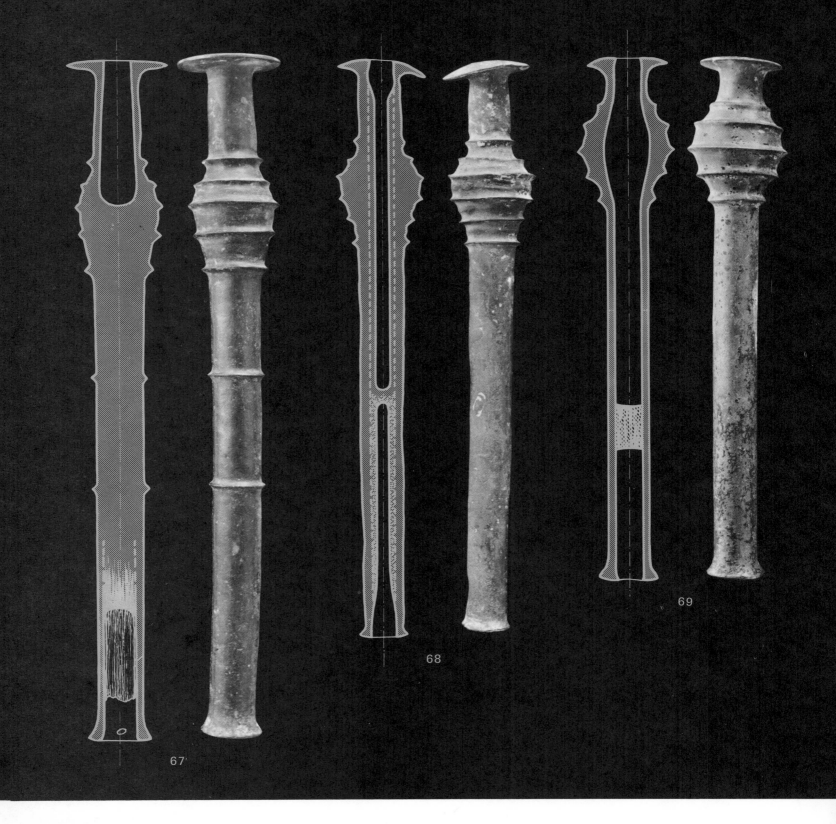

No. 67 (Reg. No. 61–17)
Standard. Partly solid. Disk-shaped upper rim and ring-shaped lower rim. Barrel-shaped head ringed with parallel ridges. Hole at lower end.
L. – 31.2 cm; Diam – 2.3 cm; Th – 0.4 cm; Wt – 608 gr.

No. 68 (Reg. No. 61–15)
Standard. Partly solid. Disk-shaped upper rim and ring-shaped lower rim. Barrel-shaped head ringed with parallel ridges.
L – 26.2 cm; Diam – 2 cm; Th – 0.4 cm; Wt – 426 gr.

No. 69 (Reg. No. 61–14)
Standard. Partly solid. Disk-shaped upper rim and ring-shaped lower rim. Barrel-shaped head with parallel ridges. Black incrustation on surface.
L – 23.5 cm; Diam – 2 cm; Th – 0.4 cm; Wt – 449 gr.

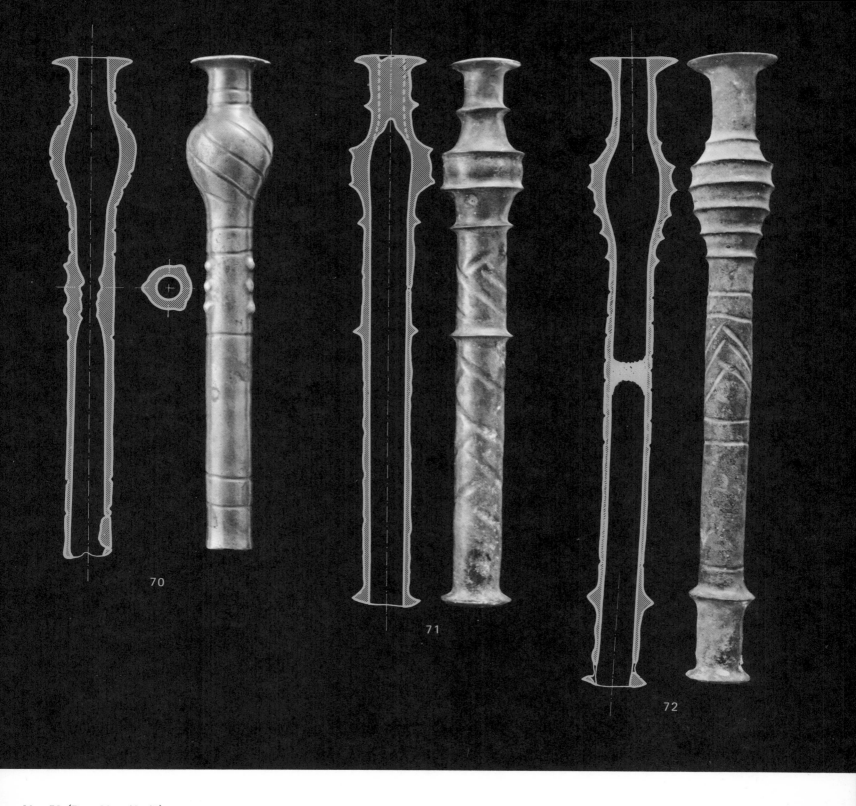

No. 70 (Reg. No. 61–60)
Standard. Hollow. Disk-shaped rim. Short neck with two horizontal grooves. Piriform head with spiral grooves. On the shaft, horizontal grooves. In the upper register, three vertical rows of small knobs.
L – 22 cm; Diam – 2 cm; Th – 0.3 cm; Wt – 430 gr.

No. 71 (Reg. No. 61–33)
Standard. Partly solid. Disk-shaped rims at both ends. Slight thickening between two parallel horizontal ridges. Above it, one horizontal ridge, and below it, two horizontal ridges and design of diagonal grooves. Two holes. Black incrustation.
L – 25 cm; Diam – 2.2 cm; Th – 0.3 cm; Wt – 476 gr.

No. 72 (Reg. No. 61–39)
Standard. Partly solid. Disk-shaped upper rim and ring-shaped lower rim. Barrel-shaped head with parallel ridges. On the shaft, grooved herring-bone design between two pairs of horizontal grooves. Near the lower end, a horizontal groove and a horizontal ridge. Three holes. Black incrustation.
L – 28.8 cm; Diam – 2 cm; Th – 0.3 cm; Wt – 469 gr.

No. 73 (Reg. No. 61–29)
Standard. Partly solid. Disk-shaped upper rim and ring-shaped lower rim. Piriform head with spiral ridges. On the shaft, between a horizontal groove and a horizontal ridge, grooved herring-bone design, and below it, closely spaced spiral groove. Black incrustation.
L – 26.1 cm; Diam – 1.6 cm; Th – 0.3 cm; Wt – 327 gr.

No. 74 (Reg. No. 61–37)
Standard. Hollow. Disk-shaped upper rim. Piriform head with spiral ridges. Near the middle of the shaft, a horizontal ridge. Near the lower end, a spiral ridge.
L – 21.7 cm; Diam – 1.9 cm; Th – 0.3 cm; Wt – 312 gr.

No. 75 (Reg. No. 61–53)
Standard. Partly solid. Disk-shaped upper rim and ring-shaped lower rim. Spherical head with spiral ridges. On the shaft, three groups of three or four horizontal grooves. Hole at lower end. Black incrustation.
L – 17 cm; Diam – 1.6 cm; Th – 0.3 cm; Wt – 317 gr.

No. 76 (Reg. No. 61–94)
Standard. Hollow. Broken, with both ends missing. Piriform head with spiral ridges. Below it, three horizontal grooves and a weave-pattern.
L – 7.6 cm; Diam – 1.8 cm; Th – 0.3 cm; Wt – 207 gr.

No. 77 (Reg. No. 61–64)
Standard. Hollow. Disk-shaped upper rim. Piriform head with diagonal grooves. On the shaft, two horizontal grooves, and below them, grooved herring-bone design. Hole at lower end.
L – 11 cm; Diam – 1.9 cm; Th – 0.3 cm; Wt – 235 gr.

No. 78 (Reg. No. 61–56)
Standard. Partly solid. Disk-shaped upper rim and damaged ring-shaped lower rim. Piriform head with diagonal grooves. On the shaft, two groups of three horizontal grooves. Hole above the lower rim.
L – 20.4 cm; Diam – 2.1 cm; Th – 0.3 cm; Wt – 417 gr.

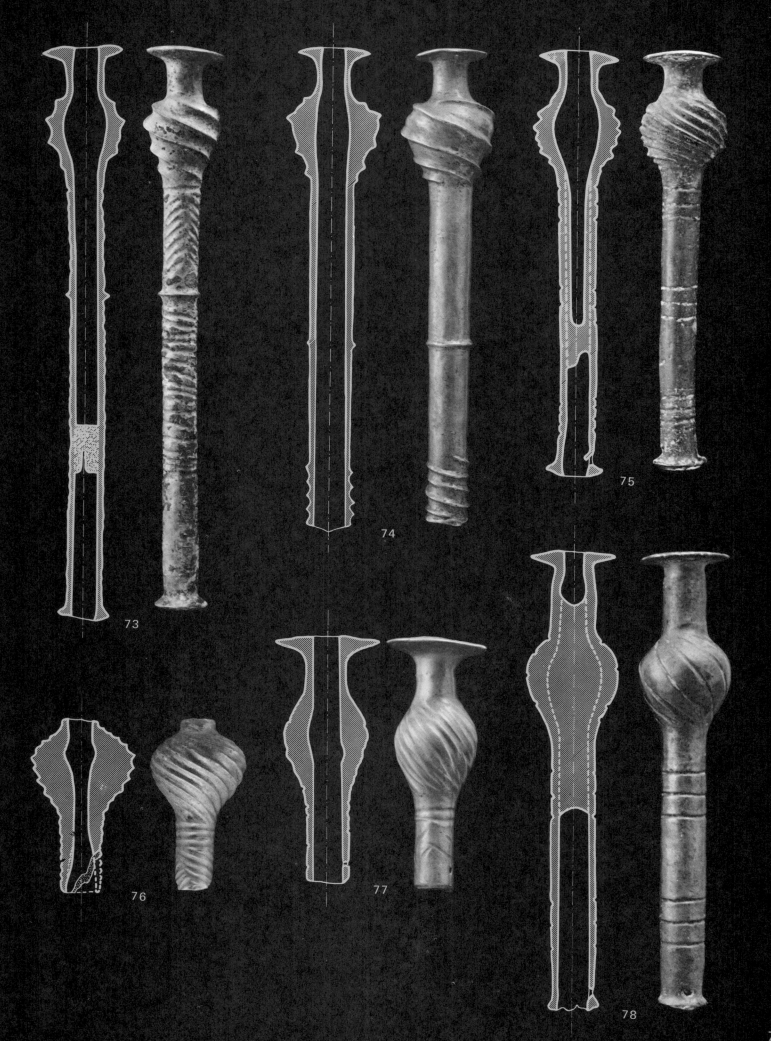

73

73

74

75

76

77

78

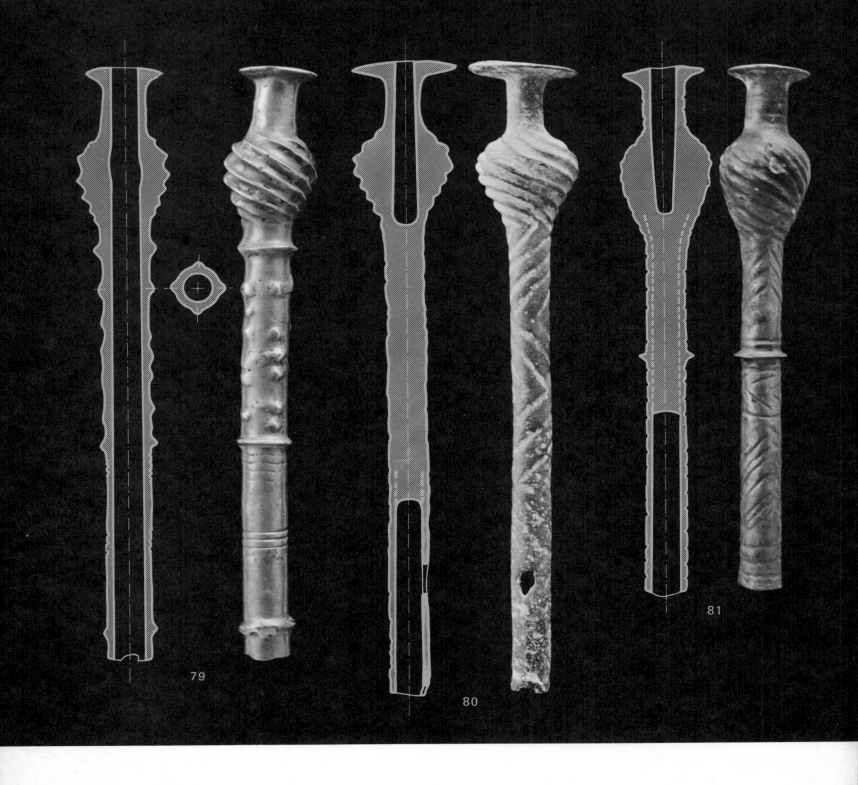

No. 79 (Reg. No. 61–50)
Standard. Hollow. Disk-shaped upper rim. Piriform head with spiral ridges. On the shaft, three horizontal ridges. In the upper register, decoration of small knobs, some damaged. In the lower register, horizontal grooves. The lower end is damaged.
L – 27 cm; Diam – 2.1 cm; Th – 0.3 cm; Wt – 418 gr.

No. 80 (Reg. No. 61–52)
Standard. Partly solid. Disk-shaped upper rim. Spherical head with spiral ridges. On the shaft, zigzag grooves. Hole in shaft. The lower end is damaged.
L – 28.9 cm; Diam – 1.7 cm; Th – 0.3 cm; Wt – 362 gr.

No. 81 (Reg. No. 61–59)
Standard. Partly solid. Disk-shaped upper rim, and below it, three horizontal grooves. Piriform head with spiral grooves. Near the middle of the shaft, a horizontal ridge; above and below it, grooved vertical and horizontal herring-bone designs. Three horizontal grooves near the lower end.
L – 24 cm; Diam – 1.8 cm; Th – 0.3 cm; Wt – 445 gr.

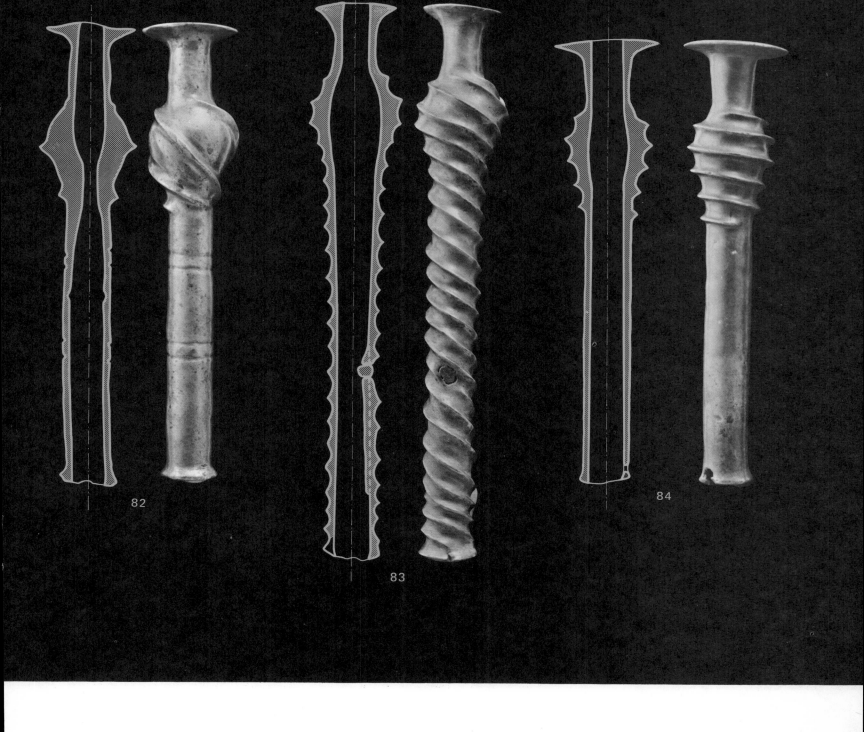

No. 82 (Reg. No. 61–35)
Standard. Hollow. Disk-shaped upper rim and ring-shaped lower rim. Barrel-shaped head with spiral ridges. On shaft, two pairs of horizontal grooves.
L – 20.8 cm; Diam – 2.1 cm; Th – 0.3 cm; Wt – 362 gr.

No. 83 (Reg. No. 61–51)
Standard. Hollow. Disk-shaped upper rim and ring-shaped lower rim. Piriform head with spiral ridges, which continue all the way down the shaft. Soldered patch in shaft.
L – 25.5 cm; Diam – 2 cm; Th – 0.3 cm; Wt – 458 gr.

No. 84 (Reg. No. 61–102)
Standard. Hollow. Disk-shaped upper rim and ring-shaped lower rim. Piriform head with spiral ridges. Hole near lower end.
L – 20.5 cm; Diam – 2 cm; Th – 0.3 cm; Wt – 347 gr.

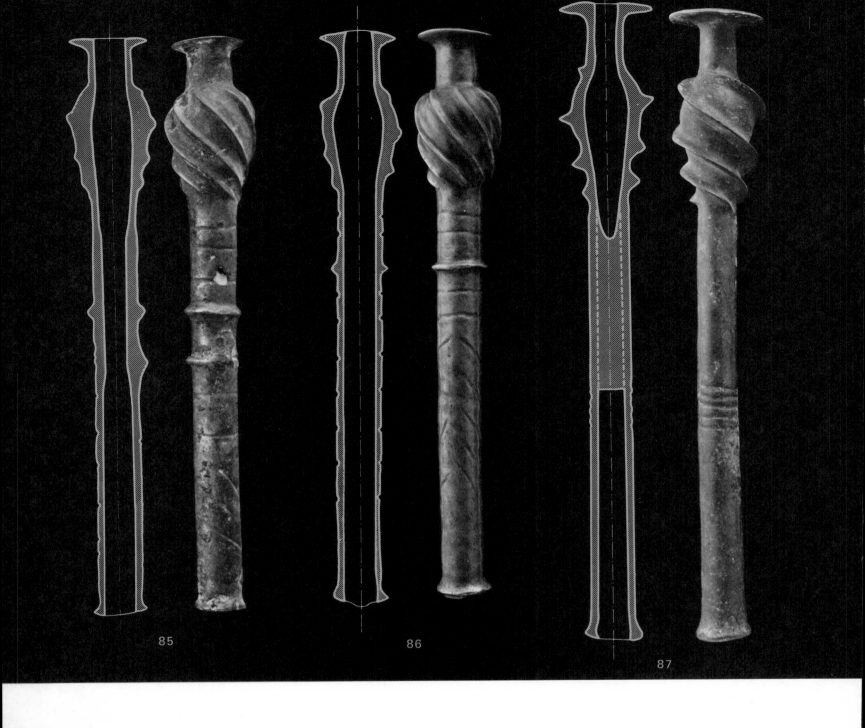

85

86

87

No. 85 (Reg. No. 61–34)
Standard. Hollow. Disk-shaped upper rim and ring-shaped lower rim. Piriform head with diagonal ridges. On the shaft, three horizontal grooves, then a horizontal ridge, and another that is part ridge and part groove. Below them, two horizontal grooves and diagonal grooves. Hole in shaft. Black incrustation.
L – 26.4 cm; Diam – 2 cm; Th – 0.3 cm; Wt – 430 gr.

No. 86 (Reg. No. 61–66)
Standard. Hollow. Disk-shaped upper rim and ring-shaped lower rim. Piriform head with diagonal ridges. On shaft, two pairs of horizontal grooves, between them a horizontal ridge, and below, design of diagonal grooves.
L – 26 cm; Diam – 1.9 cm; Th – 0.3 cm; Wt – 396 gr.

No. 87 (Reg. No. 61–36)
Standard. Partly solid. Disk-shaped upper rim and ring-shaped lower rim. Piriform head with spiral ridges. In the centre of the shaft, closely spaced spiral groove.
L – 29 cm; Diam – 1.8 cm; Th – 0.4 cm; Wt – 406 gr.

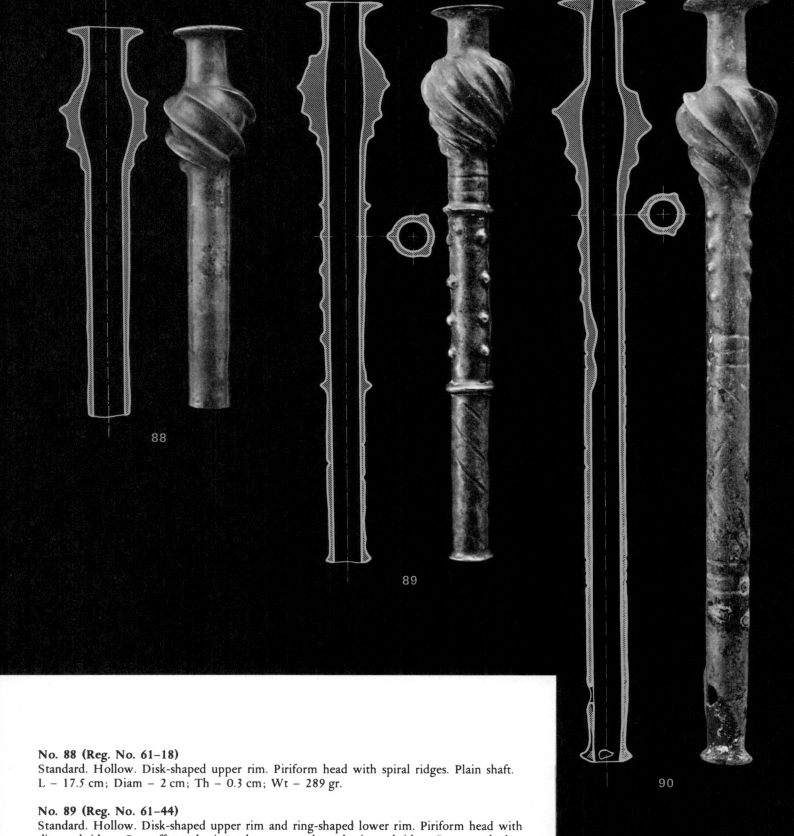

No. 88 (Reg. No. 61–18)
Standard. Hollow. Disk-shaped upper rim. Piriform head with spiral ridges. Plain shaft.
L – 17.5 cm; Diam – 2 cm; Th – 0.3 cm; Wt – 289 gr.

No. 89 (Reg. No. 61–44)
Standard. Hollow. Disk-shaped upper rim and ring-shaped lower rim. Piriform head with
diagonal ridges. On staff, two horizontal grooves and two horizontal ridges. Between the latter, three vertical rows of small knobs. In lower register, diagonal grooves.
L – 25.6 cm; Diam – 1.9 cm; Th – 0.3 cm; Wt – 375 gr.

No. 90 (Reg. No. 61–41)
Standard. Hollow. Disk-shaped upper rim and ring-shaped lower rim. Piriform head with
diagonal ridges. On shaft, two groups of three horizontal grooves. In upper register, three ver-
tical rows of small knobs. In the middle register, zigzag grooves. Two holes at lower end.
Black incrustation.
L – 35.2 cm; Diam – 1.9 cm; Th – 0.3–0.4 cm; Wt – 447 gr.

No. 91 (Reg. No. 61–20)
Standard. Hollow. Disk-shaped upper rim and ring-shaped lower rim. Spherical head with spiral ridges. On shaft, one horizontal ridge.
L – 18.5 cm; Diam – 2.1 cm; Th – 0.3 cm; Wt – 300 gr.

No. 92 (Reg. No. 61–13)
Standard. Hollow. Disk-shaped upper rim. Piriform head with spiral ridges. The lower end is broken. Plain shaft.
L – 20.3 cm; Diam – 2 cm; Th – 0.3 cm; Wt – 417 gr.

No. 93 (Reg. No. 61–19)
Standard. Hollow. Disk-shaped upper rim and damaged ring-shaped lower rim. Piriform head with spiral ridges. Plain shaft.
L – 15.3 cm; Diam – 2.1 cm; Th – 0.3 cm; Wt – 324 gr.

No. 94 (Reg. No. 61–25)
Standard. Partly solid. Disk-shaped upper rim and ring-shaped lower rim. Spherical head with diagonal ridges. On shaft, two bands of diagonal grooves between horizontal grooves. Three holes in shaft. Black incrustation.
L – 19.6 cm; Diam – 1.9 cm; Th – 0.3 cm; Wt – 221 gr.

No. 95 (Reg. No. 61–24)
Standard. Hollow. Dish-shaped upper rim and ring-shaped lower rim. Spherical head with spiral ridges. On shaft, four groups of three horizontal grooves each.
L – 18.4 cm; Diam – 1.8 cm; Th – 0.3 cm; Wt – 230 gr.

No. 96 (Reg. No. 61–23)
Standard. Hollow. Disk-shaped upper rim and damaged ring-shaped lower rim. Spherical head with diagonal ridges. Four horizontal grooves on shaft. Perforation (intentional?) at lower end.
L – 20.1 cm; Diam – 1.9 cm; Th – 0.3 cm; Wt – 303 gr.

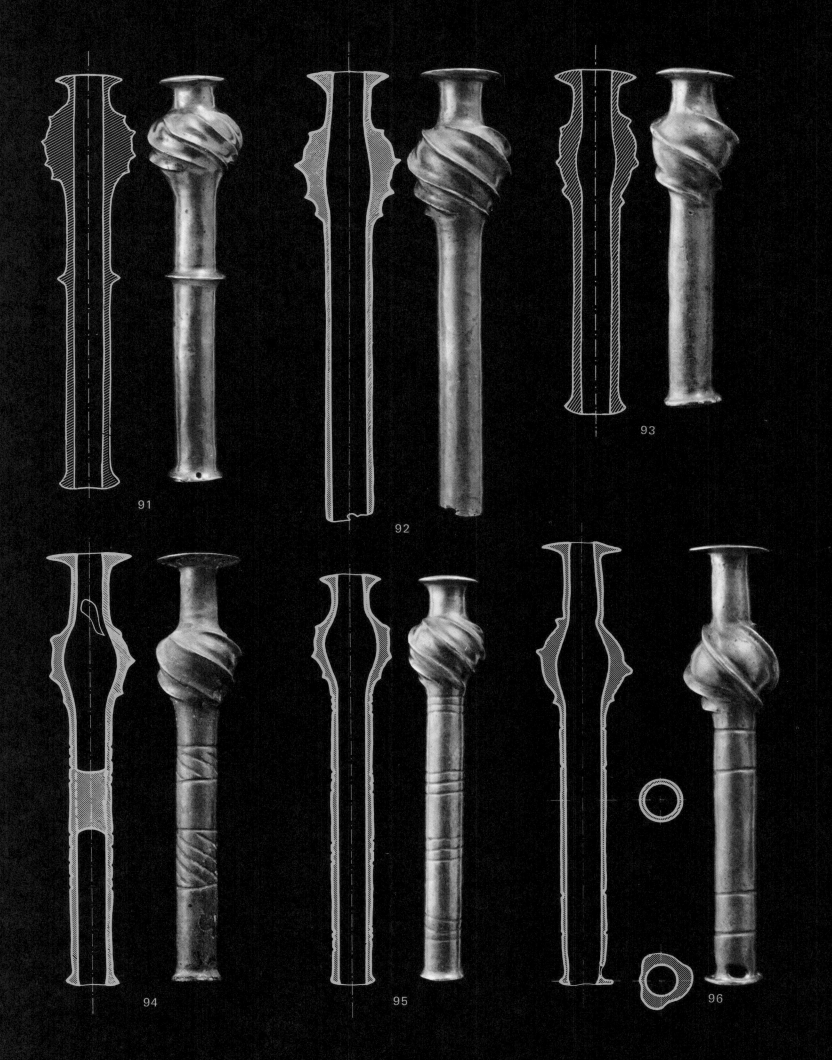

91

92

93

94

95

96

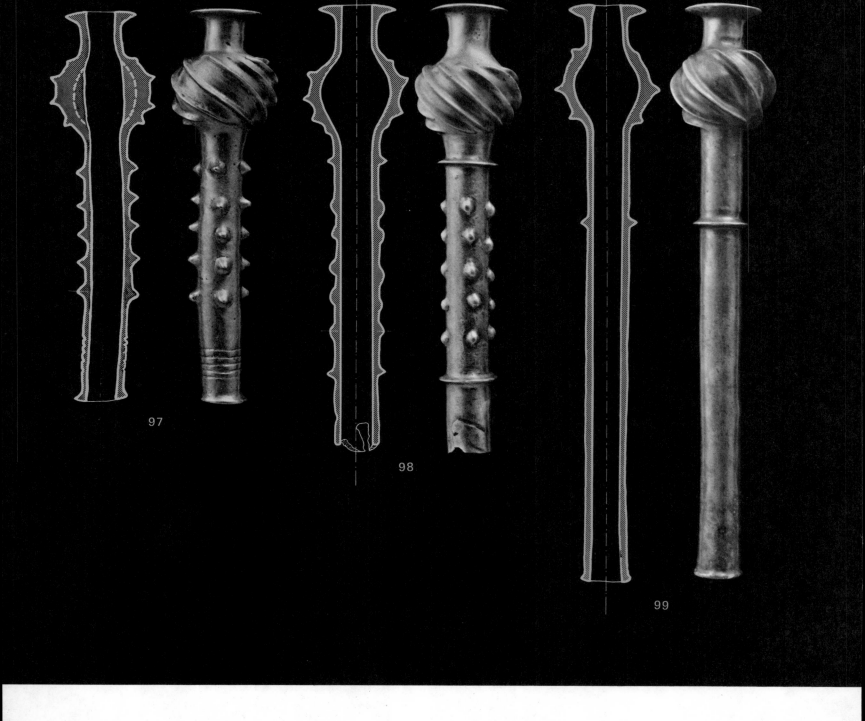

No. 97 (Reg. No. 61–47)
Standard. Hollow. Disk-shaped upper rim and ring-shaped lower rim. Flattened spherical head with diagonal ridges. On shaft, four vertical rows of small knobs. Below, five horizontal grooves.
L – 17.7 cm; Diam – 2 cm; Th – 0.3 cm; Wt – 418 gr.

No. 98 (Reg. No. 61–48)
Standard. Hollow. Disk-shaped rim. Flattened spherical head with diagonal ridges. On shaft, two horizontal ridges, and between them four vertical rows of small knobs. Below, diagonal grooves. The lower end is damaged.
L – 20 cm; Diam – 2.1 cm; Th – 0.2 cm; Wt – 356 gr.

No. 99 (Reg. No. 61–16)
Standard. Hollow. Dish-shaped upper rim and ring-shaped lower rim. Spherical head with spiral ridges. On shaft, one horizontal ridge.
L – 26.1 cm; Diam – 1.9 cm; Th – 0.3 cm; Wt – 417 gr.

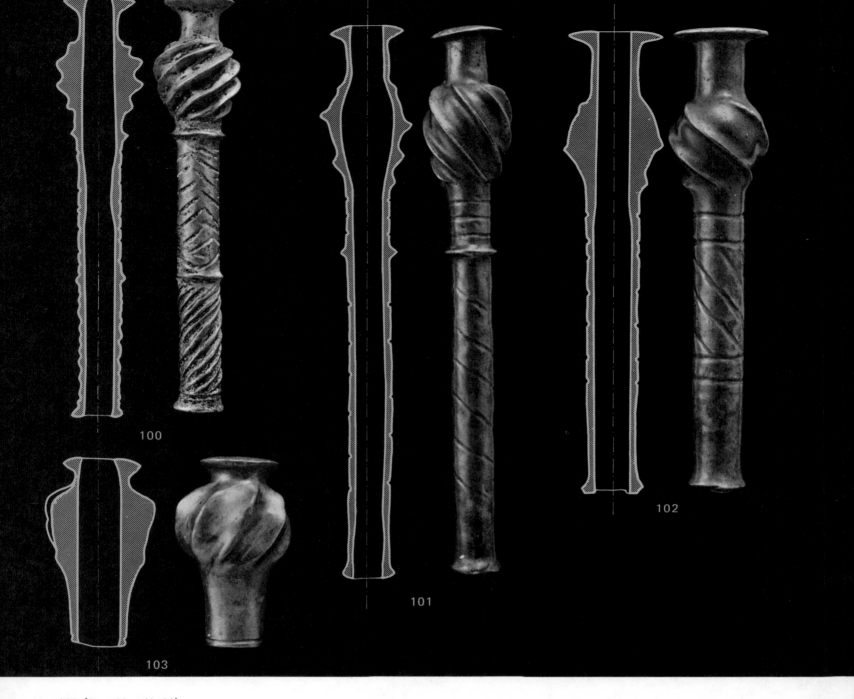

No. 100 (Reg. No. 61–83)
Standard. Hollow. Disk-shaped upper rim and ring-shaped lower rim. Piriform head with diagonal ridges. On shaft, two horizontal ridges. In the upper register, irregular grooved herring-bone design. In the lower register, spiral ridges. Black incrustation. Remains of wood inside shaft.
L – 19.1 cm; Diam – 2 cm; Th – 0.4 cm; Wt – 412 gr.

No. 101 (Reg. No. 61–28)
Standard. Hollow. Disk-shaped upper rim and ring-shaped lower rim. Piriform head with diagonal ridges. On shaft, three horizontal grooves, one ridge, and below them, diagonal grooves.
L – 25.8 cm; Diam – 2 cm; Th – 0.3 cm; Wt – 374 gr.

No. 102 (Reg. No. 61–26)
Standard. Hollow. Disk-shaped upper rim and ring-shaped lower rim. Piriform head with diagonal ridges. On the shaft, two pairs of horizontal grooves, and between them, diagonal grooves.
L – 20.9 cm; Diam – 2.3 cm; Th – 0.3 cm; Wt – 399 gr.

No. 103 (Reg. No. 61–101)
Short standard. Hollow. Disk-shaped upper rim. Piriform head with diagonal ridges. Horizontal groove near lower end.
L – 8.4 cm; Diam – 2.9 cm; Th – 0.4 cm; Wt – 420 gr.

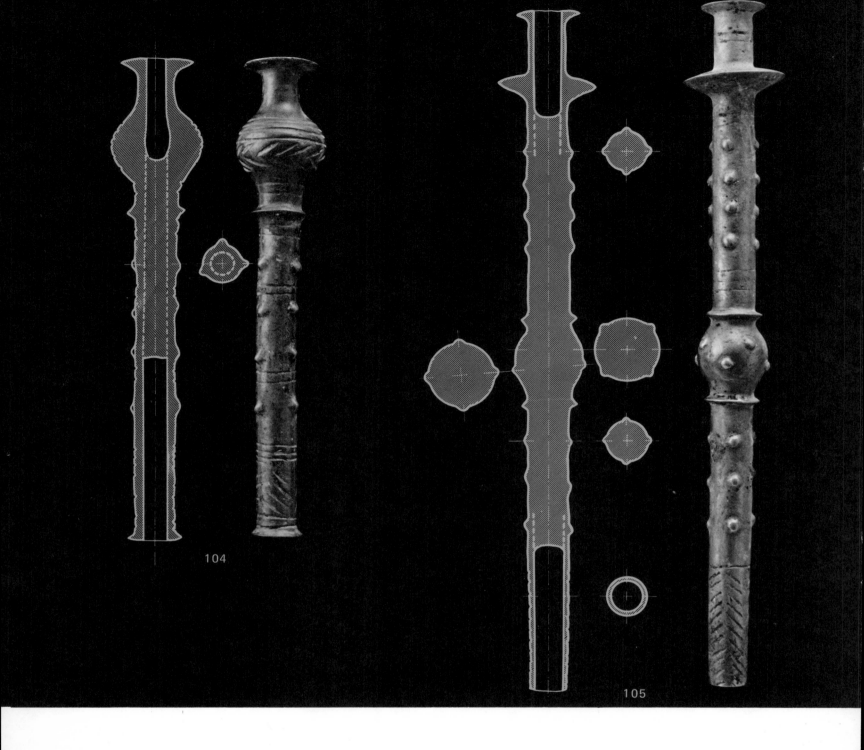

104

105

No. 104 (Reg. No. 61–61)
Standard. Partly solid. Disk-shaped upper rim and ring-shaped lower rim. Spherical head, the upper half ringed with horizontal grooves, while the lower half has grooves in a herring-bone pattern. Below it, two horizontal grooves and one horizontal ridge. On the shaft, five groups of horizontal grooves, and between them, small knobs and a herring-bone pattern.
L – 22 cm; Diam – 1.9 cm; Th – 0.4 cm; Wt – 525 gr.

No. 105 (Reg. No. 61–68)
Standard. Partly solid. Small disk-shaped upper rim. Below it, two horizontal grooves, a disk-shaped projection, two horizontal grooves, four vertical rows of small knobs and three horizontal grooves. Near the middle of the standard, between two horizontal ridges, a spherical mace-head with small knobs. Below it, four vertical rows of three small knobs each, a horizontal groove and a grooved herring-bone design. Black incrustation.
L – 31.1 cm; Diam – 1.9 cm; Th – 0.2 cm; Wt – 413 gr.

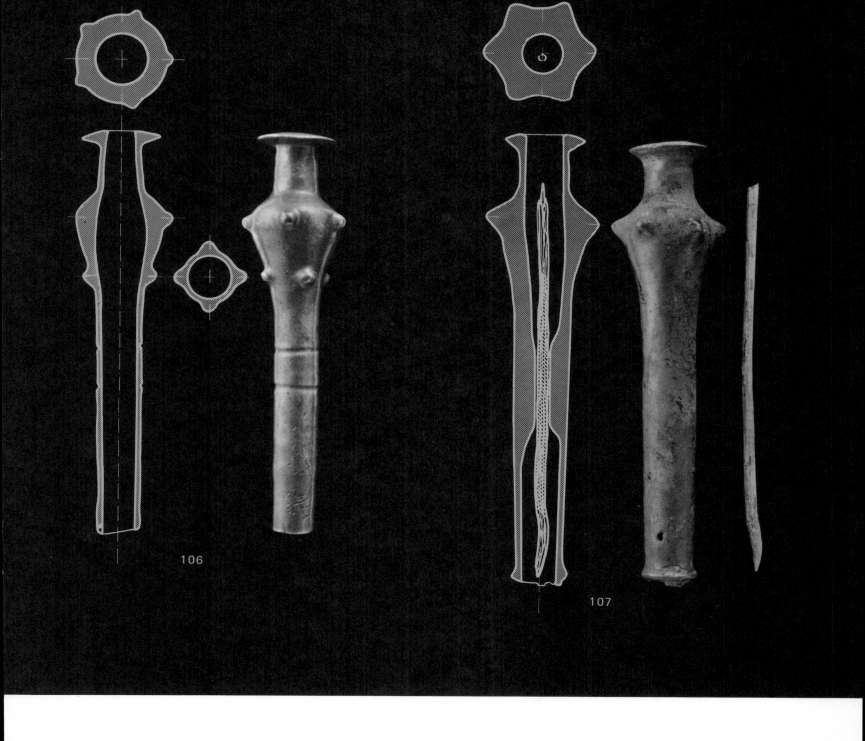

No. 106 (Reg. No. 61–70)
Standard. Hollow. Disk-shaped upper rim. Piriform head with two horizontal rows of knobs.
On shaft, two horizontal grooves.
L – 18.1 cm; Diam – 2 cm; Th – 0.3 cm; Wt – 288 gr.

No. 107 (Reg. No. 61–81)
Standard. Hollow. Disk-shaped upper rim and damaged ring-shaped lower rim. Piriform
head with a row of six knobs. Hole near lower end. Plain shaft. Inside shaft, thin wooden
stick, pointed at one end. Black incrustation.
L – 20.6 cm; Diam – 2.4 cm; Th – 0.3 cm; Wt – 470 gr.

No. 108 (Reg. No. 61–77)

Standard. Hollow. Disk-shaped upper rim. Piriform head. From this, and also from the middle of the shaft, spring four cylindrical bosses, ending in double disks, the outer smaller than the inner. One of the bosses in the middle of the shaft is broken.

L – 21 cm; Diam – 1.5 cm; Th – 0.3 cm; Wt – 325 gr.

No. 109 (Reg. No. 61–79)

Standard. Partly solid. Disk-shaped upper rim and ring-shaped lower rim. Two projections on upper rim, perhaps remains of casting process. Spherical head, from which spring four bosses, two with disk-shaped heads, the other two broken. On the shaft, petal-like grooved decoration. A large hole near the lower end. Inside the shaft, remains of wood (C-14 analysis carried out).

L – 23.2 cm; Diam – 2 cm; Th – 0.4 cm; Wt – 425 gr.

No. 110 (Reg. No. 61–73)

Standard. Hollow. Disk-shaped upper rim and small disk-shaped lower rim. Piriform head, from which spring four cylindrical bosses with disk-shaped heads, one of them broken. Below it, five small knobs. On the shaft, two horizontal grooves, and between them, two rows of diagonal grooves, and another row in lower register. Hole near lower end.

L – 18.3 cm; Diam – 1.9 cm; Th – 0.3 cm; Wt – 343 gr.

No. 111 (Reg. No. 61–190)

Standard. Hollow. Disk-shaped upper rim. Piriform head from which spring five bosses, one with a disk-shaped head. On the shaft, horizontal grooves and two horizontal ridges.

L – 15.3 cm; Diam – 2 cm; Th – 0.3 cm; Wt – 215 gr.

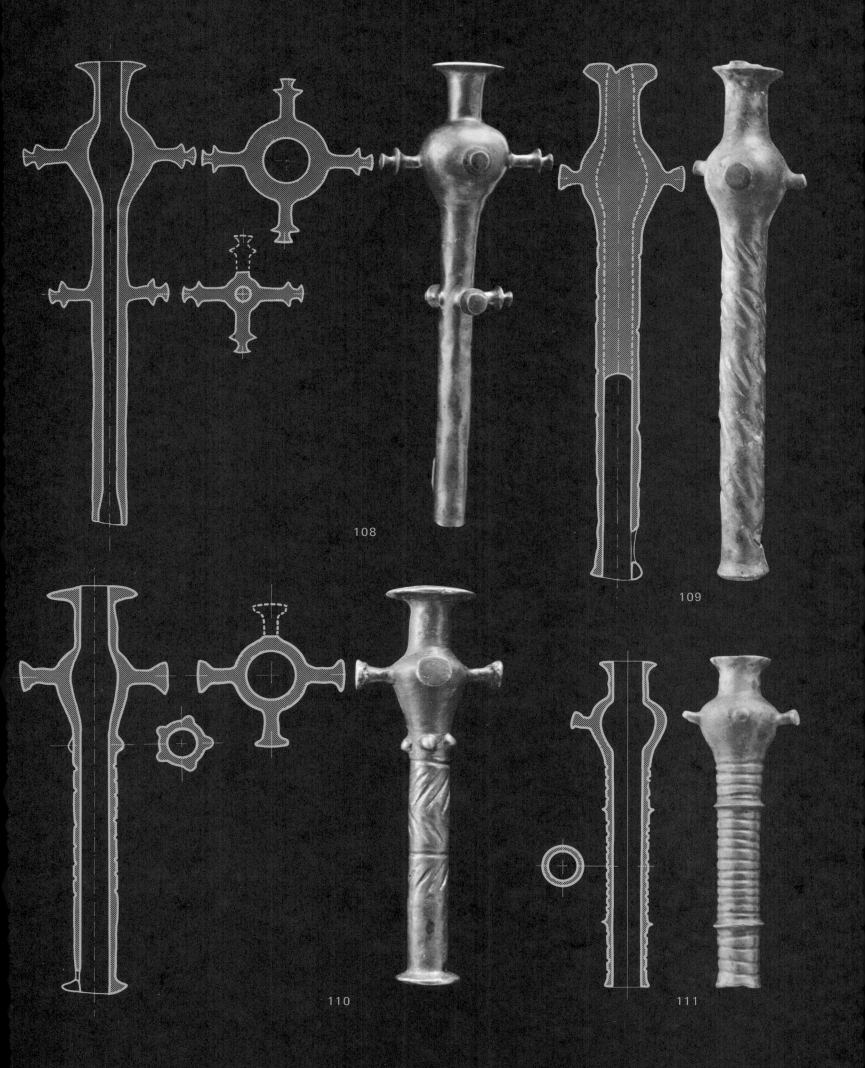

108

109

110

111

85

No. 112 (Reg. No. 61–80)
Standard. Partly solid. Disk-shaped upper rim and ring-shaped lower rim. Disk-shaped projection, divided into four petals. On shaft, horizontal ridge, and below it, closely spaced zigzag ridges. Black incrustation.
L – 22.5 cm; Diam – 1.8 cm; Th – 0.3 cm; Wt – 386 gr.

No. 113 (Reg. No. 61–69)
Standard. Hollow. Disk-shaped upper rim and ring-shaped lower rim. One large and one small disk-shaped projection, and below, spiral ridges.
L – 20.5 cm; Diam – 2.4 cm; Th – 0.4 cm; Wt – 584 gr.

No. 114 (Reg. No. 61–110)
Short standard. Hollow. Jar-shaped. Small disk-shaped upper rim. Horizontal parallel ridges.
L – 9.5 cm; Diam – 4 cm; Th – 0.3 cm; Wt – 252 gr.

No. 115 (Reg. No. 61–118)
Short standard. Hollow. Elongated jar shape. Ring-shaped upper rim. Zigzag ridges. Inside standard, remains of wood (C-14 analysis carried out).
L – 9.5 cm; Diam – 3.4 cm; Th – 0.4 cm; Wt – 195 gr.

No. 116 (Reg. No. 61–111)
Short standard. Hollow. Plain. Truncated cone shape.
L – 9.7 cm; Diam – 3.1 cm; Th – 0.2–0.3 cm; Wt – 250 gr.

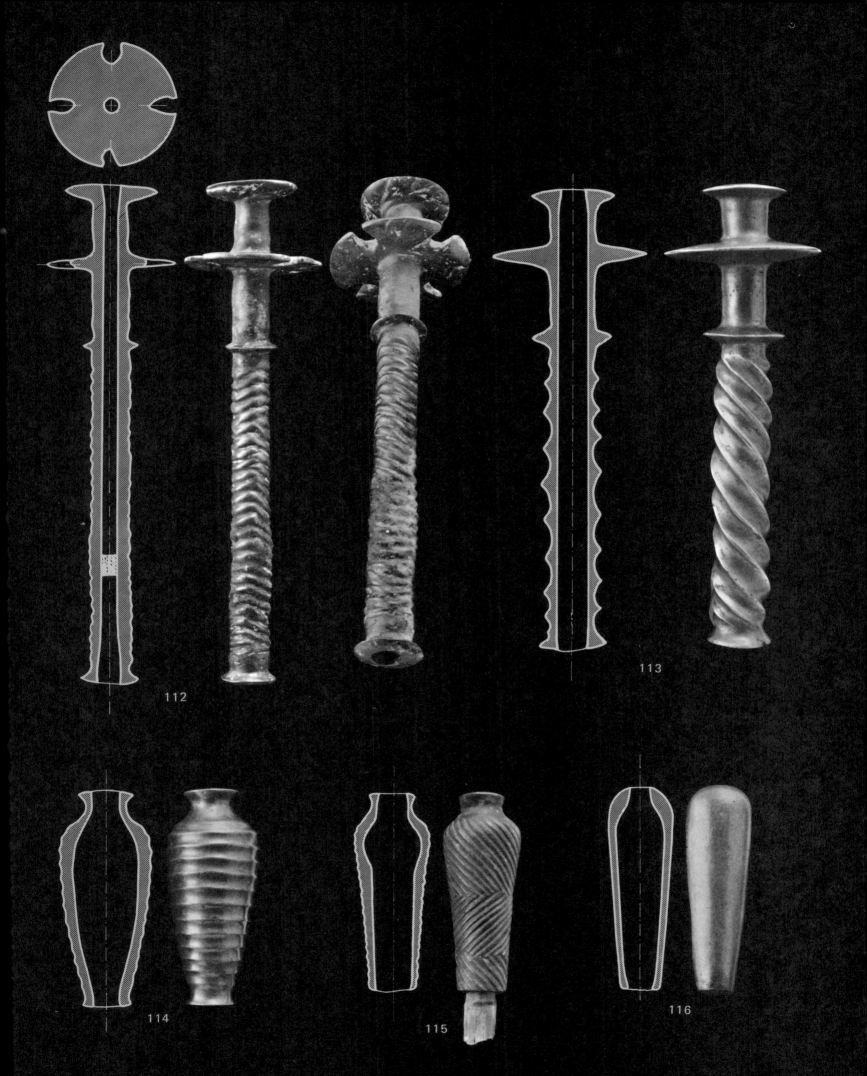

112

113

114

115

116

No. 117 (Reg. No. 61–107)
Standard. Hollow. Truncated cone shape. Six vertical rows of small knobs.
L – 14.2 cm; Diam – 3.4 cm; Th – 0.3–1.0 cm; Wt – 428 gr.

No. 118 (Reg. No. 61–109)
Short standard. Hollow. Elongated barrel-shape. Vertical rows of tooth-like knobs.
L – 8 cm; Diam – 3.2 cm; Th – 0.4–1.0 cm; Wt – 322 gr.

No. 119 (Reg. No. 61–108)
Short standard. Hollow. Barrel-shaped. Vertical rows of tooth-like knobs.
L – 7.3 cm; Diam – 3.3 cm; Th – 0.5–1.0 cm; Wt – 352 gr.

No. 120 – (Reg. No. 61–106)
Short standard. Hollow. Elongated jar shape. Four vertical rows of small knobs.
L – 11.3 cm; Diam – 2.8 cm; Th – 0.2–1.0 cm; Wt – 233gr.

No. 121 (Reg. No. 61–105)
Short standard. Hollow. Truncated cone shape. Vertical rows of small knobs.
L – 8.5 cm; Diam – 3.2 cm; Th – 0.3 cm; Wt – 291 gr.

No. 122 (Reg. No. 61–112)
Short standard. Hollow. Disk-shaped rim. Jar-shaped. Plain.
L – 6 cm; Diam – 3.5 cm; Th – 0.2 cm; Wt – 113 gr.

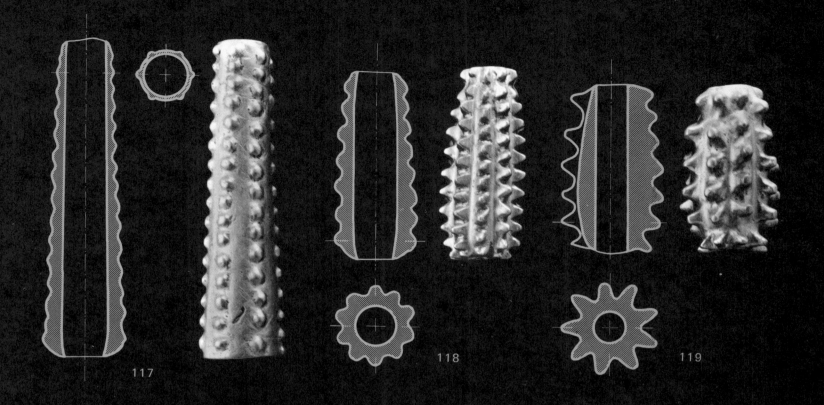

117

118

119

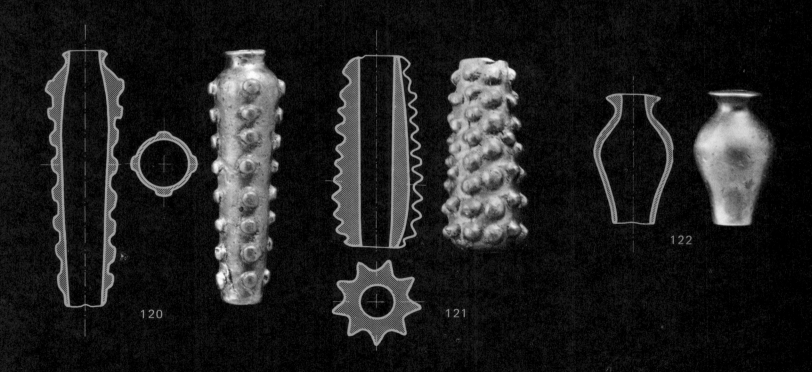

120

121

122

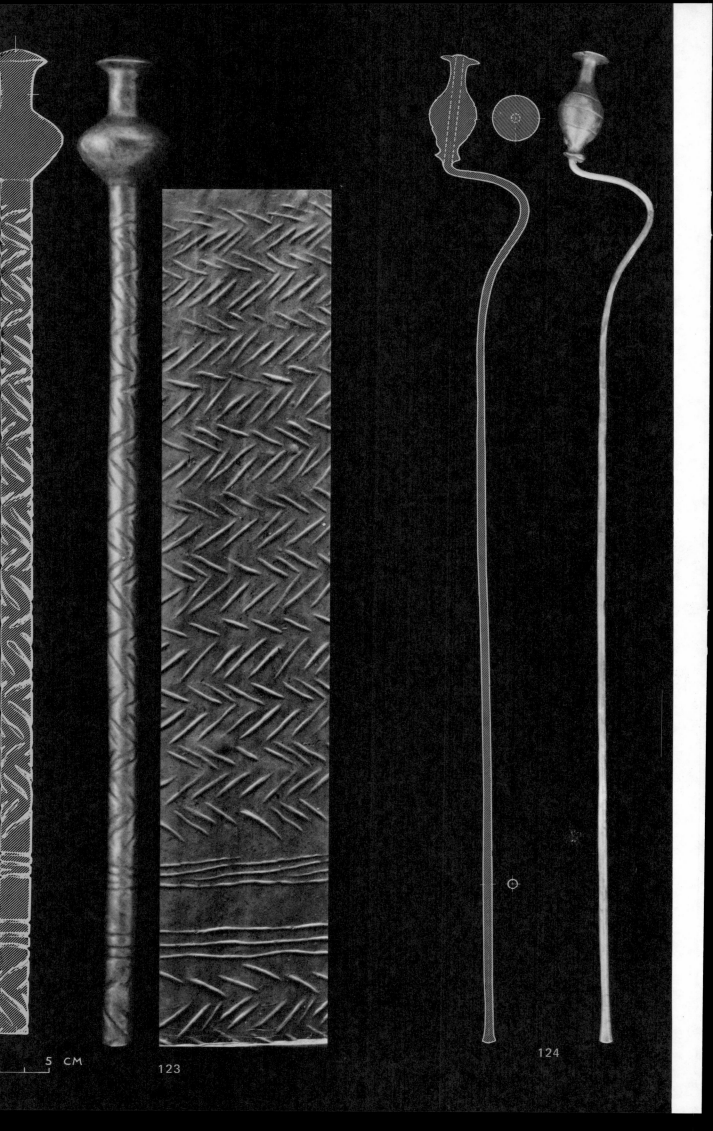

5 CM

123

124

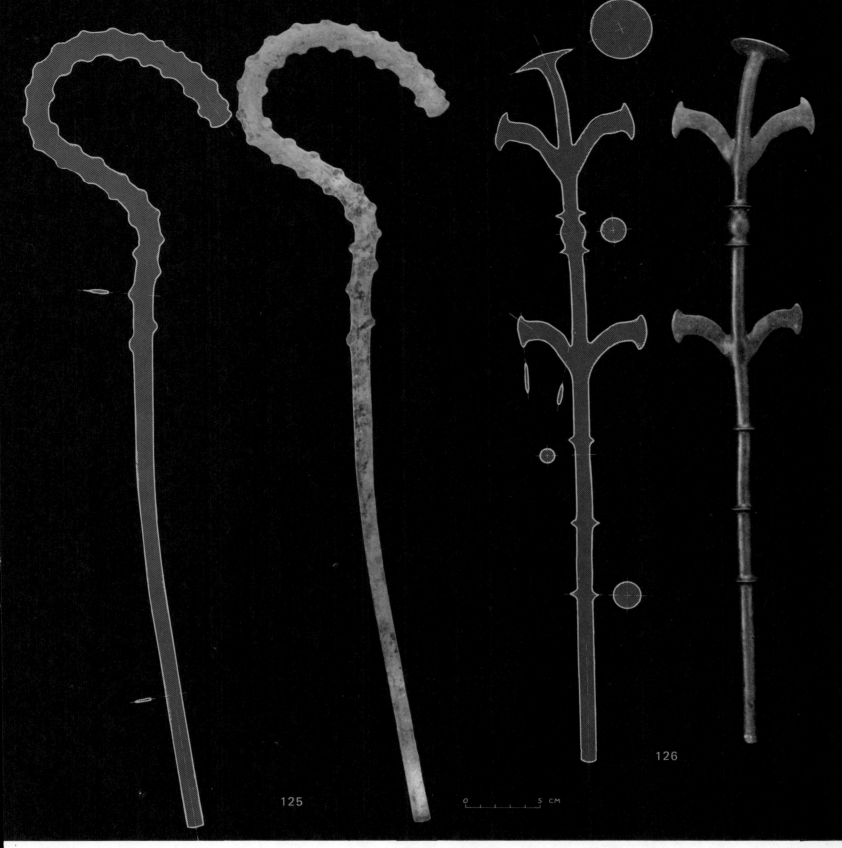

125

126

0   5 CM

No. 123 (Reg. No. 61–155)
Sceptre. Solid. Convex disk-shaped top. Plain flattened spherical head. The shaft is decorated with zigzag grooves and groups of horizontal grooves.
L – 43 cm; Diam – 1.3 cm; Wt – 499 gr.

No. 124 (Reg. No. 61–153)
Sceptre. Thin, plain, cylindrical rod, bent at upper end, which carries a jar-shaped object (length – 8.5 cm) with disk-shaped rim, elongated neck, barrel-shaped body ringed with three horizontal grooves, and slightly flaring base. The rod is threaded through this "jar" and protrudes from it slightly.
L – 77 cm; Diam of rod – 0.6 cm; Wt – 395 gr.

No. 125 (Reg. No. 61–152)
Sceptre. Solid. Long, flat and narrow, shaped like a shepherd's crook. Upper part decorated with knobs, produced by hammering the metal on both sides.
L – 57 cm; Width – 1–2 cm; Th – 0.2 cm; Wt – 185 gr.

No. 126 (Reg. No. 61–156)
Sceptre. Solid. Long shaft, resembling a tree trunk with branches. Disk-shaped top. The upper part of the shaft is slightly bent and carries two pairs of flattened arms with splayed ends. Between them, the shaft swells out into a sphere with a ridge on each side. Below the arms are three horizontal ridges.
L – 49.4 cm; Diam – 1 cm; Wt – 490 gr.

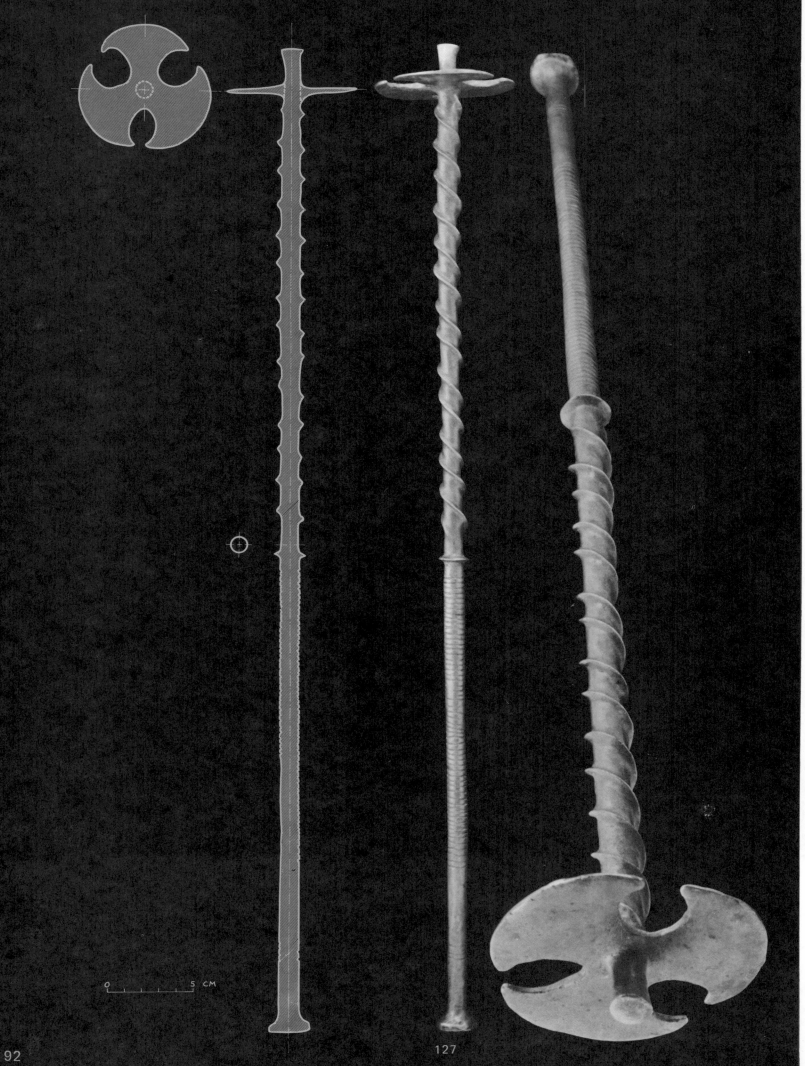

127

0   5 CM

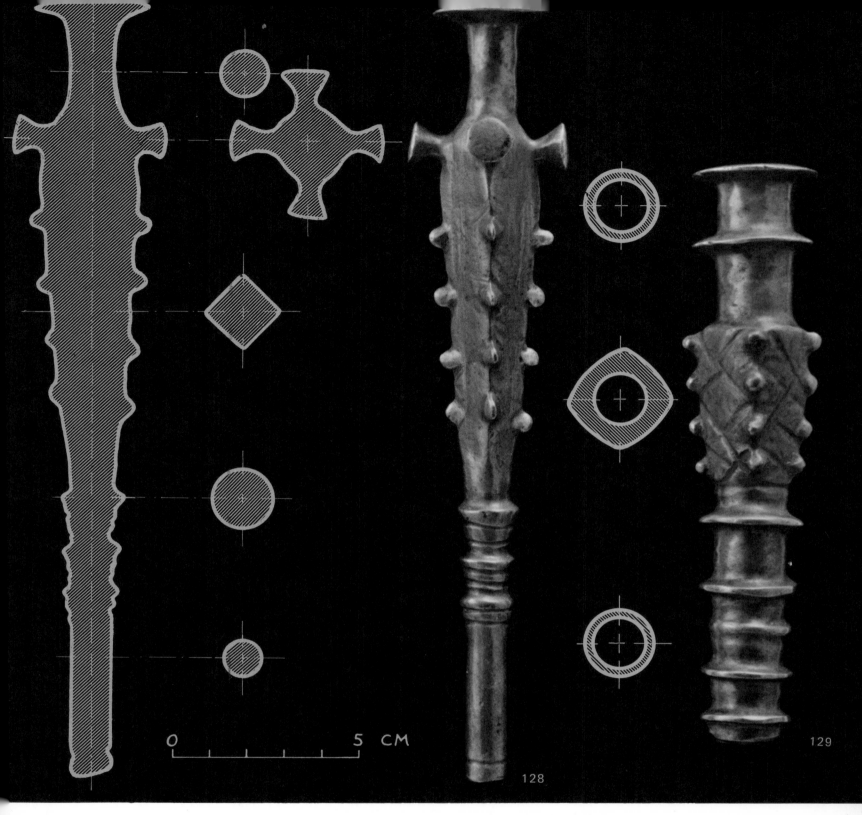

0   5 CM

128

129

No. 128 (Reg. No. 61–93)

Standard. Solid. Disk-shaped top above a cylindrical neck. The body has the shape of an elongated truncated pyramid. Each angle is decorated with four knobs. Between them, on the sides of the pyramid, a rhomboidal groove pattern, which may have been formed accidentally while filing the knobs. At the upper end of the pyramid, four bosses ending in disks, forming a shape like a Maltese cross. At the other end, three horizontal ridges and seven horizontal grooves.

L – 21 cm; Diam – 1 cm; Wt – 329 gr.

No. 129 (Reg. No. 61–192)

Standard. Hollow. Disk-shaped rim. On shaft, six horizontal ridges. Between the upper two ridges, the shaft swells out into a truncated pyramid, decorated with four knobs at each angle, and intersecting diagonal grooves on the sides.

L – 15.7 cm; Diam – 2 cm; Th – 0.3 cm; Wt – 328 gr.

No. 127 (Reg. No. 61–154)

Sceptre. Solid. Long shaft. At upper end, thin disk divided into three leaf-like parts. Above it, a cylindrical knob, and below it, a tendril-like decoration consisting of a spiral ridge, which ends near the middle of the sceptre in a small horizontal ridge. Part of the lower half is decorated with grooved spiral lines. At the lower end, a ring-shaped rim.

L – 58.5 cm; Diam – 1.2 cm; Wt – 653 gr.

No. 130 (Reg. No. 61–98)
Short standard. Hollow. Disk-shaped projections.
L – 9.3 cm; Diam – 2.1 cm; Wt – 335 gr.

No. 131 (Reg. No. 61–96)
Short standard. Hollow. Large disk-shaped projection. On the shaft, two faint horizontal grooves.
L – 7.3 cm; Diam – 2.2 cm; Th – 0.2 cm; Wt – 278 gr.

No. 132 (Reg. No. 61–97)
Short standard. Hollow. Large disk-shaped projection.
L – 8.8 cm; Diam – 2.2 cm; Th – 0.3 cm; Wt – 283 gr.

No. 133 (Reg. No. 61–99)
Short standard. Hollow. Sharp ring-shaped upper rim. Near the middle, a large disk (8.5 cm diam). Horizontal grooves on shaft. Damaged lower end.
L – 6.6 cm; Diam – 2.5 cm; Th – 0.3 cm; Wt – 381 gr.

No. 134 (Reg. No. 61–95)
Standard. Partly solid. Plain. Ring-shaped upper rim and large disk-shaped projection near upper end.
L – 18 cm; Diam – 2.1 cm; Th – 0.3 cm; Wt – 427 gr.

No. 135 (Reg. No. 61–100)
Standard. Hollow. Disk-shaped upper rim and large disk-shaped projection near centre of shaft.
L – 10.8 cm; Diam – 1.9 cm; Th – 0.2cm; Wt – 249 gr.

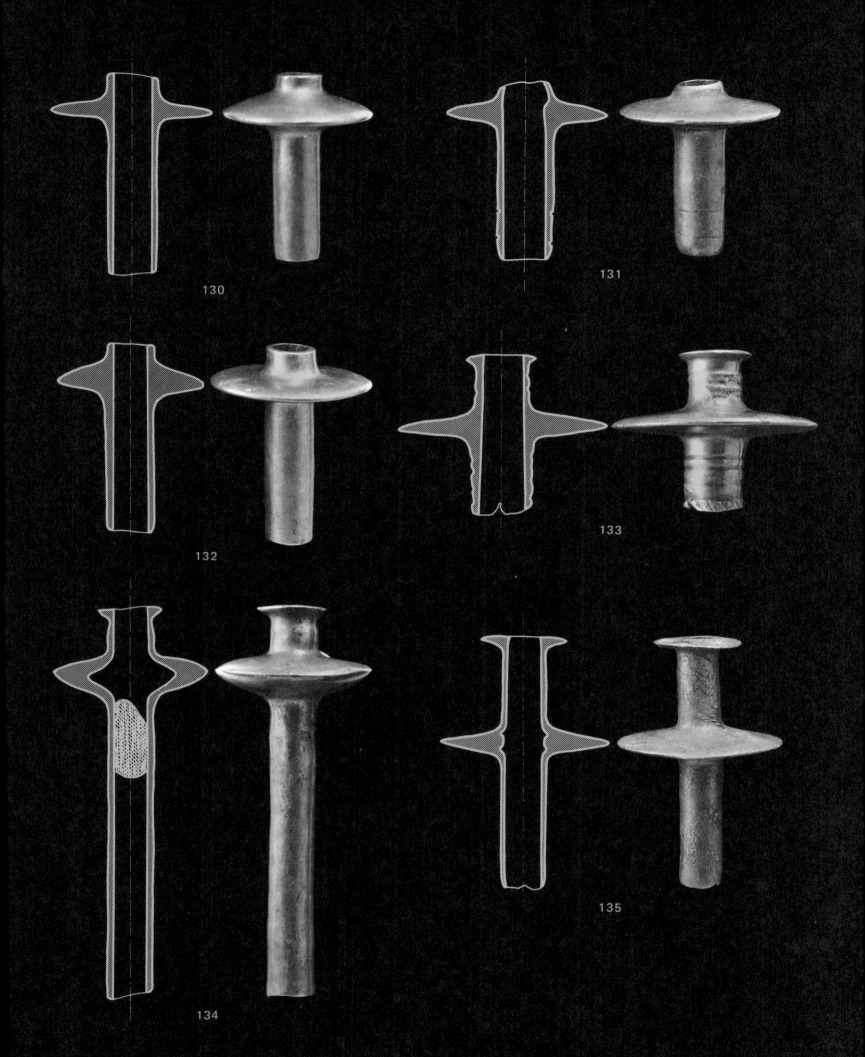

130

131

132

133

134

135

No. 136 (Reg. No. 61–121)
Triangular object. Equilateral. Perforated.
Side of triangle – 7.6 cm; Diam of hole – 1.5 cm; Th – 1.9 cm; Wt – 275 gr.

No. 137 (Reg. No. 61–129)
Disk. Perforated.
Diam – 6.1 cm; Diam of hole – 1.4 cm; Th – 1.9 cm; Wt – 195 gr.

No. 138 (Reg. No. 61–132)
Disk with short hollow shaft.
Diam – 5.9 cm; Diam of hole – 1.5 cm; Th – 2.6 cm; Wt – 151 gr.

No. 139 (Reg. No. 61–130)
Disk. Perforated.
Diam – 7 cm; Diam of hole – 1.6–1.7 cm; Th – 1.4 cm; Wt – 240 gr.

No. 140 (Reg. No. 61–180)
Disk. Perforated. Slightly damaged.
Diam – 6.1 cm; Diam of hole – 1.7 cm; Th – 2.6 cm; Wt – 103 gr.

No. 141 (Reg. No. 61–131)
Disk. Short hollow shaft.
Diam – 6.6 cm; Diam of hole– 1.6 cm; Th – 3 cm; Wt – 238 gr.

No. 142 (Reg. No. 61–124)
Disk. Perforated.
Diam – 6.4 cm; Diam of hole – 1.6–1.7 cm; Th – 2.1 cm; Wt – 250 gr.

No. 143 (Reg. No. 61–128)
Disk. Perforated.
Diam – 6.2 cm; Diam of hole – 1.7 cm; Th – 1.8 cm; Wt – 245 gr.

No. 144 (Reg. No. 61–125)
Disk. Perforated.
Diam – 5.6 cm; Diam of hole – 1.7 cm; Th – 1.5 cm; Wt – 193 gr.

No. 145 (Reg. No. 61–133)
Disk. Short hollow shaft.
Diam – 7.4 cm; Diam of hole – 1.3–1.5 cm; Th – 3 cm; Wt – 282 gr.

No. 146 (Reg. No. 61–127)
Disk. Perforated.
Diam – 5.7 cm; Diam of hole – 1.7 cm; Th – 2.2 cm; Wt – 250 gr.

No. 147 (Reg. No. 61–126)
Disk. Perforated.
Diam – 6.6 cm; Diam of hole – 1.5 cm; Th – 2.4 cm; Wt – 275 gr.

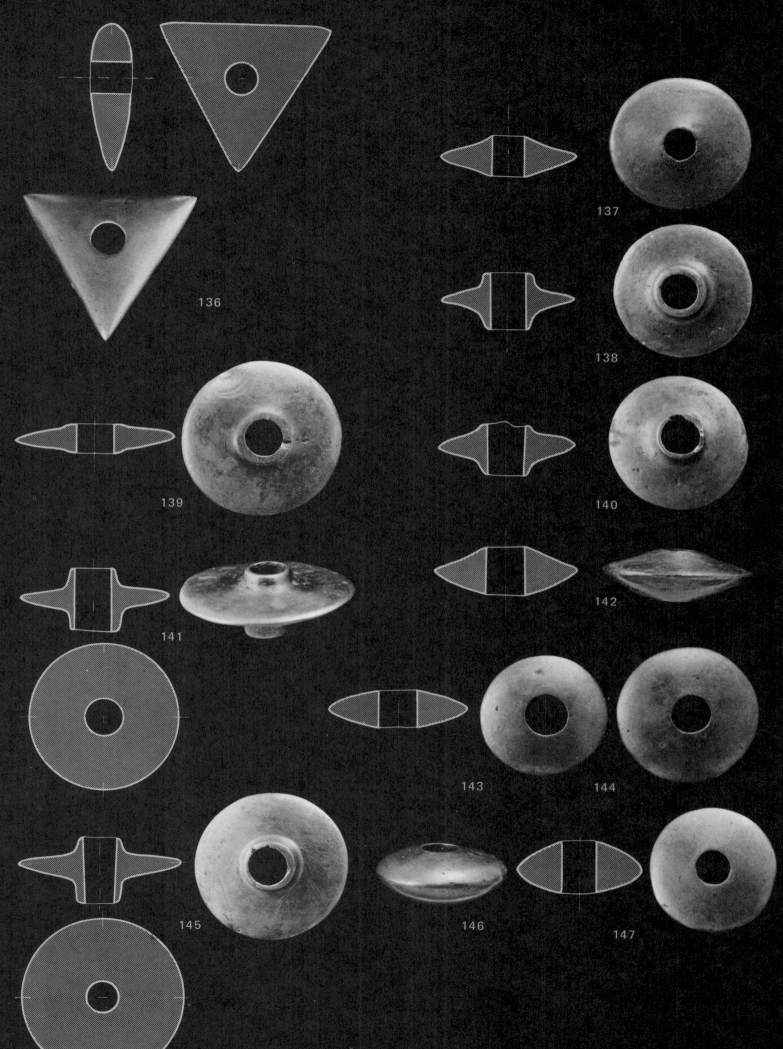

136

137

138

139

140

141

142

143

144

145

146

147

97

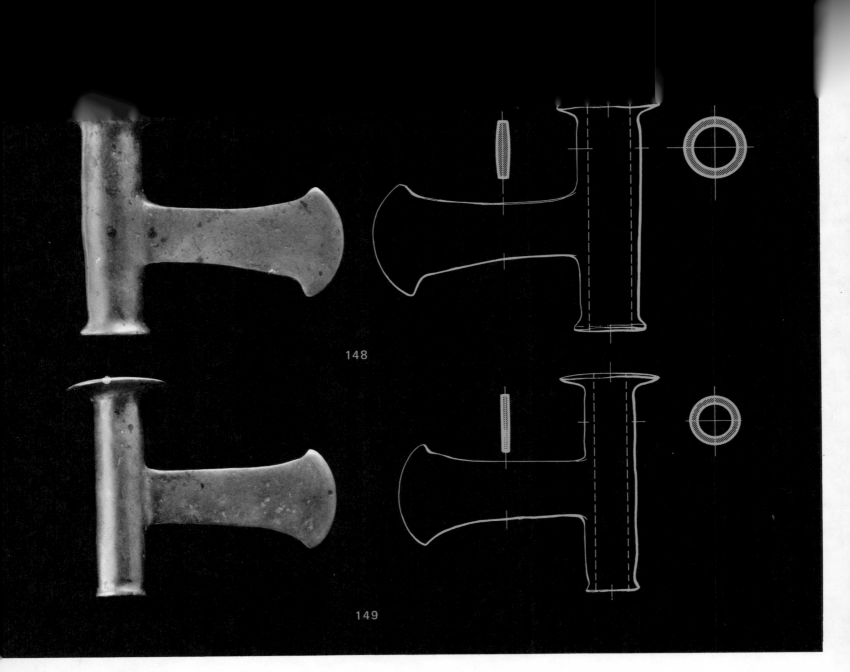

148

149

No. 148 (Reg. No. 61–122)
Standard with axe. Hollow, plain shaft. The axe is attached to the middle of the standard
(L – 8.5 cm; W – 2.6). The blade widens towards the splayed edge. Flat ledge-rim at
upper end and ring-shaped lower rim.
L – 11.3 cm; Diam – 2.5 cm; Th – 0.4 cm; Wt – 344 gr.

No. 149 (Reg. No. 61–123)
Standard with axe. Hollow, plain shaft. The axe is attached to the middle of the standard
(L – 8 cm, W – 2.5 cm). The blade widens towards the splayed edge. Flat ledge-rim at upper
end and ring-shaped lower rim.
L – 9.6 cm; Diam – 2.2 cm; Th – 0.4 cm; Wt – 240 gr.

No. 150 (Reg. No. 61–92)
Standard. Hollow. Bulbous head, from which spring: a long, sharp, beak-like projection,
pointing downwards; a boss with a disk-shaped head, pointing upwards; three similar bosses
at right angles to the shaft.
L – 14.1 cm; Diam – 2.5 cm; Th – 0.5 cm; Wt – 602 gr.

No. 151 (Reg. No. 61–116)
Standard. Hollow. Shaped like a truncated inverted pyramid. The wider end carries a sharp,
beak-like projection (L – 6.8 cm).
L – 5.7 cm; Wt – 320 gr.

No. 152 (Reg. No. 61–117)
Standard. Hollow. Cylindrical shaft carries four large cylindrical bosses with disk-like heads,
forming a kind of Maltese cross.
L – 5.4 cm; Th – 1.2 cm; Wt – 975 gr.

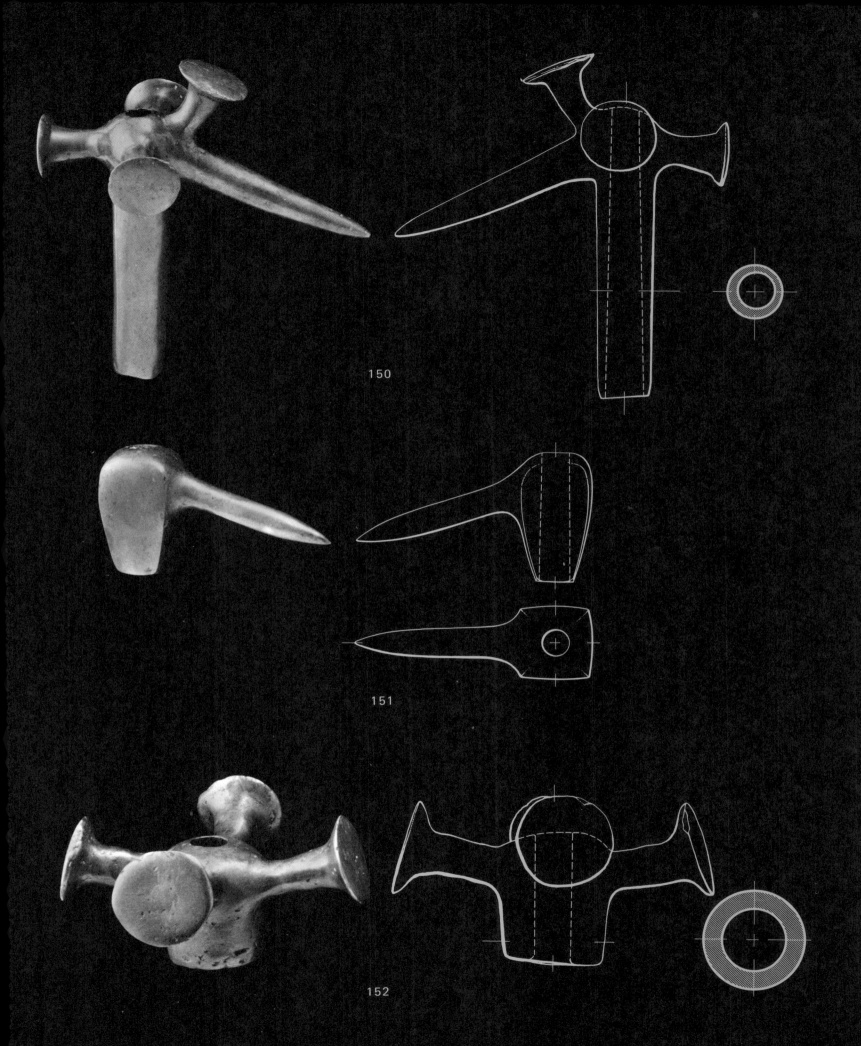

150

151

152

No. 153 (Reg. No. 61–119)
Standard. Piriform macehead surmounted by twin ibexes (foreparts only) and two arms. One has a pointed end, and the other terminates in a curved and splayed blade. The two ibex heads, which are joined to a single four-legged body, have grooved horns, projecting ears, marked eyes and nostrils and an open mouth.
Ht – 11 cm; Max W – 14 cm; Wt – 335 gr.

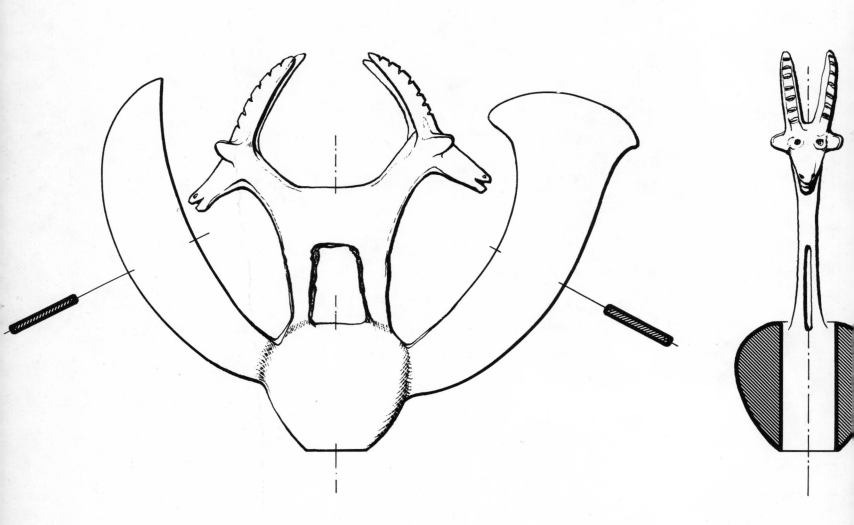

No. 154 (Reg. No. 61-151)

Eagle standard. Flat, roughly rectangular plaque. Asymmetrical spread wings, and above them, the head of the eagle, with holes marking eyes, and an open beak. Near middle of plaque, short cylindrical shaft, projecting on both sides, and enclosed on both sides by a raised rectangular frame. The plaque, both front and back, is decorated with a double zigzag line ending below in feather-like vertical grooves, and with herring-bone designs. Inside the cylindrical shaft is a 5 mm diam hole, probably the opening through which the metal was poured during casting. A soldered patch on the outside, with incisions made by a tool, was probably intended to correct a casting defect.

Ht – 15.3 cm; W – 6.5 cm; Wing-span – 12 cm; Th – 0.5-0.6 cm; L (shaft) – 4.8 cm; Th (shaft wall) – 0.3-0.5 cm; Wt – 597 gr.

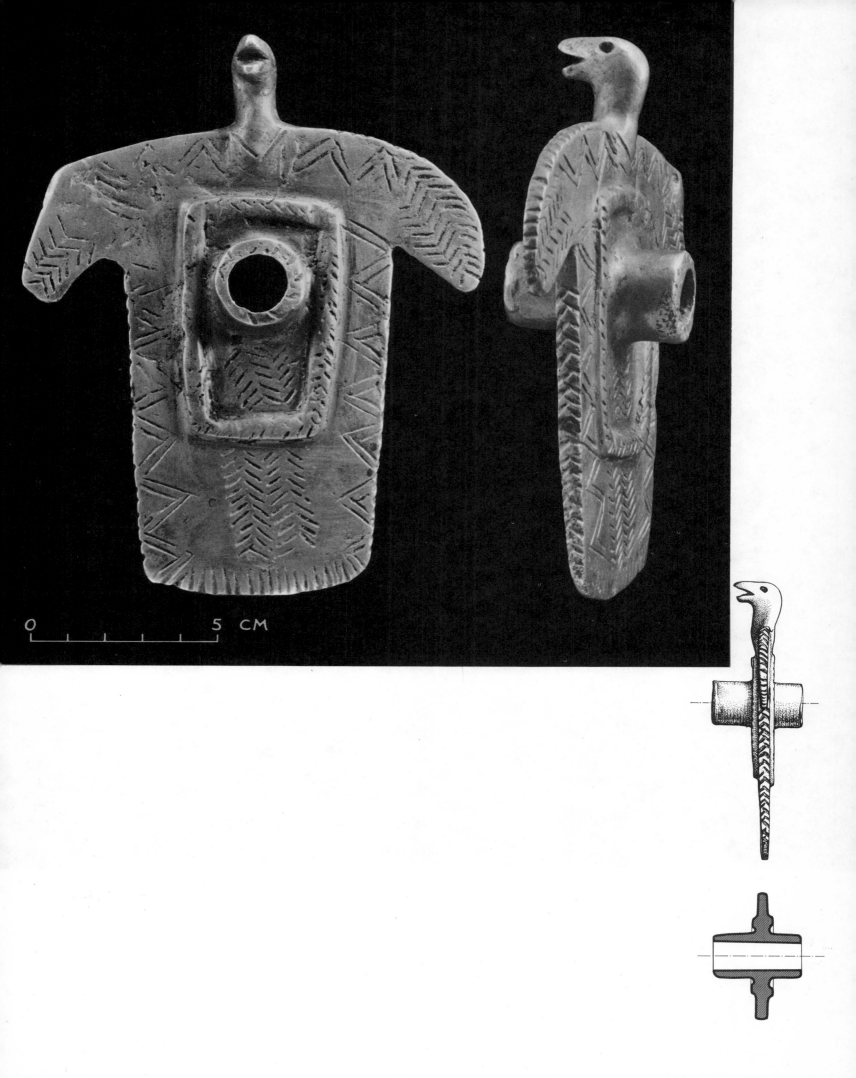

0   5 CM

103

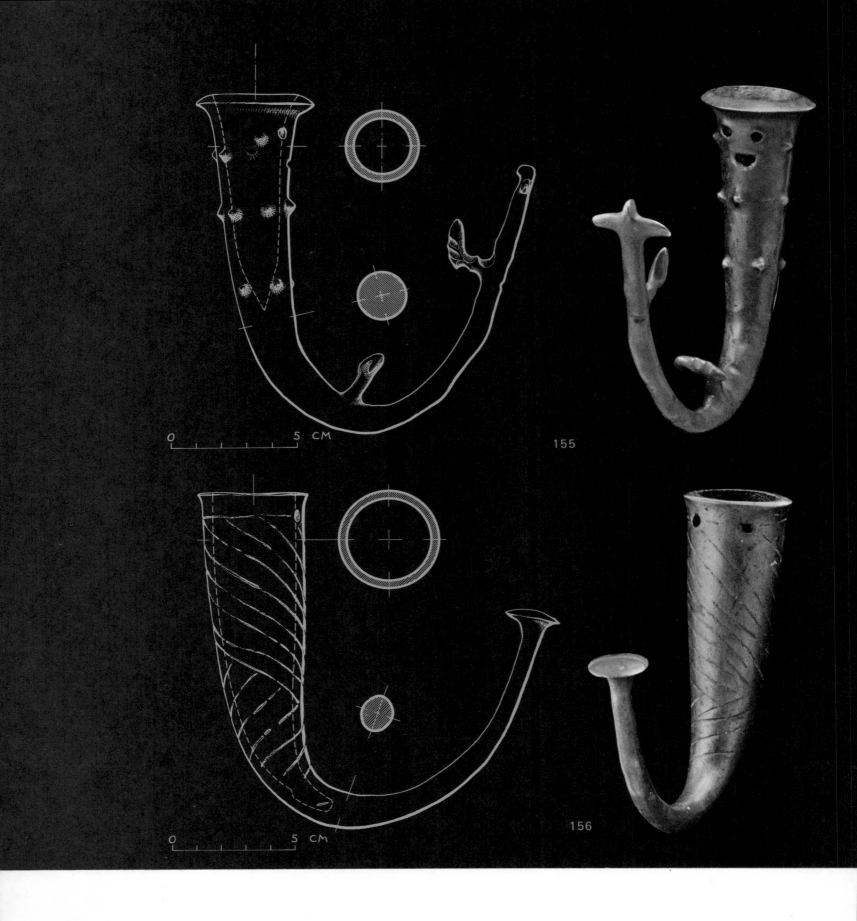

155

156

Copper Horns and Jars

The treasure includes three horn-shaped vessels. All three are solid at the narrow end, and have two holes near the rim of the mouth. In No. 157, a piece of twisted rope threaded through the holes has survived. The knobs, disks, birds and groove-patterns ornamenting these horns are familiar from the other copper artifacts in the treasure. These three objects resemble the horns of plenty of much later periods, but their purpose remains obscure.

The other vessels include two small jars, one of them resembling a pithos in shape, and three small copper baskets. Here too, a variety of grooved patterns are used to decorate the vessels.

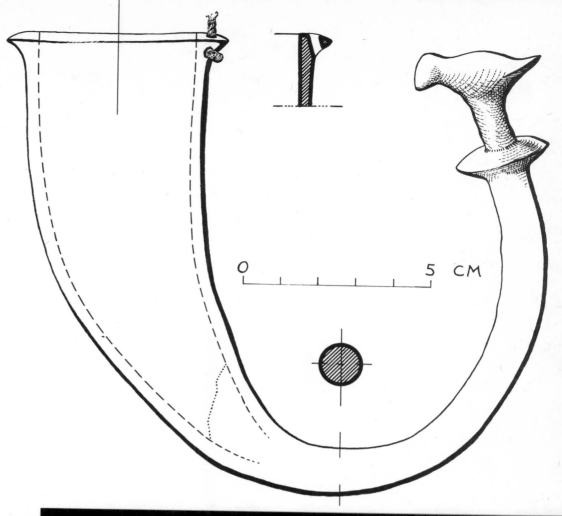

o. 155 (Reg. No. 61–169)
orn-shaped object. Partly solid. The narrow
d terminates in a schematic bird with spread
ngs. There is another schematic bird slightly
low the first, and a third at the bend of the
rn. The mouth of the horn has a flattened
erted rim. Below it, two round holes and a
angular hole, resembling two eyes and a
outh (human face?). The upper part of the
rn is decorated with small knobs.
: – 14 cm; Diam of mouth – 4.9 cm;
– 0.4 cm; Wt – 335 gr.

o. 156 (Reg. No. 61–168)
orn-shaped object. Partly solid, terminating
the narrow end in a disk-shaped head. The
outh of the horn has a flat rim, with two
les below it. The body of the horn is
corated with diagonal grooves. There are
ting defects at the bend.
– 14 cm; Diam of mouth – 4.7 cm;
– 0.4 cm; Wt – 497 gr.

No. 157 (Reg. No. 61–167)
Horn-shaped object. Partly solid, terminating at the
narrow end in a disk carrying a bird. The mouth of the
horn has a flattened everted rim, pierced by two holes.
Remains of a twisted rope are threaded into the holes
from outside.
Ht – 13.3 cm; Diam of mouth – 6 cm; Th – 0.4 cm;
Wt – 543 gr.

157

No. 158 (Reg. No. 61–166)
Jar. Ring-shaped rim. Elongated neck. Piriform body. The neck and body are decorated with grooved herring-bone and diagonal patterns. Small flat base, with a soldered patch.
Ht – 16 cm; Diam – 9.5 cm; Th – 0.3 cm; Wt – 760 gr.

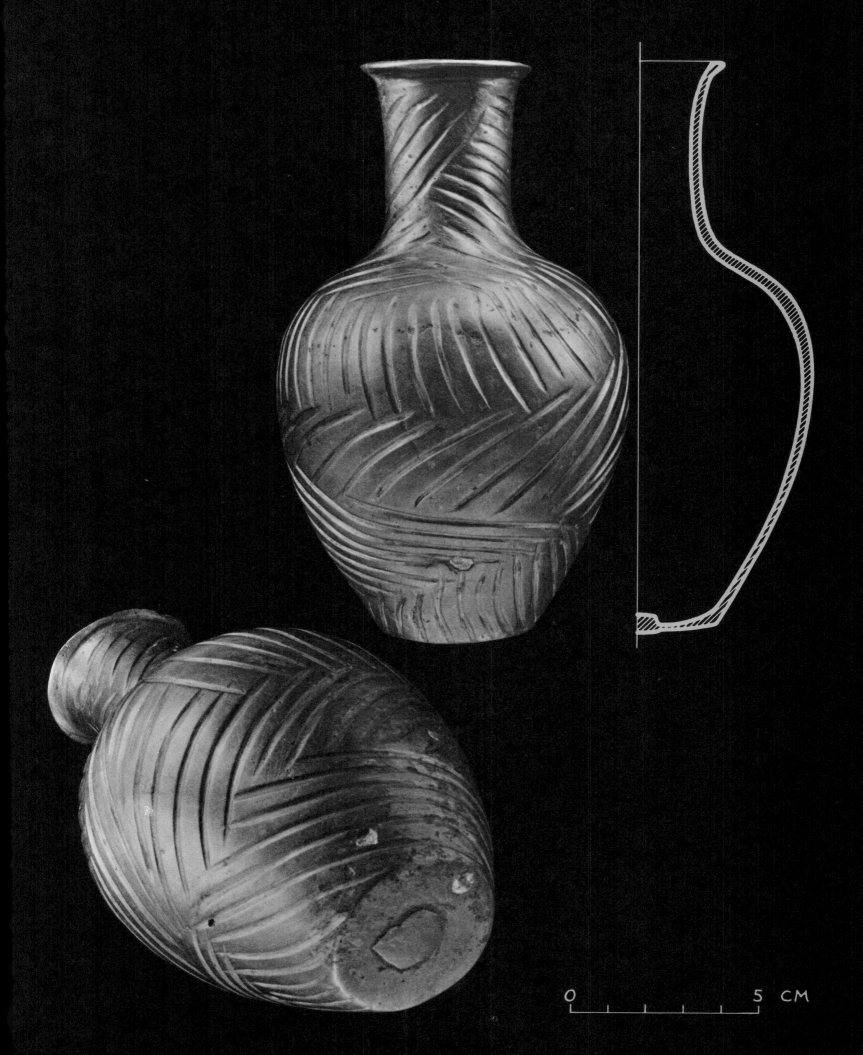

0   5 CM

No. 159 (Reg. No. 61–162)
Basket-shaped jar, cast in one piece with a high (8.5 cm) basket handle. Flattened irregular rim. Goblet-shaped body, short stump base surrounded by a soldered ring. The body is decorated with herring-bone and irregular grooved patterns between horizontal grooves.
Ht – 17.8 cm; Diam – 7.5–8 cm; Diam of base – 2.8–3 cm; Th – 0.5 cm; Wt – 671 gr.

No. 160 (Reg. No. 61–164)
Basket-shaped jar, cast in one piece with a high (9.5 cm) basket handle, which is decorated with diagonal grooves. Sharp projection at top of handle. Flattened everted rim. Two horizontal grooves below the rim and one near middle of vessel. Slightly slanting grooves converge at the rounded base, dividing the surface into segments.
Ht – 17.8 cm; Diam – 8.9 cm; Th – 0.3 cm; Wt – 672 gr.

No. 161 (Reg. No. 61–163)
Basket-shaped jar, cast in one piece with a high (9.5 cm) basket handle (cracked). Rounded projection at top of handle. Flattened everted rim. Three horizontal grooves around body. Rounded base.
Ht – 17.8 cm; Diam – 8 cm; Th – 0.3 cm; Wt – 480 gr.

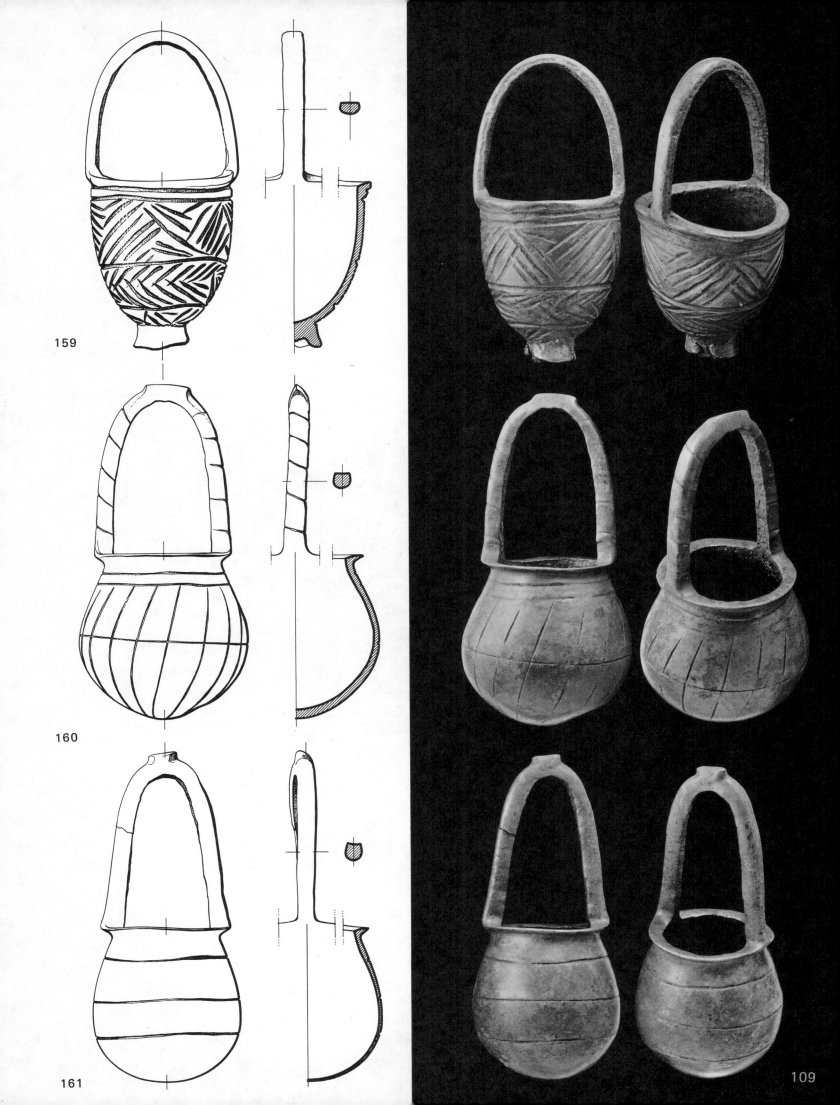

159

160

161

No. 162 (Reg. No. 61–165)

Wide-mouthed jar. Flattened, slightly everted rim. Conical body, decorated with grooved herring-bone patterns, and ringed with hoop-like horizontal ridges. Above the top ridge, four elongated vertical projections (2 × 1 cm). Rounded base. Sooty inside. (incense burner?).
Ht – 15.5 cm; Diam – 15 cm; Th – 0.3–0.4 cm; Wt – 1542 gr.

Copper Tools

The treasure also contained one axe, fifteen chisels and one hammer. The tools range in length from 15 to 30 cm, and in hue from light copper-red to very dark. The shape of the chisels is generally elongated, narrow at the top and widening towards the edge; some are thicker near the middle. One has a perforated end. The edges are sharp or blunt, straight, curved or splayed. The casting is generally of good quality; some tools show defects, either uncorrected casting faults or damage due to use, as in Nos. 167 and 178.

Similar chisels have been found in many Chalcolithic sites, such as Naḥal Ṣe'elim,[6] Teleilat Ghassul[7] and Meṣer,[8] as well as in Egypt,[9] Syria,[10] Anatolia[11] and Mesopotamia.[12]

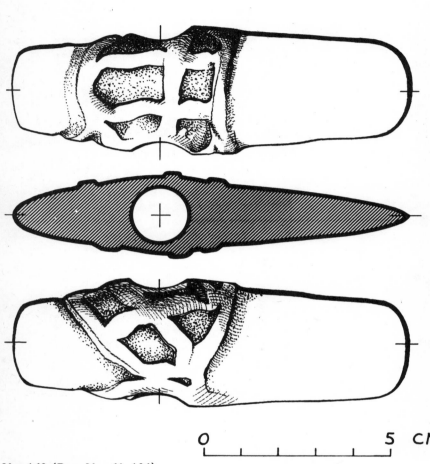

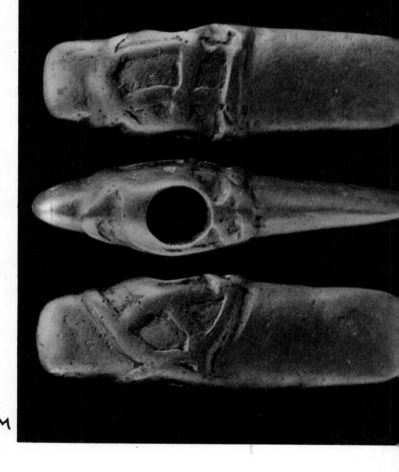

0   5 CM

No. 163 (Reg. No. 61–134)
Axe. Hole through thickest part of the elongated body. One edge sharp and the other blunt. Rope-like raised decoration around the hole, imitating the rope or leather thongs used to bind the axe to the handle. The "rope" is interlaced differently on each side of the axe. L – 10.4 cm; W – 3.5; Diam of hole – 1.5 cm; Th – 2.4 cm; Wt – 248 gr.

No. 164 (Reg. No. 61–135)
Chisel. Widening slightly towards blunt rounded edge. L – 15.3 cm; W – 3.1 cm; Th – 1.2 cm; Wt – 446 gr.

No. 165 (Reg. No. 61–136)
Chisel. Widening slightly towards blunt rounded edge. L – 16.3 cm; W – 3.8 cm; Th – 1.3 cm; Wt – 508 gr.

No. 166 (Reg. No. 61–147)
Chisel. Long and narrow. Sharp splayed edge. L – 18 cm; W – 3 cm; Th – 0.8 cm; Wt – 279 gr.

No. 167 (Reg. No. 61–146)
Chisel. Long and narrow. Blunt rounded edge. L – 32.9 cm; W – 2.8 cm; Th – 1.3 cm; Wt – 807 gr.

No. 168 (Reg. No. 61–148)
Chisel. Long and very thin. Sharp splayed edge. L – 29.5 cm; W – 2.9 cm; Th – 0.3 cm; Wt – 156 gr.

No. 169 (Reg. No. 61–145)
Chisel. Long, narrow and thin. Sharp splayed edge. L – 25.3 cm; W – 3.4 cm; Th – 0.6 cm; Wt – 325 gr.

164

165

166

167

168

169

0   5 CM

No. 170 (Reg. No. 61–150)
Hammer. Oval, with central hole. One end is blunt and thick, the other tapering.
L – 13 cm; W – 6.6 cm; Th – 2.3 cm; Wt – 836 gr.

No. 171 (Reg. No. 61–149)
Chisel. Almost rectangular. Sharp edge. Perforation near top.
L – 15 cm; W – 3.8 cm; Th – 0.8 cm; Wt – 265 gr.

No. 172 (Reg. No. 61–141)
Chisel. Almost rectangular. Sharp, rounded and slightly splayed edge. The other end is damaged.
L – 8.5 cm; W – 2.8 cm; Th – 1.6 cm; Wt – 244 gr.

No. 173 (Reg. No. 61–143)
Chisel. Almost rectangular. Sharp, rounded and slightly splayed edge.
L – 9.9 cm; W – 2.5 cm; Th – 1.6 cm; Wt – 260 gr.

No. 174 (Reg. No. 61–140)
Chisel. Widening slightly towards the sharp, rounded and slightly splayed edge.
L – 11.9 cm; W – 2.3 cm; Th – 1.6 cm; Wt – 285 gr.

No. 175 (Reg. No. 61–137)
Chisel. Widening slightly towards the rounded edge.
L – 12.5 cm; W – 2.4 cm; Th – 1.3 cm; Wt – 268 gr.

No. 176 (Reg. No. 61–139)
Chisel. Widening slightly towards the sharp, rounded and slightly splayed edge.
L – 11 cm; W – 2.5 cm; Th – 1.5 cm; Wt – 292 gr.

No. 177 (Reg. No. 61–138)
Chisel. Almost rectangular. Sharp straight edge.
L – 12 cm; W – 2.9 cm; Th – 1.1 cm; Wt – 250 gr.

No. 178 (Reg. No. 61–144)
Chisel. Widening slightly towards the rounded, splayed edge.
L – 12.5 cm; W – 2.4 cm; Th – 1.3 cm; Wt – 268 gr.

No. 179 (Reg. No. 61–142)
Chisel. Almost rectangular. Both ends are blunt and show traces of hammering and signs of casting defects.
L – 11 cm; W – 3 cm; Th – 2.1 cm; Wt – 458 gr.

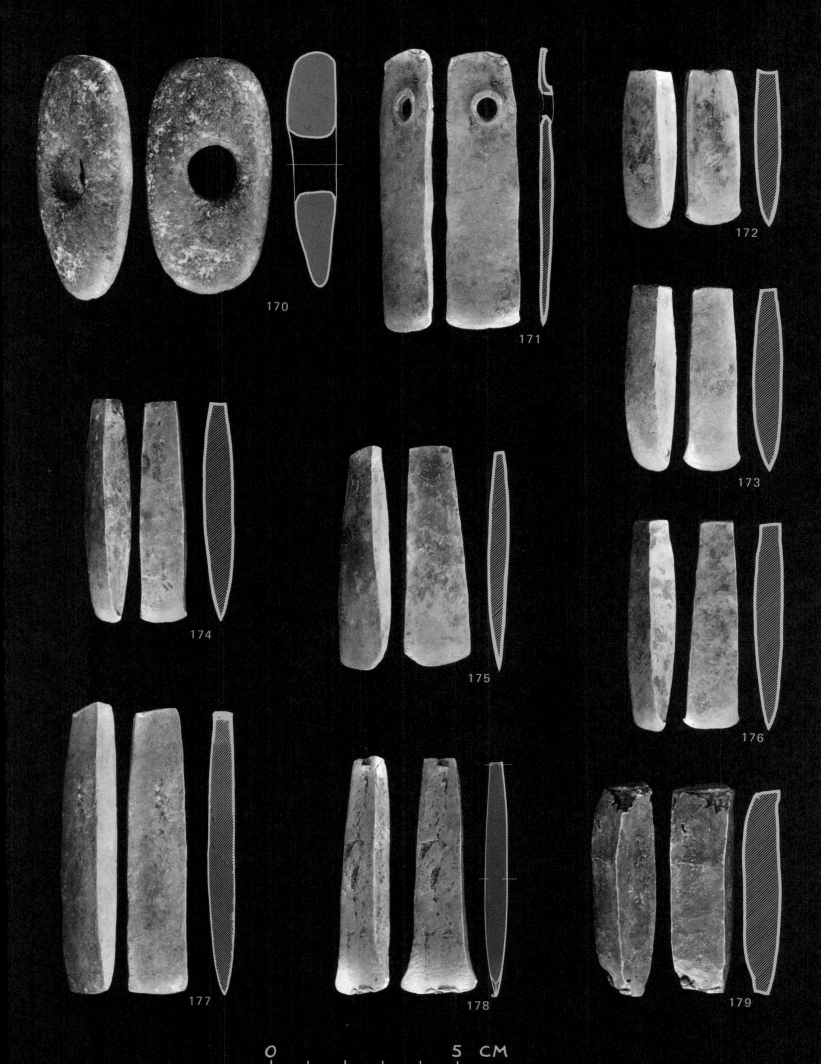

170

171

172

173

174

175

176

177

178

179

0　　　　　　　　　5　CM

115

Mace-heads

Copper. Over two hundred and forty copper mace-heads were found, no two of them exactly alike. They differ in size (3–6 cm diam), in weight (110–619 gr), in colour (from copper-coloured to dark) and in shape (spherical, flattened, piriform or disk-shaped). The majority are plain, and only a few have either grooved or ridged decorations. The perforation is either cylindrical, or wider at one end and narrower at the other. The walls vary in thickness and are either concave or straight on the inside. After testing a fairly large number of mace-heads, one was cut in half and tested in a metallurgical laboratory by R. Potashkin and K. Bar-Avi. They found that the shell formed by the walls of the mace-head was filled with ceramic material (see Appendix D). Possibly this complicated method of manufacture was invented in order to save metal. The other mace-heads tested by X-ray in the same laboratory, did not show a similar material inside the walls.

All the mace-heads are carefully polished on the outside, with the exception of one (No. 183), which has a rough surface and a perforated projection on the side. This object may perhaps provide a clue to the method of manufacture: the metal was poured through the hole in the projection into a mould filled with wax (*cire perdue* method).

Remains of wooden staffs or poles remained inside several mace-heads. In many others traces of black incrustation were found, perhaps the remains of some matter which had served to fix the mace-head firmly to the staff (see also below). A folded fragment of linen fabric survived in one of the mace-heads (No. 400).

In other sites only isolated mace-heads have so far been uncovered. For instance, a few similar spherical and piriform mace-heads were found in the Chalcolithic cave at Naḥal Ṣe'elim[13] and at Beersheba.[14] A spectrographic analysis of these mace-heads carried out by C.A. Key, shows them to be of similar composition to the mace-heads of our treasure (see Appendix E).

Haematite. Six of the mace-heads were of haematite (Nos. 184–189). They too, differ in size and in shape: one is spherical, one flattened and four are piriform. The hole is either cylindrical or narrows towards the top. Their colour is black, one matt and the others lustrous.

Similar mace-heads have been found in Naḥal Ṣe'elim,[15] Bene Beraq,[16] Azor,[17] Beersheba[18] and Megiddo.[19]

Limestone. One limestone mace-head was found (No. 423). Similar piriform mace-heads, as well as limestone mace-heads of different shape, were found at Teleilat Ghassul,[20] Beersheba,[21] Beth She'an,[22] Megiddo,[23] Stratum VII of Jericho[24] and Site H in Naḥal Besor.[25] Mace-heads of limestone, marble, basalt or granite are known from many sites in the Near East, from the Neolithic period onwards.[26]

Enlarged views of mace-heads (from left to right: No. 423, stone, showing drill marks in the hole; Nos. 416, 393, 425, copper, showing casting details.

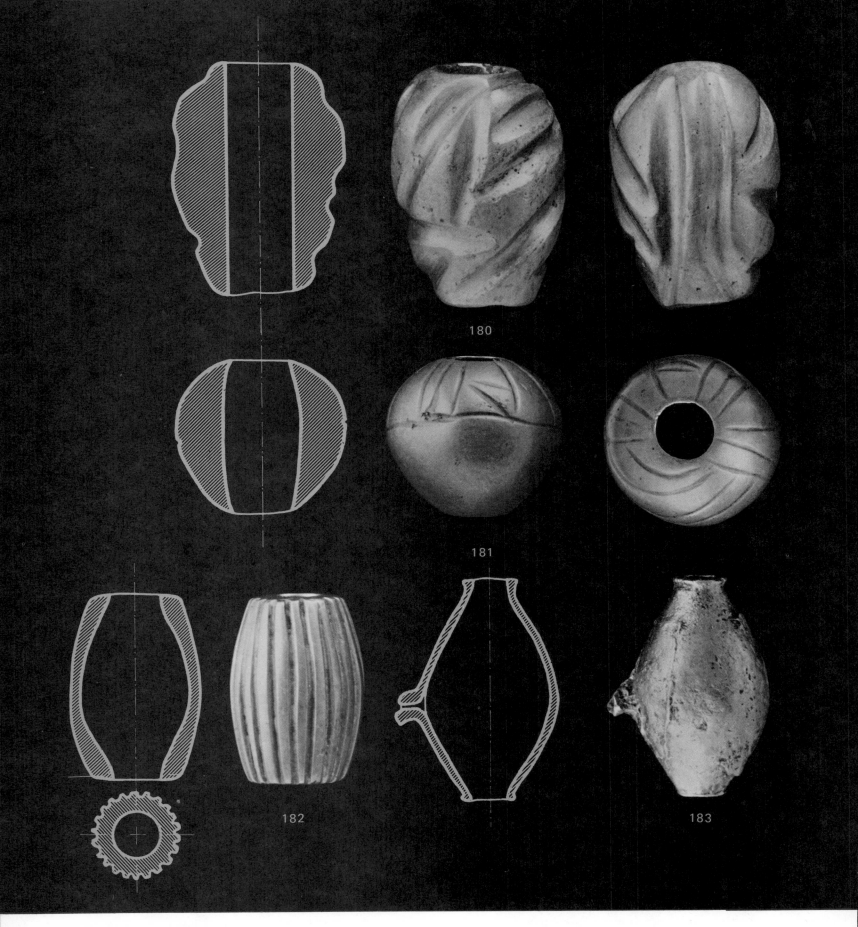

180

181

182

183

Decorated Copper Mace-heads

No. 180 (Reg. No. 61–114)
Decorated with irregular grooves.
Ht – 6.3 cm; Diam – 4.5 cm; Wt – 458 gr.

No. 181 (Reg. No. 61–120)
The upper part is decorated with irregular grooves.
Ht – 4.2 cm; Diam – 4.6 cm; Wt – 285 gr.

No. 182 (Reg. No. 61–113)
Decorated with vertical fluting.
Ht – 5.2 cm; Diam – 3.5 cm; Wt – 184 gr.

No. 183 (Reg. No. 61–115)
Ring-shaped rim at one end. Near its middle, perforated
projection, probably remains of the casting process.
Rough unfinished surface.
Ht – 6.2 cm; Diam – 3.8 cm; Wt – 145 gr.

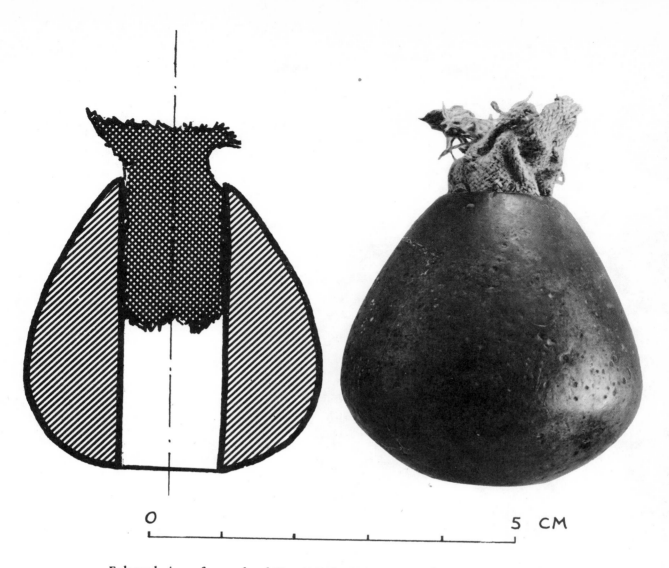

Enlarged view of mace-head No. 400, showing piece of linen fabric in the hole.

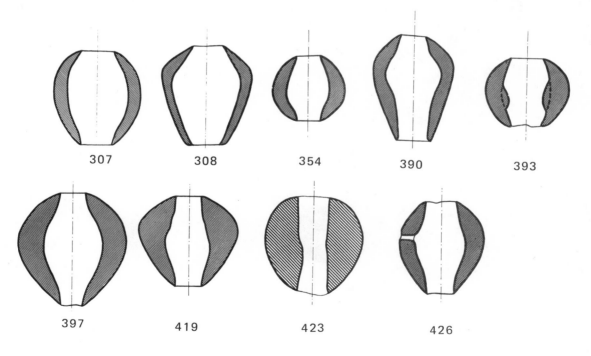

307   308   354   390   393

397   419   423   426

Section drawing of characteristic mace-heads.

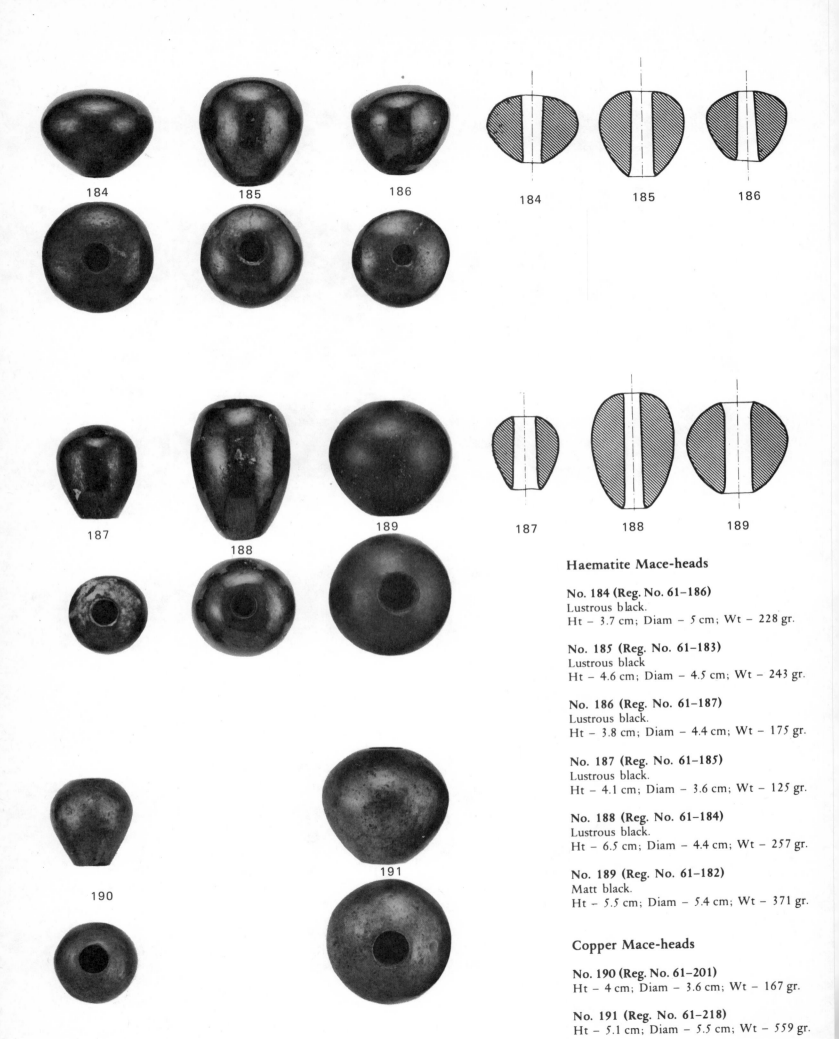

184 185 186

184 185 186

187 189

188

187 188 189

Haematite Mace-heads

No. 184 (Reg. No. 61–186)
Lustrous black.
Ht – 3.7 cm; Diam – 5 cm; Wt – 228 gr.

No. 185 (Reg. No. 61–183)
Lustrous black
Ht – 4.6 cm; Diam – 4.5 cm; Wt – 243 gr.

No. 186 (Reg. No. 61–187)
Lustrous black.
Ht – 3.8 cm; Diam – 4.4 cm; Wt – 175 gr.

No. 187 (Reg. No. 61–185)
Lustrous black.
Ht – 4.1 cm; Diam – 3.6 cm; Wt – 125 gr.

No. 188 (Reg. No. 61–184)
Lustrous black.
Ht – 6.5 cm; Diam – 4.4 cm; Wt – 257 gr.

No. 189 (Reg. No. 61–182)
Matt black.
Ht – 5.5 cm; Diam – 5.4 cm; Wt – 371 gr.

Copper Mace-heads

No. 190 (Reg. No. 61–201)
Ht – 4 cm; Diam – 3.6 cm; Wt – 167 gr.

No. 191 (Reg. No. 61–218)
Ht – 5.1 cm; Diam – 5.5 cm; Wt – 559 gr.

190

191

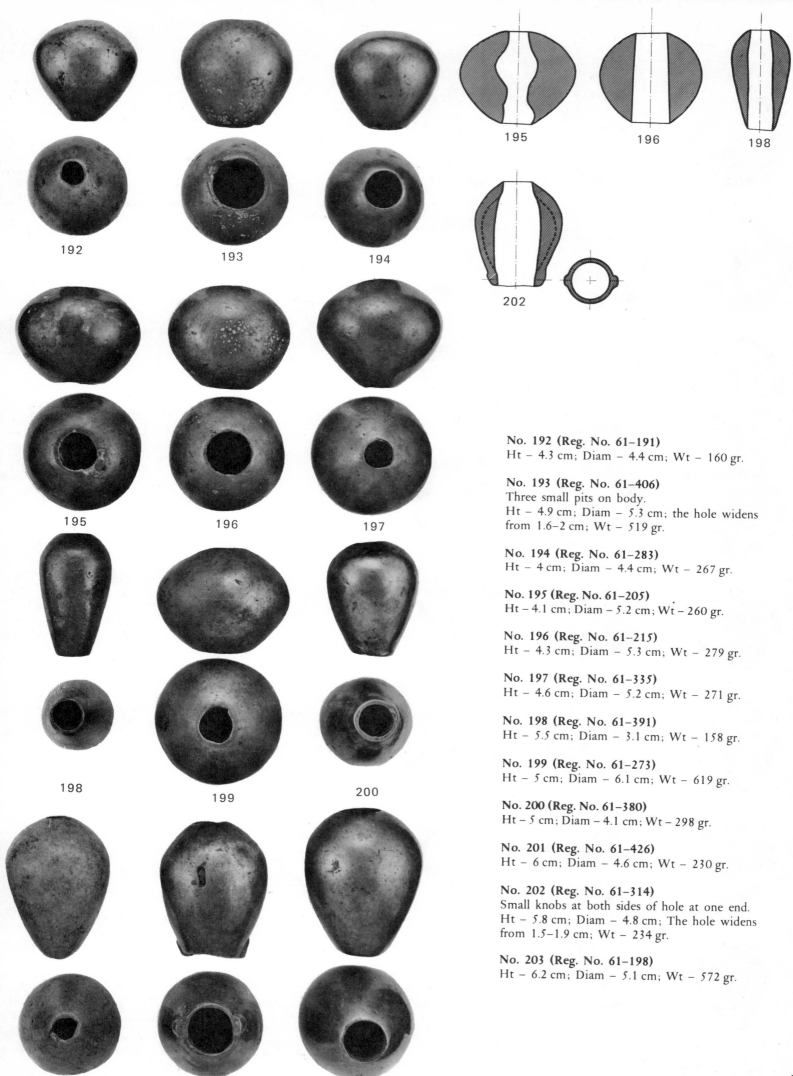

No. 192 (Reg. No. 61–191)
Ht – 4.3 cm; Diam – 4.4 cm; Wt – 160 gr.

No. 193 (Reg. No. 61–406)
Three small pits on body.
Ht – 4.9 cm; Diam – 5.3 cm; the hole widens
from 1.6–2 cm; Wt – 519 gr.

No. 194 (Reg. No. 61–283)
Ht – 4 cm; Diam – 4.4 cm; Wt – 267 gr.

No. 195 (Reg. No. 61–205)
Ht – 4.1 cm; Diam – 5.2 cm; Wt – 260 gr.

No. 196 (Reg. No. 61–215)
Ht – 4.3 cm; Diam – 5.3 cm; Wt – 279 gr.

No. 197 (Reg. No. 61–335)
Ht – 4.6 cm; Diam – 5.2 cm; Wt – 271 gr.

No. 198 (Reg. No. 61–391)
Ht – 5.5 cm; Diam – 3.1 cm; Wt – 158 gr.

No. 199 (Reg. No. 61–273)
Ht – 5 cm; Diam – 6.1 cm; Wt – 619 gr.

No. 200 (Reg. No. 61–380)
Ht – 5 cm; Diam – 4.1 cm; Wt – 298 gr.

No. 201 (Reg. No. 61–426)
Ht – 6 cm; Diam – 4.6 cm; Wt – 230 gr.

No. 202 (Reg. No. 61–314)
Small knobs at both sides of hole at one end.
Ht – 5.8 cm; Diam – 4.8 cm; The hole widens
from 1.5–1.9 cm; Wt – 234 gr.

No. 203 (Reg. No. 61–198)
Ht – 6.2 cm; Diam – 5.1 cm; Wt – 572 gr.

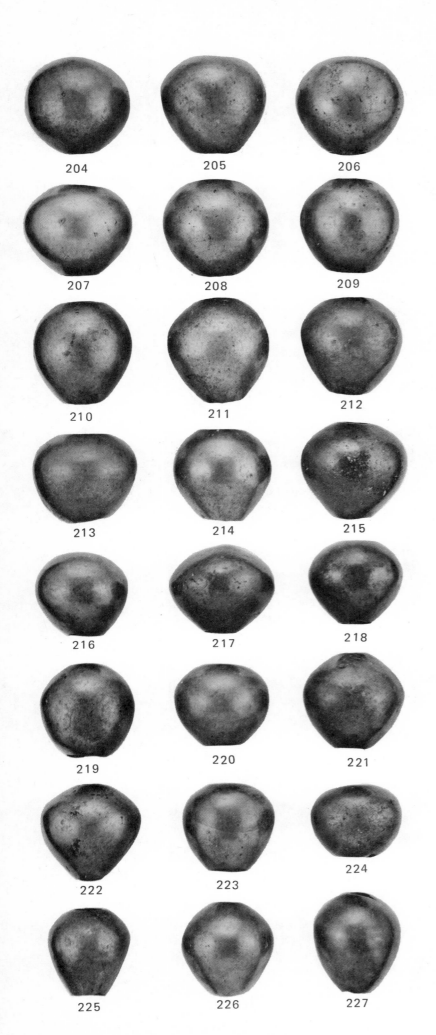

204 205 206
207 208 209
210 211 212
213 214 215
216 217 218
219 220 221
222 223 224
225 226 227

No. 204 (Reg. No. 61–360)
Ht – 4.2 cm; Diam – 4.6 cm; Wt – 242 gr.

No. 205 (Reg. No. 61–368)
Ht – 4.2 cm; Diam – 4.7 cm; Wt – 320 gr.

No. 206 (Reg. No. 61–361)
Ht – 4.2 cm; Diam – 4.6 cm; Wt – 339 gr.

No. 207 (Reg. No. 61–383)
Ht – 4 cm; Diam – 4.8 cm; Wt – 341 gr.

No. 208 (Reg. No. 61–359)
Ht – 4.5 cm; Diam – 4.6 cm; Wt – 358 gr.

No. 209 (Reg. No. 61–381)
Ht – 4.1 cm; Diam – 4.3 cm; Wt – 278 gr.

No. 210 (Reg. No. 61–354)
Ht – 4.6 cm; Diam – 4.3 cm; Wt – 260 gr.

No. 211 (Reg. No. 61–352)
Ht – 4.7 cm; Diam – 4.6 cm; Wt – 234 gr.

No. 212 (Reg. No. 61–371)
Ht – 4.3 cm; Diam – 4.5 cm; Wt – 222 gr.

No. 213 (Reg. No. 61–382)
Ht – 4 cm; Diam – 4.6 cm; Wt – 250 gr.

No. 214 (Reg. No. 61–350)
Ht – 4.1 cm; Diam – 4.3 cm; Wt – 238 gr.

No. 215 (Reg. No. 61–388)
Ht – 4.3 cm; Diam – 4.7 cm; Wt – 178 gr.

No. 216 (Reg. No. 61–408)
Ht – 4.5 cm; Diam – 4.9 cm; Wt – 240 gr.

No. 217 (Reg. No. 61–413)
Ht – 4.7 cm; Diam – 4.6 cm; Wt – 305 gr.

No. 218 (Reg. No. 61–289)
Ht – 4.5 cm; Diam – 4.7 cm; Wt – 166 gr.

No. 219 (Reg. No. 61–280)
Ht – 4.2 cm; Diam – 5 cm; Wt – 271 gr.

No. 220 (Reg. No. 61–403)
Ht – 4.3 cm; Diam – 4.5 cm; Wt – 295 gr.

No. 221 (Reg. No. 61–402)
Ht – 4.4 cm; Diam – 4.8 cm; Wt – 235 gr.

No. 222 (Reg. No. 61–306)
Ht – 4.5 cm; Diam – 4.8 cm; Wt – 330 gr.

No. 223 (Reg. No. 61–424)
Ht – 3.6 cm; Diam – 4.1 cm; Wt – 213 gr.

No. 224 (Reg. No. 61–414)
Ht – 4.2 cm; Diam – 4.5 cm; Wt – 284 gr.

No. 225 (Reg. No. 61–269)
Ht – 4.6 cm; Diam – 4.8 cm; Wt – 225 gr.

No. 226 (Reg. No. 61–407)
Ht – 4.2 cm; Diam – 4.7 cm; Wt – 280 gr.

No. 227 (Reg. No. 61–270)
Black incrustation inside hole.
Ht – 4.2 cm; Diam – 4.7 cm; Wt – 268 gr.

No. 228 (Reg. No. 61–362)
Ht – 3.8 cm; Diam – 4.3 cm; Wt – 242 gr.

No. 229 (Reg. No. 61–196)
Black incrustation inside hole.
Ht – 4.6 cm; Diam – 5.6 cm; Wt – 241 gr.

No. 230 (Reg. No. 61–425)
This mace-head was cut in half and tested in a metal-lurgical laboratory. See Appendix D.

No. 231 (Reg. No. 61–255)
Ht – 4.3 cm; Diam – 4.4 cm; Wt – 234 gr.

No. 232 (Reg. No. 61–193)
Ht – 3.7 cm; Diam – 4.1 cm; Wt – 208 gr.

No. 233 (Reg. No. 61–258)
Black incrustation inside hole.
Ht – 4 cm; Diam – 4 cm; Wt – 190 gr.

No. 234 (Reg. No. 61–230)
Ht – 4 cm; Diam – 4.3 cm; Wt – 184 gr.

No. 235 (Reg. No. 61–192)
Ht – 3.5 cm; Diam – 4 cm; Wt – 193 gr.

No. 236 (Reg. No. 61–372)
Ht – 4.2 cm; Diam – 4.2 cm; Wt – 288 gr.

No. 237 (Reg. No. 61–385)
Ht – 3.9 cm; Diam – 4.1 cm; Wt – 231 gr.

No. 238 (Reg. No. 61–212)
Ht – 3.6 cm; Diam – 4 cm; Wt – 230 gr.

No. 239 (Reg. No. 61–195)
Ht – 4.2 cm; Diam – 4.4 cm; Wt – 247 gr.

No. 240 (Reg. No. 61–261)
Ht – 3.7 cm; Diam – 4.1 cm; Wt – 203 gr.

No. 241 (Reg. No. 61–384)
Ht – 3.7 cm; Diam – 4.7 cm; Wt – 232 gr.

No. 242 (Reg. No. 61–194)
Black incrustation inside hole.
Ht – 4.4 cm; Diam – 4.5 cm; Wt – 210 gr.

No. 243 (Reg. No. 61–247)
Ht – 4.1 cm; Diam – 4.1 cm; Wt – 270 gr.

No. 244 (Reg. No. 61–266)
Ht – 3.6 cm; Diam – 4.3 cm; Wt – 166 gr.

No. 245 (Reg. No. 61–254)
Ht – 4.2 cm; Diam – 4.5 cm; Wt – 150 gr.

No. 246 (Reg. No. 61–272)
Ht – 4.4 cm; Diam – 4.9 cm; Wt – 185 gr.

No. 247 (Reg. No. 61–197)
Ht – 3.9 cm; Diam – 4.1 cm; Wt – 226 gr.

No. 248 (Reg. No. 61–207)
Ht – 4 cm; Diam – 4.4 cm; Wt – 280 gr.

No. 249 (Reg. No. 61–428)
Ht – 4.6 cm; Diam – 5 cm; Wt – 325 gr.

No. 250 (Reg. No. 61–256)
Ht – 4.2 cm; Diam – 4.1 cm; Wt – 110 gr.

No. 251 (Reg. No. 61–252)
Ht – 4.6 cm; Diam – 3.9 cm; Wt – 230 gr.

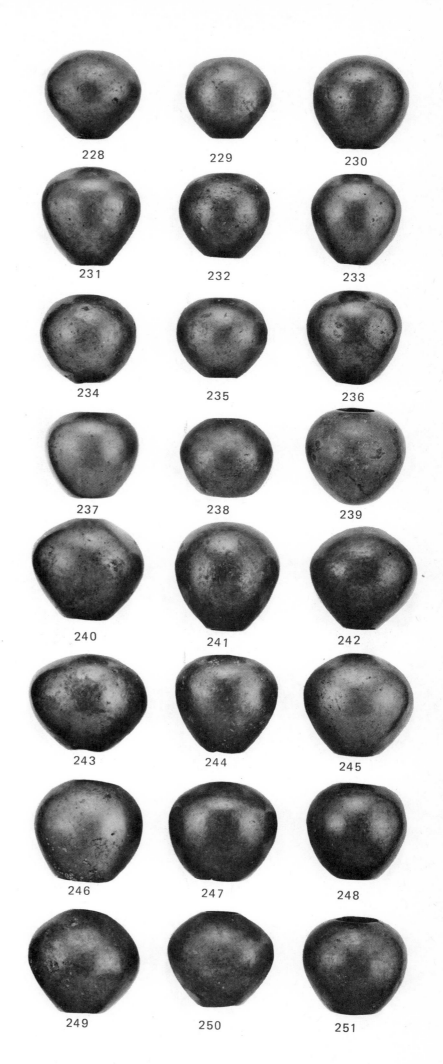

228   229   230

231   232   233

234   235   236

237   238   239

240   241   242

243   244   245

246   247   248

249   250   251

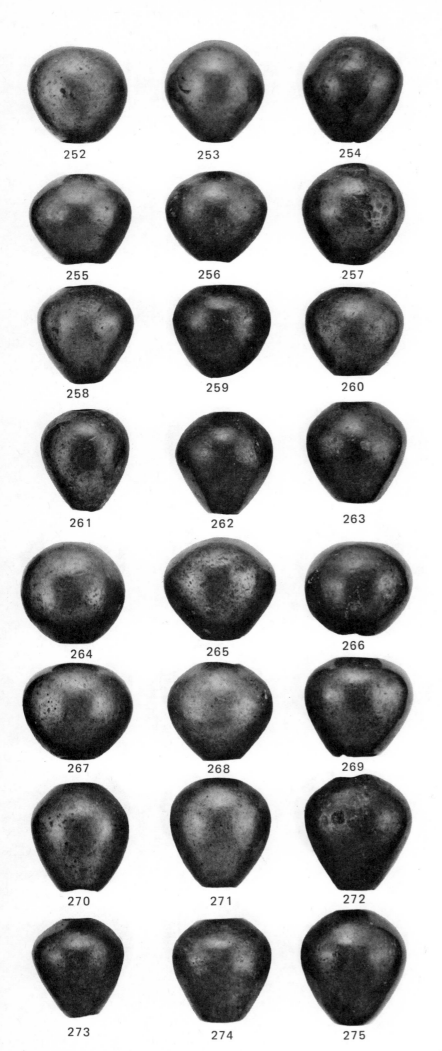

No. 252 (Reg. No. 61–208)
Ht – 4.6 cm; Diam – 4.3 cm; Wt – 222 gr.

No. 253 (Reg. No. 61–262)
Ht – 4.3 cm; Diam – 4.4 cm; Wt – 287 gr.

No. 254 (Reg. No. 61–259)
Ht – 4.4 cm; Diam – 4.3 cm; Wt – 240 gr.

No. 255 (Reg. No. 61–369)
Ht – 3.9 cm; Diam – 4.5 cm; Wt – 272 gr.

No. 256 (Reg. No. 61–263)
Ht – 4 cm; Diam – 4.4 cm; Wt – 196 gr.

No. 257 (Reg. No. 61–386)
Ht – 4.2 cm; Diam – 4.4 cm; Wt – 224 gr.

No. 258 (Reg. No. 61–222)
Ht – 4.4 cm; Diam – 4.2 cm; Wt – 221 gr.

No. 259 (Reg. No. 61–279)
Ht – 4.1 cm; Diam – 4.3 cm; Wt – 193 gr.

No. 260 (Reg. No. 61–396)
Casting defect on side.
Ht – 4 cm; Diam – 4.5 cm; Wt – 260 gr.

No. 261 (Reg. No. 61–257)
Ht – 4.5 cm; Diam – 3.9 cm; Wt – 220 gr.

No. 262 (Reg. No. 61–376)
Ht – 4.6 cm; Diam – 4.2 cm; Wt – 161 gr.

No. 263 (Reg. No. 61–240)
Ht – 4.4 cm; Diam – 4.6 cm; Wt – 344 gr.

No. 264 (Reg. No. 61–398)
Ht – 4.4 cm; Diam – 4.6 cm; Wt – 344 gr.

No. 265 (Reg. No. 61–415)
Ht – 4.4 cm; Diam – 4.8 cm; Wt – 340 gr.

No. 266 (Reg. No. 61–287)
Ht – 3.9 cm; Diam – 4.7 cm; Wt – 271 gr.

No. 267 (Reg. No. 61–410)
Ht – 4.1 cm; Diam – 4.8 cm; Wt – 375 gr.

No. 268 (Reg. No. 61–274)
Ht – 4.5 cm; Diam – 4.7 cm; Wt – 308 gr.

No. 269 (Reg. No. 61–405)
Ht – 4.3 cm; Diam – 4.7 cm; Wt – 270 gr.

No. 270 (Reg. No. 61–189)
Ht – 4.7 cm; Diam – 4.4 cm; Wt – 217 gr.

No. 271 (Reg. No. 61–275)
Ht – 4.7 cm; Diam – 4.5 cm; Wt – 228 gr.

No. 272 (Reg. No. 61–281)
Ht – 5 cm; Diam – 4.7 cm; Wt – 327 gr.

No. 273 (Reg. No. 61–340)
Ht – 4.4 cm; Diam – 4.2 cm; Wt – 195 gr.

No. 274 (Reg. No. 61–356)
Ht – 4.6 cm; Diam – 4.5 cm; Wt – 252 gr.

No. 275 (Reg. No. 61–397)
Ht – 5.1 cm; Diam – 4.6 cm; Wt – 299 gr.

No. 276 (Reg. No. 61–416)
Ht – 3.7 cm; Diam – 4.7 cm; Wt – 238 gr.

No. 277 (Reg. No. 61–278)
Ht – 3.8 cm; Diam – 3.8 cm; Wt – 173 gr.

No. 278 (Reg. No. 61–285)
Ht – 3.9 cm; Diam – 4 cm; Wt – 192 gr.

No. 279 (Reg. No. 61–423)
Ht – 3.9 cm; Diam – 4.2 cm; Wt – 178 gr.

No. 280 (Reg. No. 61–288)
Ht – 3.9 cm; Diam – 4.4 cm; Wt – 236 gr.

No. 281 (Reg. No. 61–404)
Ht – 4.3 cm; Diam – 4.1 cm; Wt – 197 gr.

No. 282 (Reg. No. 61–277)
Ht – 4.3 cm; Diam – 4.3 cm; Wt – 294 gr.

No. 283 (Reg. No. 61–401)
Ht – 4.4 cm; Diam – 4.3 cm; Wt – 223 gr.

No. 284 (Reg. No. 61–411)
Ht – 4.4 cm; Diam – 4.7 cm; Diam of
hole – 1.4–1.7 cm; Wt – 310 gr.

No. 285 (Reg. No. 61–271)
Sloping shoulder.
Ht – 5.4 cm; Diam – 4.7 cm; Wt – 314 gr.

No. 286 (Reg. No. 61–276)
Ht – 4.7 cm; Diam – 4.9 cm; Wt – 375 gr.

No. 287 (Reg. No. 61–284)
Ht – 4.3 cm; Diam – 4.5 cm; Wt – 295 gr.

No. 288 (Reg. No. 61–316)
Ht – 3.9 cm; Diam – 4.3 cm; Wt – 236 gr.

No. 289 (Reg. No. 61–309)
Ht – 3.9 cm; Diam – 4.3 cm; Wt – 260 gr.

No. 290 (Reg. No. 61–347)
Ht – 3.6 cm; Diam – 4 cm; Wt – 162 gr.

No. 291 (Reg. No. 61–339)
Ht – 4 cm; Diam – 4.5 cm; Wt – 259 gr.

No. 292 (Reg. No. 61–329)
Ht – 3.8 cm; Diam – 4.5 cm; Wt – 236 gr.

No. 293 (Reg. No. 61–324)
Ht – 4.1 cm; Diam – 4.6 cm; Wt – 249 gr.

No. 294 (Reg. No. 61–317)
Ht – 4.1 cm; Diam – 4.5 cm; Wt – 160 gr.

No. 295 (Reg. No. 61–319)
Ht – 4 cm; Diam – 4.4 cm; Wt – 200 gr.

No. 296 (Reg. No. 61–301)
Ht – 4.2 cm; Diam – 4.3 cm; Wt – 279 gr.

No. 297 (Reg. No. 61–308)
Ht – 4.1 cm; Diam – 4.5 cm; Wt – 286 gr.

No. 298 (Reg. No. 61–327)
Ht – 4.4 cm; Diam – 4.6 cm; Wt – 298 gr. ·

No. 299 (Reg. No. 61–337)
Ht – 4 cm; Diam – 4.7 cm; Wt – 286 gr.

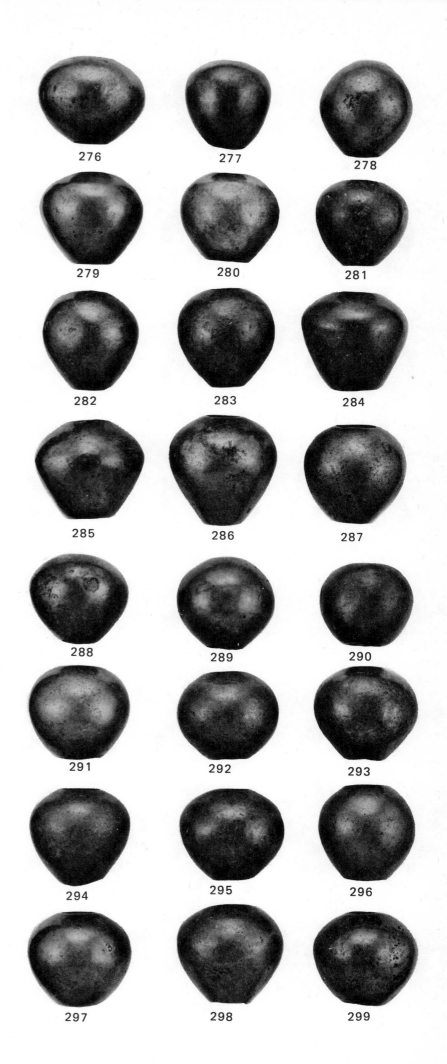

276 277 278
279 280 281
282 283 284
285 286 287
288 289 290
291 292 293
294 295 296
297 298 299

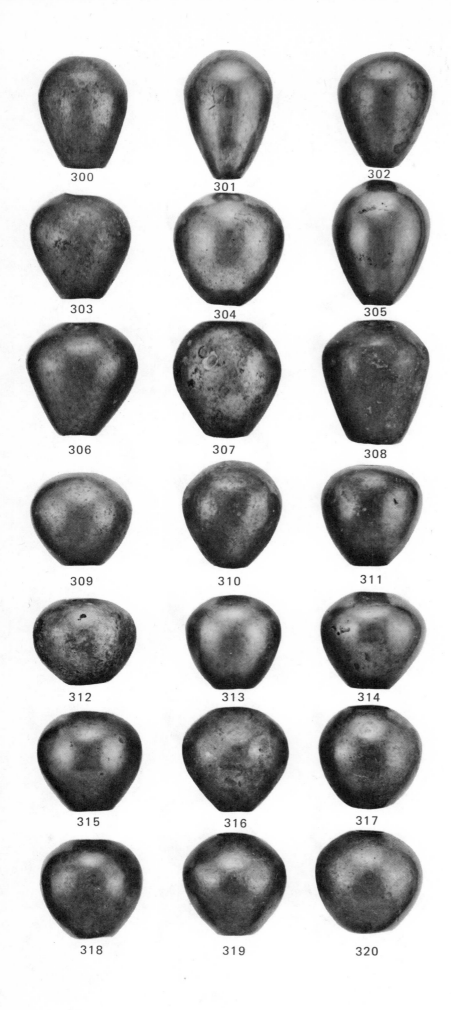

No. 300 (Reg. No. 61–200)
Ht – 4.9 cm; Diam – 3.9 cm; Wt – 203 gr.

No. 301 (Reg. No. 61–253)
Ht – 5.7 cm; Diam – 4 cm; Wt – 250 gr.

No. 302 (Reg. No. 61–346)
Ht – 5 cm; Diam – 4.2 cm; Wt – 293 gr.

No. 303 (Reg. No. 61–244)
Ht – 4.7 cm; Diam – 4.4 cm; Wt – 182 gr.

No. 304 (Reg. No. 61–322)
Ht – 5 cm; Diam – 4.8 cm; Wt – 410 gr.

No. 305 (Reg. No. 61–344)
Ht – 5.5 cm; Diam – 4.3 cm; Wt – 253 gr.

No. 306 (Reg. No. 61–268)
Ht – 5 cm; Diam – 4.9 cm; Wt – 400 gr.

No. 307 (Reg. No. 61–290)
Repair with plug.
Ht – 5.1 cm; Diam – 4.8 cm; Wt – 228 gr.

No. 308 (Reg. No. 61–297)
Ht – 5.3 cm; Diam – 4.7 cm; Wt – 312 gr.

No. 309 (Reg. No. 61–305)
Ht – 4 cm; Diam – 4.4 cm; Wt – 244 gr.

No. 310 (Reg. No. 61–331)
Ht – 4.6 cm; Diam – 4.4 cm; Wt – 249 gr.

No. 311 (Reg. No. 61–328)
Ht – 4.5 cm; Diam – 4.2 cm; Wt – 280 gr.

No. 312 (Reg. No. 61–357)
Ht – 3.8 cm; Diam – 4.6 cm; Wt – 231 gr.

No. 313 (Reg. No. 61–345)
Ht – 4.2 cm; Diam – 4.3 cm; Wt – 228 gr.

No. 314 (Reg. No. 61–333)
Ht – 4.3 cm; Diam – 4.6 cm; Wt – 320 gr.

No. 315 (Reg. No. 61–325)
Ht – 4.4 cm; Diam – 4.6 cm; Wt – 329 gr.

No. 316 (Reg. No. 61–313)
Ht – 4.6 cm; Diam – 4.7 cm; Wt – 342 gr.

No. 317 (Reg. No. 61–318)
Ht – 4.4 cm; Diam – 4.5 cm; Wt – 236 gr.

No. 318 (Reg. No. 61–338)
Ht – 4.5 cm; Diam – 4.5 cm; Wt – 302 gr.

No. 319 (Reg. No. 61–326)
Ht – 4.5 cm; Diam – 4.6 cm; Wt – 288 gr.

No. 320 (Reg. No. 61–353)
Ht – 4.5 cm; Diam – 4.8 cm; Wt – 337 gr.

No. 321 (Reg. No. 61–332)
Ht – 4.6 cm; Diam – 4.4 cm; Wt – 240 gr.

No. 322 (Reg. No. 61–343)
Ht – 4.5 cm; Diam – 5.2 cm; Wt – 360 gr.

No. 323 (Reg. No. 61–310)
Ht – 4.5 cm; Diam – 4.2 cm; Wt – 193 gr.

No. 324 (Reg. No. 61–282)
Ht – 4.8 cm; Diam – 4.9 cm; Wt – 358 gr.

No. 325 (Reg. No. 61–336)
Ht – 4.6 cm; Diam – 4.9 cm; Wt – 319 gr.

No. 326 (Reg. No. 61–312)
Ht – 4.7 cm; Diam – 4.7 cm; Wt – 299 gr.

No. 327 (Reg. No. 61–342)
Ht – 4.3 cm; Diam – 5 cm; Wt – 250 gr.

No. 328 (Reg. No. 61–323)
Ht – 4.2 cm; Diam – 5.2 cm; Wt – 348 gr.

No. 329 (Reg. No. 61–296)
Black incrustation inside hole.
Ht – 4.3 cm; Diam – 5 cm; Wt – 268 gr.

No. 330 (Reg. No. 61–286)
Ht – 4.5 cm; Diam – 5.2 cm; Wt – 283 gr.

No. 331 (Reg. No. 61–321)
Ht – 4.8 cm; Diam – 5.1 cm; Wt – 191 gr.

No. 332 (Reg. No. 61–348)
Ht – 3.9 cm; Diam – 4.8 cm; Wt – 312 gr.

No. 333 (Reg. No. 61–412)
Ht – 5 cm; Diam – 4.8 cm; Wt – 374 gr.

No. 334 (Reg. No. 61–304)
Ht – 4.9 cm; Diam – 5.2 cm; Wt – 420 gr.

No. 335 (Reg. No. 61–400)
Ht – 4.8 cm; Diam – 5.1 cm; Wt – 305 gr.

No. 336 (Reg. No. 61–320)
Ht – 4.4 cm; Diam – 5.5 cm; Wt – 259 gr.

No. 337 (Reg. No. 61–399)
Ht – 4.6 cm; Diam – 4.9 cm; Wt – 292 gr.

No. 338 (Reg. No. 61–334)
Ht – 4.8 cm; Diam – 5 cm; Wt – 250 gr.

No. 339 (Reg. No. 61–417)
Ht – 3.8 cm; Diam – 5.3 cm; Wt – 497 gr.

No. 340 (Reg. No. 61–330)
Ht – 4.7 cm; Diam – 5.1 cm; Wt – 252 gr.

No. 341 (Reg. No. 61–311)
Ht – 3.5 cm; Diam – 4 cm; Wt – 193 gr.

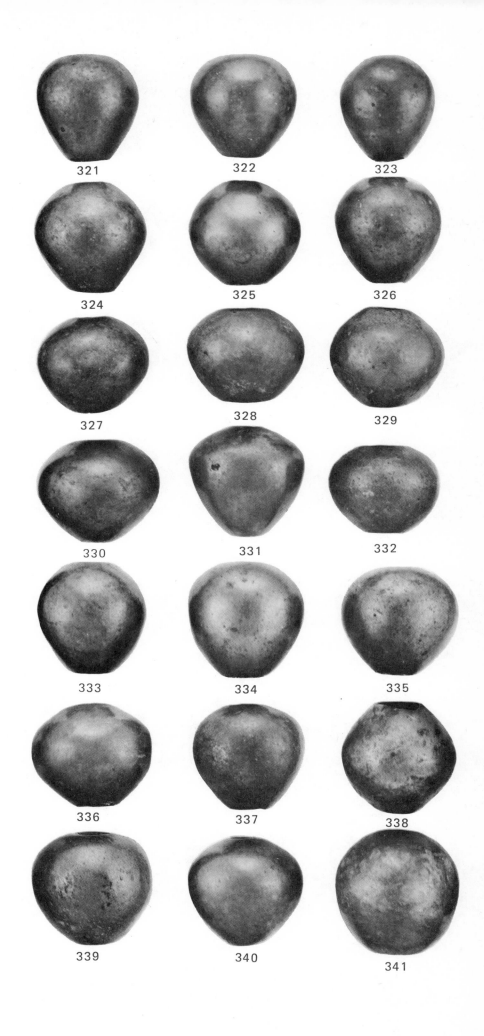

321 322 323
324 325 326
327 328 329
330 331 332
333 334 335
336 337 338
339 340 341

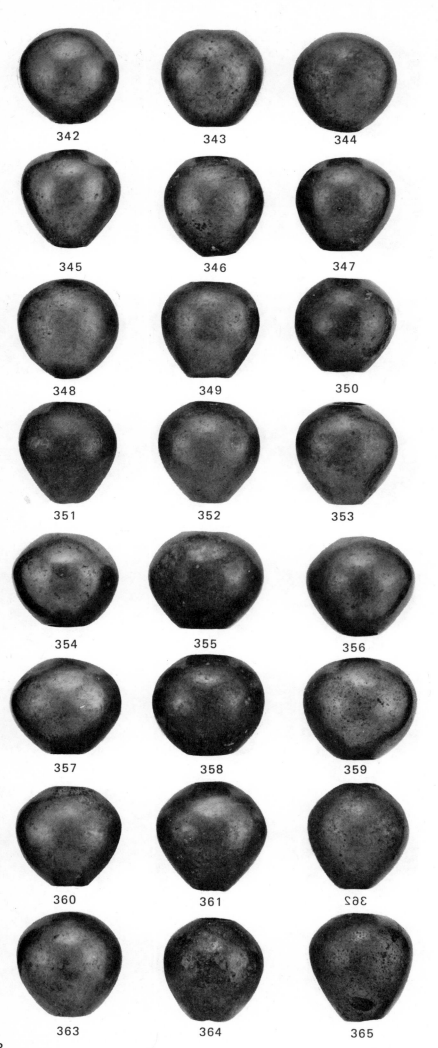

342

343

344

345

346

347

348

349

350

351

352

353

354

355

356

357

358

359

360

361

362

363

364

365

No. 342 (Reg. No. 61–260)
Ht – 4.1 cm; Diam – 4.4 cm; Wt – 292 gr.

No. 343 (Reg. No. 61–216)
Ht – 4.2 cm; Diam – 4.5 cm; Wt – 292 gr.

No. 344 (Reg. No. 61–243)
Ht – 4.1 cm; Diam – 4.6 cm; Wt – 311 gr.

No. 345 (Reg. No. 61–233)
Ht – 4.2 cm; Diam – 4.4 cm; Wt – 221 gr.

No. 346 (Reg. No. 61–245)
Ht – 4.2 cm; Diam – 4.4 cm; Wt – 224 gr.

No. 347 (Reg. No. 61–237)
Ht – 4.3 cm; Diam – 4.3 cm; Wt – 214 gr.

No. 348 (Reg. No. 61–235)
Ht – 4.4 cm; Diam – 4.4 cm; Wt – 233 gr.

No. 349 (Reg. No. 61–223)
Ht – 4.4 cm; Diam – 4.4 cm; Wt – 210 gr.

No. 350 (Reg. No. 61–245)
Ht – 4.2 cm; Diam – 4.4 cm; Wt – 224 gr.

No. 351 (Reg. No. 61–239)
Ht – 4.6 cm; Diam – 4.4 cm; Wt – 249 gr.

No. 352 (Reg. No. 61–265)
Ht – 4.5 cm; Diam – 4.5 cm; Wt – 243 gr.

No. 353 (Reg. No. 61–220)
Ht – 4.5 cm; Diam – 4.5 cm; Wt – 251 gr.

No. 354 (Reg. No. 61–231)
Ht – 3.7 cm; Diam – 3.9 cm; Wt – 164 gr.

No. 355 (Reg. No. 61–238)
Ht – 4.3 cm; Diam – 4.9 cm; Wt – 300 gr.

No. 356 (Reg. No. 61–264)
Ht – 4.2 cm; Diam – 4.7 cm; Wt – 285 gr.

No. 357 (Reg. No. 61–228)
Ht – 4.3 cm; Diam – 4.9 cm; Wt – 323 gr.

No. 358 (Reg. No. 61–251)
Ht – 4.5 cm; Diam – 4.9 cm; Wt – 368 gr.

No. 359 (Reg. No. 61–224)
Ht – 4.4 cm; Diam – 5.1 cm; Wt – 320 gr.

No. 360 (Reg. No. 61–209)
Ht – 4.7 cm; Diam – 4.3 cm; Wt – 224 gr.

No. 361 (Reg. No. 61–307)
Ht – 4.8 cm; Diam – 4.9 cm; Wt – 253 gr.

No. 362 (Reg. No. 61–315)
Ht – 4.3 cm; Diam – 4.7 cm; Wt – 235 gr.

No. 363 (Reg. No. 61–234)
Ht – 4.6 cm; Diam – 4.7 cm; Wt – 303 gr.

No. 364 (Reg. No. 61–219)
Ht – 4.5 cm; Diam – 4.5 cm; Wt – 282 gr.

No. 365 (Reg. No. 61–250)
Ht – 4.8 cm; Diam – 4.6 cm; Wt – 298 gr.

No. 366 (Reg. No. 61–395)
Ht – 4.3 cm; Diam – 4.5 cm; Wt – 250 gr.

No. 367 (Reg. No. 61–377)
Ht – 4.2 cm; Diam – 4.6 cm; Wt – 244 gr.

No. 368 (Reg. No. 61–367)
Ht – 3.8 cm; Diam – 4.6 cm; Wt – 253 gr.

No. 369 (Reg. No. 61–379)
Ht – 4.2 cm; Diam – 4.8 cm; Wt – 304 gr.

No. 370 (Reg. No. 61–378)
Ht – 4.3 cm; Diam – 4.9 cm; Wt – 265 gr.

No. 371 (Reg. No. 61–355)
Ht – 4.3 cm; Diam – 4.5 cm; Wt – 285 gr.

No. 372 (Reg. No. 61–373)
Ht – 4.5 cm; Diam – 4.7 cm; Wt – 208 gr.

No. 373 (Reg. No. 61–366)
Ht – 4.6 cm; Diam – 4.5 cm; Wt – 172 gr.

No. 374 (Reg. No. 61–390)
Ht – 4.5 cm; Diam – 4.7 cm; Wt – 289 gr.

No. 375 (Reg. No. 61–393)
Ht – 4.8 cm; Diam – 4.8 cm; Wt – 440 gr.

No. 376 (Reg. No. 61–392)
Ht – 4.5 cm; Diam – 5.2 cm; Wt – 392 gr.

No. 377 (Reg. No. 61–375)
Ht – 4.1 cm; Diam – 5 cm; Wt – 374 gr.

No. 378 (Reg. No. 61–248)
Ht – 4.2 cm; Diam – 4.8 cm; Wt – 315 gr.

No. 379 (Reg. No. 61–267)
Ht – 4.4 cm; Diam – 4.7 cm; Wt – 325 gr.

No. 380 (Reg. No. 61–213)
Ht – 4.2 cm; Diam – 4.6 cm; Wt – 165 gr.

No. 381 (Reg. No. 61–246)
Ht – 4.4 cm; Diam – 4.7 cm; Wt – 352 gr.

No. 382 (Reg. No. 61–232)
Ht – 4.7 cm; Diam – 4.8 cm; Wt – 365 gr.

No. 383 (Reg. No. 61–225)
Ht – 4.2 cm; Diam – 4.7 cm; Wt – 290 gr.

No. 384 (Reg. No. 61–236)
Ht – 4.8 cm; Diam – 4.7 cm; Wt – 310 gr.

No. 385 (Reg. No. 61–202)
Ht – 4.5 cm; Diam – 4.7 cm; Wt – 356 gr.

No. 386 (Reg. No. 61–211)
Ht – 4.8 cm; Diam – 4.7 cm; Wt – 254 gr.

No. 387 (Reg. No. 61–242)
Ht – 4.8 cm; Diam – 4.8 cm; Wt – 313 gr.

No. 388 (Reg. No. 61–206)
Ht – 4.8 cm; Diam – 4.8 cm; Wt – 211 gr.

No. 389 (Reg. No. 61–214)
Ht – 4.8 cm; Diam – 5 cm; Wt – 299 gr.

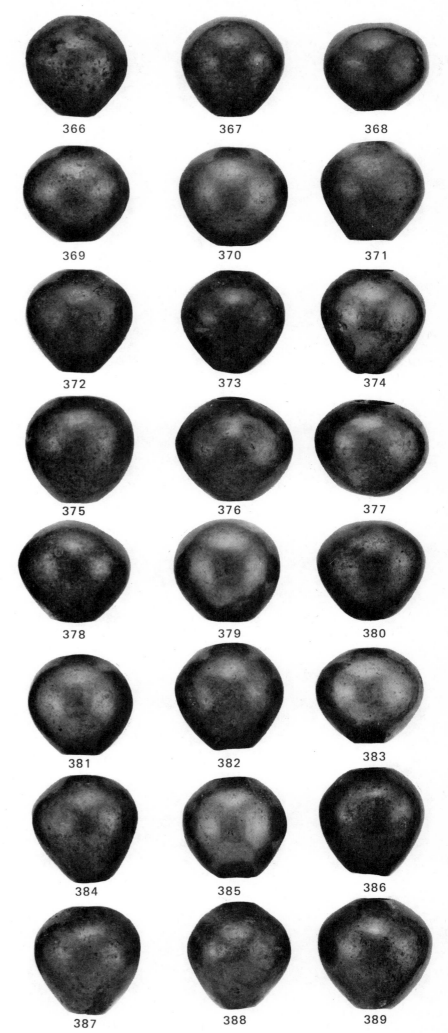

366   367   368

369   370   371

372   373   374

375   376   377

378   379   380

381   382   383

384   385   386

387   388   389

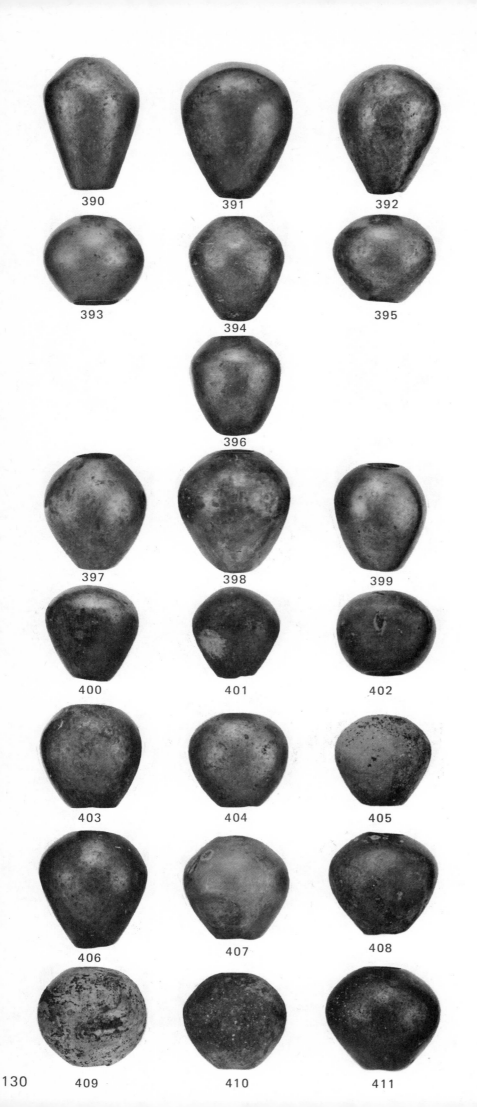

390
391
392
393
394
395
396
397
398
399
400
401
402
403
404
405
406
407
408
409
410
411

No. 390 (Reg. No. 61–374)
Ht – 5.8 cm; Diam – 4.2 cm; Wt – 280 gr.

No. 391 (Reg. No. 61–370)
Ht – 5.9 cm; Diam – 4.8 cm; Wt – 497 gr.

No. 392 (Reg. No. 61–365)
Ht – 4.7 cm; Diam – 4.4 cm; Wt – 304 gr.

No. 393 (Reg. No. 61–217)
Ht – 4 cm; Diam – 4.5 cm; Wt – 227 gr.

No. 394 (Reg. No. 61–389)
Ht – 4.6 cm; Diam – 4.1 cm; Wt – 197 gr.

No. 395 (Reg. No. 61–241)
Ht – 3.9 cm; Diam – 4.6 cm; Wt – 230 gr.

No. 396 (Reg. No. 61–349)
Ht – 4.4 cm; Diam – 4.1 cm; Wt – 218 gr.

No. 397 (Reg. No. 61–394)
Hole in wall.
Ht – 5 cm; Diam – 4.6 cm; Wt – 323 gr.

No. 398 (Reg. No. 61–210)
Ht – 5.4 cm; Diam – 5 cm; Wt – 434 gr.

No. 399 (Reg. No. 61–363)
Ht – 4.8 cm; Diam – 4.2 cm; Wt – 246 gr.

No. 400 (Reg. No. 61–419)
Linen fabric fragment inside hole.
Ht – 4.2 cm; Diam – 4.1 cm; Wt – 210 gr.

No. 401 (Reg. No. 61–295)
Ht – 3.9 cm; Diam – 3.9 cm; Wt – 130 gr.

No. 402 (Reg. No. 61–293)
Ht – 3.5 cm; Diam – 4.3 cm; Wt – 181 gr.

No. 403 (Reg. No. 61–298)
Black incrustation inside hole.
Ht – 4.5 cm; Diam – 5.4 cm; Wt – 254 gr.

No. 404 (Reg. No. 61–418)
Incrustation on body.
Ht – 4.1 cm; Diam – 4.1 cm; Wt – 276 gr.

No. 405 (Reg. No. 61–303)
Black incrustation inside hole.
Ht – 4 cm; Diam – 4.2 cm; Wt – 203 gr.

No. 406 (Reg. No. 61–422)
Incrustation inside hole.
Ht – 5.1 cm; Diam – 4.8 cm; Wt – 318 gr.

No. 407 (Reg. No. 61–300)
Black incrustation inside hole.
Ht – 4.4 cm; Diam – 4.7 cm; Wt – 325 gr.

No. 408 (Reg. No. 61–299)
Black incrustation inside hole.
Ht – 4.4 cm; Diam – 4.7 cm; Wt – 345 gr.

No. 409 (Reg. No. 61–421)
Rough unpolished surface. Incrustation inside hole.
Ht – 4.4 cm; Diam – 4.9 cm; Wt – 390 gr.

No. 410 (Reg. No. 61–291)
Black incrustation inside hole.
Ht – 4.3 cm; Diam – 4.6 cm; Wt – 271 gr.

No. 411 (Reg. No. 61–292)
Ht – 4.6 cm; Diam – 4.9 cm; Wt – 290 gr.

No. 412 (Reg. No. 61–227)
Ht – 4.3 cm; Diam – 5.1 cm; Wt – 257 gr.

No. 413 (Reg. No. 61–302)
Ht – 4.6 cm; Diam – 4.2 cm; Wt – 270 gr.

No. 414 (Reg. No. 61–203)
Ht – 4.7 cm; Diam – 5.3 cm; Wt – 253 gr.

No. 415 (Reg. No. 61–387)
Ht – 4.5 cm; Diam – 5 cm; Wt – 288 gr.

No. 416 (Reg. No. 61–364)
Ht – 4.1 cm; Diam – 5.3 cm; Wt – 388 gr.

No. 417 (Reg. No. 61–341)
Ht – 4.6 cm; Diam – 4.8 cm; Wt – 235 gr.

No. 418 (Reg. No. 61–249)
Ht – 4.6 cm; Diam – 5.5 cm; Wt – 226 gr.

No. 419 (Reg. No. 61–199)
Ht – 5 cm; Diam – 5.3 cm; Wt – 310 gr.

No. 420 (Reg. No. 61–204)
Ht – 4.7 cm; Diam – 4.8 cm; Wt – 330 gr.

No. 421 (Reg. No. 61–351)
Ht – 5.3 cm; Diam – 5 cm; Wt – 319 gr.

No. 422 (Reg. No. 61–229)
Ht – 5 cm; Diam – 5.4 cm; Wt – 288 gr.

No. 423 (Reg. No. 61–181)
Limestone, black to greyish-yellowish.
Ht – 5.1 cm; Diam – 5.2 cm; Wt – 191 gr.

No. 424 (Reg. No. 61–294)
Ht – 4.1 cm; Diam – 5.2 cm; Wt – 424 gr.

No. 425 (Reg. No. 61–420)
Remains of reed inside hole.
Ht – 4.9 cm; Diam – 4.9 cm; Wt – 299 gr.

No. 426 (Reg. No. 61–409)
Ht – 6.2 cm; Diam – 5.8 cm; Wt – 488 gr.

No. 427 (Reg. No. 61–429)
Ht – 4 cm; Diam – 4.6 cm; Wt – 332 gr.

No. 428 (Reg. No. 61–226)
Ht – 3.7 cm; Diam – 4.2 cm; Wt – 222 gr.

No. 429 (Reg. No. 61–358)
Ht – 5.5 cm; Diam – 5.2 cm; Wt – 319 gr.

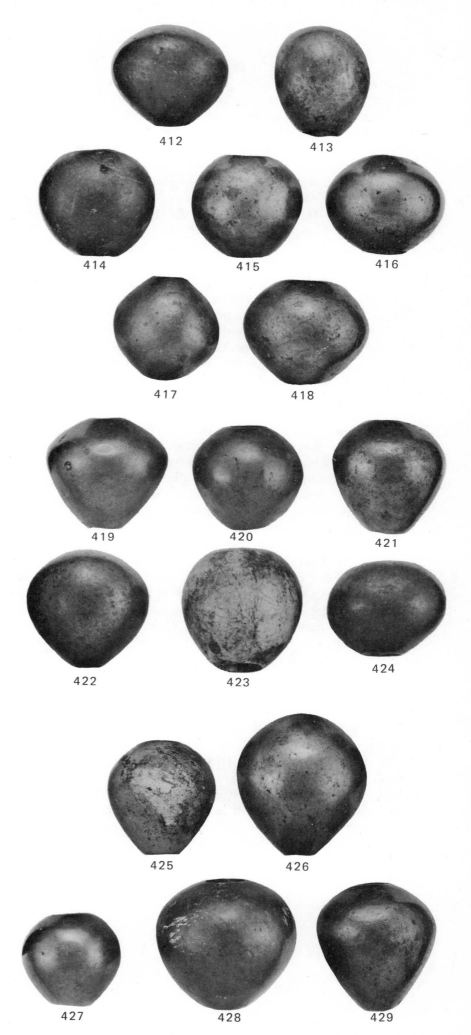

412   413
414   415   416
417   418
419   420   421
422   423   424
425   426
427   428   429

Decorative Elements

In our quest for comparative material, points of resemblance between various elements appearing on the objects and on the Chalcolithic clay ossuaries came to mind at once. For instance, the representation of the nose and eyes on "crown" No. 9 and on standard No. 21 are identical with the characteristic depiction of these features on the façades of the ossuaries from Ḥadera,[27] Bene Beraq,[28] Tel-Aviv[29] and Azor.[30] There is also a striking resemblance between the opening in "crown" No. 7 with the bosses at the top corners, and the openings of the Chalcolithic ossuaries, which are also decorated with bosses and horns.[31] Other decorative elements, such as the herring-bone pattern, floral designs and zigzag lines, also occur on ossuaries and on contemporaneous stone and pottery artifacts. In addition, Teleilat Ghassul provides a number of parallels. Birds like those on "crown" No. 7 are also found in the fresco from Ghassul[32] and on a painted potsherd from the same site.[33] The star on "crown" No. 9 is similar in conception to the eight-pointed star in the Ghassul fresco, although there are many differences.[34] The horns on the "crowns" and on the ossuaries may perhaps be compared to those in the fresco, to the right of the star (assuming that these have been preserved in their entirety). The animal heads on "crown" No. 10 are similar to those depicted in the fresco, to the left of the large building, on both sides of the elongated object. Animal heads also appear on standard No. 153, and on many of the other standards.

A Chalcolithic ossuary from Azor[35] bears decorative motifs similar to some of those found on the objects in the treasure. Flanking the sides of the opening in the ossuary façade stand shafts or posts with disk-shaped heads rising above the façade, which resemble our standards. Above the opening, next to the left-hand post, is a plastic representation of an object with a beak-shaped point. A prominent nose juts out near the top of the façade, and below it are two cylindrical bosses. Additional bosses are placed above the lintel, flanking the pointed object and the right-hand post.

Among the artifacts in the treasure is a standard with a beak-shaped point (No. 151) and a tubular standard with herring-bone designs (No. 41). If we visualize these standards carried on wooden staffs or poles (remains of wood survive inside some of them), we shall have something very similar to the objects represented on the ossuary façade.

The Significance of the Decorative Motifs

Figurines of the mother-goddess or fertility goddess are found in many forms throughout the ancient Near East. In some of these figurines the face, the nose and the eyes are emphasized, while in others the breasts and the genitalia are stressed, that is, the organs of fertility, birth, vitality and abundance. Sometimes the figure supports her breasts in her hands and her legs are bent, symbolizing the crouching position of childbirth. In other figurines only the head, the nose, the eyes and the mouth are properly fashioned, while small protuberances at the sides indicate the outstretched arms, and the body is represented by loins and a rounded belly, ending in a triangle or an inverted trapezium, with or without a line marking the vulva. At times the representation is abstract, for instance, a female body without a head, or only one of the female organs. It should be noted that in the Sumerian pictographic script the sign for "woman" is a triangle with a line marking the vulva.[36] In a later period, the triangle was used as a symbol for the fertility of the earth.[37] Indeed, one of the artifacts in the treasure is a triangular, perforated copper object (No. 136), which probably also served in ritual ceremonies.

The nose, often with exaggerated nostrils, no doubt symbolizes the breath of life, while the eyes and the fertility organs stand for renewal and growth, or for the eternal cycle of death and rebirth. Jars found in cemetery A at Kish,[38] with handles bearing female figures, illustrate this concept very clearly. This juxtaposition of fertility and death is not surprising. The concern of the living for the dead in ancient times is well known, and it found expression in the provision of gifts, food and objects of daily use and ornament, suggesting a belief in life after death. If this interpretation is correct, we can also attempt to examine the architectural and symbolic significance of the structures, of course, within the limitations of the available evidence. Sukenik suggested already in 1937,[39] and his view has been generally accepted, that the Chalcolithic ossuary was shaped like a house, and served as a substitute for the deceased's dwelling. Now, if we draw imaginary lines between the two gates of "crown" No. 7, we obtain the architectural shape of an ossuary, including the horns and the bosses. It is reasonable to assume that the ornaments on the "crown", which are unmistakable cult symbols, are not meant to represent an ordinary dwelling-house, and that both the ossuary and the "crown" symbolize a temple.

Further confirmation of this conclusion can perhaps be obtained from the large fresco at Teleilat Ghassul. A small, elaborate architectural fragment is preserved in the right-hand corner of this fresco.[40] In spite of many scholarly discussions, its exact nature has never been satisfactorily explained.[41] The restoration of this fragment offers a clue to its nature. It is suggested that the broken diagonal line above the shoulder of the building to the left, should be continued diagonally upwards; the right-hand side should be restored in the same way and a horizontal line drawn between them. This reconstruction gives us an inverted trapezium similar to the facades of the ossuaries. If we reconstruct the structure according to the surviving fragment, we shall obtain the shape of an ossuary-front with a gate, which is a common feature of ancient representations of temple gates.[42] The general character of the fresco which, in the opinion of many scholars, contains ritual symbols, indicates that the building in question is in fact a temple.

We suggest, therefore, that this is a representation of a Chalcolithic temple, which reflects local customs and beliefs connected with the ritual ceremonies of the Chalcolithic settlements (see also, below, The Culture of the Cave-Dwellers). These are also reflected in the decorations on the "crown", on the ossuary and on the fresco from Teleilat Ghassul. This cultural pattern includes, in our opinion, also other ritual symbols, such as the snake-emblem and symbols of Inanna, the mother-goddess of Mesopotamia.[43]

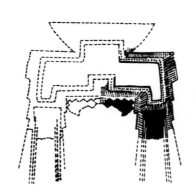

OTHER FINDS

Pottery

A considerable amount of Chalcolithic pottery of various types was uncovered in the Cave of the Treasure and in Caves 2 and 3. Most of it consists of fragments of rims, bases, handles and body-sherds of hole-mouth and other jars, deep bowls, bowls and churns. A clay spoon was also found.

Generally speaking, the pottery is well made, and some of it from well levigated clay. Most of the vessels have a slip and painted decoration. The range of colours is considerable: from light to dark brown, many shades of red, white and buff. There are also plastic thumb-indented bands, incisions and herring-bone designs. The handles are of several kinds: plain and thumb-indented ledge-handles; perforated lug-handles; bar-handles; small, medium and large loop-handles, sometimes double, thumb-indented, grooved, impressed, or plain with wide ends. Many fragments of hole-mouth jars were found, all characteristic of the Ghassulian culture, such as are known from Ghassul itself, Beersheba and other sites. However, there are also some types characteristic of the beginning of the Early Bronze Age, e.g. hole-mouth jars with thickened rims and closely spaced painted bands, showing the close relation between the two assemblages. The same picture is also true of the finds in Naḥal David and Naḥal Ṣe'elim, and to some extent in Wadi Murabba'at. We shall discuss here only the characteristic types.

Hole-mouth jars. Most of these jars bear soot-marks. They are made of gritty clay, medium to well-baked. Several types of rims and bases were found. The different diameters of the vessels and the varying thickness of their walls indicate a fairly wide range of shapes. Some of the jars, mainly the large ones, are handmade, while the smaller specimens, and especially their rims, are wheelmade. A few lug-handles were found, which are similar in ware and colour to the hole-mouth jars, and which may belong to such vessels, resembling those found at Ghassul.[1] Of special interest is a small hole-mouth jar (Ill. 1), with a spherical body and flat base. Another vessel (Ill. 2:3), of which only fragments have survived, also seems to be a hole-mouth jar, as the ware and the colour are identical with the other jars. It is decorated with vertical incisions, and zigzag lines forming triangles between them. No parallel could be found to this decoration, which was made with a sharp instrument before firing.[2] The shoulder of the jar fragment in Ill. 2:5 is ribbed up to the rim. Another vessel for which no parallel is known (Ill. 2:4) is lightly ribbed on the body. Most of the rims are of the same thickness as the body; they are rounded or sharp, a feature characteristic of finds from many Chalcolithic sites. Also found were thickened rims, similar to those from Wadi Murabba'at,[3] which are characteristic of the Early Bronze Age.[4]

Ill. 1 (Reg. No. 60–260)
Black clay; gritty; sooty inside and out; well baked; handmade.
Cave 1, A.

Ill. 2. Hole-mouth jars

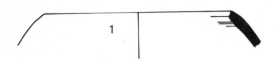

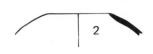

1 (Reg. No. 60–55)
Light brown clay; fine grits; sooty outside; well baked; handmade, rim wheelmade. Cave 1, A.

2 (Reg. No. 61–102/7)
Grey clay; grits and shells; sooty outside; badly fired; hand-made. Cave 1, niche 1.

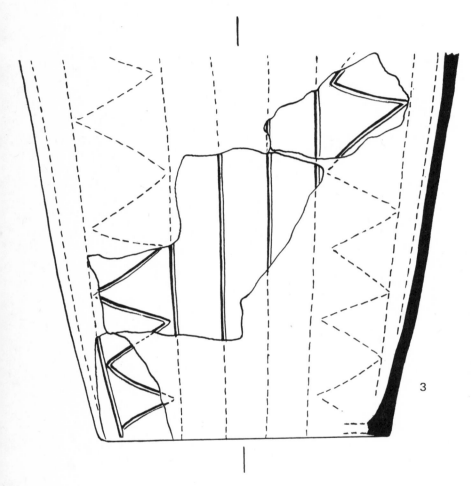

3 (Reg. No. 60–222)
Black clay; fine grits; incised lines with triangles between them; well baked; handmade. Cave 1, A.

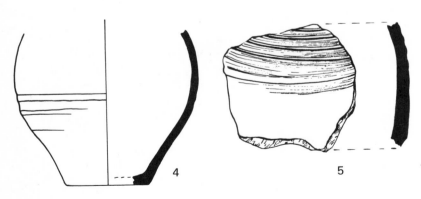

4 (Reg. No. 61–168)
Reddish-brown clay; fine grits; sooty outside; light ribbing on body; well baked; handmade. Cave 1, A.

5 (Reg. No. 60–98)
Reddish clay; fine grits; sooty outside; ribbing on upper part; well baked; wheelmade. Cave 1, A.

6 (Reg. No. 61–174/3)
Light brown clay; fine grits; two grooves around rim; well baked; handmade, rim wheelmade. Cave 1, B.

Jars. Many jar-fragments were found, both in Caves 1 and 2 and near the burials in Cave 3, where a complete jar was uncovered (Ill. 3:2). The clay is mixed with small or large grits. Some handmade cream-slipped ware was also present, and some of the rims were completed on the wheel. Generally speaking, the jars are well baked. The bases are flat and uneven. The body is pear-shaped, the neck is short and the rims are of several kinds: sharp, thickened, everted, flaring, ring-shaped, flat, rounded or thumb-indented. Some jars are decorated with plastic thumb-indented bands or irregular horizontal grooves. Several fragments may belong to jars decorated with herring-bone designs. Many body-sherds are painted with brown, white or red bands, sometimes intersecting to form a net pattern. At times, the paint trickled over the reddish slip. Large ledge-handles, probably belong-

ing to large jars, were also found; some of these are flat and wide, others are thumb-indented. One ledge-handle is still attached to a fragment of body, which bears a horizontal thumb-indented band. One of the loop-handles is decorated with white paint on a light-coloured slip and two vertical grooves with indentations between them (Ill. 16:1).

The types of the jars, the plastic thumb-indented decoration on the body, the loop-handles and the ledge-handles, the herring-bone patterns, the red and brown painted bands on a white or cream slip — all these are characteristic of the Chalcolithic period, and especially of its later part. The same assemblage is well known from Ghassul,[5] Beersheba,[6] Azor,[7] Jericho,[8] Tell Far'ah (N),[9] Samaria,[10] and the caves of Wadi Murabba'at,[11] Nahal David and Nahal Hever.[12]

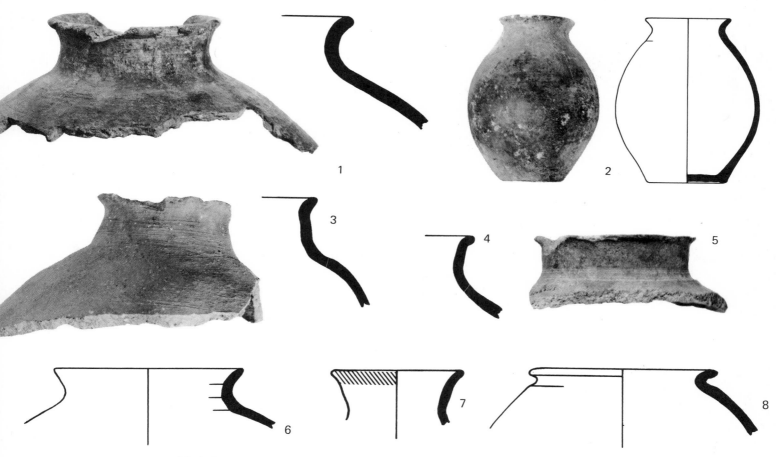

Ill. 3. Jars

1 (Reg. No. 60–201/3)
Brown clay; gritty; sooty outside; well baked; rim wheelmade. Cave 1, A.

2 (Reg. No. 62–8)
Light brown clay; gritty; soot marks inside and outside; well baked; handmade, rim wheelmade. Cave 3.

3 (Reg. No. 60–203)
Reddish clay; gritty; well baked; handmade. Cave 1, A.

4 (Reg. No. 61–121/11)
Light brown clay; dark brown slip outside and inside rim; rim wheelmade. Cave 1, A.

5 (Reg. No. 62–6)
Reddish clay; gritty; slip outside and inside rim; remains of white band at base of neck; well baked; neck and rim wheelmade. Cave 3.

6 (Reg. No. 61–109/15)
Brown clay; gritty; sooty outside; well baked; rim wheelmade. Cave 1, A.

7 (Reg. No. 60–201/7)
Yellow clay; gritty; remains of brown band below rim; well baked; rim wheelmade. Cave 1, A.

8 (Reg. No. 60–201/6)
Pink clay; gritty; medium baked; handmade. Cave 1, A.

Deep bowls. Only flat bases, flaring rims, lug-handles of various kinds and body sherds survived of the deep bowls. The vessels have no necks and the rims rise straight from the shoulders. The clay is mixed with large and small grits. The firing is medium to good. Most of the deep bowls have painted decoration on the body or on the rim, such as white paint over reddish-brown slip or red, brown or cream painted bands. The body of the vessels is handmade, while most of the rims are made on the wheel. A double loop-handle was also found.

Deep bowls similar in many characteristics have been found in other Chalcolithic sites, such as Ghassul,[13]

Naḥal Besor,[14] Beersheba,[15] Meṣer,[16] and the caves in Naḥal David,[17] Naḥal Ḥever,[18] and Naḥal Ṣe'elim.[19] However, the closely spaced painted bands on some of the sherds are also characteristic of the beginning of the Early Bronze Age.[20]

Of special interest is a straight-sided sherd (Ill. 13:10), which is too flat to belong to a bowl or a jar. The white background, which resembles a layer of plaster, is painted with brownish-red bands. The sherd must belong to a straight-sided vessel, but its shape is unknown.

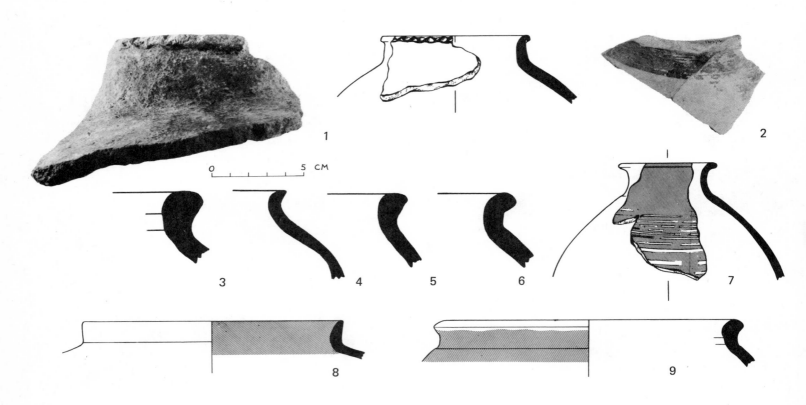

Ill. 4. Jars and deep bowls

1 (Reg. No. 61–114/4)
Grey clay; gritty; sooty outside; well baked; thumb-indented rim. Cave 1, A.

2 (Reg. No. 61–126/2)
Reddish clay; fine grits; dark brown band at base of neck; well baked; rim wheelmade. Cave 1, A.

3 (Reg. No. 61–176/22)
Pink clay; gritty; medium baked; handmade. Cave 1, B.

4 (Reg. No. 61–114/7)
Reddish-grey clay; fine grits; well baked; sooty outside; rim wheelmade. Cave 1, A.

5 (Reg. No. 60–64)
Yellow clay; fine grits; rim wheelmade. Cave 1, A.

6 (Reg. No. 61–143/19)
Light brown clay; very gritty; sooty outside and inside rim; well baked; rim wheelmade. Cave 1, A.

7 (Reg. No. 61–154/7)
Reddish clay; gritty; white painted bands; well baked; neck and rim wheelmade. Cave 1, A.

8 (Reg. No. 60–33)
Yellow clay; gritty; reddish-brown band inside neck; well baked; handmade. Cave 1, A.

9 Reg. No. 61–10/1)
Red clay; gritty; dark brown slip outside and inside rim; well baked; rim wheelmade. Cave 1, niche 1.

Small bowls. The number of bowls found was especially large. They are well baked, and their ware ranges from levigated to finely gritty. Many bowls bear wheel-marks The majority of the rims are sharp and a few are rounded. The sides of the bowls slope outwards from the base, sometimes slightly curving inwards towards the top. The bases are flat or concave. A few ring-bases and disk-bases were also found. Several bowls have faint mat-impressions on the base, and one has what looks like a textile impression (Ill. 5:7). The soot patches on some of the bowl-rims indicate that the bowls were used as lamps. The painted decoration consists of reddish or brownish bands on the rim, a spiral line inside the vessel, or horizontal bands outside and inside below the rim. Some bowls are covered with brown slip inside and out. The colour combinations vary: cream bands inside and brown or reddish bands outside, a white spiral line or white patches on a cream slip inside the bowl.

This type of bowl, in all its variations, is very common in all Chalcolithic sites, e.g. Jericho VIII,[21] Ghassul,[22] Tell Far'ah in the south,[23] Tell Far'ah in the north,[24] Beersheba,[25] Ḥadera,[26] Megiddo,[27] the caves in Wadi Murabba'at[28] and the Cave of Horror in Naḥal Ḥever.[29]

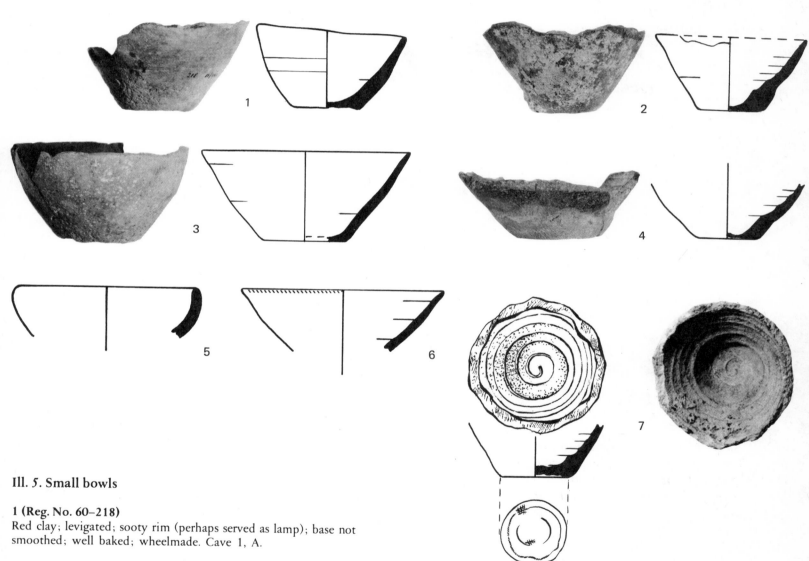

Ill. 5. Small bowls

1 (Reg. No. 60–218)
Red clay; levigated; sooty rim (perhaps served as lamp); base not smoothed; well baked; wheelmade. Cave 1, A.

2 (Reg. No. 60–216)
As above.

3 (Reg. No. 61–115/7)
Red clay; levigated; upper part sooty inside and out; well baked; wheelmade. **Cave 1, B.**

4 (Reg. No. 60–217)
Brown clay; very fine grits; base not smoothed; well baked; upper part wheelmade.
Cave 1, A.

5 (Reg. No. 61–140/1)
Grey clay; gritty; well baked; handmade. Cave 1, B.

6 (Reg. No. 61–127/6)
As above; sooty outside. Cave 1, A.

7 (Reg. No. 60–109)
Grey clay; levigated; sooty inside and out; base not smoothed; remains of textile impression(?); well baked; handmade. Cave 1, A.

139

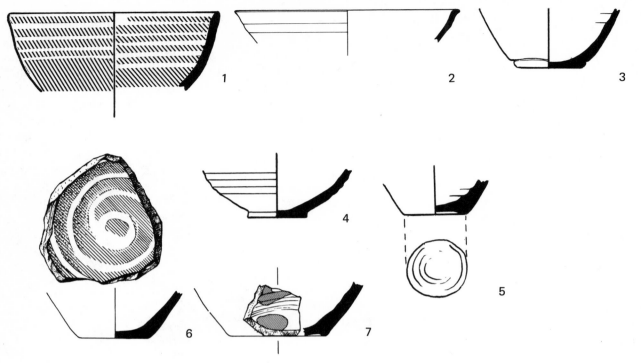

Ill. 6. Small bowls

1 (Reg. No. 61–135/2)
Brown clay; very fine grits; red painted bands inside and outside; well baked; wheelmade. Cave 1, A.

2 (Reg. No. 61–109/1)
Light brown clay; levigated; well baked. Cave 1, A.

3 (Reg. No. 61–108)
Reddish clay; very fine grits; well baked; wheelmade. Cave 1, B.

4–5 (Reg. No. 61–118/3, 61–127)
Examples of bowl bases. Cave 1, A.

6–7 (Reg. No. 60–43, 60–42/1)
Examples of painted decoration inside bowls. Cave 1, A.

Bowls. The bowls resemble in shape the small bowls, but they are larger and deeper, and their rims are more varied. Their ware is mostly gritty, and only a few are made of levigated clay. Almost all the well-baked bowls are handmade, a few have rims made on the wheel, and only a few are entirely wheelmade. The bases are flat, the sides generally sloping, but a few bowls have gently curving sides or are ribbed at the top. The rims are of great variety: sharp, rounded, flat, thickened, grooved, inverted and everted or curving inwards. One rim is thumb-indented. The painted decoration consists of brown or red bands on the rim, or of brown and white horizontal bands inside and outside, or sometimes only outside. One rim is decorated with small horizontal knobs.

Some of the bowl fragments have perforations, which most probably served to repair the vessels by means of thongs or ropes. However, it is also possible that they sometimes served other purposes (see below, p. 184, discussion of loom).

Similar, or even identical, bowls have been found in all Chalcolithic sites, such as Jericho VIII,[30] Ghassul,[31] Beersheba,[32] Lachish,[33] Ḥadera,[34] Tell Far'ah (N),[35] Megiddo,[36] the caves in Naḥal David,[37] Naḥal Se'elim,[38] Naḥal Ḥever[39] and 'En-gedi.[40]

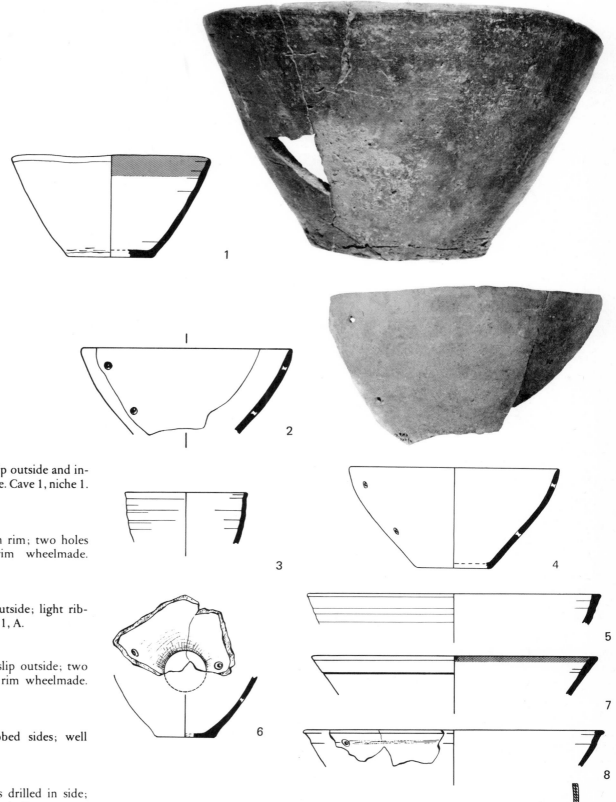

Ill. 7. Bowls

1 (Reg. No. 61–106/1)
Reddish clay; very gritty; brown slip outside and inside rim; well baked; rim wheelmade. Cave 1, niche 1.

2 (Reg. No. 61–167/1)
Reddish-grey clay; brown band on rim; two holes drilled in side; well baked; rim wheelmade. Cave 1, B.

3 (Reg. No. 61–120/4)
Reddish clay; gritty; brown slip outside; light ribbing; well baked; wheelmade. Cave 1, A.

4 (Reg. No. 61–118/2)
Reddish clay; gritty; light brown slip outside; two holes drilled in side; well baked; rim wheelmade. Cave 1, A.

5 (Reg. No. 61–120/5)
Reddish clay; very fine grits; ribbed sides; well baked; wheelmade. Cave 1, niche 1.

6 (Reg. No. 61–168/2)
Reddish clay; fine grits; two holes drilled in side; very well baked; wheelmade. Cave 1, B.

7 (Reg. No. 61–105/2)
Grey clay; gritty; brown band on rim; white slip inside; well baked; wheelmade. Cave 1, niche 1.

8 (Reg. No. 61–143/7)
Yellowish-red clay; gritty; hole in side; sooty outside; well baked; rim wheelmade. Cave 1, A.

9 (Reg. No. 61–166/2)
Reddish clay; fine grits; reddish-brown band on rim; badly fired; handmade. Cave 1, B.

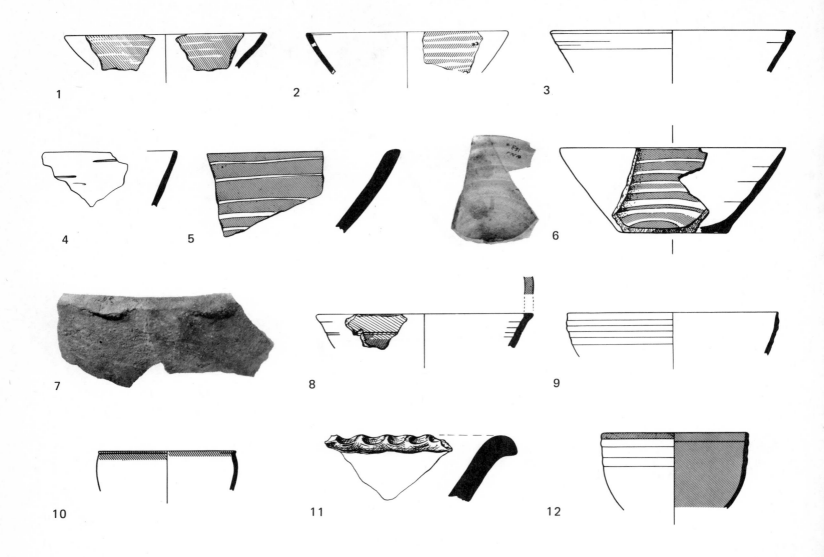

Ill. 8. Bowls

1 (Reg. No. 61–168/1)
Pink clay; fine grits, brown and white bands inside and out; well baked; handmade. Cave 1, B.

2 (Reg. No. 60–65)
Light grey clay; fine grits; brown and white bands outside; two holes drilled in side; well baked; wheelmade. Cave 1, A.

3 (Reg. No. 61–112/3)
Reddish clay; gritty; upper part ribbed; well baked; wheelmade. Cave 1, A.

4 (Reg. No. 61–160/2)
Yellow clay; gritty; brown band on rim; grooved decoration; medium baked; handmade. Cave 1, A.

5 (Reg. No. 60–40)
Yellow clay; gritty; light brown and white bands outside; well baked; wheelmade. Cave 1, A.

6 (Reg. No. 61–163)
Reddish clay; gritty; brown and white bands inside and out; well baked; wheelmade. Cave 1, A.

7 (Reg. No. 60–40)
Grey clay; fine grits; sooty outside; horizontal knobs below rim; medium baked; handmade. Cave 1, A.

8 (Reg. No. 61–127/1)
Yellow clay; gritty; red band on rim; cream and brown bands on side; well baked; wheelmade. Cave 1, A.

9 (Reg. No. 61–125/5)

Grey clay; gritty; upper part ribbed; sooty inside and out; well baked; wheelmade. Cave 1, A.

10 (Reg. No. 61–152/2)
Reddish clay; fine grits; brown band on rim; handmade. Cave 1, A.

11 (Reg. No. 61–238)
Yellow clay; gritty; thumb-indented rim; well baked; handmade. Cave 1, A.

12 (Reg. No. 60–68)
Red clay; very fine grits; red band on rim and red slip inside; ribbed on upper part; very well baked; wheelmade. Cave 1, A.

Churns. Fragments of two churns were discovered in Cave 3. A swollen, convex neck and a large pierced lug-handle belong to one specimen. A red band is painted at the junction of neck and shoulder. The clay is gritty and well baked. Of the second churn, only a large lug-handle is preserved, belonging apparently to the flat end of this vessel. The clay is light in colour, very gritty, badly fired and crumbling. Churns are common in Chalcolithic sites, e.g. Ghassul,[41] Naḥal Besor,[42] Beersheba,[43] Bene Beraq–Tel-Aviv,[44] Tell Far'ah (N),[45] Afula,[46] and many others.

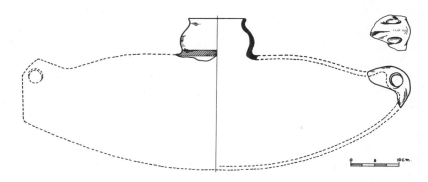

Ill. 9. Reconstruction of churn (Reg. No. 60–62)

Ill. 10. Churn fragments

1 (Reg. No. 61–186)
Large perforated lug-handle of churn. Yellow clay; gritty; very friable; badly fired. Cave 3.

2–3 (Reg. No. 60–62)
Two fragments of churn. Reddish-grey clay; gritty; red band at junction of neck and shoulder; well baked; handmade, rim wheelmade. Cave 3.

Ill. 11. Clay Figurine (Reg. No. 61–230)

Figurine. The schematic figurine of a sheep was found in Cave 1. The clay is mixed with straw and is not baked. Animal figurines, some of sheep, are frequently found in Chalcolithic sites. They probably served as cult objects.[47]

Stoppers. Two unbaked clay stoppers were found. One is concave on top, the other convex, with a slightly narrower lower part, to fit into the mouth of the jar.[48]

Composition of the clay. Not all the pottery vessels appear to have been made of local materials, as the clay of some vessels was found to contain iron and its source has not yet been discovered. The mine-detector which the army put at our disposal, and which during the first season helped to discover metal objects in the Cave of Letters, reacted also to pottery vessels in our cave. Surprisingly, the mine-detector did not show a similar reaction to pottery in the caves of Naḥal Ṣe'elim, giving rise to the assumption that the clay of the vessels in our cave contained a certain proportion of iron. A further mine-detector test was made with the kind assistance of the Israel Police Force in Jerusalem.[49] A number of pot-

sherds were submitted for analysis to the Geological Institute of the Ministry of Development, thanks to the interest shown in the material by the Director of the Institute at that time, Prof. Y. Bentor. The results of the test, given below, were kindly reported to us by Dr. Z. Bodenheimer:

"We carried out an initial examination of the sherds marked Naḥal Mishmar 66 and 67. The concentration of ferric oxide (Fe_2O_3) in sample 66 was 2.4% and in sample 67 5.42%. In sample 67 we succeeded, with the aid of a magnet, in extracting concentrations of iron (40% Fe_2O_3), a fact which explains the reaction of the mine-detector. In sample 66 we found no concentrations which could be extracted with a magnet. The qualitative proof of the presence of pyrites may possibly indicate that the vessel was produced at a relatively low temperature."

1   2

Ill. 12. Stoppers

1 (Reg. No. 60–202)
Yellow clay; mixed with straw and fine gravel; unbaked; handmade. Cave 1, A.

2 (Reg. No. 61–118/1)
As above. Cave 1, A.

Ill. 13. Thumb-indented, grooved and painted decoration

1 (Reg. No. 61–125/11)
Reddish clay; gritty; thumb-indented decoration; well baked; handmade. Cave 1, A.

2 (Reg. No. 61–110)
Brown clay; gritty; horizontal grooves; well baked; handmade. Cave 1, A.

3 (Reg. No. 61–116/14)
Grey clay; very fine grits; brownish bands on white slip; band of fine indentations; very well baked; handmade. Cave 1, A.

4 (Reg. No. 61–119)
Reddish clay; gritty; irregular grooves; well baked; handmade. Cave 1, A.

5 (Reg. No. 61–110/1)
Brown clay; gritty; horizontal groove; well baked; handmade. Cave 1, A.

6 (Reg. No. 61–109/21)
Reddish-brown clay; gritty; irregular white bands on whitish-cream slip; well baked; handmade. Cave 1, A.

7 (Reg. No. 61–109/20)
Reddish-grey clay; gritty; thin white bands on light brown slip; well baked; handmade. Cave 1, A.

8 (Reg. No. 60–23)
Brown clay; gritty; wide and narrow cream bands on reddish slip; well baked; handmade. Cave 1, A.

9 (Reg. No. 61–144/11)
Reddish clay; gritty; one broad and one narrow white band on cream slip; well baked. Cave 1, B.

10 (Reg. No. 61–166/13)
Reddish-grey clay; fine grits; flat sherd; reddish paint over thick white layer resembling plaster; handmade. Cave 1, A.

11 (Reg. No. 61–161/3)
Reddish clay; white bands on dark brown; well baked; handmade. Cave 1, A.

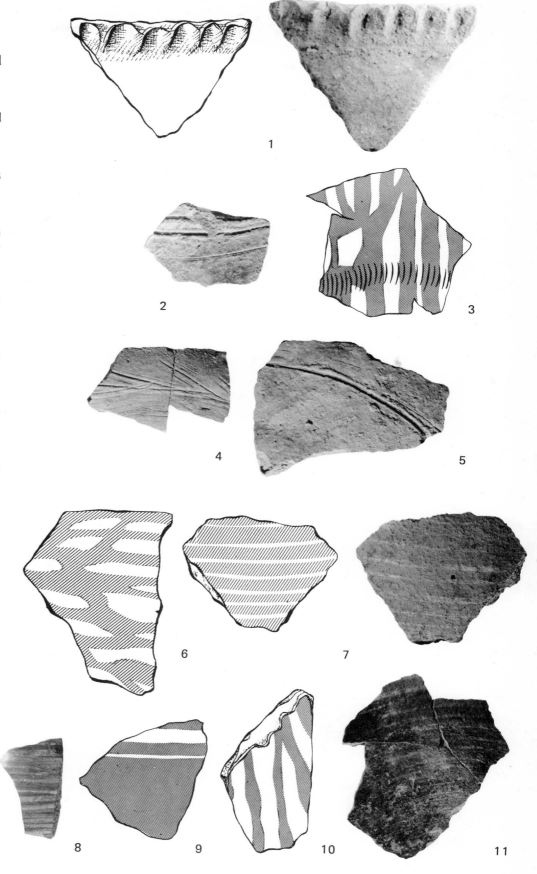

Ill. 14. Painted decoration

1 (Reg. No. 61–139/8)
Small deep bowl; reddish-grey clay; fine grits; reddish-brown **bands on white slip; well baked; wheelmade. Cave 1, A.**

2 (Reg. No. 61–169)
Reddish clay; fine grits; broad brown band on cream slip; well baked; handmade. Cave 1, B.

3 (Reg. No. 61–126/25)
Reddish-brown clay; fine grits, brown and white bands; well baked; handmade. Cave 1, A.

4 (Reg. No. 61–145/17)
Reddish-brown clay; fine grits; brown and white bands; well baked; handmade. Cave 1, A.

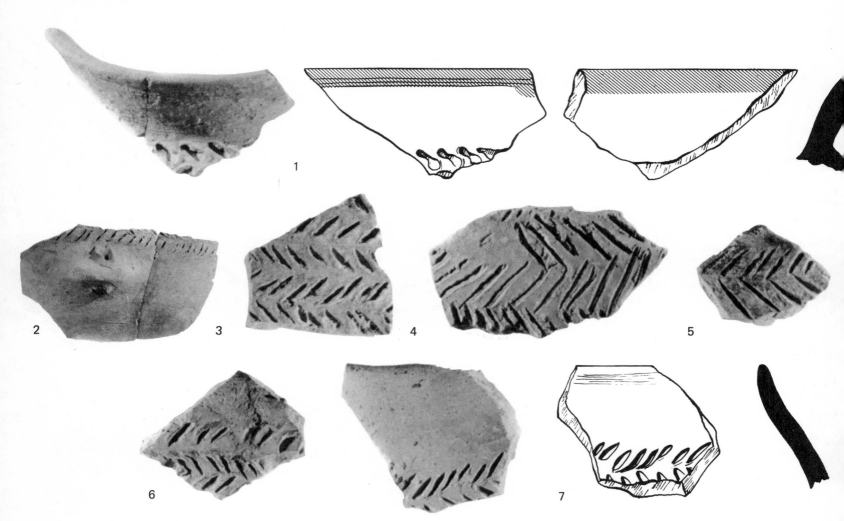

Ill. 15. Herringbone designs

1 (Reg. No. 61–168/13)
Red clay; fine grits; reddish band on rim; well baked; rim wheelmade. Cave 1, B.

2 (Reg. No. 61–138/14 + 60–33)
Reddish clay; fine grits; horizontal lug-handle; well baked; handmade. Cave 1, A.

3 (Reg. No. 61–155/1)
Light brown clay; fine grits; well baked; handmade. Cave 1, niche 1.

4 (Reg. No. 61–139/12)
Light brown clay; fine grits; well baked; handmade. Cave 1, A.

5 (Reg. No. 61–102/1)
Light brown clay; fine grits; well baked; rim wheelmade. Cave 1, niche 1.

6 (Reg. No. 61–107/1)
Reddish-yellow clay; fine grits; well baked; handmade. Cave 1, niche 1.

7 (Reg. No. 61–163/4)
Brown clay; fine grits; well baked; handmade. Cave 1, A.

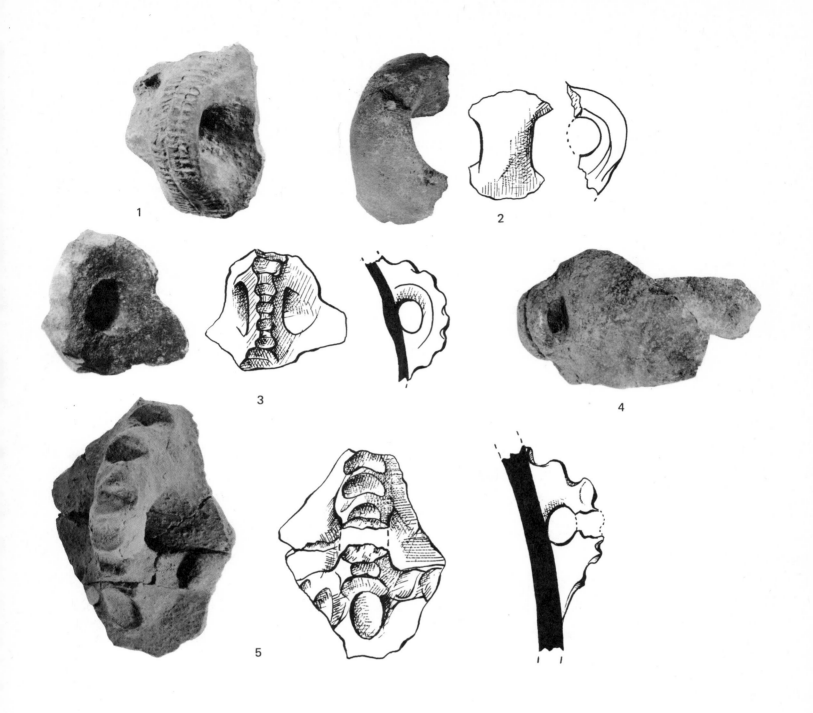

Ill. 16. Loop-handles

1 (Reg. No. 60–220)
Grey clay; very fine grits; indentations between two vertical grooves; white paint on light slip; well baked. Cave 1, A.

2 (Reg. No. 62–3)
Grey clay; levigated; very well baked; handmade. Cave 1, B.

3 (Reg. No. 61–121/2)
Brown clay; gritty; thumb-indented decoration; sooty outside; medium baked; handmade. Cave 1, A.

4 (Reg. No. 61–160/1)
Reddish clay; gritty; vertical groove; red slip; well baked; handmade. Cave 1, A.

5 (Reg. No. 61–103/1)
Reddish clay; very gritty; thumb-indented decoration on handle and body; medium baked; handmade. Cave 1, niche 1.

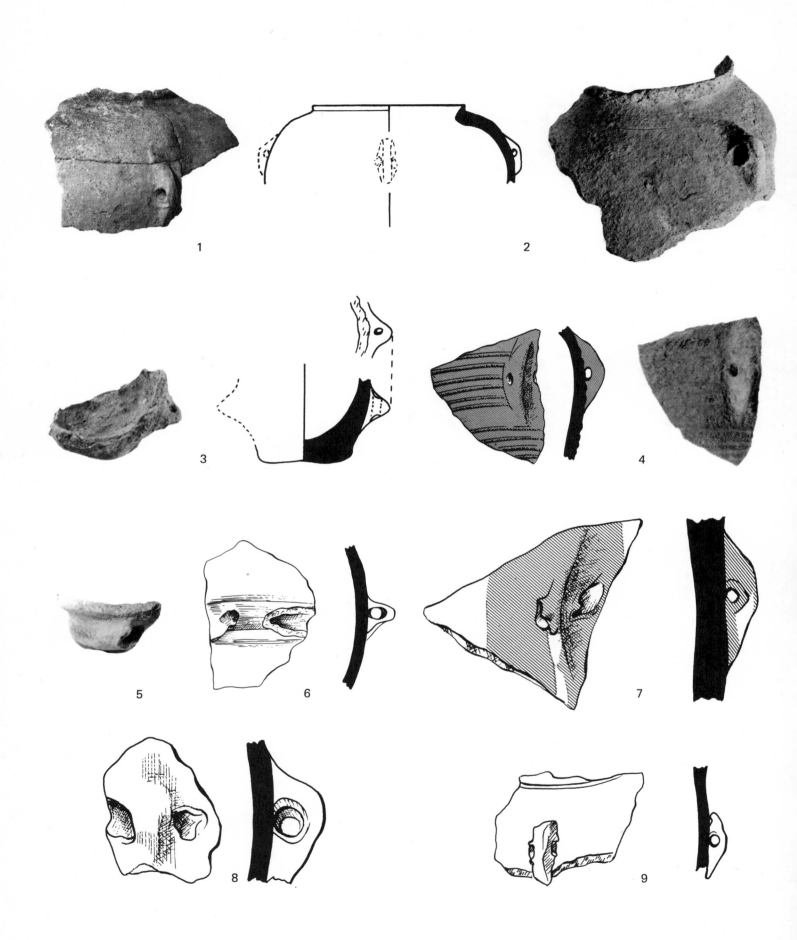

148

Ill. 17. Lug-handles

1 (Reg. No. 62–31/1)
Greyish-brown clay; gritty; cream and brown bands; medium baked; handmade. Cave 1, niche 1.

2 (Reg. No. 61–187)
Small deep bowl; brown clay; very fine grits; soot patches on rim and upper part of interior; well baked; rim wheelmade. Cave 3.

3 (Reg. No. 62–31)
Small bowl or juglet; grey clay; very fine grits; medium baked; handmade. Cave 1, niche 1.

4 (Reg. No. 61–132/3)
Reddish clay; gritty, ribbed body; sooty outside; medium baked, Cave 1, A.

5 (Reg. No. 60–219)
Bar-handle; grey clay; fine grits; well baked; Cave 1, A.

6 (Reg. No. 61–187/19)
Bar-handle; yellow clay; gritty; well baked; Cave 3.

7 (Reg. No. 61–107/8)
Red clay; gritty; brown bands on white slip; well baked. Cave 1, niche 1.

8 (Reg. No. 60–45)
Red clay; fine grits; medium baked. Cave 1, A.

9 (Reg. No. 60–127)
Reddish clay; gritty; medium baked. Cave 1, A.

Ill. 18 Ledge-handle and bases

1 (Reg. No. 60–202/2)
Reddish clay; grey core; gritty; brown bands on white slip; well baked. Cave 1, A.

2 (Reg. No. 60–178)
Stump base; grey clay; gritty; sooty outside; medium baked; handmade. Cave 1, A.

3 (Reg. No. 60–223)
Short stump base; light brown clay; gritty; medium baked. Cave 1, A.

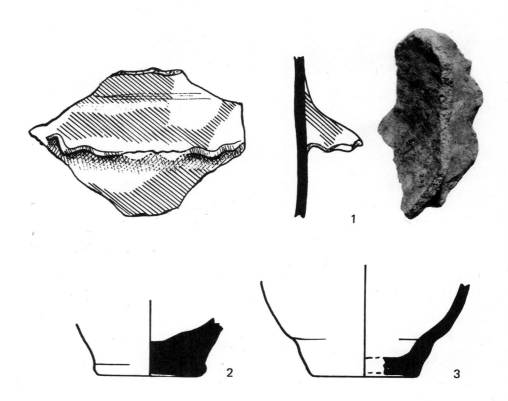

149

Miscellaneous

Stone Objects. Fragments of two querns for pounding or grinding were found. One is concave, and resembles vessels from Ghassul[50] and Beersheba.[51] The second is rectangular. Pestles bearing marks of use were also uncovered (Ill. 19:3), as well as many limestone and flint hammers of various sizes (Ill. 20). One side is generally smoothed or trimmed and all the hammers show signs of percussion. Some were found in the Intermediate level, but as similar hammers were found in the Chalcolithic level, they can be attributed with certainty to that period. Various flint implements were also uncovered (Ill. 21), including knives, chisels and arrowheads, all of types common in the Chalcolithic period.[52]

Ornaments. Among the finds was a flat perforated ivory disk (Ill. 22), ornamented on both sides with small shallow holes arranged in two concentric circles. A similar disk was uncovered at Beersheba.[53] Some pendants or amulets were also found (Ill. 24), most of them made of shell, with two perforations at the top. One amulet, trapezoidal in shape, is made of well-smoothed stone and is not perforated. Shell and stone amulets are known from other Chalcolithic sites, such as Ghassul,[54] Beersheba,[55] and the Judean Desert Caves.[56] Another find was a cylindrical curved bone pin.

Beads. Agate and faience beads of various kinds were also found. Some shell and lapis lazuli beads were found in the Intermediate level, and it is difficult to determine if they belong to the early or to the late period of occupation. Similar beads were found at Ghassul[57] and Beersheba.[58] Beads strung on a thread and a beaded purse were found in Naḥal Șe'elim and probably also belong to the Chalcolithic period.[59]

Loom accessories. A large number of bone awls of different sizes, both complete and broken, were found, as well as bone needle-shuttles and stone or pottery spindle-whorls, such as are commonly found in many Chalcolithic sites (see below, pp. 177 ff., discussion of loom).

Ill. 19. Stone objects

1 (Reg. No. 61–160/2)
Flat, rectangular mortar; hard limestone; 7×13×20 cm. Cave 1, A.

2 (Reg. No. 61–160)
Mortar, hard limestone; broken; concave surface; 8×19×26 cm. Cave 1, A.

3 (Reg. No. 61–160/1)
Pestle; hard limestone; one end worked. Cave 1, A.

Ill. 20. Hammers

1 (Reg. No. 60–206/7)
Stone hammer. Cave 1, B.

2 (Reg. No. 60–9/1)
Flint hammer. Cave 1, A.

3 (Reg. No. 60–9/2)
Flint hammer. Cave 1, A.

4 (Reg. No. 60–206/2)
Flint hammer. Cave 1, B.

5 (Reg. No. 60–206/1)
Flint hammer. Cave 1, B.

6 (Reg. No. 60–206/6)
Stone hammer. Cave 1, B.

7 (Reg. No. 60–206)
Flint hammer. Cave 1, B.

8 (Reg. No. 60–206/3)
Stone hammer. Cave 1, B.

9 (Reg. No. 60–206/4)
Stone hammer, Cave 1, B.

Ill. 21. Flint implements

1 (Reg. No. 60–9/4)
Retouched blade. Cave 1, A.

2 (Reg. No. 60–9/5)
Borer on thick blade. Cave 1, A.

3 (Reg. No. 61–208/6)
Retouched blade. Cave 1, A.

4 (Reg. No. 61–42/3)
Bladelet. Cave 1, A.

5 (Reg. No. 61–52/6)
Bladelet. Cave 1, A.

6 (Reg. No. 60–206/5)
Retouched blade. Cave 1, B.

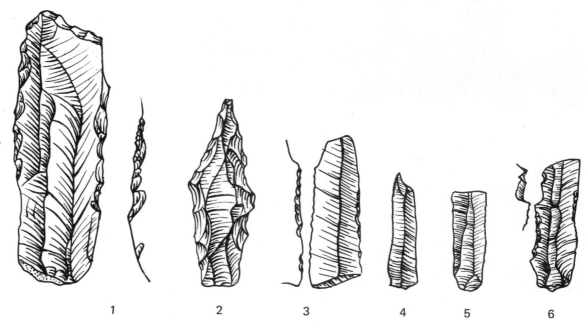

Ill. 22. Ivory disk and beads (Reg. No. 60–21)
Diam – 5.1 cm. Beads of agate, lapis lazuli, shell and faience (?). Cave I, A.

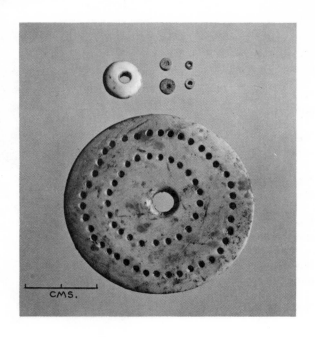

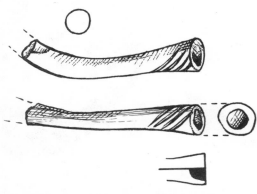

Ill. 23. Drawing of bone pin (Ill. 24:1)

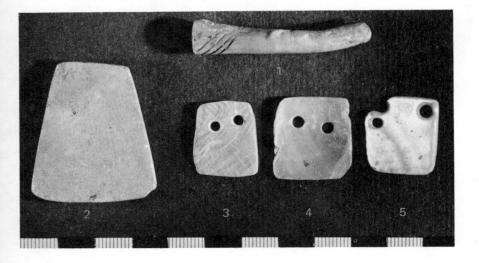

Ill. 24. Pendants, amulets and bone pin

1 (Reg. No. 61–23/7)
Cylindrical bone pin(?). Lower end broken. Upper part decorated with diagonal grooves. Small hollow on head. Cave 1, A.

2 (Reg. No. 61–167/30)
Stone amulet. Trapezoidal. Cave 1, A.

3 (Reg. No. 61–97/1 c)
Shell pendant. Two holes. Cave 1, niche 2.

4 (Reg. No. 60–228 a)
Shell pendant. Two holes. Cave 1, A.

5 (Reg. No. 61–190/2 b)
Shell pendant. Two holes, top damaged. Cave 1, niche 2.

Ill. 25. Copper awl (Reg. No. 61–33/1)
L – 7.3 cm. Cave 1, A.

Copper awl. The awl was found in Cave 1, Hall A. The body of the tool is cylindrical, one end is angular and the other pointed. A similar awl was found at Beersheba.[60] The composition of the copper is identical to that of the objects in the treasure and to that of the copper objects from Beersheba and Naḥal Ṣe'elim.

Textiles

Many textile remains were uncovered in the Cave of the Treasure and a few in the neighbouring caves, in the strata of the Bar-Kokhba and the Chalcolithic periods, as well as in the Intermediate stratum.[61] 120 samples were tested (see Appendix C, pp. 227–232), which can be divided as follows:

a) Bar-Kokhba period – 14 linen and 2 woollen samples;

b) Intermediate stratum – 46 linen and 13 woollen samples;

c) Chalcolithic period – 37 linen and 8 woollen samples.

At first is was assumed that it would eventually be possible to arrive at a typological classification. However, this turned out to be difficult, as the majority of the samples in both periods were woven from flax fibres, and only a few were made of wool, sometimes dyed. Moreover, there were no fundamental differences between the fabrics of both periods, either in type, in quality or in weaves. In Wadi Murabba'at and the Cave of Letters,[62] the linen fabrics woven from yarns with a Z-twist are very few (the more common direction of twist is S), and they are just as rare in the Nahal Mishmar caves. The only difference is that in the Roman period, the use of single-ply yarns was much more common than in the Chalcolithic period,[63] when most fabrics were woven of double-ply yarn, as shown by our finds. In the absence of additional data, it is impossible to arrive at any clear conclusions.

Textile remains of later periods were found in all the caves of the region. Special mention should be made of the rich and varied group of textiles of the Bar-Kokhba period discovered in the Cave of Letters.[64] On the other hand, only few textile remains of the Chalcolithic period have hitherto been discovered in Palestine. A carbonized fragment of clothing was found on a skeleton in the Cave of Horror in Nahal Hever, and Carbon-14 analysis proved that it is early.[65] In Wadi Murabba'at only few textile fragments were found which could be dated (with reservations) to the Chalcolithic period.[66] The textile remains found at Ghassul are carbonized to such an extent that it is impossible to determine the nature of the fibres; all that could be ascertained is that double-ply yarn was used.[67] A piece of carbonized fabric of the beginning of the Early Bronze Age was found at Jericho,[68] and at Lachish two textile impressions on Chalcolithic pottery were uncovered.[69]

This is, therefore, the first time that a large group of fairly well-preserved linen and woollen fabrics of the Chalcolithic period has been discovered in this country. The colours used on the fabrics are yellow, red, green and black.[70]

The clothing remains found on a skeleton in Cave 2 were also shown to be early by Carbon-14 analysis (see below, p. 199). The following were found inside the artifacts of the treasure: a scrap of fabric in mace-head No. 400; a twisted cord in horn-shaped object No. 157; threads inside standard No. 62 and in the perforation of hippopotamus-ivory object No. 2.

In the Fayum, too, climatic conditions helped to preserve textiles from the Neolithic period (ca. 4500 B.C.E.). In Badari, textiles were found dating from ca. 3000 B.C.E., some of which are fairly fine; the majority are linen, and the rest woollen.[71] Many textile remains, all of woollen fabrics, have been discovered at Çatal Hüyük, and are attributed to the Neolithic period (before 6000 B.C.E.). Remains of an uncarbonized red woollen fabric on a human skull were also discovered at that site.[72]

Ill. 26. Woollen fabrics – Chalcolithic Stratum

Reg. No.	Warp				Weft				Weave
	colour	ends /cm.	count	twist	colour	picks /cm.	count	twist	
1 61–22/8-d Hemmed	Red	12	7.7	Single S	Red	13	21.7	Single S	Plain
2 61–22/8-b	Yellow	14	21.7	Single S	Yellow	19	15.5	Single S	Plain
3 61–22/8-h	Yellow			Single S	Yellow			Single Z	

Strap: the weft passes over 5 warps in 3 rows.

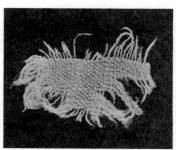

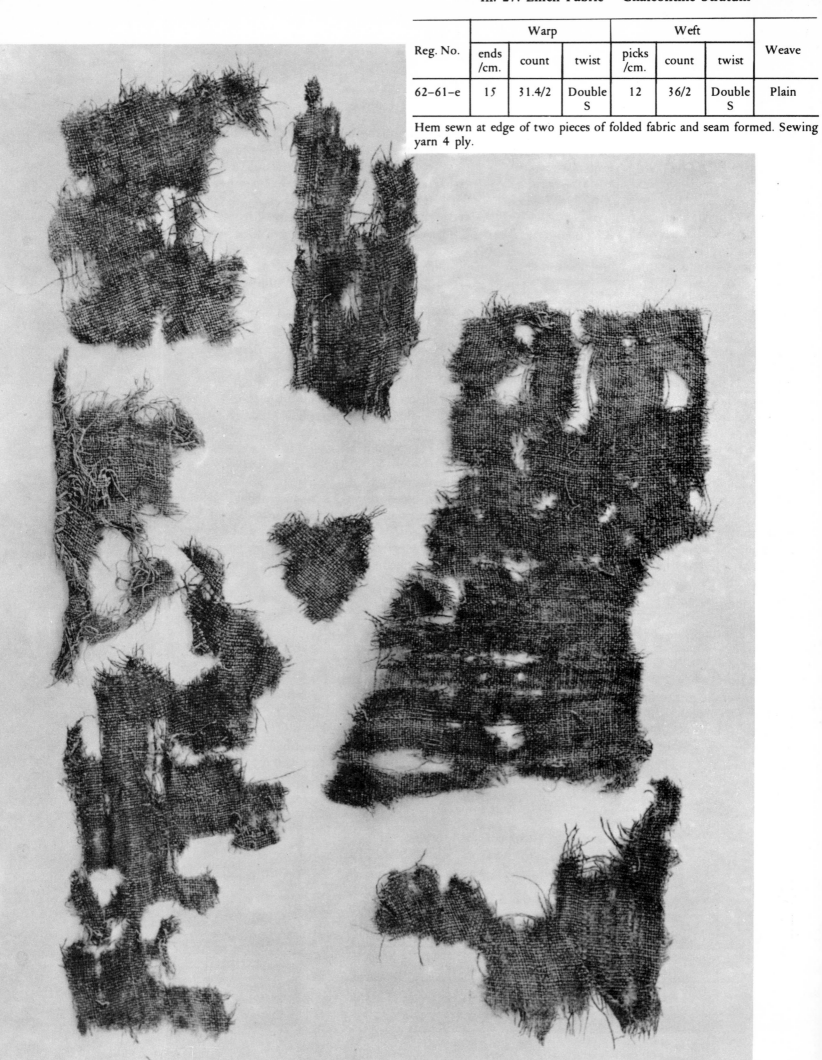

Ill. 27. Linen Fabric – Chalcolithic Stratum

Reg. No.	Warp			Weft			Weave
	ends /cm.	count	twist	picks /cm.	count	twist	
62–61–e	15	31.4/2	Double S	12	36/2	Double S	Plain

Hem sewn at edge of two pieces of folded fabric and seam formed. Sewing yarn 4 ply.

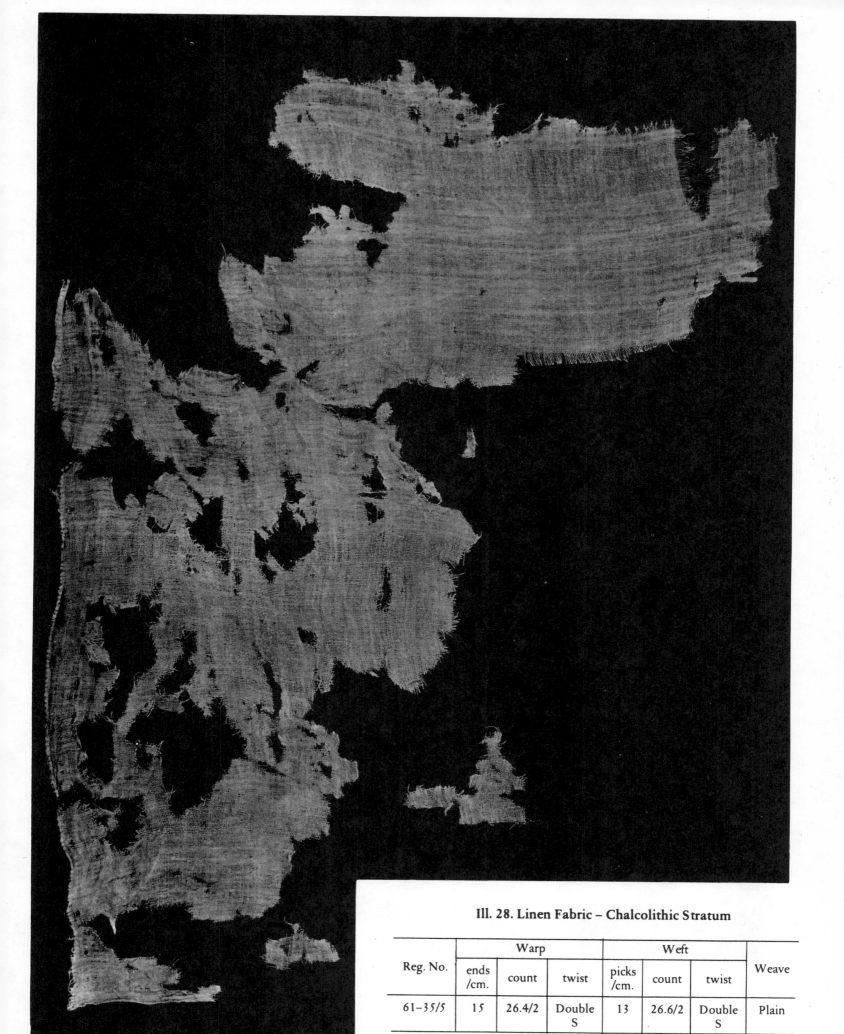

Ill. 28. Linen Fabric – Chalcolithic Stratum

Reg. No.	Warp			Weft			Weave
	ends /cm.	count	twist	picks /cm.	count	twist	
61–35/5	15	26.4/2	Double S	13	26.6/2	Double S	Plain

True selvedge. Hem: 4 warps turn round weft twice.

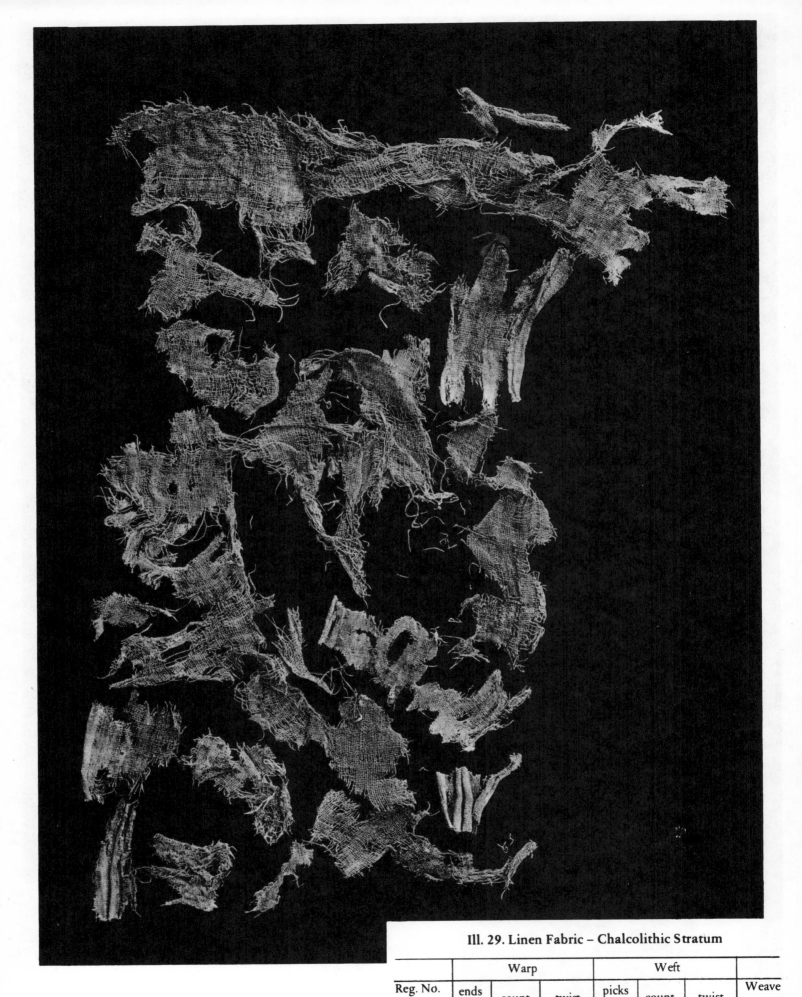

Ill. 29. Linen Fabric – Chalcolithic Stratum

Reg. No.	Warp			Weft			Weave
	ends /cm.	count	twist	picks /cm.	count	twist	
62–61–c	24	89.4/2	Double S	14-15		Double S	Plain

True selvedge.

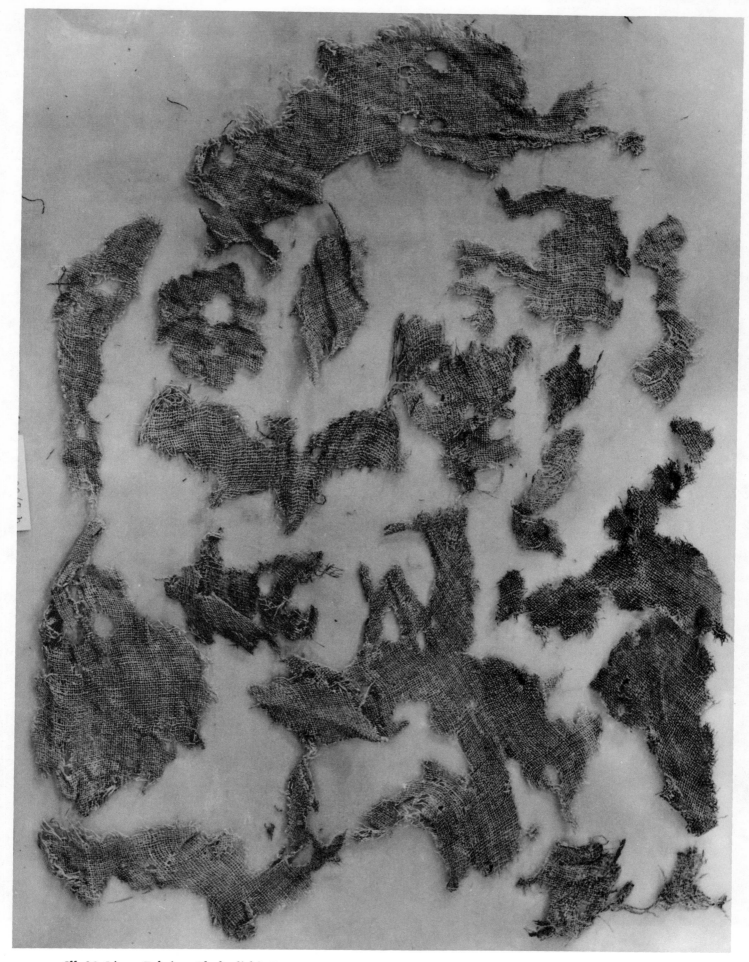

Ill. 30. Linen Fabric – Chalcolithic Stratum

Reg. No.	Warp			Weft			Weave
	ends /cm.	count	twist	picks /cm.	count	twist	
61–29/7-b	16	65.8/2	Double S	14	53.6/2	Double S	Plain

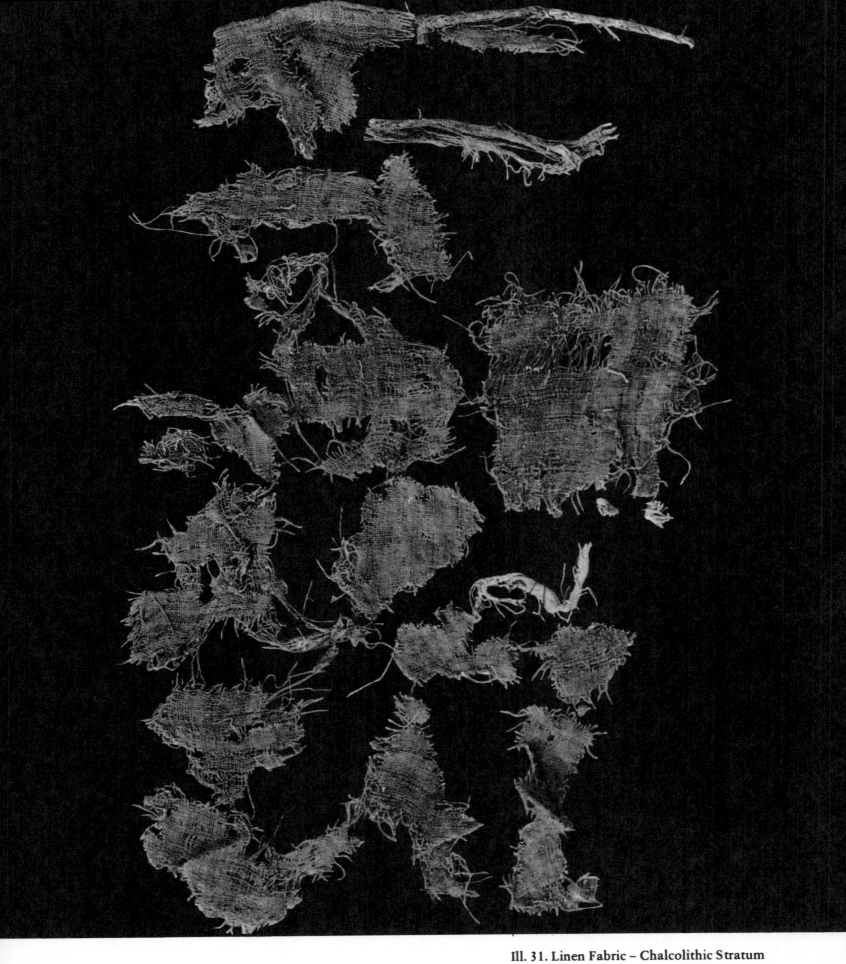

Ill. 31. Linen Fabric – Chalcolithic Stratum

Reg. No.	Warp			Weft			Weave
	ends /cm.	count	twist	picks /cm.	count	twist	
62–61–d	13	29.4/2	Double S	13	44.2/2	Double S	Plain

Two hems: 1. Weft slightly twisted into rope shape and sewn;
2. Fabric twisted slightly, rolled and sewn.

Ill. 32. Linen Fabric – Chalcolithic Stratum

Reg. No.	Warp			Weft			Weave
	ends /cm.	count	twist	picks /cm.	count	twist	
62–61–a	23	64.6/2	Double S	16	91.6/2	Double S	Plain

True selvedge.

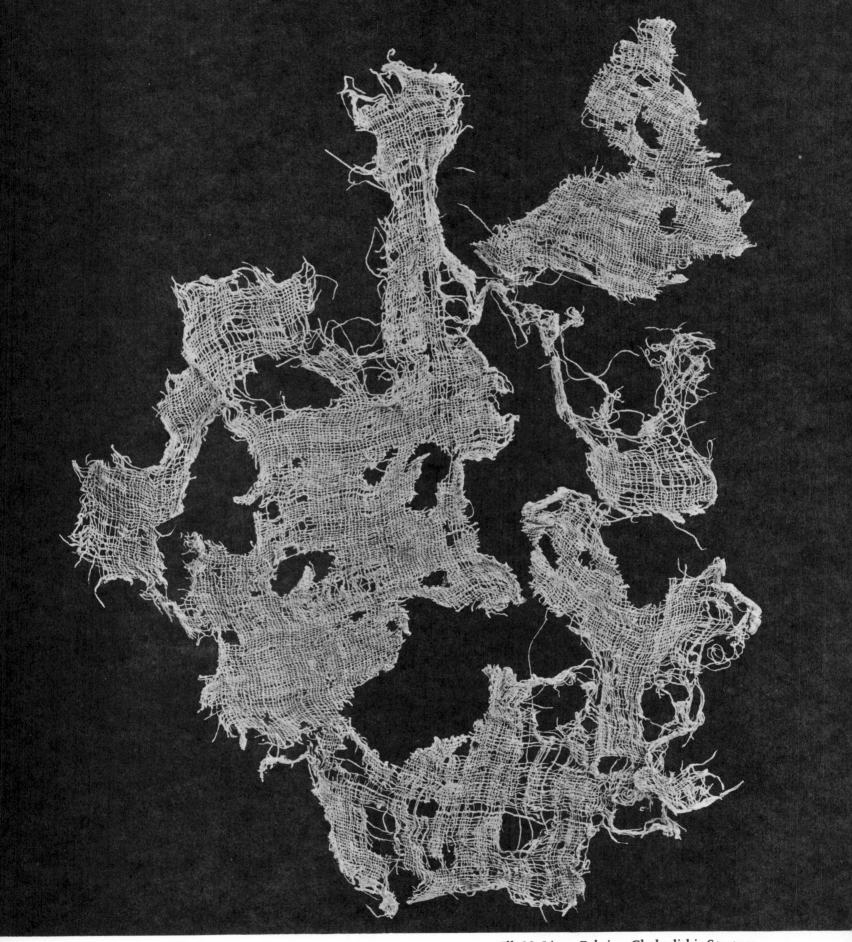

Ill. 33. Linen Fabric – Chalcolithic Stratum

Reg. No.	Warp			Weft			Weave
	ends /cm.	count	twist	picks /cm.	count	twist	
61–61/3-a	14	40.8/2	Double S	10	36/2	Double S	Plain

Ill. 34. Linen Fabric – Chalcolithic Stratum

Reg. No.	Warp			Weft			Weave
	ends /cm.	count	twist	picks /cm.	count	twist	
61–204	17	29.4/2	Double S	13	27/2	Double S	Plain

Bloodstains.

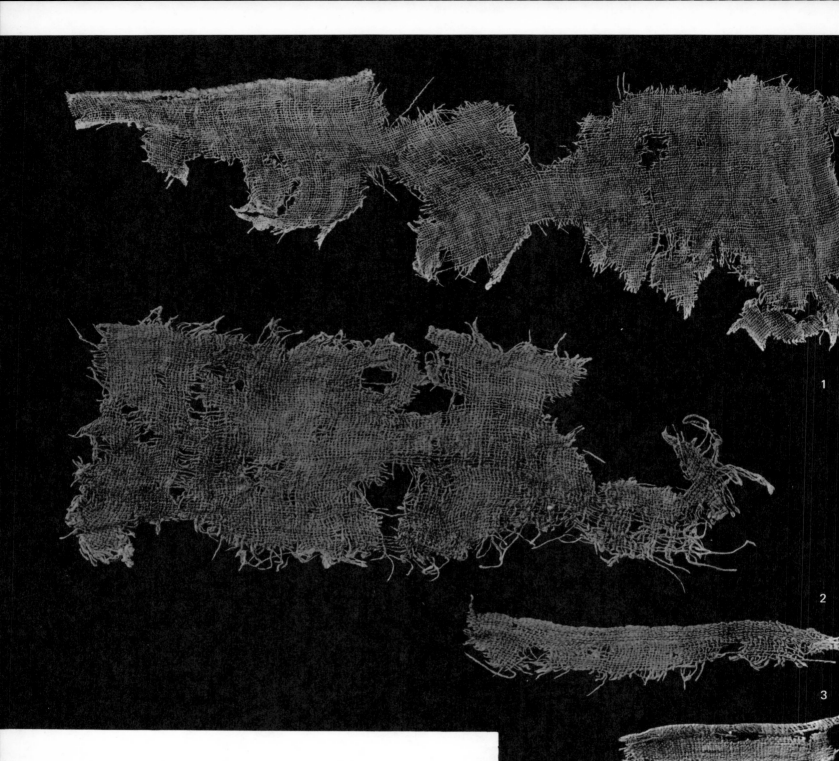

Ill. 35. Linen Fabrics – Chalcolithic Stratum

Reg. No.	Warp			Weft			Weave
	ends /cm.	count	twist	picks /cm.	count	twist	
1 62–61-b	20-21	120/2	Double S	16	78.4/2	Double S	Plain
Hem: sewn round the edge with double ply yarn, binding stitch							
2 61–61/3-c	14	30.4/2	Double S	8	22.4/2	Double S	Plain
True selvedge; 2 warps sewn along it for strengthening							
3 61–72/4-a	14	31.2/2	Double S	12	25/2	Double S	Plain
True selvedge							
4 61–29/7-a	17	31.2/2	Double S	14	36.6/2	Double S	Plain
Selvedge: weft passes over 2 warps in 3 rows. Pattern of self bands approximately every centimetre.							

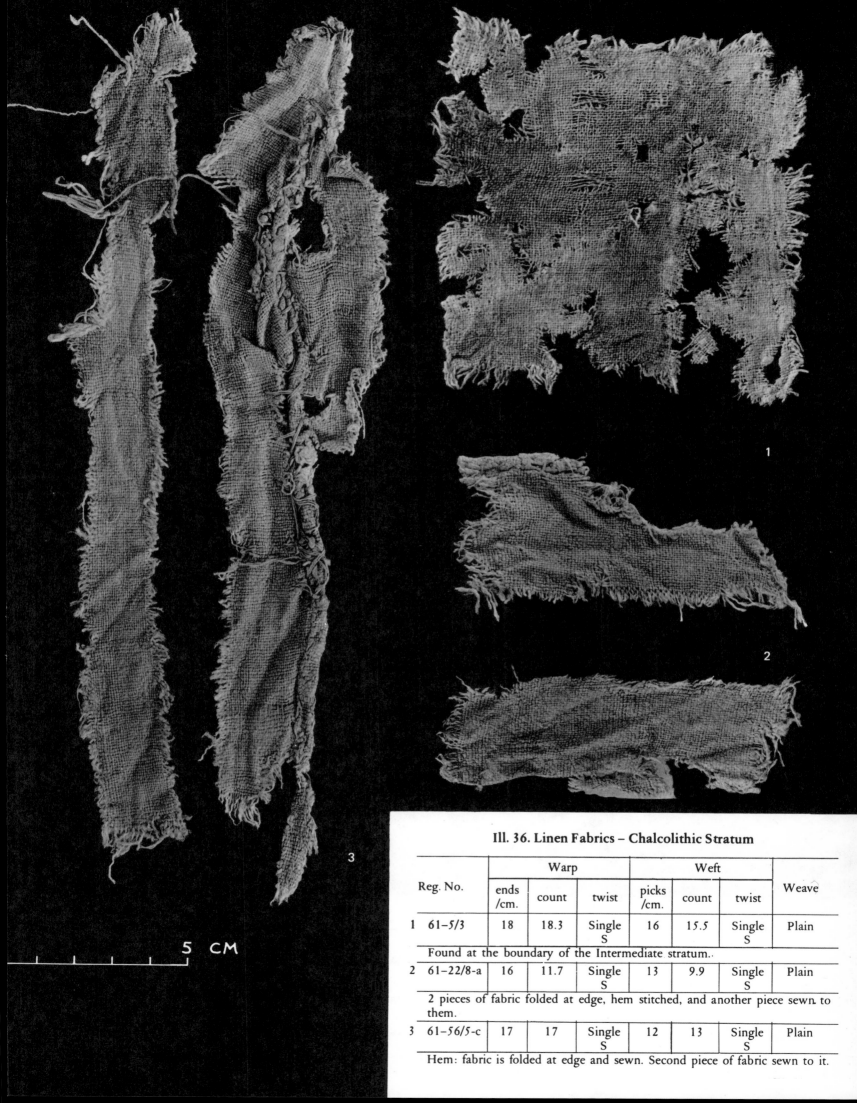

Ill. 36. Linen Fabrics – Chalcolithic Stratum

	Reg. No.	Warp			Weft			Weave
		ends /cm.	count	twist	picks /cm.	count	twist	
1	61–5/3	18	18.3	Single S	16	15.5	Single S	Plain
	Found at the boundary of the Intermediate stratum.							
2	61–22/8-a	16	11.7	Single S	13	9.9	Single S	Plain
	2 pieces of fabric folded at edge, hem stitched, and another piece sewn to them.							
3	61–56/5-c	17	17	Single S	12	13	Single S	Plain
	Hem: fabric is folded at edge and sewn. Second piece of fabric sewn to it.							

5 CM

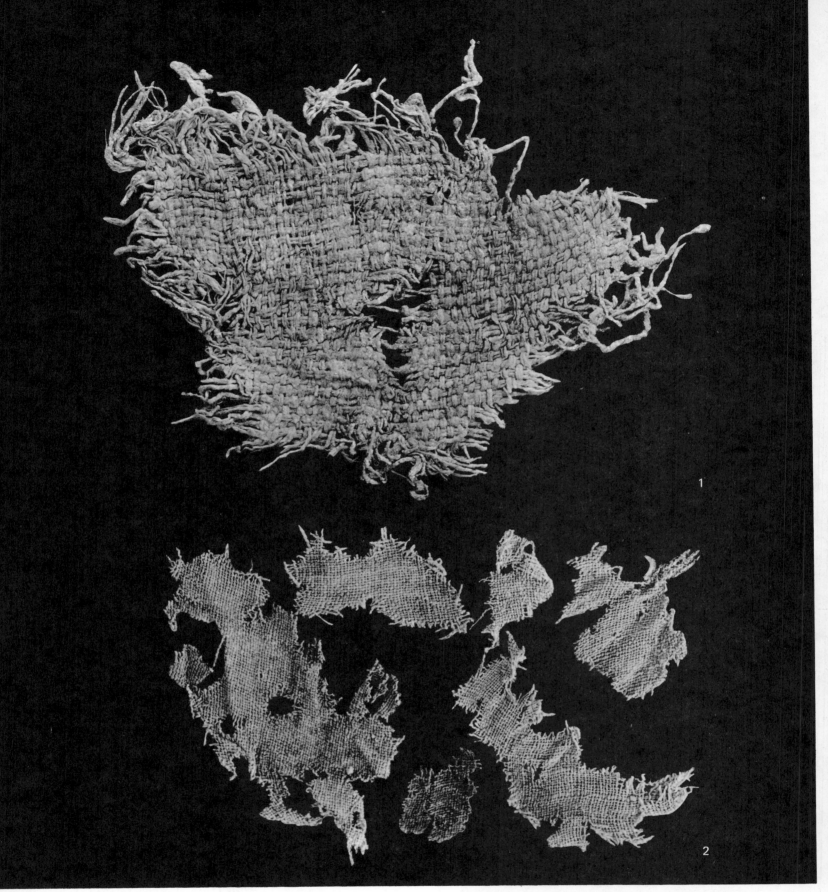

Ill. 37. Linen Fabrics – Chalcolithic Stratum

Reg. No.	Warp			Weft			Weave
	ends /cm.	count	twist	picks /cm.	count	twist	
1 62–28	12	4.3	Single S	7-8	3.1	Single S	Basket 2 × 2
2 61–29/7-e	16	35.6/2	Double S	11	44.4/2	Double S	Plain

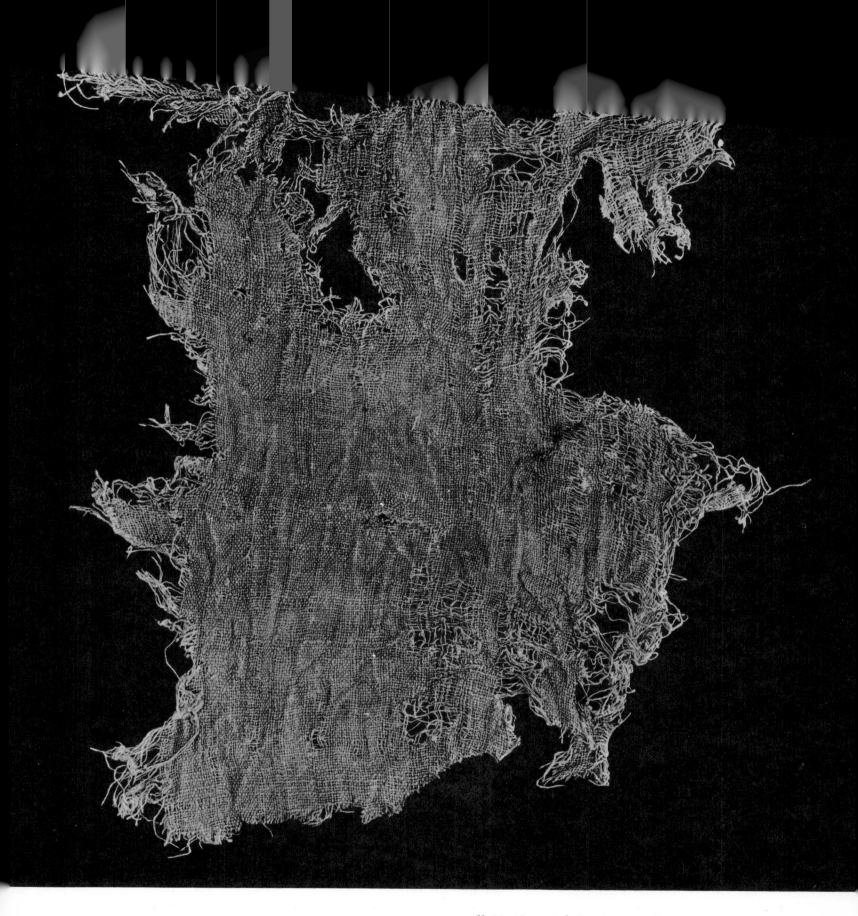

Ill. 38. Linen Fabric – Intermediate Stratum

Reg. No.	Warp			Weft			Weave
	ends /cm.	count	twist	picks /cm.	count	twist	
61–19/1-a	14	44/2	Double S	14-15	42/2	Double S	Plain

Self bands(?), not regular. Probably weaving error.

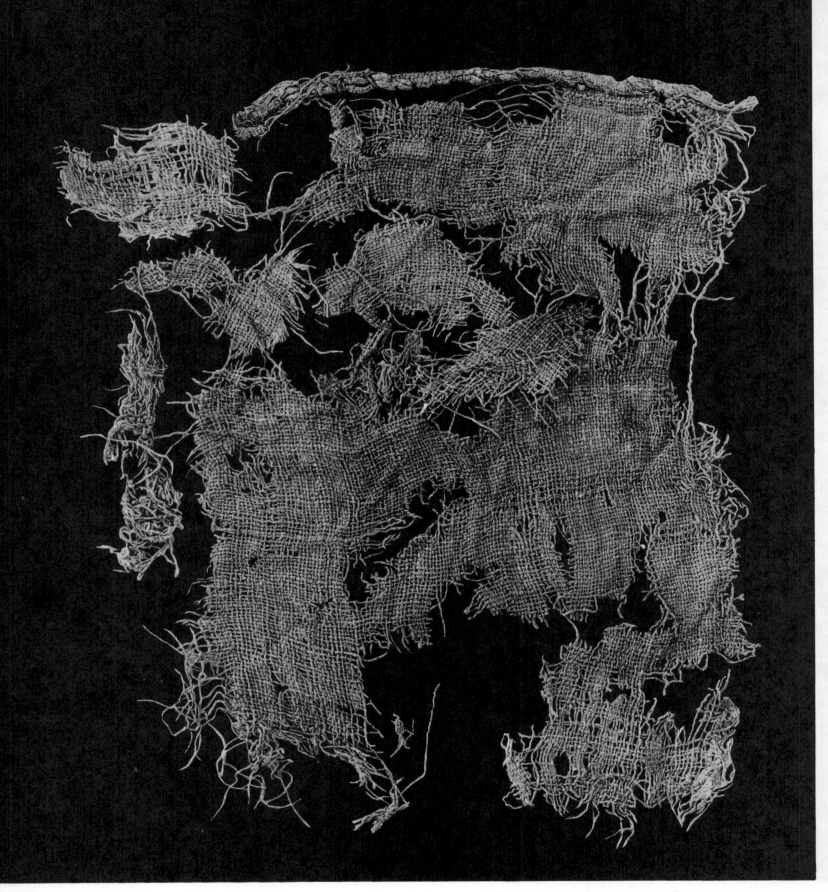

Ill. 39. Linen Fabric – Intermediate Stratum

Reg. No.	Warp			Weft			Weave
	ends */cm.	count	twist	picks /cm.	count	twist	
60–203–b	9-10	19.2/2	Double S	10-11	14/2	Double S	Plain

True selvedge. Fabric (slightly rolled) sewn on it for strengthening.

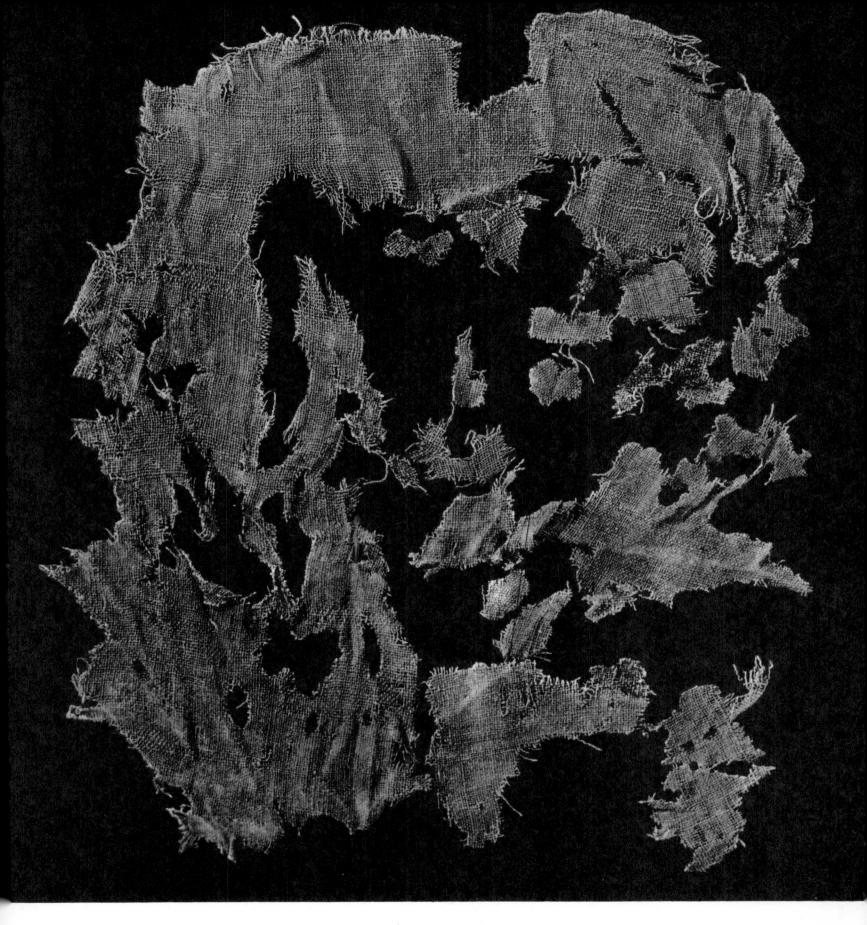

Ill. 40. Linen Fabric – Intermediate Stratum

Reg. No.	Warp			Weft			Weave
	ends /cm.	count	twist	picks /cm.	count	twist	
61–23/1-b	14	47.6/2	Double S	14	32.8/2	Double S	Plain

Ill. 41. Linen and Woollen Fabrics – Intermediate Stratum
Nos. 1–2 Linen, No. 3 Wool

	Reg. No.	Warp				Weft				Weave
		colour	ends /cm.	count	twist	colour	Picks /cm.	count	twist	
1	61–47/1-a		13	25.2/2	Double S		11	25/2	Double S	Plain
	Edge of fabric is folded and sewn with 2-ply yarn.									
2	60–151-c		18	36/2	Double S		16	29.2/2	Double S	Plain
	Selvedge: weft passes over three warps in two rows.									
3	60–201	Yellow	12	17.6	Single Z	Yellow	48	36.7	Single Z	Warp r effec
		Yellow	10	15	Single S	Yellow	17	13.8	Single S	Plain

Plain-weave fabric sewn to another piece of fabric. Both are folded. 2 small holes in fol
One layer of fabric between the folds. Hem on one side.

Ill. 42. Linen Fabric – Intermediate Stratum

Reg. No.	Warp			Weft			Weave
	ends /cm.	count	twist	picks /cm.	count	twist	
61–23/1-a	16	20	Single S	14	17	Single S	Plain
	14	8.9	Single S	14	5.3	Single S	Plain

Pocket sewn on to fabric along the selvedge of the pocket.
Selvedge: weft passes over four warps.

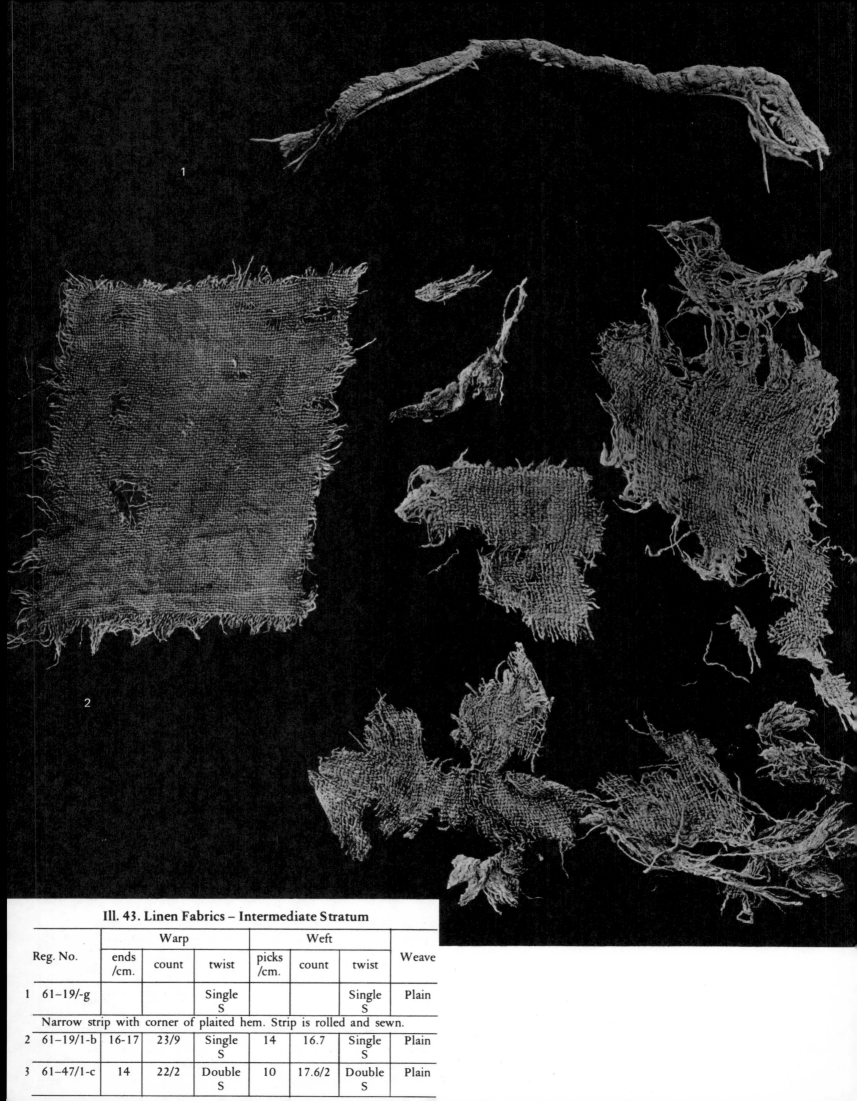

Ill. 43. Linen Fabrics – Intermediate Stratum

	Reg. No.	Warp			Weft			Weave
		ends /cm.	count	twist	picks /cm.	count	twist	
1	61–19/-g			Single S			Single S	Plain
	Narrow strip with corner of plaited hem. Strip is rolled and sewn.							
2	61–19/1-b	16-17	23/9	Single S	14	16.7	Single S	Plain
3	61–47/1-c	14	22/2	Double S	10	17.6/2	Double S	Plain

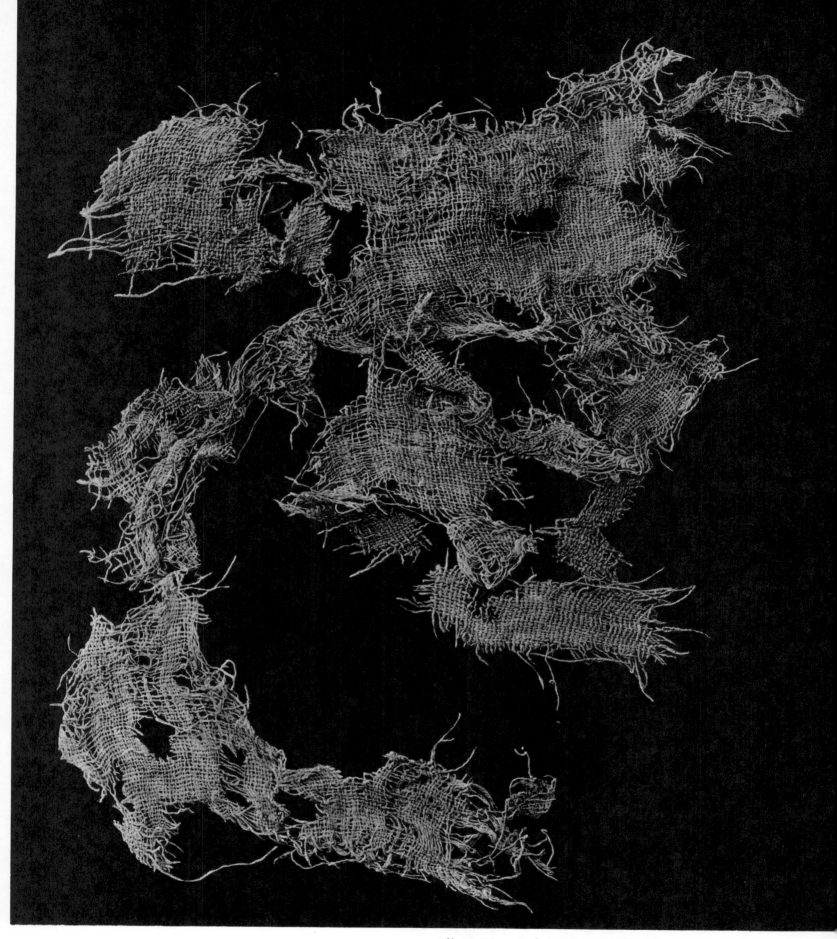

Ill. 44. Linen Fabric – Intermediate Stratum

Reg. No.	Warp			Weft			Weave
	ends /cm.	count	twist	picks /cm.	count	twist	
61–19/1-e	17	28.4/2	Double S	11	31.6/2	Double S	Plain

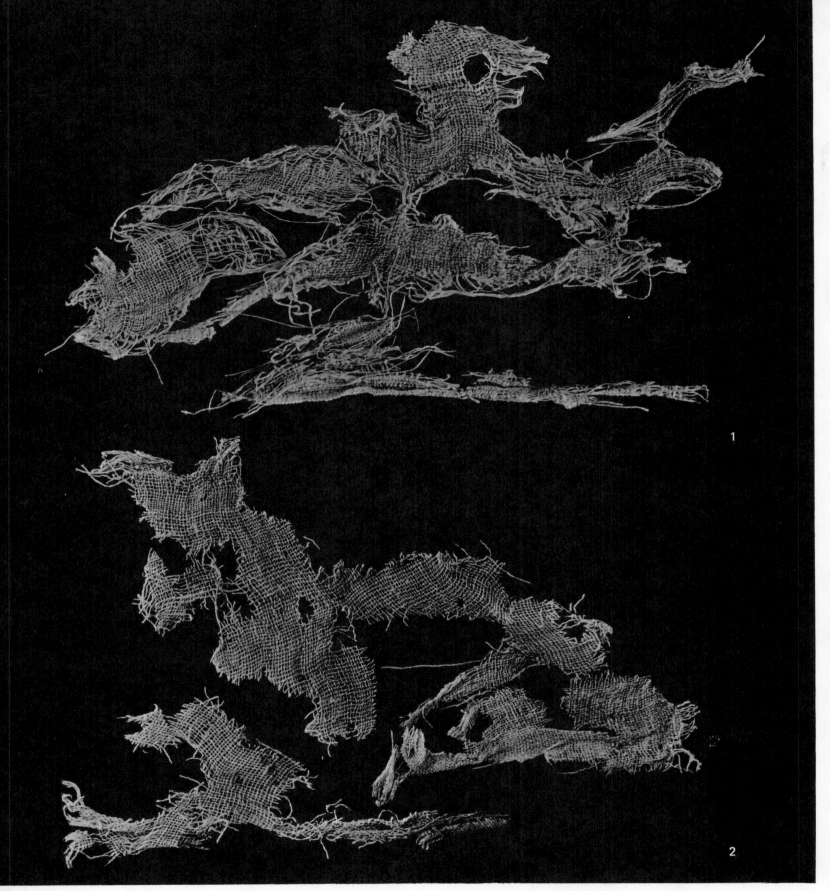

Ill. 45. Linen Fabrics – Intermediate Stratum

Reg. No.	Warp			Weft			Weave
	ends /cm.	count	twist	picks /cm.	count	twist	
1 60–151-k		34/2	Double S	16	37.8/2	Double S	Plain

Selvedge: weft passes over two warps in three rows.

Reg. No.	Warp			Weft			Weave
2 61–23/1-f	16	61.4/2	Double S	12	57.6/2	Double S	Plain

Rolled fabric 2 cm long sewn to main fragment.

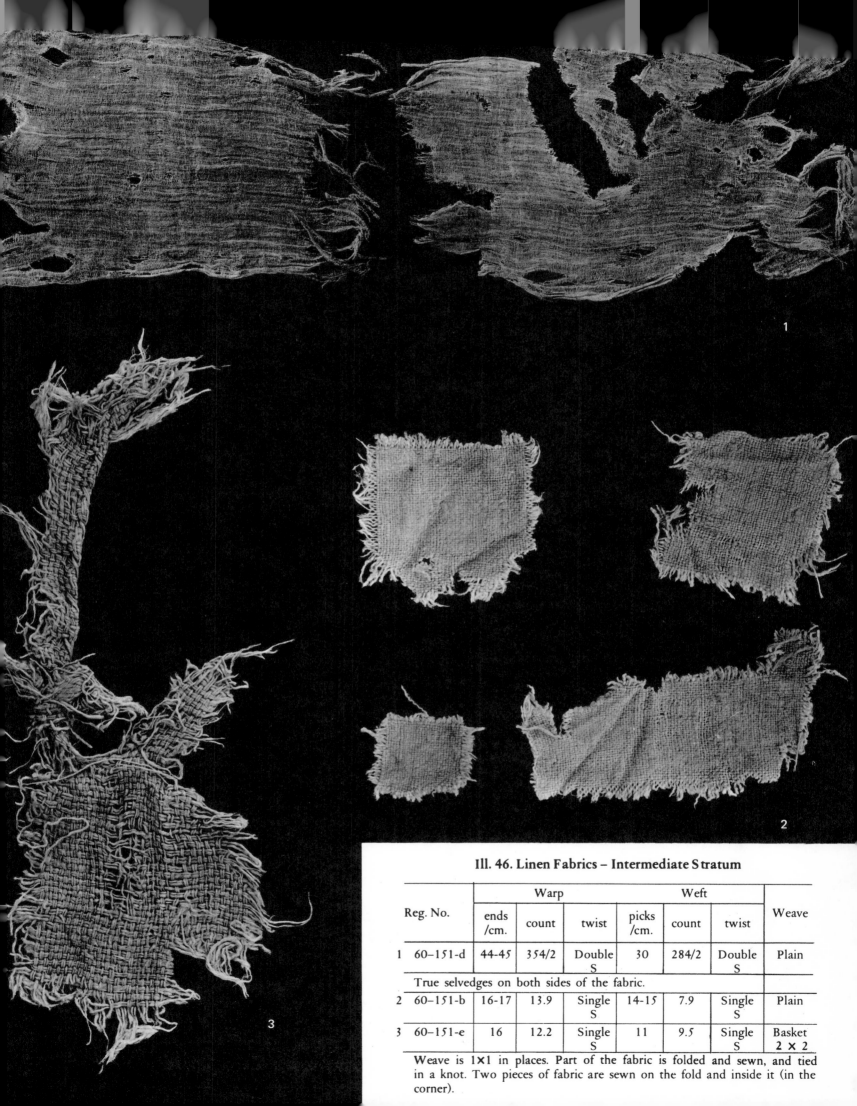

Ill. 46. Linen Fabrics – Intermediate Stratum

		Warp			Weft			
	Reg. No.	ends /cm.	count	twist	picks /cm.	count	twist	Weave
1	60–151-d	44-45	354/2	Double S	30	284/2	Double S	Plain
	True selvedges on both sides of the fabric.							
2	60–151-b	16-17	13.9	Single S	14-15	7.9	Single S	Plain
3	60–151-e	16	12.2	Single S	11	9.5	Single S	Basket 2 × 2

Weave is 1×1 in places. Part of the fabric is folded and sewn, and tied in a knot. Two pieces of fabric are sewn on the fold and inside it (in the corner).

1

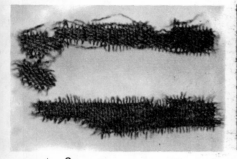

2

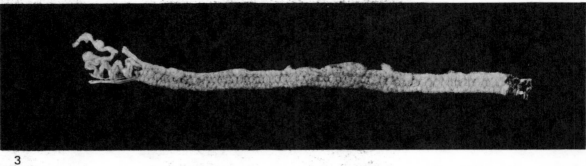

3

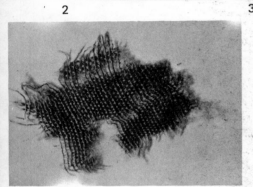

4

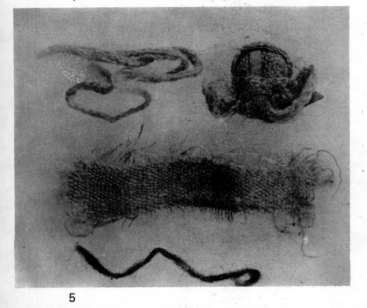

5

Ill. 47. Woollen Fabrics – Intermediate Stratum

	Reg. No.	Warp				Weft				Weave
		colour	ends /cm.	count	twist	colour	Picks /cm.	count	twist	
1	61–34/6	Black & Yellow								

Black plaited rope and knotted to it another, yellow, plaited rope. A yellow yarn is sew along the rope. Black net(?) of double-ply yarn hangs from it.

| 2 | 61–48/3 | Green | 13 | 12.2 | Single S | Green | 18 | 14.3 | Single S | Plain |
| 3 | 61–45/6-b | Yellow | | | Single S | Yellow 1/2 cm at end is red | | 3-ply | Z | Plain |

Strap: weft passes over six warps in three rows.

| 4 | 61–19/1-c | Yellow | 10 | 20 | Single S | Yellow | 20 | 29.2 | Single S | Plain |
| 5 | 60–151-n | Yellow | 10 | 14 | Single S | Yellow | 21 | 13 | Single S | Plain |

Botton wrapped in cloth. The button is round and is tied around with a strand of straw Round the straw, ten(?) turns of yellow woollen yarn. Found with another piece of red an yellow yarn.

| 6 | 61–23/1-d | Yellow | 14 | 15.6 | Single S | Yellow | 20 | 18.2 | Single S | Plain |

Edge of fabric rolled and folded twice. Hem stitched with double-ply Z-twist yarn.

| 7 | 61–49/6-a | Yellow | 16-17 | 14.6 | Single S | Yellow | 23-24 | 21 | Single Z | Plain |

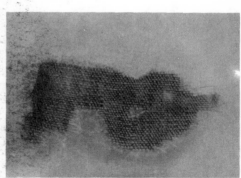

7

6

Ill. 48. Linen Fabric – Bar-Kokhba Stratum

Reg. No.	Warp			Weft			Weave
	ends /cm.	count	twist	picks /cm.	count	twist	
60–3–a	13	16.5	Single S	12	12.1	Single S	Plain

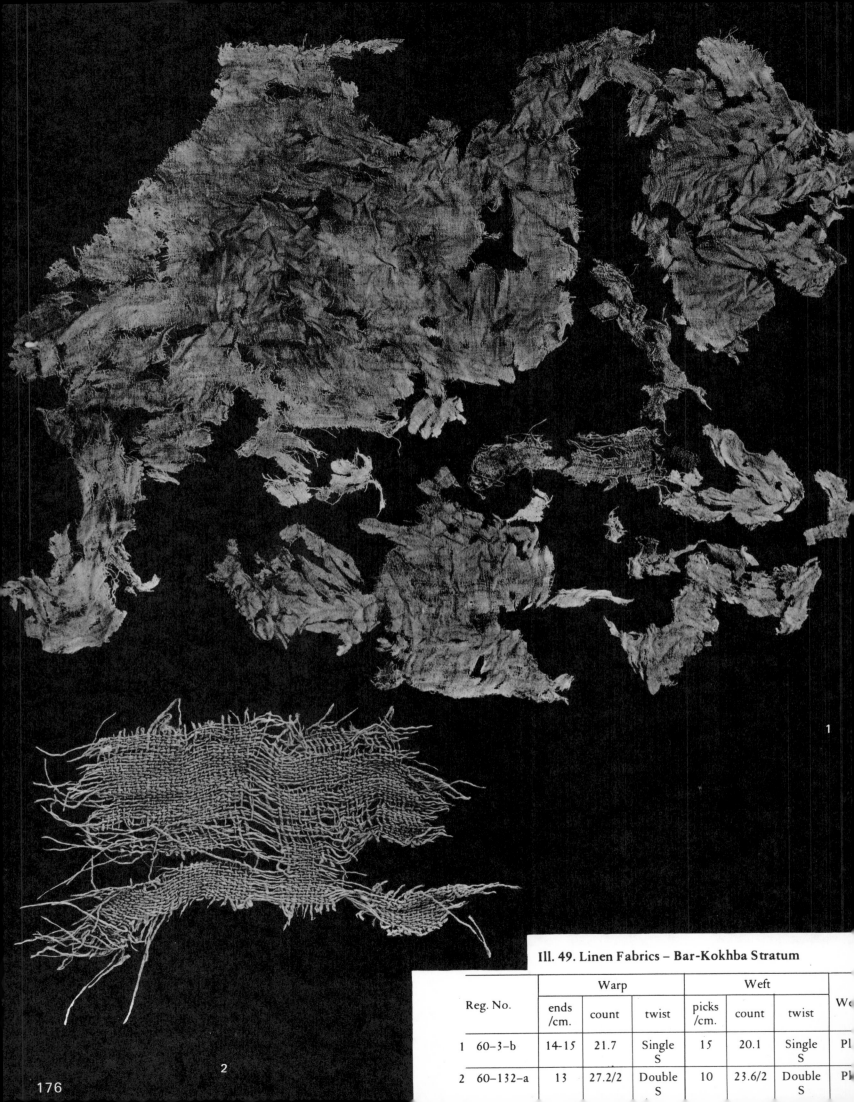

Ill. 49. Linen Fabrics – Bar-Kokhba Stratum

		Warp			Weft			We
	Reg. No.	ends /cm.	count	twist	picks /cm.	count	twist	
1	60–3–b	14-15	21.7	Single S	15	20.1	Single S	Pl
2	60–132–a	13	27.2/2	Double S	10	23.6/2	Double S	Pl

The Loom

Among the finds in the Chalcolithic layer were several groups of objects which proved to be connected with weaving. These included several two-edged bone needle-shuttles, whose one end was pointed or rounded and the other perforated. Similar needle-shuttles are known from various Chalcolithic sites, e.g. Ghassul,[73] Beersheba,[74] the Judean Desert caves and elsewhere.[75] A piece of thread has survived in the hole of one needle-shuttle (Ill. 50:2; and enlarged detail), confirming the supposition that these objects were indeed used for weaving. Fragmentary pieces of wood, either flat or D-shaped in section, and heavily worn with use, were also found in this context. The wooden implements are pointed or rounded at one end, like the bone needle-shuttles, and may have served for finer weaving. Nearby were found pieces of worked wooden sticks, some broken across the middle. Comparison with early representations of looms made it possible to recognize in our finds parts of a horizontal ground-loom.

Ill. 50. Bone shuttles

1 (Reg. No. 61–8/2)
Two-edged needle-shuttle (two fragments). Perforated. Cave 1, A–B.
L – 7 cm; W – 0.8 cm.

2 (Reg. No. 61–17/1)
Two-edged needle-shuttle. Perforated. Remains of thread in eye. Rounded end, damaged. On the side angular cut with sharp instrument. Cave 1, A–B.
L – 8 cm; W – 1 cm.

3 (Reg. No. 61–34/1)
Two-edged needle-shuttle. Perforated. Rounded end. Cave 1, A–B.
L – 11 cm; W – 1–1.4 cm.

4 (Reg. No. 61–17/2)
Two-edged needle-shuttle. Perforated. Broken. Cave 1, A–B.
L – 5 cm; W – 1–1.3 cm.

5 (Reg. No. 61–17/3)
Two-edged needle-shuttle. Top broken off. Sharp end. Cave 1, A–B.
L – 10 cm; W – 0.9 cm.

6 (Reg. No. 61–42/2)
Two-edged needle-shuttle (two fragments). Both ends broken. Cave 1, A–B.
L – 13 cm; W – 0.8 cm.

Detail of shuttle No. 2 below, showing fragment of thread in the hole.

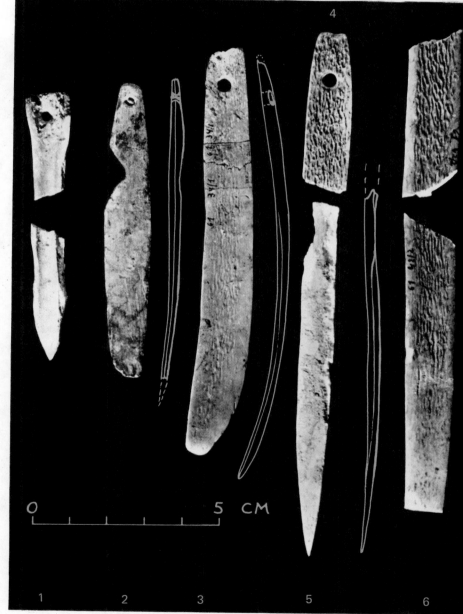

The horizontal ground-loom did not change much during the millennia since its invention, or at least, since its earliest known representation on a bowl from Badari[76] of the late fourth millennium B.C.E. (Ill. 52). Similar looms are still used today by fellahin, Beduin and primitive tribes.[77]

This type of loom consists essentially of five wooden sticks or beams: two warp beams, between which the warp is stretched, the "rod-heddle", the "shed-stick" and a rod for pressing down the weft – the "sword" or "beater-in". There are also shuttles and needles for separating and tightening the threads and for undoing knots. The warp beams are fastened to four pegs driven into the ground. The warp threads are divided into two layers, of which half, the odd threads, are attached by loops to a stick placed across the warp, the "rod-heddle", which can be thick, flat or rounded.[78] When the "rod-heddle" is raised, it separates the odd and the even threads and makes a space – the "shed", through which the weft is passed on a wooden or bone shuttle. The "shed-stick" serves to force the odd threads below the even threads. The "beater-in" serves to press home the weft at right angles to the warp. Needles, awls and combs serve to undo knots or tangles, and to tighten or loosen the weave.

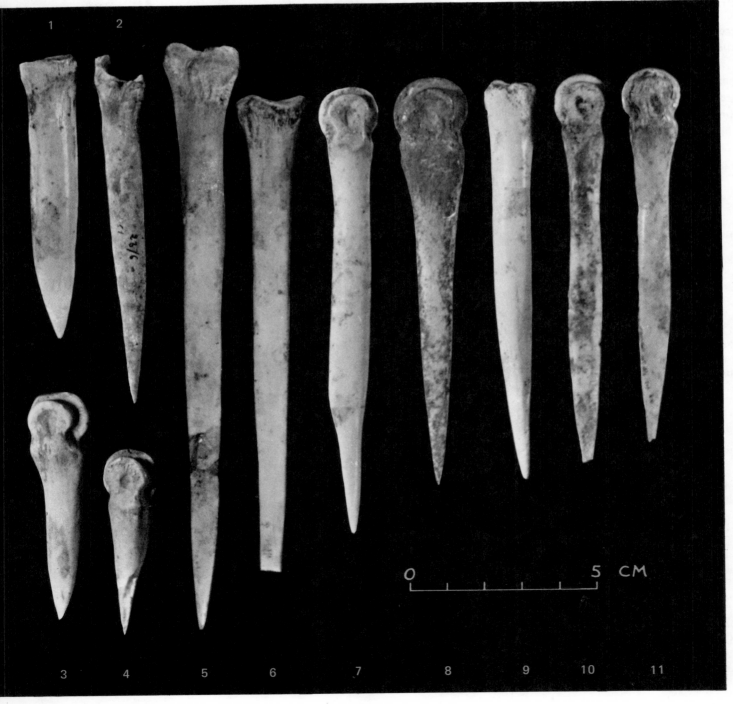

Ill. 51. Bone awls

1 (Reg. No. 61–84/
Cave 1, A. L – 7.5

2 (Reg. No. 61–23
Cave 1, A. L – 9.8

3 (Reg. No. 62–37
Cave 1, B. L – 6 c

4 (Reg. No. 61–30
Cave 1, A. L – 5 c

5 (Reg. No. 61–2
Cave 1, A. L – 16

6 (Reg. No. 61–10
Cave 1, A. L – 13

7 (Reg. No. 61–88
Cave 1, B. L – 12

8 (Reg. No. 61–6,
Cave 1, B. L – 11

9 (Reg. No. 61–5
Cave 1, B. L – 11

10 (Reg. No. 61–
Cave 1, A. L – 11

11 (Reg. No. 61–
Cave 1, A. L – 10

Ill. 55 shows the wooden sticks found in the cave, which can be identified as parts of a loom or as weaving accessories. Nos. 1 and 2 are the warp beams. The round heads at the ends and the grooves are intended to prevent the ropes lashing the beams to the pegs from slipping off. No. 3 seems to be the "rod-heddle", and No. 4 the "shed-stick", which has a grip at the end to facilitate lifting. No. 5 is probably the "beater-in". Nos. 3–5 are broken off at the ends and were originally longer. Nos. 6, 8 and 9 are wooden shuttles, which were used in addition to the bone shuttles (Ill. 50). No. 6 is a pointed stick irregularly grooved by the friction of the thread. Some of the thinner sticks may perhaps have served as spindles, together with the spindle-whorls (Ills. 57, 58). No. 7 is a needle.

Its hooked shape indicates its use for separating or tightening the threads and for untangling the yarn. Other needles are thinner, and can be identified as needles only by the way they are worked. The bone awls in Ill. 51 may have also served other purposes.

The two sticks in Ill. 54 do not seem to belong to a ground-loom and may have formed part of some other craft-appliance, perhaps a warp-weighted loom.

The above-mentioned design on the bowl from Badari shows a ground-loom with warp stretched between two beams with four pegs at the corners. At the right, three rows of weft are indicated. In the centre, three rods are shown. Next to the loom, an object resembling a bowl with a thread sticking out is represented.

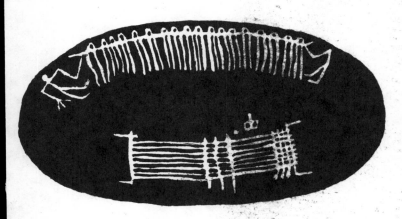

Ill. 52. Drawing of horizontal loom on bowl from Badari.

Ill. 53. Wall-painting in tomb of Khnum-hetep at Beni Hasan.

Ill. 54. Worked sticks

1 (Reg. No. 61–42/5)
Cylindrical stick. One end is knotty and rounded, the other blunt. Near the middle, hollow made by drilling and
charring.
L – 34 cm; Diam – 25 cm.

2 (Reg. No. 61–42/4)
Stick split lengthwise. One end cut diagonally, the other narrower and blunt. Cave 1, A. L – 19 cm; W – 4 cm.

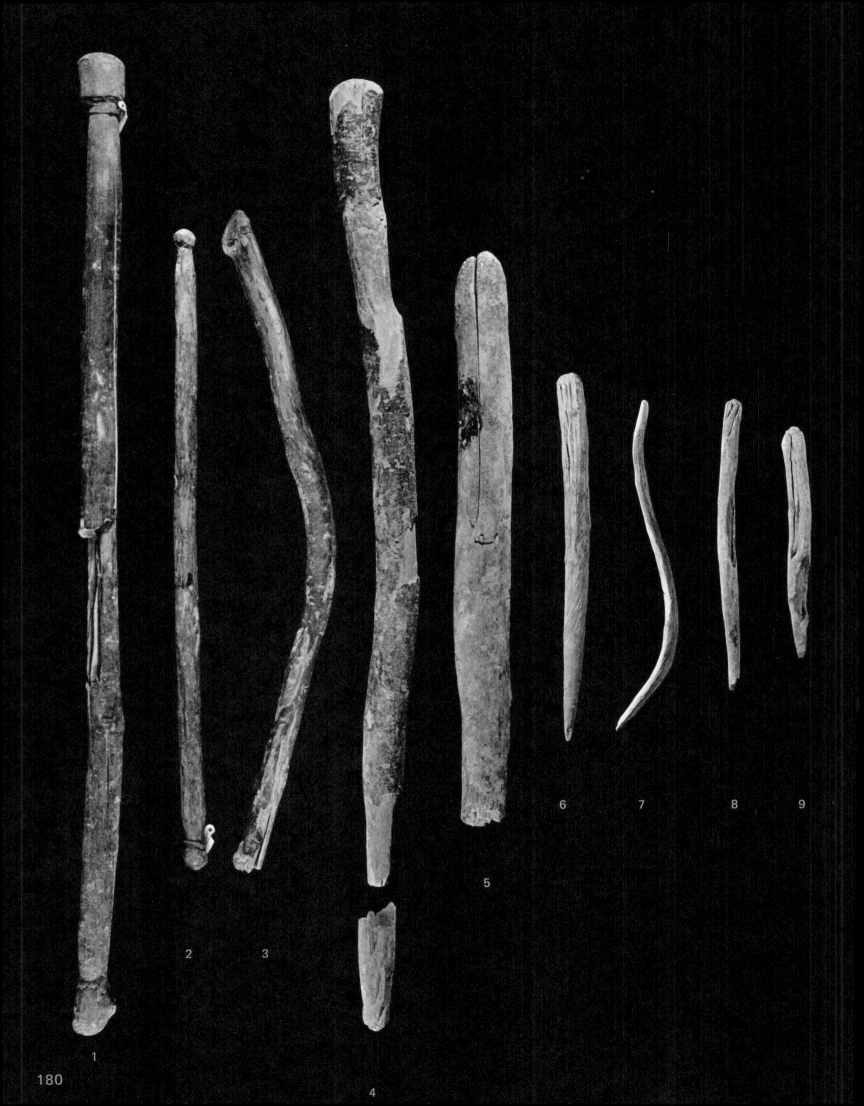

A horizontal loom also appears on a cylinder seal from Susa,[79] of the first half of the third millennium B.C.E. The seal was published in a horizontal position, so that the nature of the representation or of the objects shown on the seal remained unrecognized. It is described as an unknown object, with a figure below it and another above. However, if we place the seal in a vertical position, we can recognize a stylized loom, with two warp beams, the warp threads and a piece of woven fabric. The loom is flanked by two seated weavers, and next to each weaver is a bowl. A twisted thread (perhaps meant to represent a two-ply yarn) sticks out of one bowl. Near the warp beams stands a figure which is looping threads on pegs(?).

Arranging the threads into warps, weaving by two weavers on a loom, spinning and other related activities are known in Egypt from models and wall-paintings of the Eleventh–Twelfth Dynasties.[80] A wall-painting in the tomb of Khnum-hetep in Beni Hasan (Ill. 53) shows clearly the construction of the loom, with one short and one long warp beam.[81] On the basis of the pictorial representations and of later looms, at least one loom can be reconstructed from the various elements found in the cave.[82]

Ill. 55. Parts of the loom and accessories

1 a (Reg. No. 61–42/2)
1 b (Reg. No. 61–56/2)
Two fragments of cylindrical stick which can be joined. Round head separated from body of stick by deep groove. Cave 1, A.
L – 35.5 cm; Diam – 1.6 cm.

2a (Reg. No. 61–79/1)
2 b (Reg. No. 61–19/5)
Two fragments of stick which can be joined. Round end separated from body of stick by deep grooves. 1 a – Cave 1, A, 20 cm. below level of treasure niche; 1 b – Cave 1, A bordering on B, above level of top of treasure niche.
L – 54.5 cm; Diam – 2 cm.

3 (Reg. No. 61–79/3)
Curved stick. Partly covered with bark, with fine irregular grooves. At one end pointed head, the other end broken. Cave 1, below level of treasure. L – 37 cm; Diam – 2 cm.

4 (Reg. No. 61–79/5)
Cylindrical stick with remains of bark (two fragments). One end rounded, the other a blunt point. Elongated grip carved for easier grasping. Fine irregular grooves in bark. Cave 1, below level of treasure. L – 50 cm.

5 (Reg. No. 61–42/3)
Stick split lengthwise. One end rounded, the other broken. Cave 1, A. L – 31.5 cm; W – 3 cm.

6 (Reg. No. 61–9/2)
Conical stick with diagonal grooves. Pointed end. Friction grooves. Cave 1, A. L – 19.5 cm.

7 (Reg. No. 61–72)
Flat, crooked needle. L – 17 cm; W – 1 cm.

8 (Reg. No. 61–33/2)
Conical stick. Cave 1, A. L – 15 cm.

9 (Reg. No. 61–9/1)
Conical stick. Cave 1, A. L – 12 cm.

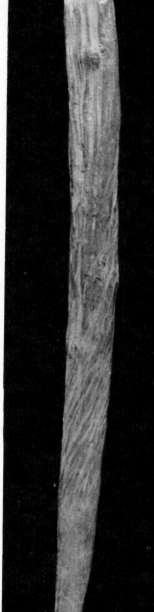

Stick No. 6, natural size, showing friction grooves.

The vertical loom was in use in Egypt by 1400 B.C.E., on the evidence of pictorial representations. On the other hand, it is generally agreed that the warp-weighted loom was known already in the mid-third millennium B.C.E., or even earlier, on the evidence of loom-weights from Troy.[83] In Palestine, this loom is thought to have appeared in the 16th century B.C.E. As loom-weights have been found in our cave and in other sites, the introduction of this loom may perhaps be dated as early as the Chalcolithic or even the Neolithic period.

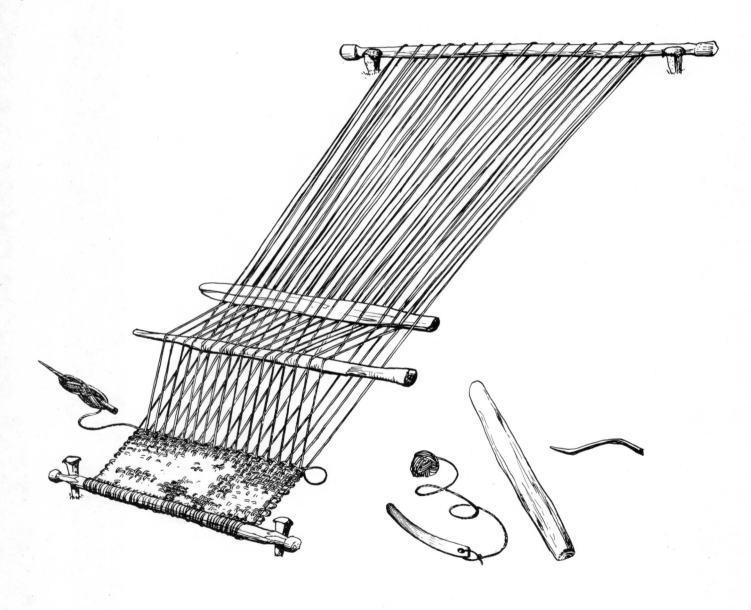

Ill. 56. Reconstruction of a horizontal ground-loom and accessories based on the finds

The spindle-whorls, both of pottery and of stone (Ills. 57, 58), are similar to those found in all Chalcolithic sites, as well as in the Judean Desert caves. Together with the spindle-whorls were found elongated, perforated, roughly shaped stones. These are probably loom-weights, such as have been found in Neolithic Jericho,[84] Ghassul[85] and Beersheba.[86]

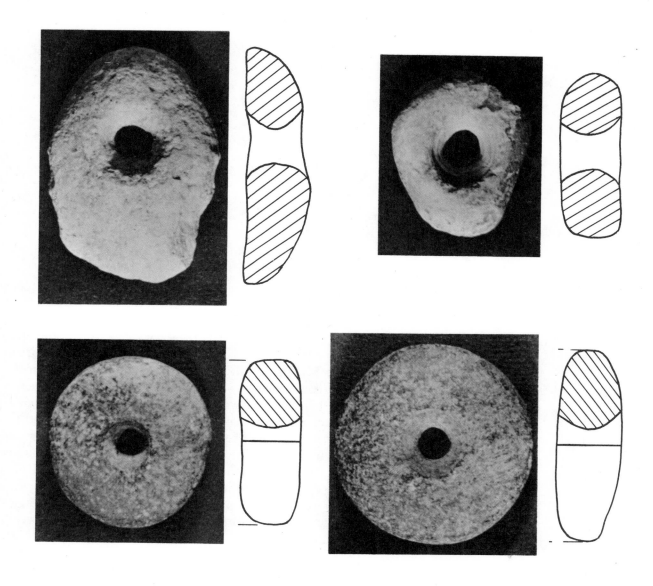

Ill. 57. Stone spindle-whorls

1 (Reg. No. 60–1)
Elongated spindle-whorl. White limestone. Friction grooves on both sides. Cave 1, A. 4.6 × 6.5 cm.

2 (Reg. No. 60–2)
Elongated spindle-whorl. Hard limestone. Drill marks on both sides of perforation. Cave 1, A. 3.8 × 4.5 cm.

3 (Reg. No. 61–56/1)
Spindle-whorl. Basalt. The perforation is funnel-shaped on both sides. Cave 1, A. Diam – 4.5 cm.

4 (Reg. No. 61–5/1)
Spindle-whorl. Basalt. The perforation is funnel-shaped on both sides. Cave 1, niche 1. Diam – 5.5 cm.

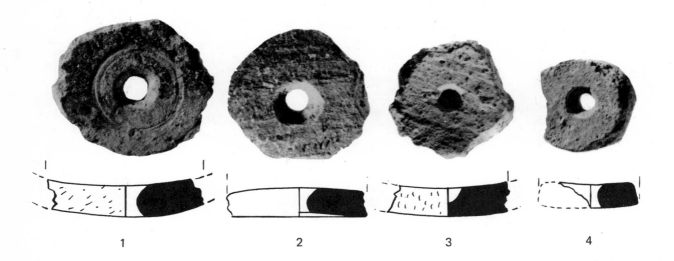

1   2   3   4

Ill. 58. Pottery spindle-whorls

1 (Reg. No. 60–173)
Cave 1, A. Diam – 4 cm.

2 (Reg. No. 60–74)
Cave 1, B. Diam – 3.7 cm.

3 (Reg. No. 60–172)
Cave 1, B. Diam – 3 cm.
Perforation incomplete.

4 (Reg. No. 60–74/1)
Cave 1, B. Diam – 2.8 cm.

Among the Chalcolithic pottery found in the cave was a bowl-fragment with a perforation near the rim (Ill. 59). Both sides are scored by irregular marks, probably the result of friction by threads. The bowl may perhaps have been used to hold thread for weaving, like on the weaver's seal from Susa mentioned above, or as a spinning bowl, like those shown in Egyptian pictorial representations.[87] In the Late Bronze and Iron Ages, pottery spinning bowls (in Egypt also stone bowls) appear in Palestine. These bowls have interior loop-handles, which served to guide the threads and to prevent entanglements.[88] Usually, perforations in pottery vessels served to repair breaks by means of cords or thongs. The perforation in our sherd seems to have served a different purpose. Another hole must have existed on the opposite side of the bowl, and a stick passed through both holes probably served much the same purpose as the loop-handles in the later spinning bowls. The representations in the tombs of Tehuti-hetep[89] and Tehuti-nefer[90] support this assumption.

In this context a roughly contemporary vessel found at Kish in Mesopotamia is of interest.[91] The bowl has a flat base and handles turned over inwards and attached to the floor of the bowl inside. The excavator was unable to find any parallels for this vessel, and he suggested that it might be a cooking-stand, without mentioning whether there were any traces of soot. He also suggested that other, less elaborate vessels with projections on the rim, served the same purpose. In my opinion, the vessel with the handles is a spinning bowl, while the projections on the rim of the other vessels may have served to separate the threads.[92]

The presence of the loom seems to indicate that at least some of the textiles found in the cave were produced there. Perhaps the flax, from which most of the textiles were made, grew at 'En-gedi, as it is the only place in the vicinity where there is sufficient water for the cultivation of this plant.

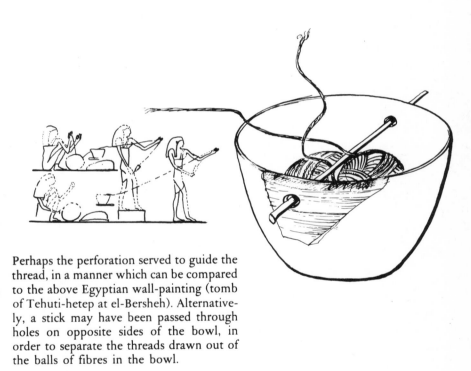

Perhaps the perforation served to guide the thread, in a manner which can be compared to the above Egyptian wall-painting (tomb of Tehuti-hetep at el-Bersheh). Alternatively, a stick may have been passed through holes on opposite sides of the bowl, in order to separate the threads drawn out of the balls of fibres in the bowl.

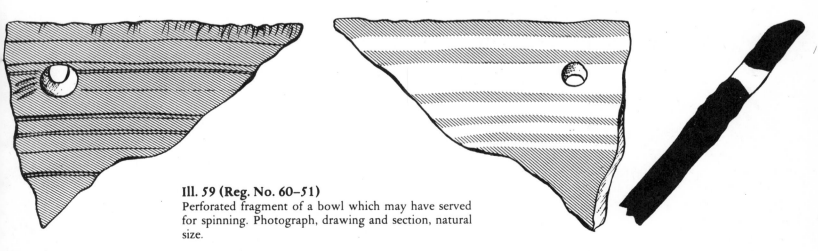

Ill. 59 (Reg. No. 60–51)
Perforated fragment of a bowl which may have served for spinning. Photograph, drawing and section, natural size.

Leather Objects

Sandals. Fragments making up one complete and one fragmentary sandal were found in Cave 1, Hall A, near the straw sieve and a jar fragment.

The sole of the complete sandal (Ill. 60) is made of layers of light-coloured coarse leather (cow-hide). Most of the layers are fastened together by threading the short, flat leather tongues of each piece through slits in the other pieces. The heel of the sandal is wide and the tip narrow. The tip is made of two pieces, joined by threading the tongue of one through a slit cut in the other. Some of the straps, through which the thong serving to tie the sandal was drawn, have been preserved, so that the sandal could be reconstructed.[93] Four wide straps are attached to the edge of the sole, two on each side. Each strap branches out into two narrow straps with a slit near the end. The left-hand front pair of straps have two slits. Still threaded through one of these is a piece of thong, probably used for tying the sandal. The shape of the slits indicates that they were probably produced by an awl made from a split bone. The sandal is 26 cm long and 7 cm wide, perhaps indicating that it belonged to a woman.

There are considerable differences between sandals of the Chalcolithic and the Bar-Kokhba periods. Our sandal is made up of many pieces, sewn or fastened together roughly, while the sandals of the later period are of better workmanship: the leather is more skilfully tanned, the sole is made of one piece of leather, the sewing is finer and sometimes there are even decorated buckles. The general shape, however, has not changed much up to this day.

This is, I believe, the first time that a sandal of the Chalcolithic period has been discovered. In contemporary representations, shoes or sandals appear only rarely; men and women, even priests and kings, are shown barefoot. Only at Ghassul, in a badly damaged fresco, can be seen what is considered by most scholars to be embroidered shoes.[94]

A leather-working shop is apparently represented on a cylinder seal of the Uruk (Warka) period. One of the objects shown has a raised and pointed tip, and Frankfort has suggested that it is a shoe,[95] a suggestion also accepted by other scholars.[96]

On each side of the Narmer palette a barefooted man is represented standing behind the king and carrying a pair of sandals.[97] The arrangement of the straps and the difference between both pairs of sandals can be clearly distinguished.

In later periods there are numerous representations of shoes and sandals in reliefs and wall-paintings.[98] An almost complete sandal of the Middle Bronze Age was found in a cave in Wadi Murabba'at.[99]

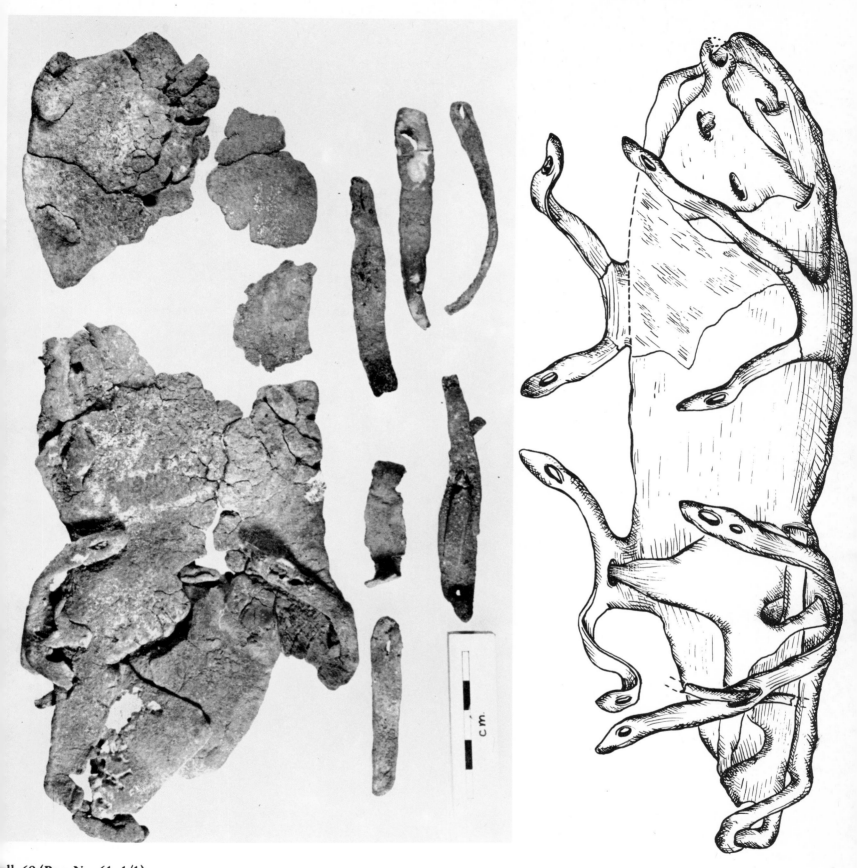

Ill. 60 (Reg. No. 61–1/1)

Fragments of leather sandal. The side-straps are cut out from the leather pieces making up the sole. Cow-hide. Tanned (?). Photograph and reconstruction.

Garments. Parts of leather garments were found near the skeletons in Cave 2.

According to Mr. Y. Fraenkel of the Fibres and Forest Products Institute, the leather is sheepskin, and is vegetable tanned(?). The leather is very fragile and even slight contact with water turns it into a squashy mass. The hair has been removed, but the roots remain up to the level of the epidermis. It is straight and not curly, as that of modern sheep. Perhaps the skin comes from a "hair-sheep".

The hair was removed either by shaving or by the use of chemicals, such as potash, K_2CO_3, or material containing sulphur, such as Na_2S or As_2S_2. These substances were known in ancient times, but it is not known when they began to be used. The Romans employed them for shaving and for cosmetics.

Ill. 61 Fragments of leather garments

1 (Reg. No. 62–36, 37)
Fragment of coat. The seams are sewn with flax fibres. Cave 2.

2–3 (Reg. Nos. 62–43, 62–43/1)
Drawing of two seams sewn with flax fibres.

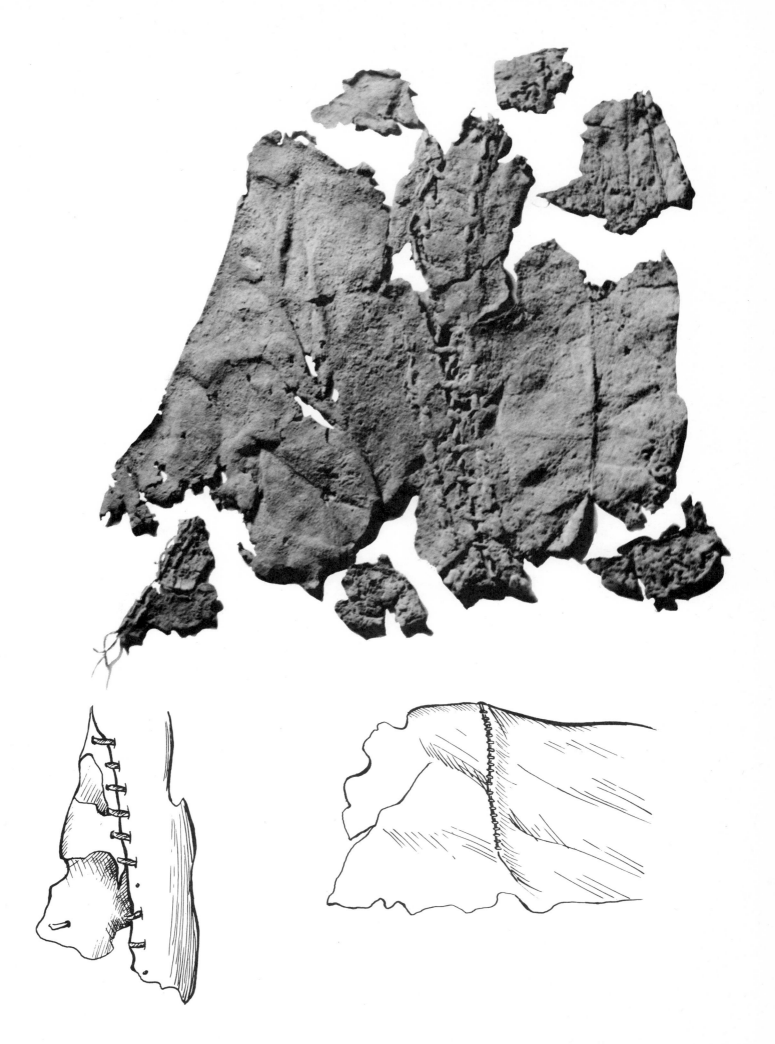

Basketry

Among the organic material uncovered in both strata, the most outstanding are the uncarbonized objects made of straw and reeds. It is likely that they were made of plants growing in the region, particularly near 'En-gedi, which has an abundance of springs.

The finds from both the early and the later strata include mats, trays, baskets and ropes. The Chalcolithic material is particularly rich and varied, and is exceptional in the number of objects found, their size and their state of preservation.[100] An outstanding example is the mat in which the treasure was wrapped (Ills. 63, 64), which measures 80 × 120 cm. The Carbon-14 analysis of this mat helped to confirm the date of the treasure (see below, p. 199). Special mention should be made of the almost complete sieve (Ill. 62), which was probably used for sifting grain.[101] Under the sieve and in its vicinity was a considerable amount of wheat and barley grains, and near it, a cooking stove and pottery of the Chalcolithic period. A variety of trays, some of fine workmanship, were also uncovered.

As with the other finds, great care was taken to distinguish between the basketware found in the Chalcolithic stratum and that found in the Intermediate stratum. Nevertheless, one fragment from the Intermediate stratum is included here because of its resemblance to mat impressions on bases of Chalcolithic pottery vessels. This is a fragment of a mat or basket (Ill. 69:2), plaited diagonally. A piece of leather is attached to it with a straw rope. Impressions of similar mats on bases of pottery vessels are known from Ghassul,

Jericho, Far'ah (S), Megiddo, etc.[102] There is no apparent difference between the plaiting technique of early and of later periods, and indeed it has not changed basically up to this day. The quality of workmanship, too, has always depended mainly on the skill of the craftsman. Nevertheless, our basketware contains, in addition to the usual wrapped coil technique, a technique characteristic of the Chalcolithic period, to which, so far, I have been unable to find parallels. Several mats made in this technique have been found (Ills. 63–64, 67, 68 and Reg. No. 62–38). This technique consists of passing the weft through a slit in the warp in such a manner as to conceal the joint, so that on the outside only a ridge is visible.

The mats whose impressions are found on the bases of pottery vessels seem to have been made in a similar technique, as the warp is not interrupted by the protuberant pattern produced by the ties of the weft. This is the case in the mat-impression on the base of a large pithos from Ashdod-Ya'aqov,[103] except that the concealed weft seems to be spaced more closely. The coil technique of our trays, even of the finer ones, can be found, for example, in the impressions on the bases of vessels from Jericho, Murabba'at, Lachish and Ghassul,[104] and on the base of a small ossuary found at Tel-Aviv.[105]

Some of the mats were used for burial (see above, p. 6), like the mats found in the Cave of Horror in Naḥal Ḥever.[106] A burial in a basket has been discovered in Anatolia.[107]

Ill. 62 (Reg. No. 61–207)

Basketwork sieve. The sloping sides of the bowl-shaped sieve consist of nine coiled rounds. The coil is made up of bundles of fibres wrapped with straw sewing strips, which are passed through the edge of the next round. The bottom of the sieve is made of flat reeds(?) plaited into a mesh, each strand fastened into the bottom round of the coiled sides. Cave 1, A. Top diam – 38 cm; Bottom diam – 20 cm; Depth – 6 cm; interstices of sieve 2–3 × 2–3 cm.

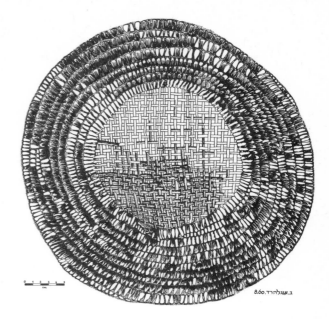

Ill. 63 (Reg. No. 61–430)
The mat in which the treasure was wrapped. The mat is made of reeds (Cyperus). The two-ply weft is passed through slits produced by splitting the reeds of the warp. The ridges formed by the concealed weft are spaced at regular intervals, adding both strength and beauty to the mat. The rim is bound by straw ropes which issue from the bundle of straw ropes below the rim. 80 × 120 cm.

Ill. 64. Enlarged photograph of part of the mat

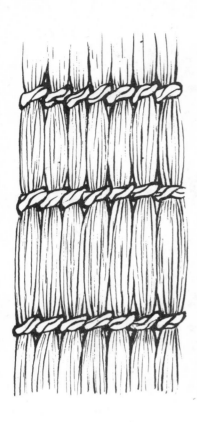

Ill. 65 (Reg. No. 61–208)
Mat fragment made of closely packed bundles of straw stalks twined in figure-of-eight stitches by two-ply straw cords at irregular intervals (2–3.5 cm). Cave 1, A. L – 25 cm; W – 16 cm; Th – 4 cm.

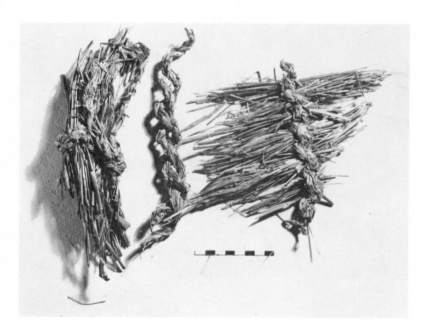

Ill. 66 (Reg. No. 61–61/1)
Mat fragment made of bundles of straw twined in figure-of-eight stitches by two-ply straw cords. Cave 1, B. ca. 10 × 17 cm.

Ill. 67 (Reg. No. 61–5/4)
Mat fragment made in the same technique as the mat in which the treasure was wrapped. The warp consists of reeds, the weft of two-ply straw rope, which is passed through slits in the warp at intervals of 5–6 cm. Cave 1, B.

Ill. 68 (Reg. No. 62–7)
Mat fragment made in same technique as the mat in Ill. 67 and the mat in which the treasure was wrapped. Intervals between ridges formed by concealed weft – 5 cm. Cave 3.

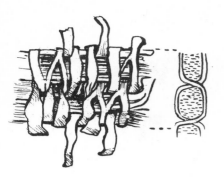

1

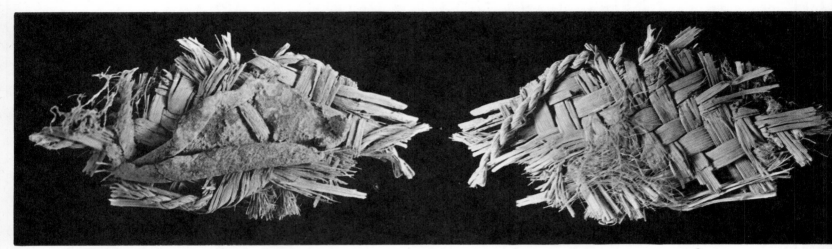

2

3

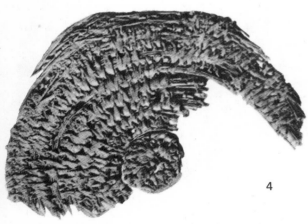

4

Ill. 69. Basket and tray fragments.

1 (Reg. No. 61–63)
Basket fragments. The remains of two rounds have been preserved. Technique similar to sieve. Cave 1, niche 1.

2 (Reg. No. 61–13/1)
Basket fragment. Front and back views. Diagonally plaited reeds. Pieces of leather are attached to the fragment with a straw rope. Cave 1, niche 1.5 × 9 cm.

3 (Reg. No. 61–209)
Basket or tray. Five coiled rounds have been preserved, starting from a snail centre. The coil consists of bundles of straw stalks wrapped with sewing strips passed through the edge of the adjoining round. Cave 1, A. Diam of fragment – 12 cm; Th – 2 cm.

4 (Reg. No. 61–211)
Fragment of basketwork tray of ten coiled rounds, starting from a snail centre. The coil consists of bundles of straw stalks closely wrapped with straw sewing strips, passed through the edge of the adjoining round. Cave 1, A. Diam of complete tray – 14 cm; Th – 8 mm.

Ill. 70. Tray and rope fragments

1 (Reg. No. 61–212)
Tray fragment of seven coiled rounds, similar in technique to the fragment in Ill. 69:4. Cave 1, A. Diam of complete tray – 32 cm.

2 (Reg. No. 61–5/5)
Tray of seven coiled rounds, starting from a snail centre. The coil consists of bundles of straw closely wrapped with straw sewing strips, passed through the edge of the adjoining round. Cave 1, B. Diam – 10.5 cm.

3 (Reg. No. 61–12/8)
Straw rope plaited from three strands. Cave 1, niche 1. W – 1 cm.

4 (Reg. No. 69–12/8(3))
Two two-ply straw ropes knotted together. Cave 1, niche 1. W – 2 and 3 cm.

5 (Reg. No. 61–91/1(3))
Three-ply straw rope. Cave 1, A. Diam – 1.5 cm.

6 (Reg. No. 61–91/1)
Straw rope plaited from three strands. Diam – 1.7 cm.

7 (Reg. No. 62–51)
Two-ply straw rope, tied into a knot. Cave 1, A.

8 (Reg. No. 61–5/6)
Two-ply straw rope, Cave 1, B. Diam – 6 cm.

Plant remains

Dr. D.V. Zaitschek, of the Hebrew University, who joined the expedition in the first week of the second season, gathered the plant remains and examined them (see below, Appendix A).

Some plant remains could be assigned with certainty to the Chalcolithic period, as they were found in Cave 1 under stones which had fallen from the ceiling after the Chalcolithic occupation and before the use of the cave in Bar-Kokhba's time. Of great interest are the cereal remains, found here for the first time in a non-carbonized state, which are of special importance for studying the origin and historical development of cultivated wheat.

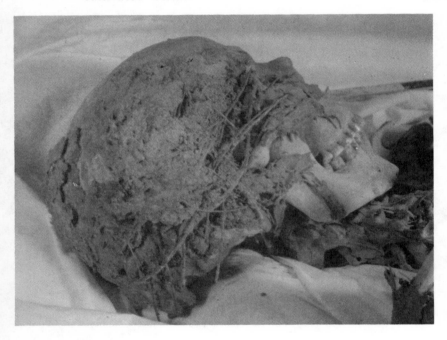

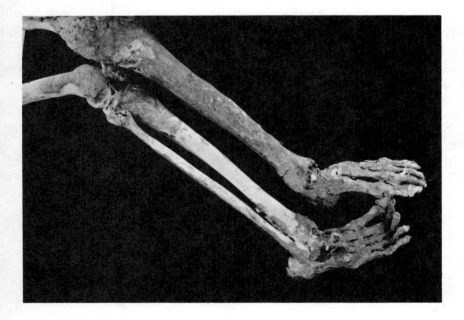

Other plant remains were found during all three seasons of excavations, mainly in Cave 1, but also in Caves 2 and 3.

The cereal remains found in the occupation level of the Bar-Kokhba period differ somewhat from those in the Chalcolithic level. The fruit remains, though representing the same species (olives, dates, pomegranates, walnuts, acorns), also show some differences.

Plant remains which could not be attributed with certainty either to the Chalcolithic or to the Roman level, were assigned to the Intermediate level.

Burials

The skeletons found in Caves 1–3 reflect the composition of the population in the Chalcolithic period. The following skeletal remains were found: Cave 1 – two children, one woman and two men (5 burials); Cave 2 – four children, one woman and one man (6 burials); Cave 3 (the excavation of this cave has not been completed) – one child, four women and five men (10 burials). Burial-caves 2 and 3 were certainly connected with Cave 1, which served for habitation, and formed together one unit.

The 21 individuals whose remains were uncovered were of the following ages: 7 children aged 2–12; 6 women aged 18–50; 8 men aged 18–45. The height of the men was over 1.70 m; the height of the women, over 1.65 m. The teeth found were all without caries. 12 of the individuals seem to have been in good health. The others suffered from various ailments, but it is only in a few cases that any of these can be considered as the cause of death.

Most of the skeletons were found in an extended position, and only a few were in a contracted position. Some of the burials were oriented with the head to the south. Chalcolithic vessels (for instance, Ill. 3:2) were found next to them. Dr. N. Haas of the Hebrew University, Hadassah Medical School, Jerusalem, who participated in the third season, studied the skeletal remains and a full report has been published elsewhere.[108]

The individuals all belong to the meso-dolicho-cephalic type, with very long faces, strong jaws and aquiline noses. They conform to the southern proto-Mediterranean type. This type has been found, inter alia, at Jemdet Nasr, and in this country at Beersheba and Ghassul.

CONCLUSIONS

The Date of the Treasure

The problem of dating the treasure arose immediately after its discovery. The fact that the hoard was wrapped in a mat and hidden in a deep crevice suggested from the first that it constituted a homogeneous collection of artifacts belonging to one period. Only two occupation levels could be distinguished in the cave, one of the time of Bar-Kokhba, and the other of the Chalcolithic period, and there were no signs of occupation, even of the most transitory nature, between the two periods.

The first clue to their date was furnished by the resemblance of some of the objects, such as the mace-heads, chisels, axes, standards and ivories, to objects known from other sites, and dated there to the late Chalcolithic period or to the beginning of the Early Bronze Age. Furthermore, the decorative motifs on some of the artifacts, particularly on the "crowns", were recognized as characteristic of that period.

Fortunately, remains of organic material were also found in the cave. They not only furnished valuable evidence of the cave-dwellers' way of life, but also helped in determining the date of the treasure. C-14 analyses were made of the mat in which the treasure was wrapped, and of the pieces of wood that had remained inside the standards. The results of these analyses (though they should be accepted with caution) confirm the archaeological conclusions.

A C-14 analysis of the mat in which the treasure was wrapped was made in 1963 in the British Museum[1] (BM 140), with the following results:

5390±150, i.e. between 3577 and 3277 B.C.E.[2]

The mat was analysed again in 1964 in the Department of Geology of the United States Government in Washington (WR-1341), with the following results:

4880±250, i.e. between 3166 and 2666 B.C.E.

Different results were obtained in the analyses of the mat made in 1961 by the Isotopes Inc. Laboratories, New Jersey, U.S.A. (No. I-285):

4780±100, i.e. between 2919 and 2719 B.C.E.

The same laboratory also analysed in the same year the remains of wood preserved inside the standards (No. I-353). The results were:

4760±120, i.e. between 2919 and 2679 B.C.E.

The laboratory also analysed in 1963 (No. I-1819) a piece of fabric adhering to one of the skeletons in Cave 2, with the following results:

4725±230, i.e. between 2992 and 2532 B.C.E.

Clearly, the lower date of this last analysis does not agree with the stratigraphical evidence of Cave 2, since neither in our caves nor in any other caves of this region, have occupation remains of that period been found. The upper date is also open to doubt, in view of the results of the analysis of the mat in the British Museum. A charred piece of fabric, which was found by Aharoni and his expedition in the Cave of Horror, was analysed in 1961 at the Isotopes Inc. Laboratories, which gave its age as 5460±125, i.e. between 3624 and 3374 B.C.E.[3] Aharoni already remarked in his report that the Naḥal Ḥever date seems to be a little early, while the Naḥal Mishmar date appears to be somewhat late. The best course seems to be to take a mean date between the results obtained by the British Museum and those of laboratories in the United States. This would also agree with the dates for the three strata of the Beersheba Chalcolithic assemblage, as determined by C-14 analyses carried out at the Laboratories of the University of Michigan:[4]

Stratum A – 5420±350, i.e. between 3820 and 3120 B.C.E.

Stratum B – 5270±300, i.e. between 3620 and 3020 B.C.E.

Stratum C – 5120±350, i.e. between 3520 and 2820 B.C.E.

Although no C-14 analyses have been made of the material from Teleilat Ghassul, the close similarity between the two cultures allows us to assign both, broadly speaking, to the same horizon.

The generally accepted provisional dates are as follows: Ghassulian culture – from the mid-fourth millennium to 3300 B.C.E.; Jezreel culture – 3300–3100 B.C.E.; Early Bronze Age – 3100–2900 B.C.E. These dates correspond to the Ubaid, Uruk-Warka and Jemdet-Nasr cultures in Mesopotamia, which are generally agreed to have influenced the Ghassulian cultures and the beginnings of the Early Bronze Age in Palestine. The few known parallels to the objects in our treasure also point to the connection with the Uruk-Warka and Jemdet-Nasr periods.[5]

The Civilization of the Cave-Dwellers

Since the excavation in the thirties of Teleilat Ghassul near the Dead Sea, many Chalcolithic sites have been discovered throughout Palestine. These were unfortified settlements, comprising houses with courtyards, silos and livestock pens, or subterranean dwellings. Their inhabitants, whose main livelihood was agriculture, possessed technical skill and a feeling for art, as is evidenced by the superb frescoes discovered at Ghassul, the ivory figurines and the characteristic bone objects found at Beersheba, the decorated clay ossuaries known from sites such as Hadera, Azor, Bene-Beraq, Ben-Shemen, etc., the richly decorated clay vessels, fine basalt incense stands, and a few copper objects, such as mace-heads and chisels.

Traces of this culture have also been found in all the Judean Desert caves excavated so far – in Wadi Murabba'at, Naḥal David, Naḥal Ḥever, Naḥal Mishmar, Naḥal Ṣe'elim, and also, as our surveys have shown, further south, in Naḥal Ḥemar and Naḥal Zohar. There must certainly be other caves that have not yet been discovered. A large sacred enclosure of the same period has been uncovered in the 'En-gedi oasis,[6] but no traces of a settlement have yet been found in its vicinity. The character of the finds testifies to the homogeneous culture of all these cave-settlements.

Obviously this culture did not mature suddenly, but was the result of gradual growth and development. Since there is no evidence to indicate that this growth was solely a local phenomenon, we have to try and trace its origins, probably somewhere in the wider region. However, we have little comparative material, as most of the objects in the treasure are unique, and we can only try to reconstruct, detail by detail, as complete a picture as possible of this culture. The anthropological and metallurgical evidence, and a comparison of the treasure with the art of the ancient Near East, and in particular with cult objects symbolizing fertility, such as the eagle, birds and other living creatures,[7] the jar,[8] the deep bowl,[9] the horn-shaped vessels,[10] the horns,[11] the Maltese cross[12] etc., lead the author to the conclusion that the origins of this culture must be sought in the north. This subject will be dealt with in more detail in a special article.

The temple uncovered at 'En-gedi may supply the background to support our conclusions concerning the character of the artifacts in the treasure. However, the finds in the caves of the region do not always include the whole range of the characteristic Chalcolithic assemblage. This fact should be borne in mind when considering other Chalcolithic sites, such as Teleilat Ghassul and Beersheba, and when attempting to draw conclusions from such evidence. Thus, for example, cornets were found in Wadi Murabba'at, but not in Naḥal Mishmar.[13] On the other hand, clay spoons and churns occur in Naḥal Mishmar, but not in Wadi Murabba'at, while in the caves copper mace-heads were found only in Naḥal Ṣe'elim and Naḥal Mishmar. In addition, the composition of the copper mace-heads found at Beersheba is identical to that of the mace-heads from our treasure (see Appendix E). Clearly a close link existed between all the sites mentioned above.

No distinctive features can be recognized which would set apart the pottery found in the Judean Desert caves (Naḥal Mishmar, Wadi Murabba'at, Naḥal David,

Naḥal Ḥever, Naḥal Ṣe'elim, Naḥal Ḥemar and Naḥal Zohar), in 'En-gedi and in the Negev,[14] from that found at other sites of the Chalcolithic culture, nor can any substantial differences be shown between them. The points of resemblance between pottery from the southern and the northern parts of this country and from the mountains of Transjordan, is greater than the differences in detail, which are only natural among tribes and families that valued the preservation of their individuality.

Dress and Footwear

The fine collection of textiles and the fragmentary leather garments and sandals are the earliest discovered so far in this country, and they give us some idea of the cave-dwellers' dress. There is no doubt whatever that most of the fabrics belong to the late Chalcolithic period, as some of them were found inside artifacts. Furthermore, clothing fragments, some of them of two-coloured fabric, found on one of the bodies in Cave 2, were submitted to C-14 analysis (see above). Another piece of fabric was found adhering to a characteristic Chalcolithic potsherd. In addition, many of the linen and woollen textile remains were uncovered in the Chalcolithic stratum.

The spindle-whorls and the loom with its accessories prove that spinning and weaving were practiced by the inhabitants of the caves.

The cave-dwellers also wore leather coats, for which they used goatskins, sheepskins, or the hides of other, as yet unidentified, animals. The pieces were sewn together very neatly with thongs, while some of the repairs were made with linen thread. Goatskins with hair still attached, were found on some of the skeletons. Jewellery made of ivory, decorated bone and shell, and beads of faience, agate and shell served for personal adornment. Only two sandals were found, implying perhaps that most of the cave dwellers went barefoot.

Food

The numerous animal bones and other food remains of this period found here for the first time in such quantity, bear witness to a fairly rich diet: wheat and barley, olives and lentils, onions and garlic, pomegranates and dates, acorns and nuts, meat of sheep, goats, gazelles, and various kinds of birds (see Appendices A, B). The churns show that dairy products were also used. Water was probably brought from the spring in the cliff-side, and during the winter months from rock-pools.

Cooking played an important role, as evidenced by the sooty hole-mouth jars. The main utensils were large and small bowls, storage jars, jugs and pithoi. The straw sieve and the pounding and grinding utensils are also an indication of the manner in which food was prepared.

The fuel used for cooking consisted of twigs, shrubs, pieces of wood and branches, which were probably carried down from the hills by the seasonal flow of water in the valleys. Dried dung was perhaps also used, as it still is today.

Crafts

Various implements found in the cave indicate that the inhabitants also practised crafts such as spinning and weaving. We do not know if the flax fibres were also prepared and dyed on the spot. On the other hand, there is no doubt that the skins were prepared and sewn in the cave (as evidenced by the bone awls, and perhaps also the copper awl). The cave-dwellers also made baskets, trays and mats, and perhaps produced the various pottery vessels, decorating them with pigments obtained from the earth in the vicinity of the cave.

Copper Industry

Up to the present it was generally accepted that copper objects first appear in Sialk I, and that, beginning in the early Chalcolithic period, the use of copper spread in Iran and in Mesopotamia, in the Halafian, Ubaid, Uruk (Warka) and Jemdet-Nasr cultures. Some scholars are of the opinion that copper metallurgy originated in north-west Iran and in the mountains of Armenia and the Caucasus.[15] However, the interesting finds at Çatal Hüyük in Anatolia, which the excavator, Mellaart, ascribes to the middle of the seventh millennium B.C.E., also included copper objects,[16] and it would therefore appear that it began to be used earlier than was hitherto supposed.

Part of the copper objects in the treasure have a high arsenic content (up to 11.9%). At first glance this would appear to support the theory that the ore came from the Armenian mountains, whose copper ore is known to be rich in arsenic (see Appendix E). However, it has also been suggested that we have here perhaps the beginnings of an attempt to make a copper and arsenic alloy[17] for the manufacture of practical and durable artifacts, attempts which eventually led to the discovery of bronze. Perhaps the ceramic material found inside the copper shell of one of the mace-heads (No. 230, see Appendix D), can also serve as evidence of this striving towards improved methods.

It is difficult to determine where the copper ore was mined. Prof. Bentor has informed me that among the data he collected from geologists in the countries of the region, with the exception of the Armenian deposits mentioned above, there are no deposits of copper ore of similar composition to that of our artifacts. The Timna deposits, too, have a different composition. It has also been established that the Punon (Feinan) ore has a similar composition to the ores worked in the Elath region,[18] thus refuting the theory that the ore from which the copper objects found at Beersheba were made, came from the Punon mines.[19] Tests made by C.A. Key have shown that the metal of our mace-heads is identical with that of the objects found in Naḥal Şe'elim and Beersheba. Small crucibles for smelting copper, as well as copper ore and slag, were discovered in the Beersheba excavations,[20] indicating the existence of a copper industry in Palestine at that period, although the origin of the copper ore is as yet unknown. If the copper was not mined in the vicinity, as might reasonably be assumed, it may well have been brought from afar in the form of sheet-copper.[21] We have no way of knowing if the artifacts in the treasure, and in particular the more elaborate items, were manufactured in Palestine or elsewhere. Metal objects of a high technical standard are known to have been produced during this period in Mesopotamia and in Iran, but perhaps we can assume that at least the mace-heads and the tools were made in Palestine.

The design and workmanship of the decorated artifacts found in the hoard is substantially different from that of the objects whose shape and character indicate their practical purpose. The decorated objects are distinguished by their delicate workmanship, meticulous design, good finish and harmonious proportions. The hammer and most of the chisels, on the other hand, are of coarse workmanship, without any particular accuracy of shape or measurement. Moreover, the decorated objects are made of copper high in arsenic content, while the tools are made of purer copper (see below, Appendix E). From a technical point of view this seems illogical, as it is more important for the tools to be made of a harder material.

If we accept the theory that the decorated objects were made of copper derived from ore mined in the Armenian mountains, it can be argued that the tools were manufactured from copper produced in another mine, and were made by less accomplished craftsmen. Alternatively, if it is true that the arsenic was added intentionally, it cannot be ruled out that the tools were deliberately made of a softer material so that they could not be used for everyday purposes. As long as the question whether arsenic could be produced at that time and added intentionally remains unsolved, it seems reasonable to consider the copper from which the artifacts in the hoard were made as derived from natural copper ores.

Arts

The numerous works of art of the Chalcolithic period, such as sculpture, carving and painting, which have come to light both in Palestine and elsewhere, bear witness to a highly developed aesthetic sense. Until the discovery of our treasure, however, nothing had been found to equal such a level of artistic design and craftsmanship, particularly in metalwork.

These special works of art must have been inspired by a religion still wrapped in mystery, and by a belief in the magic properties of these objects, which may explain the care devoted to their design. The abstract style or the realistic representation that is only hinted at, are appropriate to cultic symbols which are meant to fire the religious imagination.

The artifacts of the treasure, in all their variety, are for the present, the first material evidence of the symbols that appeared in ancient art. The highly developed artistic sense and technical proficiency did not, of course, come into being all at once, but evolved over many generations. They were the fruit of a long and rich tradition, which is only partly revealed in the finds.

Cult and Religion

All the known facts indicate that the treasure, including the tools, is an assemblage of ritual objects. The wealth of symbols used is rooted in the mysteries of nature, such as fertility and birth, life and death, growth and perpetual rebirth in the universe, all connected with the cult of the mother-goddess. The type of burial – at times in a contracted position – and the gifts placed near the deceased, give expression to the ancient belief in life after death.

The sacred enclosures at 'En-gedi, Naḥal Mishmar and other sites, the burials in dolmens and ossuaries, the multitude of ritual objects found in other Chalcolithic sites in Palestine – all these reflect the character of the religion of that period and provide the background to the use of the ritual objects in the temples. The existence of temples testifies to an advanced social, economic and political structure, and to a religious leadership perhaps comparable to that of the priest-kings of Mesopotamia, who played a central role in the life of the community.

From where were the ritual objects brought to the cave? It seems probable that they came from a temple in the vicinity. However, none of the finds so far confirm the theory that they were brought from the sacred enclosure at 'En-gedi, although the enclosure was destroyed at about the time when the treasure was hidden in the cave, probably as a result of the same event that brought about the destruction of all the Chalcolithic settlements.

The ritual objects may have been used in ceremonies and public assemblies held on fixed festivals, such as those celebrating the change of the seasons, the sowing or the harvest. The hundreds of standards, which were probably carried on poles or staffs,[22] are evidence of the large number of participants in these impressive processions. Perhaps, it can be suggested that the degree of splendour of the ritual objects reflects the rank of the bearers – priest-king, priests, tribal chiefs, heads of families – or their age. However, it may also well be that the various objects symbolized different occupations, such as farmers, shepherds, hunters and craftsmen.

The Character of the Cave Settlements

The finds in the Naḥal Mishmar caves point to a degree of prosperity and cultural development that is unexpectedly high for cave-dwellers. The question arises, therefore – what was the basis of their economy, and what led these people to settle in this desert region, in caves difficult and dangerous of access, even in those days. Did they live there of their own volition, or were they fugitives from some danger, as were others in the days of Bar-Kokhba?

Any attempt to give an answer to these questions requires an examination of the finds from the cave and from the whole region, in the light of what we know of the period and its background.

1. As far as we know, all Chalcolithic settlements were unfortified, indicating that peaceful conditions prevailed in the country. Had the settlers been in danger, they would surely have surrounded their settlements with fortifications, as was done by settlers in the Neolithic period (for instance Jericho), and from the Early Bronze Age onwards.

2. There is no doubt that the large sanctuary at 'En-gedi was a central cult-place for the people of the entire region. No remains of contemporary settlements could so far be traced in the vicinity, although the area has been thoroughly explored, and no doubt the sanctuary served the inhabitants of the caves of the valleys to the north and to the south. The same applies to the large enclosure above the Naḥal Mishmar caves, which, too, was probably a cult-place, perhaps of a local character.

3. Living in caves seems to have been a characteristic of the people of that period. At Lachish, too, the Chalcolithic settlement is located in natural caves, some of them enlarged by the settlers, and the objects found in them point to a direct connection with the cave-dwellers of the Judean Desert. At Beersheba, the culture of the people who dwelt in the subterranean houses is similar to that of the inhabitants of the Judean Desert caves.

4. The thick layer of debris, ashes and potsherds, and the fairly numerous skeletons of men, women and children that were discovered in the Naḥal Mishmar

caves, can serve as evidence of a prolonged period of occupation.

We can, I believe, infer from the above facts that these people lived in the caves in peaceful times, and did not use them in times of emergency only. However, it is still an open question whether this was a permanent settlement, marked by continuous occupation, or if settlement was seasonal, in accordance with economic needs. A clue may perhaps be provided by an enquiry into the sources of livelihood that enabled the inhabitants to maintain the high standard of living reflected in the finds.

Sources of Livelihood

The data in our possession do not enable us to draw any definite conclusions regarding the sources of livelihood of the cave-dwellers. We can, however, consider three categories of finds from the Naḥal Mishmar caves:

1. Finds that are directly connected to the occupations of the cave-dwellers, such as the breeding of livestock, probably goats, who have the agility necessary for climbing steep slopes and rocks and reaching every inch of available pasture. The goats ensured the supply of dairy products and meat. Other animals were hunted for their meat and their skins, which were made into leather or fur.

However, the grazing season in the Judean Desert is very short and is dependent on the amount of rainfall. During the first excavation season, towards the end of the dry winter of 1960, we found the desert completely bare. There was no water in any of the rock-pools, and the Beduin wandered with their flocks and their camels to the west and to the north of the country. 1961 and 1962, on the other hand, were years of plentiful rainfall, and the desert sprouted forth an abundance of grass and even of flowers. The rock-pools filled with water, and the Beduin brought their flocks and their camels to graze on the hills and in the valleys.

The remarkable state of preservation of the objects found in the cave, and other considerations, have led the experts to conclude that there have been no substantial changes in the climate of the Judean Desert, from the Chalcolithic period to this day. Then, too, there were years of drought, which forced the owners of flocks to migrate to other parts of the country. Even in rainy years, the grazing season lasts only for a few months, after which the flocks must be driven northward. This must also have been the case in ancient times, and it may help to explain the similarity of a great part of the assemblages found in the southern and in the northern parts of the country. Thus, the shepherds must have migrated with their entire families, and it is very likely that there were seasonal interruptions in the occupation

of the caves. This assumption is also strengthened by the burials found in the Cave of the Treasure. As far as we know, at that period the dead were no longer buried in the places of habitation, as is also shown by the use of the neighbouring caves for burial only.

2. Finds of which it cannot be definitely said whether they were produced locally or brought into the cave from elsewhere. Cereals, fruit, vegetables, reeds and flax belong to this category. According to de Vaux, the Chalcolithic cave-dwellers of Wadi Murabba'at, in addition to stockbreeding and hunting, also engaged in dry farming on a small scale. This could not have been the case in Naḥal Mishmar, unless climatic conditions in those days were very different from what they are now. Today the Beduin graze their flocks in the desert during the rainy season, and also cultivate patches of land on the fringes of the desert and the hill country. Did the cave-dwellers do likewise?

As for vegetables and fruit, it is doubtful if they were grown by the cave-dwellers. If the flow of the two springs was as sparse then as it is today, they could not have supplied enough water both for the flocks and for cultivation. The same applies to flax, used for thread and textiles, and to reeds, from which the baskets and mats were woven, and which is a plant requiring large quantities of water.

'En-gedi is the only place in the whole region where there is abundant water for cultivating these crops. All economic life must have centered around the sanctuary, and 'En-gedi probably served as the supply centre of all the cave-dwellers in the vicinity.

3. Finds that are beyond doubt of foreign origin, such as the ivory and shell ornaments, the beads and the metal awl, which at that period must have been expensive items, and of course, the splendid copper, ivory and haematite objects forming the treasure. However, these were probably not private property, but belonged to the temple, and had been purchased by a wealthy community. How did they acquire their wealth? Surely not only from stockbreeding, nor from small-scale agriculture. We are led to the conclusion that they must have had additional sources of livelihood, which perhaps forced them to remain in their cave-dwellings the whole year round.

Is it possible that their economy was based on the production of salt, either by mining or by evaporation, and its transportation to distant markets? There is no doubt that salt was important, both for everyday use and for the preservation of food. If this assumption is correct, why did these people live in almost inaccessible caves, relatively far from the places where salt could be extracted? Did they perhaps settle in the caves in order to control the trade routes from the east, which crossed the Lisan peninsula, and continued through the Judean Desert to the Hebron hills and beyond? If so, what was the nature of this trade, and did the route pass this way? No evidence has been found of the cultivation at 'En-gedi at that time of costly plants, such as the balsam tree (*aparsamon*), which are known to have been grown there in a much later period, and from which were derived precious perfumes and medicines, cosmetics and sacramental ointments. We also do not know if at that time there was already a trade in bitumen extracted from the Dead Sea, which was in great demand in Egypt in dynastic times.

The temple at 'En-gedi was not rebuilt after it had been abandoned, and settlement in the caves of this region was not renewed after its destruction. What then were the particular economic circumstances during the Chalcolithic period which made settlement in the Judean Desert caves possible and which did not recur in later periods?

We have no reasonable economic explanation for this phenomenon. In view of the discovery of such a large number of finds of a religious and ritual nature dating to this period (the Ghassul fresco, ritual objects in Beersheba, numerous ossuaries, figurines from many Chalcolithic sites, our magnificent treasure and the sanctuaries), would it be too venturesome to suggest that the religious motive was one of the incentives for settling in the desert?

The data in our possession are too scanty even to suggest an answer to this problem. Let us hope that continued excavations in the Judean Desert caves will bring us nearer to the solution.

The Destruction of the Chalcolithic Settlements

We have shown that the people who lived in the Naḥal Mishmar caves did so by choice and were not forced to do so as the result of an emergency. As this occupation was undoubtedly of a permanent nature, the question arises: what made the cave-dwellers cache this treasure of ritual artifacts in a remote cave? What was the event which prevented them from recovering it later, an event which appears to have caused the sudden destruction of the Chalcolithic settlements in the Judean Desert and in other parts of Palestine?

Significant considerations lead me to believe that the destruction which overtook these settlements came from the direction of Egypt. A detailed discussion of these important questions is outside the scope of an archaeological report, and I shall deal with them later in another context.

THE BAR-KOKHBA PERIOD

PAPYRI AND OSTRACA

Three papyrus fragments were found in the upper layer of the Cave of the Treasure. They are inscribed in black ink, one in Hebrew and two in Greek. Only fragmentary lines, individual words or letters could be deciphered. In addition, several narrow strips and tiny fragments of papyrus bore undecipherable traces of writing. The content of the inscribed fragments and the calligraphic character of the script indicate that these are the remains of official documents.

Five ostraca were also found, four inscribed in Hebrew and one in Greek. Four of these are fragments of typical Roman jars, such as have frequently been uncovered in the caves of this region. It cannot be said whether the inscriptions were written on the jars when still complete or on fragments. One of the Hebrew inscriptions is written on a large jar-fragment. Undecipherable traces of writing were also found on other jar-fragments, as well as on a Chalcolithic sherd uncovered in the upper layer. Fragments of parchment may belong to scroll margins.

Papyrus No. 1 (Reg. No. 60–214)

The small fragment which came to light in Hall A, measures 2.7 × 4 cm. The Hebrew letters ניתנו can be read,[1] meaning some act connected with "giving", either in the past or in the future, if we assume that the first *nun* belongs to the preceding word. The shape of the *taw* is unusual, as both strokes are bent outwards, apparently as a result of the speed at which the scribe wrote, as he began writing it from below, immediately after completing the *yod*.

Papyrus No. 2 (Reg. No. 60–213)

When discovered in Hall B, this papyrus was folded many times over. After opening, it was found to be damaged below and on the left side. The fragment measures 7.5 × 8.5 cm. It is inscribed in Greek on both sides. Many letters are blurred and complete lines are almost entirely undecipherable. Dr. B. Lifshitz published this papyrus.[2] On the recto, four lines have been preserved, of which two can be read as follows:

$$\theta\iota\alpha \; \varphi\varepsilon\iota\lambda\omega\nu o[\varsigma] \; \dot{\alpha}\delta\varepsilon\lambda\varphi\dot{o}\varsigma$$
$$E\iota[o]\dot{\upsilon}\delta[a] \; \dot{\alpha}\delta\varepsilon\lambda\varphi[\dot{o}\varsigma]$$

According to Lifshitz, the patronymics are also given here. In line 1 the name *Ματθία*, a Greek transliteration of Mattatyahu, may perhaps be restored.

On the verso, the remains of eight lines have been preserved, but most are illegible. The sign 4 appears four times, always with a number to its right. It can be

assumed that in every line this sign was preceded by a name. In line 1, the number $\beta\lambda'$ (32) is written to the right of the sign. In line 2, which is separated from line 1 by a considerable space, the number is illegible, and in line 3 the number appears to be $\varepsilon\iota'$ (15). The last two lines also contain unclear traces of names. Traces of writing can also be discerned in the upper part of the fragment, perhaps IN on the left and Δ on the right. All the letters are accented. The sign 4 also appears in papyri from Naḥal Ṣe'elim[3] and in documents from Wadi Murabba'at. According to Benoit, this sign represents wheat.[4]

The word $\dot{\alpha}\delta\varepsilon\lambda\varphi\dot{o}\varsigma$ appears also in documents from Naḥal Ṣe'elim[5] and the Cave of Letters.[6] Who were the people who were called by the title "brothers"? Lifshitz conjectures that this appellative indicates membership in an organization similar to the Essene sect, or holders of a certain position of authority in an organization, perhaps in Bar-Kokhba's army.[7]

Papyrus No. 3 (Reg. No. 61–192)

When discovered in Hall A, the papyrus was folded and very crumpled; after it was opened, it was found to be fragmentary and split into strips. The papyrus measures 8–10 × 11.8 cm. It is a palimpsest, written in Aramaic and Greek. Most of the letters are blurred. The remains of nine lines can be discerned, one of which is in Greek.

The top strip is certainly part of the same papyrus, but its correct place cannot be determined. Most of the letters are cut in half, with the exception of three letters at the end of the line: רדחן or דמן Before these letters the remains of a *he* and *pe* (or *qof*) can be distinguished.

In Strip 4, the letter *he* can be read, preceded by *waw* or *yod*, and *resh* or *dalet*. Remains of three undecipherable lines can be discerned below, though perhaps an *alef* can be read at the end of the third line.

The last fragment of this papyrus is continuous and contains four lines:

Line 1. At the end of the line, the word נפשה "in person" can be read. This is the edge of the papyrus and there is no room for another word. It can be assumed that it was preceded by the name of the signatory of the document – X son of Y – with the addition of the formula usual in the documents from Wadi Murabba'at and the Cave of Letters: על נפשה "in person", or the word כתב or כתבה — "wrote".[8]

Line 2. At the left can be clearly read בר דרמנס שהד "son of Darmanas, witness". The name Joseph, son of Darmanas or Darmonas, appears in Aramaic document No. 6 from the Cave of Letters.[9]

Papyrus No. 1.

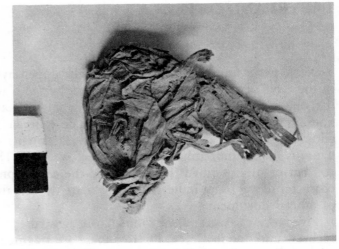

Photograph of papyrus No. 2 folded, as discovered.

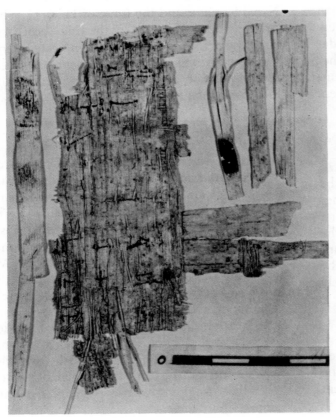

Both sides of papyrus No. 2.

Line 3. Near the beginning of the line, the letters שה can be distinguished. Since there is room before them for one or two letters, perhaps we can complete the word to read מנ[שה.[10] However, the form of the *shin* is difficult, since the long stroke appears here on the right instead of on the left, as usual. The remains of a *nun* are visible above and below the tear. Yadin proposed the reading עיה, which could be completed as [ב]עיה or [שמ]עיה, names which appear in documents from the

Cave of Letters,[11] followed by שחד...בר "son (of)..., witness". The letters in this line are twice as large as those in line 2 and measure 6 mm instead of 3 mm. In view of the signatures of two witnesses and the formula [על] נפשה "in person" preceding the signature of the first witness, the papyrus was certainly an official document. Unfortunately it is so fragmentary that we are unable to determine its contents.

Papyrus No. 3.

Line 4. The line contains only Greek letters, but their reading is mostly doubtful.

$$\iota\alpha/\iota\mu o\upsilon\mu\underset{\cdot}{\alpha}\sigma\gamma\alpha\lambda\iota\alpha\varsigma \quad \kappa\beta\delta \; \varepsilon \; . \; 4 \sim$$
$$\underset{\cdot}{\nu} \; \underset{\cdot}{o} \quad \beta \quad \alpha? \quad \underset{\cdot}{\kappa}$$
$$\iota\alpha\rho o\upsilon$$

As the papyrus is a palimpsest, line 4 has no connection with the other lines. Between the letters faint traces of the obliterated original can be seen.

The sign **4**, a symbol for wheat, is clearly visible, like in papyrus No. 2. The letter κ, which stands for the measure *kor*, appears also in documents from Wadi Murabba'at.[12] The number to the right seems to be a 4.

Ostracon No. 1 (Reg. No. 61–188/1)

The small ostracon, which was found in Hall A, is triangular and measures 3 × 3.3 cm. The letters are inscribed in black ink on the ribbed sherd. They average only 3 mm in height, and therefore it can be assumed that they were inscribed on a potsherd and not on a complete jar. Our fragment appears to be part of a larger ostracon. The inner side of the sherd is covered with shiny dark brown incrustation, which also appears on other sherds. Laboratory tests of this incrustation have been inconclusive up to the present.[13]

The letters begin in the centre of the fragment and continue to the left-hand edge. There are no traces of other letters. The reading is difficult and three alternative proposals have been put forward:

1. Prof. Y. Yadin – זוזין; 2. the author – דיין that is, די יין or דייין "of the wine"; 3. Prof. S. Abramson – דהן that is, "oil" or "fat".

Yadin's suggested reading fits the appearance of the letters on the ostracon. According to Yadin, the word זוזין was followed by a number, like in other documents. However, infra-red photography has shown that between the *zayin* and the *waw* of Yadin's reading, there is a connecting line, and the letter looks like a *dalet*.[14] Another difficulty is the different form of the letters *zayin* – the first is straight, while the second has a small projecting stroke in the centre. If this stroke is considered to be the result of writing on the ribbed sherd, it should be noted that the first *zayin* is straight, though it

Ostracon No. 1.

Ostracon No. 2.

was written on the same ribbing. However, there is no doubt that in many documents, the same letter appears in different forms, even within the same word.

The author's suggested reading also presents difficulties, as according to Lieberman, the די should be followed by the Aramaic חמרא or חמר for wine, like in other documents of this period. The author has been unable to find confirmation in other documents for his suggestion that the letter preceding the word יי signifies a measure.

Abramson considers the projecting stroke in the third letter to be a connecting line with the fourth letter, and reads *he,* as in documents from Wadi Murabba'at.[15] Up to the present the word דהן "oil" has not been found on jars, but it is known in various sources, e.g. Shebuoth 47.2 (cf. Rashi); Targum, Proverbs 3:8; Targum, Isaiah 34:6, 43:24; Targum Jonathan,[16] cf. in Aruch Completum, s.v. דהן. In Arabic, the word دهن means "fat", "ointment" and the root has the meaning "to anoint".[17]

Ostracon No. 2 (Reg. No. 61–175/7+128/8)

The ribbed jar-fragment, which was found in Hall B, measures 4.5 × 5 cm. On the inside, the sherd is covered with dark brown incrustation. On the lower third of the sherd, three Greek letters have been preserved, which extend to the bottom edge of the sherd. The letters are 1.5–2.2 cm high. The reading is clearly *ιακ* and may perhaps be completed as *ιακω* or *ιακωβος*.[18] Palaeographically, the form of the letters corresponds to the scripts of the period.[19]

Miscellaneous ostraca

In the other ostraca, only blurred and illegible Hebrew letters can be discerned. For instance, No. 3 (Reg. No. 61–101/4) has two lines of undecipherable writing. No. 4 (Reg. No. 61–193), a Chalcolithic sherd of gritty clay, bears three lines of writing. Perhaps |ס| can be read in line 2, meaning possibly "one, *seah* one". On No. 60–163 a few unconnected letters can be distinguished and the same is true of a few other sherds.

Ostracon No. 3

Ostracon No. 4.

OTHER FINDS

Pottery

All the pottery vessels were found broken and only a few could be restored. The number of rims, handles, bases and body sherds indicates that there must have been several dozen vessels in the cave. The commonest vessels are store-jars and cooking-pots.

Store-jars. All the jars are wheelmade, well baked and all belong to one type, with slight variations.[1] They have flat, ring-shaped or slanting rims, slightly everted or inverted. The mouth measures 7–8 cm in diameter and the neck is about 4–5 cm high. At the base of the neck is a slight ridge. The loop-handles are slightly ridged. The oval body tapers towards the top and is ribbed, either partly or entirely. The convex base is slightly pointed in the centre. On some fragments, traces of writing can be distinguished (see above). In some of the jars, there are remains of a dark brown, often shiny, incrustation.

These store-jars have been found in quantities in many caves of this region, such as Qumran,[2] 'Ain Feshkhah,[3] Wadi Murabba'at,[4] Naḥal David,[5] Naḥal Ḥever[6] and Naḥal Ṣe'elim.[7] They are also common on other sites of this period.[8]

Cooking-pots. Very numerous fragments of cooking-pots, mostly blackened by soot, were found. Most of the rims are grooved and a few are ridged. Two slightly ridged loop-handles extend from rim to shoulder, and sometimes there is a ridge on the shoulder. The body is ribbed and the convex base is often slightly pointed in the centre. The thin-walled pots are wheelmade, well baked, of dark brown, levigated clay.

This type of cooking-pot, with slight variations, is common in the Hellenistic and early Roman periods,[9] also in the caves of this region, such as Wadi Murabba'at,[10] Naḥal David,[11] Naḥal Ḥever[12] and Naḥal Ṣe'elim.[13]

Jugs. Many jug-fragments were found, but only one jug could be restored (No. 9). All the vessels are of well levigated clay, wheelmade, well baked and thin-walled. With some variations, all the jugs belong to one type: a piriform body, partly or entirely ribbed; wide cup-like rim projecting from the neck, or ledge-rim with a ridge below, or collar rim; plain or ridged loop-handles stretching from the rim or from just below the rim to the shoulder; ring-base or concave base.

Selected vessels of the Bar-Kokhba period.

209

These jug-types, which were common in the first century C.E., have been found at Qumran II,[14] Ramat Raḥel,[15] as well as in Naḥal Ḥever[16] and in Wadi Murabba'at.[17]

Juglets. Many juglet-fragments were found, but no complete specimen could be restored. Some of the characteristic sherds have a triangular rim and a wide, flat handle springing from rim to shoulder; others have a straight rim and a rounded handle springing from rim to shoulder; the squat body is lightly ribbed; the small base is flat; the juglets are wheelmade, of light brown or dark brown levigated clay, and well baked. Although the material is scanty, these juglets represent a ceramic tradition which continued into the Bar-Kokhba period.[18]

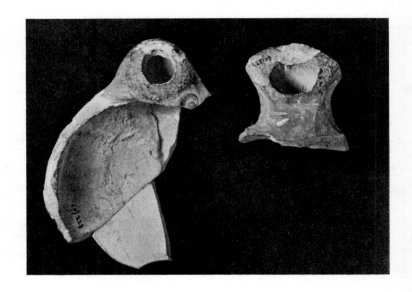

Lamps. Many fragments of pottery lamps were found, but only two are of sufficient size for identification. One lamp is made in two parts; near the short, rounded nozzle are traces of a moulded floral design; it has a flat ring-base, with traces of brownish-red slip; it is made of light, levigated clay and is well baked. This type of lamp is characteristic of the second half of the first century C.E. and it continued to be produced in the early second century.[19] The second lamp fragment has a splayed nozzle; it is wheelmade and knife-pared, of levigated, dark brown clay and well baked. This is a typical "Herodian" lamp,[20] generally thought to have been current from Herod's reign until the mid-first century C.E.[21] For instance, at Ramat Raḥel this type of lamp was found in Stratum IV, which ends with the destruction of the Second Temple,[22] and whose material resembles the finds from Samaria.[23] A similar lamp was found together with pottery and coins of the first century C.E. in Wadi Murabba'at, in a cave which, according to de Vaux, served as a place of refuge during the First Revolt and during Bar-Kokhba's revolt.[24] As this type of lamp has now been found, together with material from Bar-Kokhba's time, in a number of caves,[25] in Naḥal David,[26] Naḥal Ṣe'elim,[27] in the Cave of Horror,[28] in the Cave of Letters and in the Roman camp which laid siege to this cave during Bar-Kokhba's revolt,[29] it is now possible to continue its span to the mid-second century C.E.

Stone Vessels
Several fragments of a limestone vessel with a bar-handle near the rim were found in Hall A. The sides of the vessel are knife-pared. Though the fragments are too few to enable restoration of the complete vessel, this type, which is known as a "measuring cup", is well known from other sites. Some specimens have two

loop-handles, others have none. Our vessel continues the tradition of the characteristic "measuring cup" of the Herodian period.[30] Similar vessels have been found in Wadi Murabba'at,[31] and in the Cave of Letters.[32]

A stone mortar (13 × 18 × 28 cm) was found in the upper layer of Hall A, between the two large rocks in the southern part of the cave, near the square oven. A stone pestle was found with it, as well as several stones which must have served as pestles, as they bore marks of use.

Glass vessels

Many fragments of glass vessels were found, but few can be attributed to definite types. One is the upper part of a juglet of bluish-green glass, with a folded everted rim, elongated neck and high folded handle. The other fragment probably belongs to a "candlestick" unguentarium of greenish glass with a ring-rim. A conical spout of greenish glass may belong to a third vessel. A folded fragment belongs to a vessel which could not be identified.

A similar juglet with a folded handle was found in the Cave of Horror; the type is dated to the Bar-Kokhba period.[33] "Candlestick" unguentaria were common in the first through third centuries C.E.[34] The bottle with spout fits in well with this date.[35]

Miscellaneous

In addition, a few iron objects were also found: a hook and part of a narrow strip 20 cm long and grooved at the ends, which was perhaps used to reinforce a wooden box. Among the textile remains should be mentioned a ball of fine linen thread wound around a small stone.

CONCLUSIONS

The evidence shows clearly that the material from the upper layer in the Cave of the Treasure is identical with that found in other caves of this region, where it is dated to the Bar-Kokhba period. We can safely assume, therefore, that our material belongs to the same period, when rebels and fighters took refuge in the cave.[36]

The numerous finds on both floors, the ovens and hearths, the ash-heaps, grinders and mortars, indicate that a considerable number of people inhabited the cave over a fairly long period of time. The varied finds give us a glimpse of their daily life – what they wore, how they were shod, what they ate and what goods they owned. The luxury goods which the cave-dwellers had brought with them, such as glass vessels, fine pottery and lamps, delicate textiles, as well as the fragments of documents found, indicate that they abandoned well-established homes when they fled to the caves.

The large number of jars and containers indicates that the people reached the cave in relatively quiet times and that they had time to prepare stores of food and water. In this context, a tiny cave 10–12 m below the Cave of the Treasure and about 2 m south of it, should be mentioned. This cave contained a fairly thick layer of burnt organic matter, probably cereals.[37]

No doubt the waters of the two springs could be used in more or less peaceful times, if their flow was the same as it is now. In winter and in spring, water could be obtained from rock-pools filled by local rains or by flood waters pouring down from the mountains.

A small square structure (2 × 2 m) on the cliff-edge, above the cave, was probably used by the cave-dwellers as a look-out post or for communication with people living in other caves. The fieldstone walls are 0.60 m wide and three courses have been preserved. About 0.50 m to the south is another parallel wall, with a curving row of stones at the east end, perhaps a fireplace. With the exception perhaps of a levelled space nearby, there are no traces of a fortified Roman camp,[38] such as those on both sides of Naḥal Ḥever.[39] A few Roman sherds were found west of the structure.

There are no indications that the inhabitants died in the cave, as they did in the caves of Naḥal Ḥever, where many skeletons were discovered. In this respect, there is some similarity between the Cave of the Treasure and the Cave of the Pool, which was apparently abandoned by its inhabitants.[40] The unused wood and twigs, the stone vessels left standing, the broken pottery and the store of burnt cereals(?), all indicate that the cave was abandoned in a hurry, perhaps as a result of the Romans gaining control of strategic heights and roads in the Judean Desert. It may well be that before leaving their place of refuge, the cave-dwellers broke the pottery and burned their store of cereals, so as to leave nothing which could be used by the enemy.

Something of the fear and awe of the days of Bar-Kokhba's revolt still clings to this cave, which is a further link in the chain of caves in Naḥal Ḥever, Naḥal Ṣe'elim, and the valleys to the north, in which the rebels sought refuge from the Roman army of conquest. Additional caves may still be awaiting discovery in these valleys.

NOTES

THE EXCAVATIONS
pp. 1–13

1. Y. Aharoni and B. Rothenberg, *In the Steps of Kings and Rebels*, Tel Aviv, 1960, plans 4–6, 12 (Hebrew); *IEJ* 11 (1961), pp. 15–16; *Archaeological News* 26 (Apr. 1968), pp. 24–28 (Hebrew); P. Bar-Adon, in *Judea, Samaria and the Golan, an Archaeological Survey in 1967–68*, Jerusalem, 1973, pp. 92–149 (Hebrew).
2. *Murabba'at*, pp. 23 ff.
3. *Ibid.*, pp. 26–28, Fig. 6:1–7, Pl. VI:6; Aharoni, *IEJ* 11 (1961), pp. 15–16; *IEJ* 12 (1962), p. 174.
4. Aharoni, *'Atiqot* III, pp. 148–162; *IEJ* 11 (1961), pp. 11–24.
5. *IEJ* 11 (1961), pp. 3–5; Y. Aviram, in appendix "Among the Cave-Dwellers" to S. Abramsky, *Bar Kokhba – Prince of Israel*, Jerusalem, 1961, pp. 234–254 (Hebrew); Yadin, *Cave of Letters*, pp. 1–6.
6. The following took part in the first season: D. Bahat, Y. Ben-Israel, H. Cohen, Y. Ginnat, Irit Goldstein, G. Ilani, R. Judenfreund, B. Momis, Nehama Moussaief, B. Rabinowitz, Y. Reifenberg, Z. Shapira, Y. Shmida, A. Shob, Y. Tsor, Y. Zafrir, A. Zalmanovitz. Soldiers: D. Bar-Adon, Y. Finkelstein, M. Flankenflik, Z. Gefen, D. Goren, D. Levi, D. Naaman, N. Ozerko, Y. Rabinowitch, K. Shweitzer, S. Shendor, D. Shevah, M. Trachtman, Y. Yagar.
7. Aharoni, *IEJ* 12 (1962), p. 186; idem, *'Atiqot* III, pp. 159 ff.; Yadin, *Cave of Letters*, pp. 11–12.
8. The following took part in the second season: J. Alva, D. Bar-Adon, J. Birak, I. Cabilio, Deborah Dov, Y. Ginnat, A. Goren, Helen Greber (U.S.A.), G. Ilani, J. Jehezkiel, R. Judenfreund, Dalia Karpman, J. Lemberg, J. Lishanski, J. Naor, P. Ofri, Ruth Pecherski (Argentine), D. Paritzki, M. Rafaeli, Y. Reifenberg, J. Saliternik, J. Schwartz, J. Shipon, Mira Spilberg, Dr. S. Strauss (U.S.A.), L. Yudkin, Dr. D. Zaitchek, Y. Zafrir, S. Zeidlich-Eran. Soldiers: N. Adler, E. Amitzur, E. Esh (in charge of the camp), Y. Avigdor, R. Ben-Hamo, M. Cohen, A. Haibi, A. Halperin, I. Israel, M. Lander, A. Luebeck, O. Naveh, S. Nissim, S. Sami, D. Samirah, A. Shabtai, Y. Shamir, I. Shaubi, L. Solomon, M. Tiomkin.
9. *IEJ* 12 (1962), pp. 167–168.
10. The following took part in the third season: Y. Abkasis, E. Ash, D. Bar-Adon, M. Ben-Dov, Y. Ben-Efraim, R. Berkowitz, Y. Better, N. Burg, Duncan and Elizabeth Burbridge (U.S.A.–France), I. Cabilio, G. Cohen, H. Cohen, Esther Derekh, F. Di Denato (Italy), Deborah Dov, Zionah Dov, S. Eran, A. Gal, G. Galinor, M. Goldberg (U.K.), Dr. N. Haas, A. Halperin, C.A. Key (geologist), G. Kiulik, Nina Lazar, Ruth Levin, J. Lishanski, Rachel Livneh, Y. Luzi, M. Magen, Y. Mandel, Esther Mann, T. Messing, G. Mezad, R. Mines, B. Moses, A. Navon, P. Ofri, I. Pianko, M. Piletzki-Pan, A. Rabinowitz, M. Rafaeli, J. Saliternik, K. Shweitzer, J. Shipon, M. Sklar, A. Sternberg, E. Vicario (Italy), Y. Vites, Y. Zafrir. Soldiers: Abu Assam, A. Ali, M. Amitai, T. Azem, A. Azulaos, U. Fink, N. Hamud, B. Hassan, O. Harizi, S. Hussein, F. Mansur, H. Murshid, S. Muhsan, D. Nabia, H. Naif, K. Saleh, A. Sakman, S. Salman, M. Samir, S. Sliman, Y. Siegelman, G. Wertheim, S. Yonah, H. Yussuf, M. Zeid.
11. M. Stekelis, *Les monuments mégalithiques de Palestine* (Archives de l'Institut de Paléontologie Humaine, Mémoire 15), Paris, 1935, p. 68, Fig. 15; idem, *La necrópolis megalítica de Ala-Safat, Transjordan*, Instituto de Prehistoria y Arqueología, Monografías, 1), Barcelona, 1961, pp. 49–128, Figs. 1–12.

THE CHALCOLITHIC PERIOD
THE TREASURE
pp. 15–133

1. The object (IDAM Reg. No. 56–1218) is exhibited in the Israel Museum, Jerusalem.

2. A horn-shaped or sickle-shaped object was found in the excavations of the early temple (VIII) at Eridu, decorated with painted circles, cf. S. Lloyd, The Oldest City of Sumeria – Establishing the Origins of Eridu, *ILN*, 11 Sept. 1948, p. 305, Fig. 10. In a letter to me of January 6, 1962, Prof. Lloyd wrote: "Regarding the purpose of the painted horn, I myself concluded that it was a wall-ornament of the sort which we still know very little about." Cf. also Frankfort, *BCNE*, Pl. V:7 b, pp. 46–47.
3. J. Perrot, Les ivoires de la 7è campagne de fouilles à Safadi près de Beershéva, *EI* 7 (1964), pp. 92*–93*, Pl. LI:1.
4. Perrot, *IEJ* 5, p. 172, Fig. 20:24 b-c; idem, *Syria* 34, p. 27, Fig. 23:24 b-c.
5. E.F. Schmidt, *Excavations at Tepe Hissar*, Philadelphia, 1937, Pl. XXIX: H. 1200, H. 2021; cf. also a granite standard plated with gold at the top, found in an early stratum at Uruk (Warka), *Uruk* IX, 1938, Pl. 29:b.
6. Aharoni, *IEJ* 11, Pl. 8:A.
7. *TG* I, Pl. 34:2.
8. M. Dothan, Excavations at Meṣer, *IEJ* 7 (1957), p. 226, Pl. 37:C-D For tools of a slightly later period, see Stratum XVI at Beth Shean, cf. Fitzgerald, *EPBS*, Pl. III:21, 23; Ruth Hestrin and Miriam Tadmor, A Hoard of Tools and Weapons from Kfar Monash, *IEJ* 13 (1963), pp. 265 ff.
9. W.M.F. Petrie, *Tools and Weapons*, London, 1917, Pl. XVI.
10. R.J. and L.S. Braidwood, *Excavations in the Plain of Antioch* I, Chicago, 1960, Fig. 185:6 (Phase F); M.E.L. Mallowan, Excavations at Brak and Chagar Bazar, *Iraq* 9 (1947), Pl. XXXI:9.
11. H. Koṣay and M. Akok, Preliminary Report on Test Excavations at Büyük Güllücek, *Belleten* 12 (1948), pp. 479 ff., Pl. XCIX:18–19, Fig. 36.
12. Speiser, *Tepe Gawra* I, p. 107 f., Pl. XLVIII:8 (Str. VIII); Tobler, *Tepe Gawra* II, Pl. XCVIII:1–2 (Str. XII–XI); M.E.L. Mallowan, *The Excavations at Tell Arpachiya, 1933*, London, 1935, Pl. X:1.
13. Aharoni, *IEJ* 11, p. 14, Pl. 8:B.
14. Perrot, *IEJ* 5, p. 79, Pl. 15:A; idem, *Syria* 34, pp. 1 ff., Pl. I:3.
15. Aharoni, *IEJ* 11, p. 14, Pl. 8:B.
16. J. Kaplan, Excavations at Benei Beraq, 1951, *IEJ* 13 (1963), pp. 300 ff.
17. Perrot, *Azor*, p. 83, Fig. 43:4.
18. Dothan, Ḥ. Beter, p. 29, Pl. VII:4; Perrot, *IEJ* 5, p. 189, Pl. 14:A.
19. *Megiddo* II, Pl. 270:11.
20. *TG* I, pp. 71–72, Pl. 35.
21. Dothan, Ḥ. Beter, Figs. 11:14, 18:47, 56, Pl. VII:2; Perrot, *IEJ* 5, p. 189.
22. Fitzgerald, *EPBS*, Pl. III:26–27.
23. *Megiddo* II, Pls. 270:2 ff.
24. Garstang, *AAA* 23, Pls. XXX:19, XXXVI:25.
25. *Beth Pelet* II, Pls. XXVII:78, 79, 81, 82, XXVIII:9.
26. W.M.F. Petrie, *Prehistoric Egypt*, London, 1920, pp. 22–24, Pls. XXV, XXVI; Speiser, *Tepe Gawra* I, Pl. XL:a; Tobler, *Tepe Gawra* II, Pl. CLVII:a.
27. Sukenik, Hadera, pp. 15 ff.
28. J. Ory, A Chalcolithic Necropolis at Benei-Braq, *QDAP* 12 (1946), pp. 54–57, Pl. XVIII:1–3.
29. J. Kaplan, *The Archaeology and History of Tel-Aviv–Jaffa*, Ramat Gan, 1959, pp. 30–31, Fig. 7 (Hebrew).
30. Perrot, *Azor*, pp. 1 ff., Figs. 8 ff., Pls. III ff.
31. Perrot, *Azor*, Figs. 16:D, 32:9. The place of the bosses (which are usually represented in pairs) over the lintel and the jambs of the ossuary-opening, and not at roof level, leads me to the conclusion that Perrot (*op. cit.*, p. 12) was mistaken in explaining these bosses as beams.
32 *TG* I, Pl. 57.

33. *TG* II, Pl. 13:2.
34. *TG* I, frontispiece: La grande peinture à l'étoile.
35. Perrot, Azor, Fig. 21:1, Pl. III:1,2.
36. A. Falkenstein, *Archaische Texte aus Uruk*, Berlin, 1936, p. 25, Fig. 4:e; D. Diringer, *The Alphabet*, London, 1968, II, p. 19.
37. Van Buren, *Symbols*, pp. 14 ff.
38. E. Mackay, *A Sumerian Palace and the "A" Cemetery at Kish, Mesopotamia*, Chicago, 1929, pp. 142–144, Pls. XLV:6, 8, 11–13; cf. also Frankfort, *SCS Diyala*, Pl. 84:880.
39. Sukenik, Hadera, pp. 26 ff.
40. *TG* I, frontispiece.
41. Cf., e.g., E. Unger, Die Erde als Stern des Kosmos im vierten Jahrtausend am Toten Meer (Telēlāt Ghassul), *ZDPV* 77 (1961), pp. 72 ff. and bibliography.
42. Frankfort, *BCNE*, pp. 53 ff.; idem, *Encyclopaedia Biblica* II, Jerusalem, 1954, col. 720 (Hebrew).
43. In the Ghassul fresco, to the left of the large star, there is a gate with rings next to the gate-posts, which has remained unexplained. I believe this representation can be identified on cylinder seals as the posts bearing rings at the top or at the sides, with or without streamers, which are shown on the seals next to the temple gates, and which symbolize Inanna, the mother goddess.. This symbol appears either singly or in pairs, sometimes together with other religious symbols, such as jars, animals, etc., and sometimes by itself. A line connects the bound or ringed posts at the bottom, like in the Ghassul fresco. Sometimes this symbol is carried like a standard towards the gate of the temple, with birds represented above it. Cf. Frankfort, *CS*, Pls. III:a-e; V:c,i, p. 36, Fig. 13; Amiet, *GMA*, Pls. 13:229, 46:652–667; *Uruk* IX, 1938, Pl. 31:c-e; Van Buren, *Symbols*, C 3, pp. 48–49. A pair of snakes' heads is represented on the front of a rectangular ossuary from Tel Aviv, cf. Kaplan (above, n. 29), p. 31, Fig. 7. A snake is also represented on a small jar-ossuary from Ben-Shemen, J. Perrot, Les ossuaires de Ben-Shemen, *EI* 8 (1967), Pl. XIII. At the top of this ossuary there is a broken loop which may be the remains of horns. On the body are two lines of pointed knobs, and some holes between the knobs of the bottom line. The snake is coiled around the body of the ossuary, and its head is near the opening. The snake appears in various forms in ancient art as a cult symbol signifying procreation and fertility, cf., e.g., Frankfort, *CS*, p. 17, Pls. III:b, IV:h; Van Buren, *Symbols*, B 7, pp. 40–42.

THE CHALCOLITHIC PERIOD
OTHER FINDS
pp. 135–198

1. *TG* I, p. 98, Figs. 46–47; II, Pl. 77:4–5. In Stratum XVI at Beth Yeraḥ (Kh. Kerak), large hole-mouth jars with high loop-handles were found (unpublished).
2. A similar decoration, but executed in lines of burnishing, was found on a vessel from Stratum XV at Beth Yeraḥ, together with grey-burnished ware (unpublished). For a decoration of painted triangles, see, e.g. *TG* I, Pls. 42:17, 54:15; II, Pl. 80:13, 20. For incised hatched triangles and other incised decoration on basalt vessels, see, e.g. Dothan, Ḥ. Beter, pp. 18, 29, Figs. 11:18, 19:1.
3. *Murabbaʻat*, p. 16, Fig. 2:1; Farʻah, *RB* 54 (1947), p. 411, Fig. 3:2, 5; *Megiddo* II, Pl. 3:3.
4. *PPEB*, pp. 19, 47; Fig. A-VIIIb.
5. *TG* I, p. 110, Fig. 50:3–4, Pl. 43:4, 104; II, Pl. 77:8; for early herring-bone designs see, e.g. M. Stekelis, *IEJ* 1 (1950–51), Pl. I.
6. Perrot, *IEJ* 5, Pl. 17:B–C; Contenson, *IEJ* 6, Fig. 5:1–12; Dothan, Ḥ. Beter, Figs. 9:19–20, 22, 26, 11:29 ff., 18:23 ff.
7. Perrot, Azor, Figs. 40:1–3, 16, 41:12, 22.
8. Garstang, *AAA* 22, Pl. LXIII:17.
9. Farʻah, *RB* 54 (1947), Fig. 1:1–3; *Beth Pelet* II, Pl. XXXI:A, B, M; cf. also *Lachish* IV, Pls. 11–12.
10. J.W. Crowfoot, G.M. Crowfoot, K.M. Kenyon, *Samaria–Sebaste* III. *The Objects*, London, 1957, p. 92, Fig. C.
11. *Murabbaʻat*, p. 16, Fig. 2.
12. Avigad, *IEJ* 12, p. 173, Fig. 3:5; Aharoni, *IEJ* 12, p. 189, Fig. 1:12–15; idem, *ʻAtiqot* III, p. 160, Fig. 10:3–4.
13. *TG* I, p. 90, Fig. 39.
14. *Beth Pelet* II, Pl. XXXI.
15. Dothan, Ḥ. Beter, Fig. 9:27–30; Perrot, *Syria* 34, pp. 19–25; *IEJ* 5, Fig. 16:8, Pl. 16:A–B; Contenson, *IEJ* 6, p. 166, Fig. 2:1–9.
16. M. Dothan, Excavations at Meṣer, 1957, *IEJ* 9 (1959), p. 27, Fig. 8:17; cf. also *Lachish* IV, Pls. 11–13.
17. Avigad, *IEJ* 12, p. 173, Fig. 3:9.
18. Aharoni, *ʻAtiqot* III, p. 160, Fig. 10:2.
19. Idem, *IEJ* 12, p. 189, Fig. 1:2–6.
20. *PPEB*, p. 45.
21. Garstang, *AAA* 22, Pl. XL:16–17.
22. *TG* I, pp. 95–96, Figs. 42:6–7, 43:1–2, Pl. 41:2, 4, 23–24; II, p. 58, Pl. 79:8–9.
23. *Beth Pelet* II, Pls. XXXVIII:12, XXXIX:15, XL:40–41.
24. Farʻah, *RB* 58 (1951), Fig. 11:7; 59 (1952), Fig. 12:2.
25. Dothan, Ḥ. Beter, Figs. 7:1–16, 12:1; Perrot, *IEJ* 5, pp. 81–83, Fig. 16:10; Contenson, *IEJ* 6, p. 174, Fig. 6:7–11.
26. Sukenik, Hadera, Fig. 6:a-c, Pl. IV:1.
27. *Megiddo* II, Pl. 2:2, 6, 11.
28. *Murabbaʻat*, p. 32, Fig. 8:20–21, Pl. VIII:10, 12, and discussion on p. 34.
29. Aharoni, *IEJ* 12, p. 189, Fig. 1:3–4.
30. Garstang, *AAA* 22, Pls. XXXIX:19, XL:21–25; *AAA* 23, Pl. XXXII: 33 B, 34 B.
31. *TG* I, p. 89, Fig. 38, p. 97, Fig. 43:4; II, Pl. 79:10, 12.
32. Dothan, Ḥ. Beter, Figs. 7:20–32, 8:1–2, 12:27–38; Contenson, *IEJ* 6, pp. 163 ff., Figs. 6:7–25; 7–8.
33. *Lachish* IV, Pl. 12:59, 62.
34. Sukenik, Hadera, p. 21, Fig. 6:C.
35. *RB* 59 (1952), p. 581, Fig. 12:11.
36. *Megiddo* II, Pl. 1:27–28 (Str. XX).
37. Avigad, *IEJ* 12, p. 173, Fig. 3:6.
38. Aharoni, *IEJ* 12, p. 189, Fig. 1:1–2, 5–6.
39. Yadin, *Cave of Letters*, p. 111, Fig. 43:A6.
40. J. Naveh, *BIES* 22 (1958), p. 48, Fig. 2:2–4 (Hebrew); idem, An Archaeological Survey of Ein Gedi, *Phoenix*, Dec. 1958, p. 60, Fig. 40.
41. *TG* I, p. 111, Fig. 59:3.
42. *Beth Pelet* II, Pls. XXXIX:19, XL:35.
43. Perrot, *IEJ* 5, Pl. 14:C; Contenson, *IEJ* 6, p. 178, Fig. 9:7–12; Dothan, Ḥ. Beter, Figs. 10:2–3, 16:1 ff., Pl. V:4.
44. J. Kaplan, *The Archaeology and History of Tel-Aviv–Jaffa*, Ramat Gan, 1959, p. 35, Fig. 10 (Hebrew); idem, *PEQ* 86 (1954), pp. 97–100.
45. Farʻah, *RB* 54 (1947), p. 407, Fig. 1:20, Pl. XIII:10.
46. E.L. Sukenik, *JPOS* 21 (1948), Pl. 1:2, 5; Ruth Amiran, Pirhiya Beck, Uzza Zevulun, *Ancient Pottery of the Holy Land*, Jerusalem, 1969, p. 33, Pl. 7.
47. *TG* I, p. 85, Fig. 35; Albright, *STC*, p. 98.
48. Similar clay stoppers were found in Wadi Murabbaʻat and in Naḥal Ḥever in mixed layers. Those in Wadi Murabbaʻat were attributed by de Vaux to the Roman stratum. The stopper of unbaked clay found in Cave 1 in Wadi Murabbaʻat together with Chalcolithic small bowls should probably also be attributed to that period; cf. *Murabbaʻat*, p. 32, Fig. 8:2–3; Aharoni, *ʻAtiqot* III, p.155, Pl. XXI:4.
49. I should like to take this opportunity of thanking Mr. D. Rosolio, at the time Inspector General, Israel Police and the Bomb-Disposal squad of the Israel Police, Y. Habib and H. Yosef.
50. *TG* I, p. 66; II, p. 112.
51. Dothan, Ḥ. Beter, Fig. 19:9, 19.
52. Cf. e.g., Ephrath Yeivin, in *ibid.*, pp. 43–47, Fig. 1 (and bibliography).
53. J. Perrot, *Syria* 36 (1959), p. 15, Fig. 8; Aharoni, *IEJ* 11, Pl. 8:A.
54. *TG* I, p. 80, Fig. 32:5; II, p. 63, Pl. 97:13.
55. Perrot, *IEJ* 5, p. 172, Fig. 20:1–11; Dothan, Ḥ. Beter, Fig. 11:23.
56. Aharoni, *IEJ* 11, Pl. 8:C.
57. *TG* I, Fig. 32:2, 21, 22.

58. Perrot, *IEJ* 5, p. 172, Fig. 20.
59. Aharoni, *IEJ* 11, Pl. 7:A, B.
60. Perrot, *Préhistoire*, Fig. 849; compare also Tobler, *Tepe Gawra* II, Pl. XCVIII:a,3 (Str. XI).
61. The textile remains were tested in the Institute of Fibre and Forest Research, Jerusalem. The descriptions of the textiles in Illustrations 26–49 are taken from the report in Appendix C. Originally, the number of textile items was larger, but between their discovery and their treatment, they deteriorated, some too much for examination.
62. Yadin, *Cave of Letters*, p. 252.
63. Yael Israeli, Crafts: Spinning, Weaving and Dyeing, in *Encyclopaedia Biblica*, IV, Jerusalem, 1962, cols. 998–1010, and literature (Hebrew).
64. Yadin, *Cave of Letters*, pp. 204 ff., 252 ff. and literature.
65. Aharoni, *IEJ* 12, pp. 189–190; see also above, p. 199, The Date of the Finds in Naḥal Mishmar.
66. G.M. & E. Crowfoot, The Textiles and Basketry, in *Murabba'at*, p. 51.
67. G.M. Crowfoot, Textiles, Basketry and Mats, in C. Singer et al., eds., *A History of Technology* I, Oxford, 1955, p. 432.
68. K.M. Kenyon, *Excavations at Jericho* I, London, 1960, pp. 519 ff.
69. *Lachish* IV, Pl. 13:93, 94. A clay stopper of EB III bearing a textile impression was found at Beth Yeraḥ (Kh. Kerak).
70. For pigments and dyes, their origin, preparation and use in Palestine and in other countries of the Near East, from the Predynastic to the late periods, see R.J. Forbes, Chemical, Culinary and Cosmetic Arts, in C. Singer et al., eds., *A History of Technology*, (above, n. 67), pp. 238 ff. and literature; cf. also Yadin, *Cave of Letters*, pp. 204 ff., 252 ff.
71. Crowfoot (above, n. 67), pp. 431 ff.
72. J. Mellaart, *Anatolian Studies* 13 (1963), pp. 99–101, Pls. XXVIII-XXIX; H. Helbaek, *Archaeology* 16 (1963), pp. 39–46.
73. *TG* I, p. 78, Fig. 31:6, 7, 12–15.
74. Dothan, Ḥ. Beter, p. 20, Fig. 11:25; Aharoni, *IEJ* 11, Pl. 8:A.
75. E.g. *Megiddo* II, p. 140, Pls. 165:1, 198:3; *Beth Pelet* II, Pl. XXVI: 57.
76. G. Brunton, G. Caton-Thompson, *The Badarian Civilization*, London, 1928, Pl. XLVIII:6; Crowfoot, (above, n. 67), p. 432, Fig. 272.
77. H. Ling Roth, *Ancient Egyptian and Greek Looms*, 2, Halifax, 1951, p. 13, Fig. 12; Lucas, *AEMI*, p. 142 (and literature).
78. According to Yadin's proposal, cf. Y. Yadin, Goliath's Javelin and the *manor orgim, PEQ* 87 (1955), pp. 58–69.
79. R. de Mecquenem, *Mémoires de la Mission Archéologique de la Perse*, XXV, Paris, 1934, p. 183, Fig. 7; L. le Breton, *Iraq* 19 (1957), p. 106, Fig. 20, Pl. 24:5; Amiet, *GMA*, Pl. 16, Fig. 275.
80. Lucas, *AEMI*, pp. 140–141; Ling Roth (above, n. 77), p. 3.
81. Ling Roth, (above, n. 77), **Figs.** 3–6.
82. I wish to thank Prof. A. Fahn and Miss Ella Werker of the Hebrew University, Jerusalem for the following identifications of the tree species from which some of the loom parts were made: Reg. No. 61–9/3: tamarisk (Tamarix), grows in the vicinity of the Dead Sea; Reg. No. 61–42/3 (Ill. 54:5): tamarisk; Reg. No. 66–32/2 (Ill. 54:8): tamarisk; Reg. Nos. 61–65/2 + 61–42/1 (Ill. 54:1): tamarisk; Reg. No. 61–27/1: desert broom (Retama), grows in the sands and valleys of the Negev and the Aravah; Reg. No. 61–79/5 (Ill. 54:4): Acacia (Acacia), grows in the valleys of the Negev and the Aravah; Reg. Nos. 61–79/1 + 61–19/5 (Ill. 54:2): olive (Olea).
83. Crowfoot (above, n. 67), p. 427, Fig. 269 C.
84. K.M. Kenyon, *Digging up Jericho*, London, 1957, p. 57; cf. also J. Kaplan, Teluliot Battashi, *EI* 5 (1958), pp. 15, 23, Fig. 9:32 (Hebrew).
85. Among the round spindle-whorls from Ghassul kept at the Pontifical Biblical Institute in Jerusalem are also some weights, such as No. 1038, but the perforation is too small for them to be used on a spindle. No. 1103 is angular. I should like to thank Father Skira for his helpfulness.
86. Dothan, Ḥ. Beter, p. 19, Fig. 11:7.
87. G.M. Crowfoot, *Methods of Hand Spinning in Egypt and the Sudan*, Halifax, 1931, pp. 21 ff., Figs. 5–8 (and literature).
88. For a thorough study, see Trude Dothan, Spinning Bowls, *IEJ* 13 (1963), pp. 97–112.
89. Crowfoot (above, n. 87), p. 23, Fig. 6; cf. also Yael Israeli (above, n. 63), *loc. cit.*; P. Bar-Adon, *ibid.*, col. 1168 (and literature).
90. Crowfoot (above, n. 87), p. 16, Fig. 4.
91. E. Mackay, *A Sumerian Palace and the "A" Cemetery at Kish, Mesopotamia*, Part II, Chicago, 1929, p. 150, Pls. XLIV:12/2000, LII:25–26n. The excavator dates these vessels to 3500 B.C.E., but now it is generally agreed that these finds should be dated to the third millennium B.C.E.
92. I should like to quote here part of a Sumerian poem, as it contains a technical account of the process of weaving – picking the flax, combing, spinning, braiding, weaving and dyeing. The poem is from the first half of the second millennium B.C.E., but it probably reflects an earlier tradition. Most of the poem consists of an intimate dialogue between Inanna and her brother, the sun god Utu: "Sister mine, I will bring you plucked(?) flax, / Inanna, I will bring you plucked(?) flax, / Brother, after you have brought me the plucked(?) flax, / who will comb it for me, who will comb it for me, / That flax, who will comb it for me? / Brother, after you have brought it to me combed, / who will spin it for me? / .... / .... / .... / .... / Brother, after you have brought it to me spun, / who will braid it for me? / .... / .... / .... / .... / Brother, after you have brought it me braided, / who will warp it for me? / .... / .... / .... / Brother, after you have brought it to me warped, / who will weave it for me? / .... / .... / .... / .... / Brother, after you have brought me the woven flax, / who will dye it for me? ... / ... / ..." From S.N. Kramer, The Biblical "Song of Songs" and the Sumerian Love Songs, *Expedition*, Bull. of the Univ. of Pennsylvania, Fall 1962, vol. 5, 1, pp. 28–29.
93. I wish to thank Y. Shenhav for his patience and skill in restoring the sandal.
94. *TG* I, Pl. 66; Albright, *STC*, p. 102.
95. Frankfort, *CS*, p. 20, Pl. IV:h.
96. Porada, *NES*, p. 2, Pl. 1E.
97. W.M.F. Petrie, *Prehistoric Egypt*, London, 1920, p. 31; Pritchard, *ANEP*, Pls. 296–297 (and literature).
98. P.E. Newberry, *Beni Hasan* I, London, 1893, Pl. XXXI; J. Capart, *L'art égyptien*, Bruxelles, 1942, p. 21, Pl. 445; N.M. Davies, A.H. Gardiner, *Ancient Egyptian Paintings*, I. Chicago, 1936, Pls. 10–11; idem, *La peinture égyptienne*, Paris, 1954, Pls. I–II; Pritchard, *ANEP*, Pl. 3.
99. *Murabba'at*, II, Pl. VII:1.
100. Avigad, *IEJ* 12, p. 174, Pl. 17:B; Aharoni, *ibid.*, p. 188, Pl. 24:A.
101. The earliest sieves found in Egypt are from the 18th–20th dynasties onwards, cf. Lucas, *AEMI*, p. 133.
102. *TG* I, p. 91, Fig. 40, Pl. 39:1; II, Pl. 84:9–11; Garstang, *AAA* 22, Pl. LV:a; *Beth Pelet* II, Pl. XXXIV:11–12; *Megiddo* II, Pl. 2:16–17.
103. N. Tsori, Two Pithoi from the Beth-Shean Region and the Jordan Valley, *PEQ* 99 (1967), pp. 101–103.
104. Garstang, *AAA* 23, Pl. XXXII:33 B; *Murabba'at*, p. 16, Fig. 2:29, Pl. IV:15; *Lachish* IV, Pl. 13:91, 92; Bar-Adon, *IEJ* 11, p. 33, n. 15.
105. Unpublished. I wish to thank Dr. J. Kaplan for his kindness in supplying the information. The number of the ossuary is BM/H.125. For techniques cf. M. Stekelis, *The Yarmukian Culture of the Neolithic Period*, Jerusalem, 1972, p. 25.
106. Aharoni, *IEJ* 12, pp. 188–189.
107. J. Mellaart, *Earliest Civilizations of the Near East*, London, 1956, p. 89, Pl. 60; idem, Excavations at Çatal Hüyük, *Anatolian Studies* 13 (1963), Pls. VII, XVI; Crowfoot (above, n. 67), pp. 413 ff.
108. N. Haas, H. Nathan, An Attempt at a Social Interpretation of the Chalcolithic Burials in the Naḥal Mishmar Caves, *Excavations and Studies, Essays in Honour of Prof. S. Yeivin*, Tel Aviv, 1973, pp. 132–154 (Hebrew, English Summary). Their conclusions are different from those published in the preliminary report, cf. H. Nathan, Skeletons from Naḥal Mishmar, *IEJ* 11, p. 68.

THE CHALCOLITHIC PERIOD
CONCLUSIONS
pp. 199–204

1. I should like to thank Dr. R.D. Barnett of the British Museum, Dr. M. Rubin and Dr. G. Sonn of the Geological Department of the United States Government, Washington, and the Isotopes Laboratories, Inc., as well as the staff of these institutions.

2. The two mat-fragments sent to the United States were taken from the outer edge, while the fragment sent to the British Museum was taken from the inner part of the mat.

3. Aharoni, *IEJ* 12, pp. 189–190.

4. Perrot, *Préhistoire*, col. 439.

5. Recently, the question of the division of the early periods has been re-examined. While working on the material uncovered in the lowest strata (XVI–XV) of Beth Yeraḥ (Kh. Kerak), excavated in 1949–1955, and the comparative material from the lowest strata at Megiddo, Afula, Beth Shean and Tell el-Far'ah (N), I reached the conclusion that the "Esdraelon culture", which at that time was assigned to the end of the Chalcolithic period, should be placed within the EB I framework. This implies that the Ghassulian culture continued until the end of the Chalcolithic period. Prof. G.E. Wright saw the material from Beth Yeraḥ and Far'ah during a visit to Israel, and reached similar conclusions, which do not accord with de Vaux's views, cf. R. de Vaux, Les Fouilles de Tell el-Far'ah, Rapport préliminaire sur les 7e, 8e, et 9e campagnes, 1958–1960, *RB* 68 (1961), pp. 588 ff; G.E. Wright, The Problem of the Transition between the Chalcolithic and Bronze Ages, *EI* 5 (1958), pp. 37* ff. The Beth Yeraḥ material is still unpublished, with the exception of a few pottery types from the early strata in Ruth Amiran et al., *Ancient Pottery of the Holy Land*, Jerusalem, 1969. Miss Kathleen Kenyon agrees with Wright's conclusions, but proposes to change the terminology and to call this period Proto-Urban, cf. K.M. Kenyon, Some Notes on the Early and Middle Bronze Age Strata of Megiddo, *EI* 5 (1958), pp. 51* ff.; idem, *Excavations at Jericho*, I, London, 1960, pp. 4–10. It seems to me that the material available is still insufficient to validate Wright's proposal to divide this period into three phases (A, B, C), cf. de Vaux, *loc. cit.*

6. Y. Aharoni, *BIES* 22 (1958), p. 39, Fig. 11 (Hebrew); J. Naveh, *ibid.*, pp. 46–48, Fig. 1 (Hebrew); B. Mazar, *Archaeology* 16 (1963), pp. 99–107; *Encyclopedia of Archaeological Excavations in the Holy Land*, II, Jerusalem, 1976, pp. 371–2.

7. Cf., e.g., Frankfort, *SCS Diyala*, Pl. 6:34; idem, *CS*, Pls. III b, V h, VII j–k; Delaporte, *CC*, Pl. 64:3; Weber, *AS*, p. 59, Fig. 278; Amiet, *GMA*, Pls. 45:650, 46:658. Compare also in the Ghassul fresco, R. North, A unique new Palestine Art Form, *Estudios Eclesiásticos* 34 (1960), pp. 381–390, Pl. III. The eagle represents the god as bringer of the fertilizing rain, while birds symbolize the clouds of the storm. For the dove and its close connection with the mother goddess, see H. Frankfort, *Art and Architecture in the Ancient Orient*, Baltimore, 1954, p. 17; Van Buren, *Symbols*, p. 30; Albright, *STC*, p. 98.

8. The jar, in its many forms and variety of decorations, appears on cylinder seals among the symbols of the mother goddess. In representations of ceremonies, it is carried by offering-bearers as a container of water, and thus became a symbol of abundance and fertility. Cf. Porada, *NES*, Pls. 1:3 E, V:22; Frankfort, *CS*, p. 36, Fig. 12, Pls. III C, VIII C; idem, *SCS Diyala*, Pls. 4:12–13, 19:201; Amiet, *GMA*, e.g. Pl. 16:264; Heinrich, *Kleinfunde*, Pls. 2–3; H.H. von der Osten, *Ancient Oriental Seals in the Collection of Mr. Edward T. Newell*, Chicago, 1934, Pls. XXVII:398 ff.; Van Buren, *Symbols*, pp. 124 f., 133. Thus it seems to me that there are sufficient grounds for understanding the symbolism of the jar-shaped ossuary.

9. The deep copper bowl (No. 162) resembles the basket represented in cult scenes on cylinder seals, next to the symbols of the mother goddess. In the pictographic script, it means "food". Cf. e.g., Heinrich, *Kleinfunde*, Pl. 18; Amiet, *GMA*, Pl. 20:322; D. Diringer, *The Alphabet*, p. 46, Fig. 19. The large pithoi from Ghassul, which are ringed by plastic bands or ropes, resemble our deep bowl, cf. *TG* I, p. 103, Fig. 53.

10. The decorated horn-shaped vessels resemble the horns of plenty and rhyta of much later periods. Scholars are of the opinion that initially, such vessels served for drinking, but that already in an early period they came to symbolize abundance and fertility. Cf. E. Mackay, *A Sumerian Palace and the "A" Cemetery at Kish*, II, Chicago, 1929, Pl. LII, Type JA:29–31; Ruth Amiran, The Arm-shaped Vessel and its Family, *JNES* 21 (1963), pp. 161–174, Figs. 1–5; C. Daremberg & E. Saglio, *Dictionnaire des antiquités*, I, 2, Paris, 1887, p. 1514, *s.v.* cornucopia.

11. The horns are an early cult symbol, an expression of the god's vitality and power, cf. J. Mellaart, Excavations at Çatal Hüyük, *Anatolian Studies* 13 (1963), Figs. 4, 9 ff; Heinrich, *Kleinfunde*, Pl. 38.

12. Both the Maltese cross and the straight-sided cross are frequently found in ancient art, from the Halaf period onwards. The cross appears on pottery vessels, amulets, painted in red on the arm of a female figurine, on seals and cylinder seals, either by itself or together with other symbols of religious significance. It has also been found in a fresco at Çatal Hüyük in Anatolia, dated by the excavator to about 6500 B.C.E. Attempts have been made to explain the early significance of the cross in its various forms as a symbol for a settlement, a water reservoir or a lake, and thus also as a symbol of the god who brings down the rain, cf., e.g., *TG* I, Pl. 37:6; M.E.L. Mallowan and J.C. Rose, *The Excavations at Tell Arpachiya, 1933*, London, 1935, p. 81, Fig. 45:10; Frankfort, *SCS Diyala*, 12:95, 30:297; Delaporte, *CC*, Pl. 24:8, 25:10; J. Mellaart, Excavations at Çatal Hüyük, *Anatolian Studies* 12 (1962), Pl. X:a, 13 (1963), Pl. XII; Van Buren, *Symbols*, H 1, pp. 110 ff., 114.
Our standards, with their spherical, disk-shaped or spindle-shaped "heads", their spiral and herring-bone patterns, their decorations of nipples or knobs, buds, fruit, branches and leaves, recall the three phases of representing trees – presumably the "tree of life" – on cylinder seals. Cf., e.g., Van Buren, *Symbols*, A 4, pp. 22–29 and bibliography; Amiet, *GMA*, Pl. 41:622; Frankfort, *SCS, Diyala*, pp. 16, 20, 25, Pls. 5:24; 18:191, 193, 22:225. Cf. also trees or branches painted on Chalcolithic ossuaries from Azor.
The objects resembling mace-heads, which are carried as standards by figures bringing offerings to the temple, certainly symbolize fruit, in view of the context in which they appear. Cf., e.g., Frankfort, *CS*, Pl. VIII:e; Amiet, *GMA*, Pls. 18:302, 306, 43:637 B, 45:651; Weber, *AS* II, p. 103, Fig. 515; Delaporte, *CC*, Pl. 20:15; P. Delougaz, S. Lloyd, *Pre-Sargonid Temples in the Diyala Region*, Chicago, 1942, pp. 237–238, Figs. 184–185; Heinrich, *Kleinfunde*, Pl. 38; Van Buren, Religious Rites, *AfO* 13 (1939–40), p. 36, Fig. 3; idem, *Symbols*, p. 173.

13. *Murabba'at*, p. 16, Fig. 2:15–16, Pl. IV:9, 13.

14. N. Glueck, *BASOR* 131 (1953), pp. 6–15; 137 (1955), pp. 10–22; 138 (1955), pp. 7–20; 142 (1956), pp. 17–35; 145 (1957), pp. 11–25; *BA* 18 (1955), pp. 2–9.

15. R.J. Forbes, *Metallurgy in Antiquity*, Leiden, 1950, pp. 18, 358–360; idem, Beginnings of Metal Working, in *History of Technology* I, London, 1956, pp. 576 ff., Fig. 378.

16. J. Mellaart, *Çatal Hüyük, A Neolithic Town in Anatolia*, London, 1967, pp. 22, 212, 217.

17. Lucas, *AEMI*, pp. 214, 216.

18. C.A. Key, Note on the Trace-Element Content of the Artifacts of the Kfar Monash Hoard, *IEJ* 13 (1963), p. 290.

19. Perrot, *IEJ* 5, p. 84.

20. Dothan, Ḥ. Beter, p. 32; cf. also S. Abramski, *Metallurgy in Eretz-Israel in the Late Canaanite and Israelite Monarchy Periods*, Ph.D. Thesis, Hebrew University, 1957 (Hebrew), pp. 1–40, chapter on metallurgy from its beginnings to the second millennium; B. Rothenberg, Ancient Copper Industries in the Western Arabah, *PEQ* 94 (1962), pp. 5–71.

21. Lucas, *AEMI, loc. cit.*, n. 17; Forbes, *loc. cit.*, n. 15.

22. The remains of wood found in some of the standards and mace-heads indicate that they were carried on wooden poles. On the other hand, it is not clear how the "crowns" were carried. Were they perhaps placed on the backs of animals, like the temple models with the symbols of

the goddess Inanna represented on cylinder seals of the Proto-literate periods? Cf., e.g., Frankfort, *CS*, Pl. V:c; Amiet, *GMA*, Pls. 44:643, 46:652–655; Heinrich, *Kleinfunde*, Pls. 2, 3, 38; *Uruk* VII, Pl. 25:e. Alternatively, it is also possible that the "crowns" were worn on the head by those who officiated in cult ceremonies, cf. a stone figurine from Elam, which is dated to the third millennium B.C.E.: *Kunstschätze aus Iran*, Kunsthaus Zürich, 1962, p. 4, Fig. 1. As far as weight is concerned, the "crowns" can be worn on the head. However, in a letter of June 6, 1965, Prof. Edith Porada doubts whether the head and the body of this figurine belong together, as represented on the photograph quoted above, and she dates it to a later period. Perhaps the "crowns" were carried in the hands, like the standards?

BAR-KOKHBA PERIOD
PAPYRI AND OSTRACA
pp. 205–208

1. Cf. *Murabba'at*, Pl. XLVI.
2. B. Lifschitz, The Greek Documents from Naḥal Ṣe'elim and Naḥal Mishmar, *IEJ* 11 (1961), pp. 53–62, Pl. 23.
3. *Ibid.*, p. 56.
4. *Murabba'at*, pp. 213, 219–220.
5. Lifschitz, *IEJ* 11, pp. 54–55.
6. Yadin, *IEJ* 11, p. 44.
7. Lifschitz, *IEJ* 11, pp. 60–61; J. Schwartz, Remarques sur des fragments grecs du désert de Juda, *RB* 69 (1962), pp. 61–63.
8. Yadin, *IEJ* 12, pp. 253–254.
9. Y. Yadin, Documents from the Cave of Letters (in preparation).
10. Yadin, *IEJ* 11, p. 48; *Murabba'at*, p. 110, Pl. XXX.
11. Yadin, *IEJ* 11, pp. 43–44.
12. Cf. P. Benoit, *Murabba'at*, p. 214.
13. I wish to thank Dr. Lina Ben-Dor and Prof. P. Feigel of the Inorganic Chemistry Department in the Hebrew University, Jerusalem, for these tests. Earlier tests were also carried out at the laboratories of the Shemen Industries.
14. Cf. *Murabba'at*, Fig. 24.
15. *Ibid.*, loc. cit.
16. A. Sperber, ed., *The Bible in Aramaic*. III. *The Latter Prophets according to the Targum Jonathan*, Leiden, 1962.
17. E.W. Lane, *Arabic-English Lexicon*, London, 1867, col. 926.
18. *Murabba'at*, p. 232.
19. Cf. Comparative table, C.B. Welles, *The Inscriptions*, in C.H. Kraeling, *Gerasa*, New Haven, 1938, Fig. 12:122, 125, 135.

BAR-KOKHBA PERIOD
OTHER FINDS
pp. 209–211

1. According to Kahane's classification, based on the shape of the body, our store-jars belong to type B: P.P. Kahane, Rock-cut Tombs at Huqoq, *'Atiqot* III (1961), pp. 140–141.
2. R. de Vaux, Qumran, *RB* 60 (1953), p. 97, Fig. 2:1, 3, 6.
3. Idem, Fouilles de Feshkha, *RB* 66 (1959), p. 239, Fig. 1:1.
4. *Murabba'at*, p. 31, Fig. 7 (and bibliography).
5. Avigad, *IEJ* 12, p. 174, Fig. 5:1–3.
6. Yadin, *Cave of Letters*, p. 114, Fig. 43; Aharoni, *'Atiqot* III, p. 156, Fig. 7:16–24.
7. Aharoni, *IEJ* 11, Pl. 10:A–B.
8. For detailed discussion and bibliography see Kahane (above, n. 1), loc. cit.
9. *Ibid.*, p. 134, Pl. XVIII:4; Y. Aharoni, *Excavations at Ramat Raḥel, Seasons 1959–1960*, Rome, 1962, Fig. 20:9 (Str. IV).
10. *Murabba'at*, p. 32, Fig. 8:16.
11. Avigad, *IEJ* 12, p. 175, Fig. 5:15–18.
12. Yadin, *Cave of Letters*, p. 112, Fig. 41; Aharoni, *'Atiqot* III, p. 160, Fig. 10:8–10.

13. Aharoni, *IEJ* 11, Pl. 9:D–E.
14. De Vaux, Qumran, *RB* 61 (1954), p. 223, Fig. 4:12.
15. Aharoni, *Ramat Raḥel* (above, n. 9), Fig. 6:26.
16. Idem, *IEJ* 12, p. 191, Fig. 2:14–22.
17. *Murabba'at*, p. 32, Fig. 8:9–10; P.P. Kahane, Pottery from Ossuary Tombs around Jerusalem, *IEJ* 3 (1953), pp. 48 ff., Pl. 4:B2.
18. Aharoni, *Ramat Raḥel* (above, n. 9), Fig. 20:12 (Str. IV); idem, *IEJ* 12, p. 191, Fig. 2:11–13; L.Y. Rahmani, Jewish Rock-cut Tombs in Jerusalem, *'Atiqot* III, p. 99, Fig. 5:20; see also detailed discussion by Kahane (above, n. 17), pp. 48–54, Pl. 4:B1.
19. Kahane, Huqoq (above, n. 1), p. 134, Fig. 3:21, Pl. XVIII:5.
20. Bar-Adon, *IEJ* 11, p. 29, n. 6; cf. also R.H. Smith, The Herodian Lamps of Palestine – Types and Dates, *Berytus* 14 (1961), p. 53; P.W. Lapp, *Palestinian Ceramic Chronology, 200 B.C.–A.D. 70*, New Haven, 1961, p. 193.
21. For a detailed discussion of Herodian lamps, with references to all the material published up to 1961, see Kahane, Huqoq (above, n. 1), pp. 135–139, Fig. 3:18. Our fragment of lamp is too small for attribution to one of Kahane's five types.
22. Aharoni, *Ramat Raḥel* (above, n. 9), p. 27, Figs. 3:24, 20:26–30.
23. J.W. Crowfoot, G.M. Crowfoot, K.M. Kenyon, *Samaria–Sebaste* III. *The Objects*, London, 1957, pp. 365–366, Fig. 86:3.
24. *Murabba'at*, pp. 31 ff., Fig. 8:12; pp. 47–48.
25. De Vaux, Feshkha (above, n. 3), p. 241, Fig. 2:3.
26. Avigad, *IEJ* 12, p. 177, Fig. 5:19–20.
27. Found by Aharoni (unpublished).
28. Aharoni, *IEJ* 12, p. 194, Fig. 4.
29. Yadin, *Cave of Letters*, pp. 114–115, Fig. 42:CD 1, RC 4, Pl. 35. Yadin considers that the span of this type can now be continued to the mid-second century C.E., cf. p. 115, n. 14.
30. Rahmani, *'Atiqot* III (above, n. 18), p. 104, Fig. 5:26. According to Rahmani the capacity of the vessel, which is similar to ours, is 0.54 litres, that is, the equivalent of one *log*. Our vessel is too fragmentary to measure its capacity. Cf. also Aharoni, *Ramat Raḥel* (above, n. 9), Fig. 6:5.
31. *Murabba'at*, Fig. 8:6, Pl. VIII:3.
32. Yadin, *Cave of Letters*, p. 115, Fig. 43:A 7, Pl. 35. The vessel has a bar-handle; its restored capacity is 0.55 litres.
33. D. Barag, *IEJ* 12, p. 209, Figs. 11–12, Pl. 33:C.
34. Yadin, *Cave of Letters*, p. 104 (and bibliography); cf. also Kahane, Huqoq (above, n. 1), p. 133–134.
35. Kahane, *ibid.*, p. 126, Fig. 3:14.
36. Bar-Adon, *IEJ* 11, p. 30, where it was suggested that the cave was also occupied during the Second Temple period. However, since then it has become clear that the Herodian vessels, on whose presence this suggestion was based, have in fact a span down to the mid-second century C.E.
37. Yoram Zafrir, at that time a student, reached the cave with great difficulty. He described it as follows: "The small cave is not suitable for habitation. It is 2 m wide, 1.5 m deep and 1.2 m high at the highest point. In front of the cave is a small terrace. I found signs of human occupation: just under the surface a Roman sherd was found. At a depth of 10 cm, in the debris, a 5 cm deep burnt layer was discerned. In this layer a small textile fragment was found, and a little below it, a Chalcolithic sherd. My impression is that the small cave or niche served as a store for the cave-dwellers. The burnt layer does not give the impression of being the remains of successive fires, but of one conflagration, either accidental or intentional."
38. Cf. Josephus, *War*, III, v(1): "The Romans... whatever hostile territory they may invade, they engage in no battle until they have fortified their camp."
39. Aharoni, *IEJ* 12, p. 186; idem, *'Atiqot* III, pp. 151 ff.; Yadin, *Cave of Letters*, pp. 11–14.
40. Avigad, *IEJ* 12, p. 181; in the Cave of the Pool no valuable articles or written documents were found. Avigad writes that "this may be taken as a sign that these fugitives survived the period of turmoil and danger and, when they finally left the cave, took away with them everything worth taking."

ABBREVIATIONS

Diam	Diameter (maximum outer diameter)
Ht	Height
L	Length
Th	Thickness (of wall)
W	Width (at widest point)
Wt	Weight

Aharoni, *'Atiqot* III	Y. Aharoni, The Caves of Naḥal Ḥever, *'Atiqot* III (1961), pp. 148–162.
AfO	*Archiv für Orientforschung.*
Albright *STC*	W.F. Albright, *From the Stone Age to Christianity,* Baltimore, 1940.
Amiet *GMA*	P. Amiet, *La glyptique mésopotamienne archaïque,* Paris, 1961.
BA	*Biblical Archaeologist.*
BASOR	*Bulletin of the American Schools of Oriental Research.*
Beth Pelet II	E. Macdonald, *Prehistoric Fara,* in *Beth Pelet* II, London, 1932.
BIES	*Bulletin of the Israel Exploration Society* (Hebrew).
Contenson, *IEJ* 6	H. de Contenson, La céramique chalcolithique de Beersheba, *IEJ* 6 (1956), pp. 163–179; 226–238.
Delaporte, C.C.	L. Delaporte, *Catalogue des cylindres, cachets et pierres gravées de style oriental* II, Paris 1923.
Dothan, Ḥ. Beter	M. Dothan, Excavations at Ḥorvat Beter (Beersheba), *'Atiqot* II (1959), pp. 1–42.
EI	*Eretz-Israel,* Archaeological, Historical and Geographical Studies, published by the Israel Exploration Society (Hebrew).
Fitzgerald, *EPBS*	G.M. Fitzgerald, The Earliest Pottery of Beth-Shan, *Museum Journal* 24 (1935), pp. 5–32.
Frankfort, *BCNE*	H. Frankfort, *The Birth of Civilization in the Near East,* London, 1951.
Frankfort, *CS*	H. Frankfort, *Cylinder Seals,* London, 1939.
Frankfort, *SCS Diyala*	H. Frankfort, *Stratified Cylinder Seals from the Diyala Region,* Chicago, 1955.
Garstang, *AAA* 22	J. Garstang, J.P. Droop, Joan Crowfoot, Jericho, Fifth Report, *Annals for Archaeology and Anthropology, Liverpool* 22 (1935).
Garstang, *AAA* 23	J. Garstang, I. Ben-Dor, G.M. Fitzgerald, Jericho, Report for Sixth Season, *Annals for Archaeology and Anthropology, Liverpool* 23 (1936).
Heinrich, *Kleinfunde*	E. Heinrich, *Kleinfunde aus den archaischen Tempelschichten in Uruk* (Ausgrabungen der Deutschen Forschungsgemeinschaft in Uruk-Warka I), Berlin, 1936.
IDAM	Israel Department of Antiquities and Museums.
IEJ	*Israel Exploration Journal*
IEJ 11	The Expedition to the Judean Desert, 1960, by N. Avigad, Y. Aharoni, P. Bar-Adon, Y. Yadin et al., *IEJ* 11 (1961), pp. 1–72.
IEJ 12	Do. 1961, *IEJ* 12 (1962), pp. 165–262.
ILN	*Illustrated London News.*
JNES	*Journal of Near Eastern Studies.*
JPOS	*Journal of the Palestine Oriental Society.*
Lachish IV	Olga Tufnell et al., *Lachish* IV, *The Bronze Age,* London, 1958.
Lucas, *AEMI*	A. Lucas, *Ancient Egyptian Materials and Industries,* 4th ed., London, 1962.
Megiddo II	G. Loud, *Megiddo* II, *Seasons of 1935–1939,* Chicago, 1948.
Murabba'at	P. Benoit, J. Milik, R. de Vaux, *Les Grottes de Murabba'at,* Oxford, 1961.
PEQ	*Palestine Exploration Quarterly.*
Perrot, Azor	J. Perrot, Une tombe à ossuaires du IVe millénaire à Azor, près de Tel Aviv, *'Atiqot* III (1961), pp. 1–83.
Perrot, *IEJ* 5	J. Perrot, The Excavations at Tell Abu Matar near Beersheba, *IEJ* 5 (1955), pp. 17–40; 73–84; 167–189.
Perrot, Préhistoire	J. Perrot, Préhistoire Palestinienne, in *Dictionnaire de la Bible* VIII, Supplément, Paris, 1972, col. 286–441.
Perrot, *Syria* 34	J. Perrot, Les fouilles d'Abou Matar près de Beersheba, *Syria* 34 (1957), pp. 1–38.
Porada, *NES*	E. Porada, *Corpus of Ancient Near Eastern Seals in North American Collections,* New York, 1948.
PPEB	G.E. Wright, *The Pottery of Palestine from the Earliest Times to the End of the Early Bronze Age,* New Haven, 1937.
Pritchard, *ANEP*	J. Pritchard, *The Ancient Near East in Pictures Relating to the Old Testament,* Princeton, 1954.
QDAP	*Quarterly of the Department of Antiquities in Palestine.*
RB	*Revue Biblique.*
Sukenik, Hadera	E. Sukenik, A Chalcolithic Necropolis at Hadera, *JPOS* 17 (1937), pp. 15–30.
Speiser, *Tepe Gawra* I	E.A. Speiser, *Excavations at Tepe Gawra* I, Philadelphia, 1935.
Tobler, *Tepe Gawra* II	A.J. Tobler, *Excavations at Tepe Gawra* II, Philadelphia, 1950.
TG I	A. Mallon et al., *Teleilat Ghassul* I, Rome 1934.
TG II	R. Koeppel et al., *Teleilat Ghassul* II, Rome, 1940.
Uruk	*Vorläufige Berichte über die von der deutschen Forschungsgemeinschaft in Uruk-Warka unternommenen Ausgrabungen,* Abhandlungen der Preussischen Akademie der Wissenschaften, Phil.-Hist. Klasse, Berlin.
Van Buren, *Symbols*	E.D. Van Buren, *Symbols of the Gods in Mesopotamian Art,* Rome, 1945.
Weber, *AS*	O. Weber, *Altorientalische Siegelbilder,* Leipzig, 1920.
Yadin, *Cave of Letters*	Y. Yadin, *The Finds from the Bar-Kokhba Period in the Cave of Letters,* Jerusalem, 1963.
ZDPV	*Zeitschrift des Deutschen Palästina-Vereins.*

APPENDICES

PLANT REMAINS FROM THE CAVE OF THE TREASURE

D.V. ZAITSCHEK
Hebrew University, Jerusalem

Remains of a great variety of cultivated plants were found in all strata of the caves of Naḥal Mishmar: the Chalcolithic, the Intermediate, and the Roman (time of Bar Kokhba).

The most important finds were made in Cave No. 1 ("The Cave of the Treasure") in 1961, during the second season of the excavations. In Hall A there were three large, heavy stones, which had fallen from the ceiling of the cave in ancient times, in the span of time between the occupation of the cave in the Chalcolithic and in the Roman periods. All the material found under one of these stones (measuring about 2 × 2 m), therefore certainly belonged to the Chalcolithic level. This was later confirmed by Carbon-14 analysis of the organic remains.

Ancient cereal remains preserved in a non-carbonized state were found here for the first time in Palestine, due to the aridity of the Judean Desert region. The remains included: (1) whole spikelets and grains of emmer — *Triticum durum* (Schrank.) Schübl. (the cultivated two-grained glume wheat, called 'kussemet' כֻּסֶּמֶת in the Bible) and (2) spike fragments, triplets of spikelets and grains of cultivated two-rowed barley — *Hordeum sativum* Jess. ssp. *distichum* L. pr.p. var. *nutans* Schübl. The discovery of emmer, identified here with certainty, owing to the presence of whole, non-carbonized spikelets,[1] is of special importance in studying the origin and historical development of cultivated wheat. Emmer was the "missing link" between the wild emmer, *Triticum dicoccoides* Körn. — the "ancestor of cultivated wheats", which was discovered in Palestine more than sixty years ago by Aaronsohn — and Durum wheat, *Triticum durum* Desf., which has been cultivated in this area for the last several hundred years.

The intermingled occurrence of cultivated emmer and cultivated two-rowed barley in this area is interesting in itself, for this is also the area of the simultaneous occurrence of wild emmer and wild two-rowed barley (*Hordeum spontaneum* C. Koch). We may mention here Aaronsohn's conjecture, that the ancient farmer began cultivating wheat (emmer) and barley simultaneously and intermingled, just as he found them in nature in a wild state. This conjecture has been considerably substantiated by our finds.

Other food remains from the Chalcolithic level were: olive stones (*Olea europaea* L.), date seeds (*Phoenix dactylifera* L.), fragments of pomegranate fruits (*Punica granatum* L.), endocarp fragments of walnut (*Juglans* sp.), broken endocarps of Atlantic pistachio (*Pistacia atlantica* Desf.), shell fragments of acorns of the Tabor oak (*Quercus ithaburensis* Decne.), probably used for food; a bulb and single bulblets (cloves) of garlic (*Allium sativum* L.) and bulb scales of onion (*Allium cepa* L.).

A great number of items were classified as belonging to an Intermediate level, because it was difficult to assign them with certainty to either the Chalcolithic or the Roman level. The great majority of this material showed a close resemblance to the finds of the Chalcolithic level listed above.

The remains found in the Roman level showed some remarkable differences in comparison to those from the Chalcolithic stratum. Besides spikelets of emmer (non-carbonized), there were also carbonized grains which might be classified as a naked species of wheat (*Triticum durum* Desf.). The spikes, spikelets and grains of two-rowed barley showed clear morphological differences from the kind of two-rowed barley found in the Chalcolithic level and mentioned above, and a part of them was tentatively identified as *Hordeum sativum* Jess. ssp. *vulgare* L. (six-rowed barley). Some fruit remains in this level showed slight differences in comparison with the items of the more ancient levels. These were olive stones, date seeds, pomegranate fruit fragments, endocarp fragments of walnut and acorn-shell fragments of the Tabor oak. In this level we found also some leguminous seeds, of broad bean (*Vicia faba* L. var. *minor* Beck.) and small-seeded lentil (*Lens esculenta* Mönch. ssp. *microsperma* Bar.).

---

[1] Earlier finds examined by the writer were carbonized grains only, in which the lack of paleae and glumes made the identification as emmer uncertain, while being confined only to the shape and the size of the kernel.

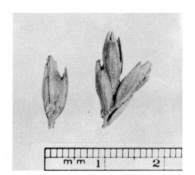

Selected Plant Samples

Reg. No. 61–29/3 (Chalcolithic level)
Emmer — *Triticum dicoccum* (Schrank.) Schübl.
Single spikelet and fragment of spike.

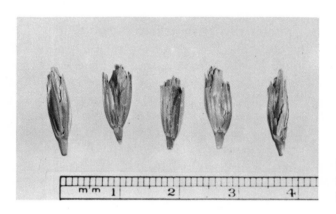

Reg. No. 61–80/3 (Chalcolithic level)
Emmer — *Triticum dicoccum* (Schrank.) Schübl.
Spikelets.

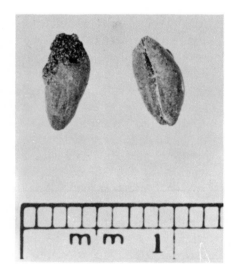

Reg. No. 60–180 (Roman level)
Durum wheat ? — *Triticum durum* Desf.
Carbonized grains.

Reg. No. 61–29/3 (Chalcolithic level)
Two-rowed barley — *Hordeum sativum* Jess.
ssp. *distichum* L. pr.p. var. *nutans* Schübl.
Spike fragments and units of three spikelets (one fertile
median and two infertile lateral spikelets) with attached
rachis internode.

Reg. No. 60–12 (Roman level)
Two-rowed barley — *Hordeum sativum* Jess. ssp. *distichum* L. pr.p.
Spike fragments, spikelet triplets and grains of fertile spikelets.

Reg. No. 60–180 (Roman level)
Two-rowed barley — *Hordeum sativum* Jess. ssp. distichum L. pr. p.
Carbonized grains.

Reg. No. 61–72/3 (top); **Reg. No. 61–37/3** (bottom)
(Chalcolithic level)
Date palm — *Phoenix dactylifera* L.
Seeds.

Reg. No. 61–69/2 (Chalcolithic level) (top row)
Reg. No. 61–46/2 (Chalcolithic level) (lower left)
Reg. No. 61–32/2 (Chalcolithic level) (lower centre)
Reg. No. 61–40/1 (Chalcolithic level) (lower right)
Tabor oak — *Quercus ithaburensis* Decne.
Shell fragments of acorns.

Reg. No. 60–12 (Roman level) (top row)
Reg. No. 61–62/2 (Intermediate level) (lower left)
Reg. No. 61–37/3 (Chalcolithic level) (lower centre)
Reg. No. 61–72/3 (Chalcolithic level) (lower right)
Pomegranate — *Punica granatum* L.
Fruitpeel fragments.

Reg. No. 61–92/1 (Intermediate level)
Olive tree — *Olea europaea* L.
Fruit stones.

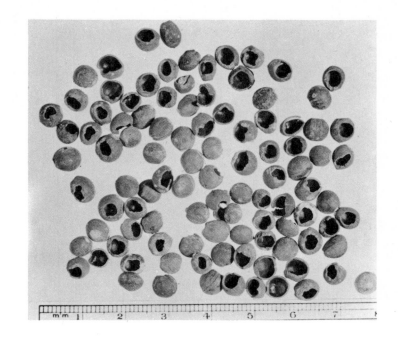

Reg. No. 61–92/1 (Intermediate level)
Atlantic pistachio — *Pistacia atlantica* Desf.
Broken endocarps.

Reg. No. 60–180 (Roman
level)
Lentil — *Lens esculenta* Mönch.
ssp. *microsperma* Bar.
Carbonized seeds.

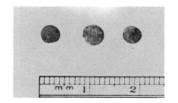

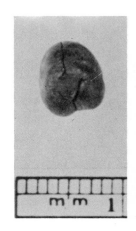

Reg. No. 60–85 (Roman level) (top) rough endocarp
Reg. No. 60–12 (Roman level) (bottom) smooth endocarp
Walnut — *Juglans* sp.
Endocarp fragments.

Reg. No. 60–12 (Roman level)
Broad Bean — *Vicia faba* L.
var. *minor* Beck.
Seed (without testa).

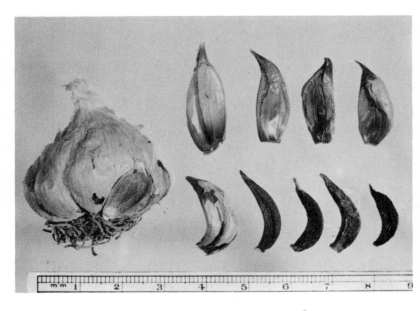

Reg. No. 61–92/2 (Intermediate level) whole bulb
Reg. No. 61–92/3 (Intermediate level) single bulblets (cloves)
with and without skin
Garlic — *Allium sativum* L.

FAUNAL REMAINS FROM THE CAVE OF THE TREASURE
(Chalcolithic Stratum)

Identified by Prof. G. Haas

Reg. No.	Cave 1	Description
61–52	Hall A	Goat.
61–61	Hall B	Bird, small bovid.
61–83	Niche 2	Probably hare (Lepus), small ruminant, ibex(?), pigeon(?), coney (Procavia syriaca), gazelle.
61–26	Hall A	Goat.
61–88	Betw, niches 1 and 2	Gazelle (?).
61–72	Hall B	Bovidae, pigeon(?), hare, goat.
61–68	Hall B	Vertebra of snake, hares, fragmentary ribs of bovidae.
61–66	Hall B	Bovidae.
61–63	Hall B	Birds, goat.
61–32	Hall A	Snakes, gazelle.
61–12/4	Niche 1	Hare (Lepus), pigeon (rock-pigeon?), goat, vertebra of snake, mole-rat (Spalax), mandibles of gerbil, one small and one large snake, gazelle(?).
61–14/1	Niche 2	Bird, hare (Lepus), mandible of large bird (pigeon?), goat, large bird, large snake, skull of medium-sized bird.
61–42	Hall A	Goat, medium-sized bird.
61–54	Hall A	Pigeon, pigeon-sized bird.
61–44	Hall A	Kid.
61–37	Hall A	Goat.
61–39	Hall A	Gazelle, hare, goats, bovidae, roedeer.
61–40	Betw. Halls A and B	Goat, hare, horn-core of goat, birds (6–7 kinds).
61–59	Hall B	Bird, small bovid.
61–48	Hall A	Large bird, goat, rib of bovid.

Reg. No.	Cave 1	Description
61–25	Hall A	Goat, hare, large bird of prey.
61–49	Hall A	Goats, birds, porcupine (Hystrix?), small bird, hare, gazelle.
61–51	Hall A	Murid or hamster (Cricetid), goats, birds.
61–55	Hall A	Goat.
61–80	Niche 1	Bird, cervical vertebra of goat(?), large bird, gazelle.
61–57	Betw. Halls A and B	Birds, hare(?), large bird of prey, bovid, goat.
61–31	Hall A	Roedeer, pigeon.
61–6/1	Debris Hall A	Ibex or wild goat.
61–7/2	Niche 1	Rodents (Microtus, gerbil).
61–10–1	Niche 1	Hare (Lepus), goat/sheep, medium-sized snake, gazelle.
61–15/1	Niche 2	Hare, bird, tooth of gerbil, tooth of hare, small bird, gazelle.
61–21/1	Hall I	Goats, hares, birds, bovidae, badger (Meles), bird of prey.
61–91	Hall A	Falcon-sized bird.
61–45	Hall A	Gazelle.
61–47	Hall A	Hare (Lepus), large bird, roedeer(?), bird, goat or roedeer, gazelle, small vulture(?), pigeon(?), bird of prey, marten, perhaps Vormela.
61–13	Hall A	Hare (Lepus), gazelle(?), pigeon-sized bird, goat.
61–41	Hall A	Hare(?), birds, gazelle or goat, pigeon, bovidae(?).
61–40	Betw. Halls A and B	Goat, roedeer(?).

TEXTILE REMAINS FROM THE CAVES OF NAḤAL MISHMAR

ESSA CINDORF, S. HOROWITZ and R. BLUM
Institute of Fibre and Forest Research, Jerusalem

Samples of textiles were received from the Chalcolithic and the Roman strata, and from the Intermediate stratum between them. Both wool and linen samples were found in all three strata. No wool-flax blends were found.

The samples were first photographed in their original state. Some of them were fully decomposed, rendering any testing impossible, but most of the samples, while appreciably weakened, were in a condition suitable for the investigation of their properties.

After photographing, the samples were washed. In order to prevent further decomposition of the cloth and to straighten it during washing, a double wooden frame (30 × 50 cm) with plastic netting was built, into which the cloth was inserted. The cloth was washed in a solution of distilled water with a small amount of non-ionic detergent. The samples were first soaked in this solution for 1 hour and cleaned with a soft brush. This was followed by two rinsings of 2 hours each in clear distilled water. The fabric was then unfolded, straightened and spread to dry on blotting paper. After cleaning and straightening the samples were again photographed.

Testing was carried out for:
1) Identification of the material — by microscope;
2) Direction of twist — S or Z;
3) Count of warp and weft — in all cases the count is expressed as a metric number, both for flax fibres and wool;
4) Number of ends and picks per cm;
5) Design of the weave.

Chalcolithic Stratum

The samples from the Chalcolithic period were made of wool and linen but in no case were blends of the two fibres found.

All the wool fabrics were piece dyed (one colour). One of the samples (Ill. 26:1; No. 61–22/8–d) is a finely preserved wool fabric dyed a rich red colour.

The linen samples were not dyed. There are differences in shade which may be attributed to differences in retting methods and possibly to aging.

Forty-five samples were tested, 37 of linen and 8 of wool. In addition, some 10 samples from the Chalcolithic period were completely decomposed or in a state which did not allow testing. Some of the samples tested could be analysed only in part because of their poor state of preservation.

Yarn count. The thickness of yarns varied from a count of 3 to 120/2 for the linen and from a count of 7.7 to 21.7 for the wool.

Twist. In the linen samples, the yarns were double-ply with an S-twist in both warp and weft. Single-ply was found in only five samples in warp and weft; these also showed an S-twist. Three of the samples with single-ply yarns could not be clearly attributed to the Chalcolithic period; one was a basket-weave.

Of the 8 wool samples, 5 were woven, all of single-ply yarns with an S-twist. In one sample (No. 61–22/8–h) the weft consisted of double-ply yarns with a Z-twist.

Design of the Weave. All the wool and the linen samples were in plain weave, except for one sample of a 2/2 basket weave.

Number of ends and picks per cm. In the linen fabrics the number of ends was always greater than the number of picks. In the few wool samples, on the other hand, the number of picks exceeded the number of ends.

Selvedges. The common type of selvedge in the linen fabrics was the true selvedge. This is the selvedge which is used today. The selvedge is flat and formed by one weft passing over the warp and returning into the cloth. Of the 11 selvedges from the Chalcolithic period, 9 were of this type. Three were true selvedges strengthened by supplementary yarns.
1) In sample No. 61–29/7-c two doubled yarns were sewn round the true selvedge and these also passed round two additional warp yarns inserted along the selvedge.
2) In sample 61–61/3-c (Ill. 35:2) two warp yarns were sewn to the cloth with a double-ply yarn.
3) In sample No. 61–82/4 brown yarn was sewn round the selvedge.

Other selvedges: the weft passes over two warp yarns in three rows in sample No. 61–29/7-a (Ill. 35:4), and in sample No. 61–56/5-d (Chalcolithic?) the weft passes over eight warp yarns in one row.

Two of the woollen fabrics had selvedges: in No. 61–80/6 the weft passes over three warps in three rows, and the strap No. 61–22/8-h (Ill. 26:3) was made by a weft passing over five warp yarns in three rows.

Hems. Hems of several types were found both in the linen and in the wool samples, e.g.: the edge of the cloth is folded and sewn with a hem stitch; the edge of the cloth is sewn round with a binding stitch. In another sample the fabric is twisted, rolled and sewn down (Ill. 31; No. 62–61-d). In sample No. 61–35/5 (Ill. 28) four warp yarns are twisted twice round several weft yarns along the hem.

Patterns. The only pattern found was that of self bands (Ill. 35:4; No. 61–29/7-a). The bands, which are four weft yarns wide, are made of wefts thicker than the ordinary weft of the cloth. The pattern is repeated at intervals of approximately one cm.

Miscellaneous

1) In sample No. 61–204 (Ill. 34) blood stains were observed.
2) Sample No. 62–33 consists of a white flax-fibre net made of knotted ropes.
3) Samples Nos. 62–2 and 62–24 of linen were completely charred and disintegrated. Two shades of colour could be noted: the warp was dark brown and the weft light brown. A pattern of three light brown yarns was apparently woven into the fabric, but the poor state of the sample did not allow a thorough examination.

Conclusions

Linen fabrics. All fabrics were woven in plain weave except for one sample of basket weave. The yarns were twisted in an S direction. The common type of selvedge was the true selvedge. The yarn count ranged from 3/1 to fine yarns of 120/2. The fabrics were not dyed, and varied in shade from white and light yellow to dark brown.

Woollen fabrics. Eight samples were found in yellow, red, green and black. As in the linen specimens, these fabrics were also woven in plain weave. All yarns were single-ply and not double-ply, as in the linen samples, and had an S-twist (except one case of a Z-twist).

From the few samples tested it appears that the number of picks exceeded the number of ends. (The opposite was found in the linen samples). The yarn count ranged from 7.7 to 21.7.

In addition to the woven fabrics a plaited rope of yellow wool (No. 61–72/4-b) was found as well as a sample of black netting (No. 61–22/8-f). The net is made of two double-ply yarns and was apparently sewn with a needle. Between the twist of the yarns additional yarns were inserted. The sample is too small to be examined more throughly. In the method of sewing it is similar to samples No. 61–34/6 (Ill. 47:1) and 60–151–m, both from the Intermediate stratum.

The strap No. 61–22/8-h (Ill. 26:3), made of yellow wool, is almost identical with the strap No. 61–45/6-b (Ill. 47:3) from the Intermediate stratum.

Intermediate Stratum

Linen

1) Two samples of a 7 cm wide ribbon were found, preserved in one sample for a length of 20 cm. Both samples are light brown in colour. The ribbon is made of double-ply yarns in plain weave. The fabric is very fine and has the appearance of fine silk. The yarn count in sample 60–151–d (Ill. 46:1) is 354/2 for the warp and 184/2 for the weft, with 44–45 ends per cm and 30 picks per cm. Two true selvedges run along both sides of the ribbon.

Sample No. 60–203–a is identical to the above in method of weaving and in general appearance, and may be part of the same ribbon. The test results, however, differ slightly: the yarn count of the warp is 334/2 and of the weft 244/2, with 43 ends and 28 picks per cm.
2) Together with the fine fabric described above, a sample of very coarse fabric was found (Ill. 39; No. 60–203–b). The warp count was 19.2/2 and the weft count 14/2. The number of ends was 9–10 per cm and the number of picks 10–11 per cm. A rolled piece of cloth was sewn onto the true selvedge, for strengthening.
3) Three samples of yarns were found: a) No. 60–151–i, a ball of yarn; b) No. 60–151–1, consisting of about 25 white yarns, not rolled up but straight and tied in the middle; c) No. 60–151–n, a ball of yarn partly unravelled.
4) Two samples were woven in a warp-rib effect. In both samples half the fabric is woven more tightly in the warp than in the second half (30:20 and 36:22). This may be a weaving error.
5) A pocket was found sewn onto a piece of fabric (Ill. 42; No. 61–23/1-a). Both the pocket and cloth are made of single-ply yarns in plain weave, but the yarns used for the pocket are thicker than those of the cloth. The pocket has a selvedge which is sewn onto the cloth and the fragment which has been preserved is 18 cm wide and 8 cm long.
6) Sample No. 61–19/1-g (Ill. 43:1) apparently represents the edge and corner of a pocket or a garment. The sample consists of a strip of rolled fabric with a corner of a plaited hem.
7) A sample of basket weave was found (Ill. 46:3; No. 60–151–e). In several places the weave is 1/1, apparently a weaving error. The sample consists of two parts; the fabric is tied by a knot to a second narrow piece of fabric which is folded and sewn. Two other pieces of fabric are sewn on and in the fold, but only a small part of these has been preserved.

Wool

1) Sample No. 61–151–m, is black netting of double-

ply yarn. The fabric is not woven and was apparently made by needlework. Threads were passed by a needle through the twist of the yarn and the yarn was twirled to form squares. This method is identical to that used in Chalcolithic sample 61–22/8-f and in sample 61–34/6 (Ill. 47:1) of the Intermediate Stratum.

2) A button (Ill. 47:6; No. 60–151–r) made of yellow wool was found wrapped in a piece of plain-weave fabric (the button is of similar weave). The button is round and tied about with a strand of straw, which also passes over the centre of the button. The straw on the sides is hidden by about 10 strands of yellow woollen yarn which are wrapped around it, so that the straw is visible only in the centre of the button and round the edges of the yarn. In the button cover a single yarn of red wool was found together with several strands of yellow woollen yarn.

3) Sample No. 60–201 (Ill. 41:3) consists of a piece of plain-weave fabric, which is folded and sewn onto a second piece of fabric woven in a warp rib effect, which is also folded. Two little holes appear in the fold, at a distance of 5 cm between them. In the centre of the fold there is only one layer of plain-weave fabric. A hem is sewn along one end of the piece.

4) A plaited rope of black wool (Ill. 47:1; No. 61–34/6) was found with another shorter plaited rope of yellow wool tied to it and ending in a knot. The black rope is partly sewn with a yellow woollen thread, and black threads hang down from it, sewn by the method used in sample No. 60–151–m. The rope may have served as an ornament.

6) Sample No. 61–23/1-d (Ill. 47:7) may represent the edge of a garment or a sleeve and is made of yellow wool, in plain weave. The fragment is rounded in shape, folded twice and sewn.

7) A strap (Ill. 47:3; No. 61–45/6-b) made of yellow wool was found, in which the weft passes over six warp yarns in three rows. At one end of the sample the weft consists of red wool for a length of 0.5 cm. This strap is similar to No. 61–22/8-h (Ill. 26:1) of the Chalcolithic period.

Bar-Kokhba Stratum

Sixteen samples were found which may be clearly dated to the Bar-Kokhba Stratum (Roman period) – 14 made of linen and two of wool. As in the fabrics from the Chalcolithic period, no blend of wool and flax was found.

Yarn count. The thickness of the yarns in the linen samples ranged from a count of 7.8 to 52.3/2, while that in the wool samples ranged from 18 to 19.8 (only one woven sample was found).

Twist. The linen fabrics were woven from both double-ply (7 samples) and single-ply (6 samples) yarns. In both cases the direction of the twist was S. The one woven wool sample was made of single-ply yarn with an S-twist.

Design of weave. As in the Chalcolithic fabrics the common weave was the plain weave; two samples of basket weave were also found.

Number of ends and picks per cm. In the flax fibres the number of ends per cm exceeded the number of picks.

Selvedges. Three selvedges were found; all were of the true selvedge type. In one sample (No. 61–85/1-a) yarn was sewn round the selvedge to strengthen it.

Hems. Sample No. 60–79–c had a plaited hem – the warp yarns were gathered at the end of the fabric and twisted in the form of a plait.

Two samples of wool fabric were found: 1) A small dark brown sample, woven in a plain weave; 2) Two plaited ropes tied together, make of pink wool.

Conclusions

The few samples from the Bar-Kokhba period did not essentially differ from those dating from Chalcolithic times. The main difference is the more widespread use of single-ply yarns in the Bar-Kokhba period as compared with the Chalcolithic period, when according to our samples most fabrics were woven from double-ply yarns.

List of Textile Remains

The list includes all samples examined which are not shown in Illustrations 26–49 (pp. 155–176)

Linen Fabrics – Chalcolithic Stratum

Reg. No.	Warp			Weft			Weave
	ends /cm.	count	twist	picks /cm.	count	twist	
61–12/3	14		Double S	14		Double S	Plain
At the boundary of Intermediate Stratum.							
61–22/8–e	18	42.4/2	Double S	13	47.6/2	Double S	Plain
61–29/7–c	14-15	24/2	Double S	12	35.2/2	Double S	Plain
True selvedge: two yarns sewn around it, and also around two yarns inserted along warp for strengthening.							
61–29/7–d	16	64.4/2	Double S	14	73.4/2	Double S	Plain
The cloth is white.							
61–29/7–f	14	31.2/2	Double S	14		Double S	Plain
61–38/1	26	34.6/2	Double S	10	32.6/2	Double S	Plain
True selvedge.							
61–56/5–b	26	113.2/2	Double S	17	90.2	Double S	Plain
True selvedge.							
61–56/5–d	16(?)		Single S	16(?)		Single S	Plain
Selvedge: weft passes over eight warps in one row.							
61–61/3–d	19	23.4/2	Double S	11	34.4/2	Double S	Plain
61–61/3–e	19	31.2/2	Double S	10	–	Double S	Plain
61–61/3–f	11	18.2/2	Double S	11	17.6/2	Double S	Plain
Edge is folded and sewn with 3-ply yarn.							
61–61/3–g	10	25.8/2	Double S	10	26.2/2	Double S	Plain
61–63/5–b			Single S				
Yarn.							
61–82/4	16(?)		Double S	12(?)	26/2	Double S	Plain
True selvedge. Brown yarn sewn round it. Very small sample.							
62–2	28(?)		Double S	5(?)		Double S	
Dark and light brown(?) Cloth completely charred and decomposed. Hard to tell original colours.							
62–24	28(?)		Double S	5(?)		Double S	
Identical to 62–2 and in same state.							
62–33			Z			Z	
White. Net(?) Knotted ropes.							
62–39–a			Double S				
Three strip of cloth sewn together. Too small to test.							

Woollen Fabrics – Chalcolithic Stratum

Reg. No.	Warp				Weft				Weave
	colour	ends /cm.	count	twist	colour	picks /cm.	count	twist	
61–22/8–c	Yellow	11	20	Single S	Yellow	18	14.3	Single S	Plain
61–22/8–f	Black								
Net(?) Made of two double-ply yarns. Other yarns inserted inside the twist of the yarns.									
61–22/8–g	Red-Yellow								
Yarns.									
61–72/4–b	Yellow								
Plaited rope made of three double-ply yarns.									
61–80/6	Green	12-13	8.5	Single S	Green	18-19	10	Single S	Plain
Selvedge: weft passes over three warps in three rows.									

Linen Fabrics – Intermediate Stratum

Reg. No.	Warp			Weft			Weave
	ends /cm.	count	twist	picks /cm.	count	twist	
60–151–a	16	9.3	Single S	12	10.1	Single S	Plain
60–151–f	13	25/2	Double S	11	24.4/2	Double S	Plain
60–151–g	16	48.6/2	Double S	10	28.6/2	Double S	Plain
White cloth. True selvedge.							
60–151–h	23	87.6/2	Double S	17	58.2/2	Double S	Plain
60–151–i			Double S				
Ball of thread.							
60–151–j	17	45/2	Double S	13	22/2	Double S	Plain
60–151–l		40.6/2	Double S				
About 25 white yarns tied in middle.							
60–151–n		37.4/2	Double S				
Yarns.							
60–151–o	19	33.4/2	Double S	11	31.6/2	Double S	Plain
60–151–p	20	43.2/2	Double S	15	42/2	Double S	Plain
True selvedge.							
60–151–q		25.6/2	Double S			Double S	Plain
Selvedge(?) Weft passes over two warps in three rows. Yarn sewn round selvedge for strengthening. Sample too small to test.							
60–151–s			Single S				
Yarns.							
60–203–a	43	334/2	Double S	28	224/2	Double S	Plain
True selvedges on both sides of the cloth.							
60–203–c	21	51.2/2	Double S	14		Double S	Plain
True selvedge.							
61–11/3	17	21.6/2	Double S	14	20.8/2	Double S	Plain
61–11/3–a	19	29.4/2	Double S	11	28.8/2	Double S	Plain
61–19/1–d	20–30	27/2	Double S	7	26/2	Double S	Warp-rib effect
Part is woven more tightly (30 as against 20).							
61–19/1–f	16	20	Single S	14	19.8	Single S	Plain
61–23/1–c	16	19.3	Single S	15	13.8	Single S	Plain
True selvedge. It is folded and the hem is stitched.							
61–23/1–e	16	26.4/2	Double S	10	27.4/2	Double S	Plain
61–23/1–h	17	41/2	Double S	12	38/2	Double S	Plain
61–28/2	17	33.4/2	Double S	14	26.4/2	Double S	Plain
61–47/1–b	22–36	27.6/2	Double S	8		Double S	Warp-rib effect
Part is woven more tightly (36 as against 22).							
61–50/5	25	21.7	Single Z	12	8.3	Single Z	Plain
61–51/4	16	43/2	Double S	13	43.6/2	Double S	Plain
61–55/2–a	16	22/2	Double S	15	27.6/2	Double S	Plain
61–55/2–b	17	17.2/2	Double S	11	19.4/2	Double S	Plain
61–55/2–d	17	58.6/2	Double S	14	49/2	Double S	Plain
61–57/4	13	21/2	Double S	12	30/2	Double S	Plain
Selvedge: weft passes over two warps in two rows.							
61–94/5	16	31/2	Double S	13	32/2	Double S	Plain
60–200	25	44.4/2	Double S	15	27.2/2	Double S	Plain
True selvedge.							

Woollen Fabrics – Intermediate Stratum

Reg. No.	Warp				Weft				Weave
	colour	ends /cm.	count	twist	colour	picks /cm.	count	twist	
60–151–m	Black			Double Z 4-ply S					

Net(?) of double and 4-ply yarns. Apparently needlework. Threads pass first through other threads and then twirl round them.

Reg. No.	Warp				Weft				Weave
61–23/1–g	Yellow			Single S Double Z	Yellow				Plain

Two cloths sewn together. In bad condition.

Reg. No.	Warp				Weft				Weave
61–45/5	Green	12	20.6	Single S	Pink	20	17.6	Single S	Plain

Warp and weft are in different colours.

Reg. No.	Warp				Weft				Weave
61–49/6–b	Red	8–9	20	Single S	Red	16	16.8	Single S	Plain
61–55/2–c	Green	10	18.9	Single S	Green	16	12.5	Single S	Plain

Linen Fabrics – Bar-Kokhba Stratum

Reg. No.	Warp			Weft			Weave
	ends /cm.	count	twist	picks /cm.	count	twist	
60–3–c	14	24.2/2	Double S	12	26.2/2	Double S	Plain

True selvedge.

Reg. No.	ends /cm.	count	twist	picks /cm.	count	twist	Weave
60–3–d	17	17.6/2	Double S	9	22.2/2	Double S	Plain

True selvedge.

Reg. No.	ends /cm.	count	twist	picks /cm.	count	twist	Weave
60–3–e			Single Z Double S				

Rope.

Reg. No.	ends /cm.	count	twist	picks /cm.	count	twist	Weave
60–3–g	15	52.2/2	Double S	13	37.8/2	Double S	Plain
60–3–h	13	33.2/2	Double S	13	41.2/2	Double S	Plain
60–79–a	17	13.1	Single S	13–14	11.4	Single S	Plain
60–79–b	24	18	Single S	10	7.8	Single S	Basket 2 × 2

1/2 cm long hem on one side. Cloth sewn on the other side to prevent unravelling. A sewn corner is formed at the junction of the two sides.

Reg. No.	ends /cm.	count	twist	picks /cm.	count	twist	Weave
60–79–c	16	17.5	Single S	14	10.1	Single S	Plain

Plaited hem. Warps gathered and plaited.

Reg. No.	ends /cm.	count	twist	picks /cm.	count	twist	Weave
60–79–e	13	19.3	Single S	11	8.1	Single S	Basket 2 × 2
60–132–b	15	31/2	Double S	10	37.8/2	Double S	Plain
61–85/1–a		37.4/2	Double S			Double S	Plain

True selvedge sewn round with a brown yarn.

Woollen Fabrics – Bar-Kokhba Stratum

Reg. No.	Warp				Weft				Weave
	colour	ends /cm.	count	twist	colour	picks /cm.	count	twist	
60–79–d	Dark brown		18.1	Single S	Dark brown		19.8	Single S	Plain
60–79–f	Pink			Single S					

Two plaited ropes of three yarns, knotted together at one end.

A MATERIAL INVESTIGATION OF METAL OBJECTS
FROM THE NAḤAL MISHMAR TREASURE

R. POTASZKIN and K. BAR-AVI
The Metallurgical Service, Israel Military Industry

This investigation was carried out on two specimens, representative samples of groups of different types of objects:

Specimen A, mace-head No. 61–425, is a casting manufactured with care. Its surface is highly polished and has an excellent appearance. The colour is a bronze-like dark brown. The shape of the mace-head and its very uniform dimensions were obtained without the use of technologies requiring plastic deformation. It belongs to a group of items intended apparently for ceremonial or ornamental purposes (Photo 1).

Specimen B, chisel No. 61–137, is a forging whose shape, dimensional uniformity and surface quality are rather crude, of copper-like red colour. It is part of a collection of tools (Photo 2).

Preliminary examinations (X-rays, specific gravity measurement) showed that specimen A is a composite, consisting of a hollow metallic shell filled with ceramic matter, while specimen B is made of solid metal.

The chemical compositions (%) and densities of the two metals are:

Specimen	Cu	As	Ni	Ag	Si	Density
A	95.1	4.1	0.3	0.2	0.2	8.6
B	99.5	0.27	nil	nil	nil	8.9

Photo 1. Photo 2.

Photo 3.

Apart from these major constituents, the metal of A contains traces of lead and antimony and is almost free from zinc, iron and aluminium. The metal of B contains 0.07% iron and is virtually free from lead.

Hardness values, Vickers 5 Kg, were determined on the surfaces and at several cross-sections of the metallic parts:

Specimen	Surface	Section
A	70–90	45–65
B	75–90	40–50

Some results of the metallographic examinations are shown in Photos 4 and 5 for A and in Photos 6 and 7 for B.

It is evident that specimen A has a definitely dendritic microstructure, typical of castings, while the structure of specimen B is polyhedric and recrystallized, characteristic for wrought products.

The ceramic filling of specimen A has the following approximate composition (%): Ca-carbonate 57, anhydrite 8, silica 10, iron oxides 3.5, alumina 7.5, free carbon 1.5. Its density is 2.3.

The material distribution between metallic shell and ceramic core in specimen A is shown in Photo 3. The central channel of the mace-head, for the introduction of a handle, has a raw and unpolished surface, ruptured at several places. At two diametrically opposite locations, approximately at mid-height of the object, there are circular perforations of the channel wall through which the ceramic core emerges, and in their centres are located round holes. The convex outer shell-wall is obviously much thicker than the straight channel wall. The

physical soundness both of the metal casting and of the ceramic filling is fairly good. While there are numerous clusters of pores and blow-holes of various sizes, none of them reaches the surface, which has an unblemished appearance.

The following remarks and conjectures are based on the foregoing facts and on the examination results:

Specimen A

It is highly probable that it was manufactured, in sizeable series, by the lost-wax investment casting process, using as core material a refractory mixture of oxides with charcoal, which on burning and volatilizing, permitted ventilation for the escape of entrapped gases. This approach, not dissimilar to present-day techniques, was fairly successful, as evidenced by the sound quality of the product. The original ceramic core consisted of a toroidal part, which remained intact and permanently enclosed in the metallic shell, and a cylindrical section, to provide the central channel. Both parts, the toroid and the cylinder, were linked by a circular beam, reinforced by a rigid piece of wood or bone, which burned on contact with the molten metal, leaving a hole at its original location in the ceramic mass. The precise circular shape of the core may have been obtained on a potter's wheel. This complex core was probably coated with wax to the desired thickness and shape, and around it the outer clay mould was kneaded and then hardened by firing. At this stage the wax pattern was melted out and the mould cavity became ready for teeming. After solidification of the casting, the outer moulding and the central cylinder of the core were removed, leaving the

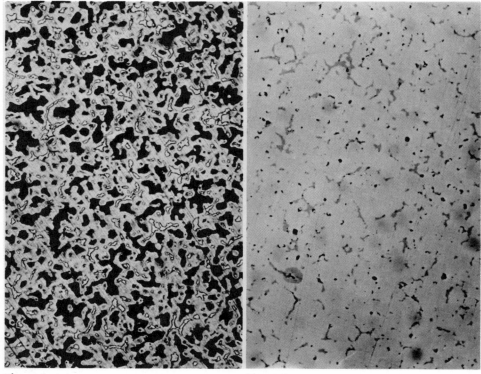

Photo 4.   Photo 5.

final product, whose outer surface appearance was then improved by grinding and polishing.

The alloy employed in this casting is essentially copper, found in many or most of the objects of the group from which specimen A was sampled. The presence of arsenic, which appears in the present instance at a concentration of about 4%, is technologically favourable for several reasons: it lowers temperatures for melting and casting and also improves the fluidity of the rather viscous copper melt and thus allows the easy filling of narrow spaces; it is an energetic reducing agent, removing oxides from the melt, and it therefore improves the soundness of the casting and makes it possible to obtain clean, unblemished surfaces by polishing. Nothing can of course be said about the origin of the arsenic in the alloy, whether it was added intentionally during melting, or was due to the impurity of the copper ores employed in particular batches of manufacture.

The motivation of the ancient craftsman who used an extremely intricate technology to obtain hollow bodies is shrouded in mystery. Material scarcity does not seem very satisfactory as an explanation, since the saving of metal was not great and could hardly outweigh the enormous amount of labour required to build the necessary complex cores. Perhaps it was just art for art's sake, the pleasure of solving difficult problems or of impressing society. Whatever their motives, these artisans had a definite sense of aesthetics and a feeling for regularity of shapes and smooth surfaces, which brought them to raise their final product to an impressive degree of perfection.

Specimen B

This is a solid piece of unalloyed copper, whose mediocre cleanliness and soundness reflect the state of the craft at that time. It is a forging, probably obtained by cold hammering, finished by a softening anneal at approximately 600 C. The surface is untouched by any process meant to improve its appearance. However, while the shape and appearance are purely functional, the heat treatment applied as a final manufacturing process defeats its own end, as it reduces considerably the usefulness of the tool by destroying the original hardness obtained by cold-working. It is unlikely that the tool-makers were unaware of this softening effect, but probably in this instance too, there may have been other considerations which motivated the application of a superfluous and damaging step to the manufacturing process. Of course, other explanations could also be offered: the tools having been exposed at one time of their long existence to accidental heat, by a firestorm or some other source, or perhaps even the possibility of spontaneous recrystallization at relatively low temperatures during a period of more than 5000 years. So far metallurgical knowledge in this respect is incomplete.

It is evident that the two specimens examined reflect very different approaches in conception, the use of materials and in technology. This may be due to the existence of two different schools of craftsmen; one manufacturing ceremonial objects, and the other tools and the like. Alternatively, perhaps the two classes of objects were produced at different times and in different geographical areas.

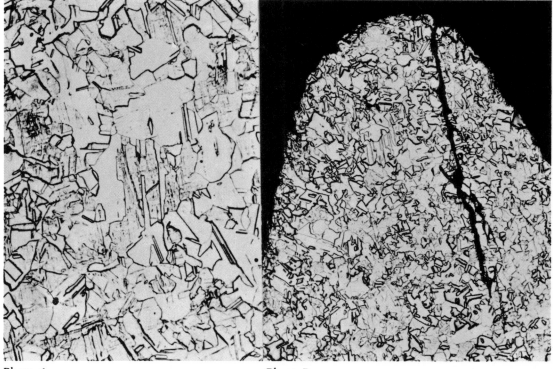

Photo 6.   Photo 7.

THE TRACE-ELEMENT COMPOSITION OF THE COPPER AND COPPER ALLOYS ARTIFACTS OF THE NAḤAL MISHMAR HOARD

C.A. KEY

Prehistory Department, Institute of Advanced Studies, Australian National University

The full results of trace element analyses of thirty artifacts from the Naḥal Mishmar Hoard and three related ones are presented. They are discussed because of their great age, approximately 5000 years (see above, p. 199), and the light they throw on the problem of early metallurgical techniques.

The artifacts analysed were chosen according to their shape and the colour of their tarnish, which ranged from yellowish born to dark brown. Few artifacts other than the tools of the hoard had the reddish-brown tarnish of copper, but two specimens, Nos. 54 and 404, a standard and a mace-head, were included in the analysis to make up a representative sample. Three groups of artifacts were analysed, consisting of eleven mace-heads, eleven standards and eight tools. The Director of the Department of Antiquities placed three similar objects from other sites at our disposal for comparison. These were a mace-head and an axe, found in a cave in Naḥal Ṣe'elim by Aharoni (1961, p. 14) and a standard fragment excavated at Tell Abu Matar by Perrot (1955, p. 172, Fig. 20).

Full chemical analyses were not attempted, and only optical spectrographic determinations were made. These were carried out by the author in the spectrographic laboratory of the Geological Survey of Israel by kind permission of the Director, Prof. Y.K. Bentor.

The following elements were determined: Arsenic (As); Antimony (Sb); Silver (Ag); Bismuth (Bi); Lead (Pb); Nickel (Ni); while Tin, Zinc and Cobalt were looked for but not found to be present in any of the objects examined. These elements are those most likely to be of use in making comparisons between the composition of the manufactured object and that of the original ore, if ever found. Furthermore there are certain known geochemical relationships which can help to decide which ores were used.

The following apparatus and working conditions were used:

Apparatus — Hilger-Watts large Littrow automatic quartz/glass spectrograph.
Excitation — Hilger high voltage condensed spark unit.
Wave-length range — 2470–3500 A.
Slit width — .02 mm.
Optics — Spark-image focussed on a diaphragm, then on the collimating lens of the spectrograph, with a seven-step sector interposed.

Upper electrode — "National Spectrographic" graphite, regular grade.
Lower electrode — The specimen.
Spark — .03 mh., 15 KV, condensed spark.
Spark-gap — 2 mm.
Exposure time — 60 seconds.
Plates — Kodak 103–0, developed in the usual manner.

The following lines were read, using the Hilger non-recording photo-electric micro-photometer:

Antimony	Sb	2598.3
Lead	Pb	2833.0
Tin	Sn	2839.9
Arsenic	As	2860.4
Copper	Cu	2961.1
Bismuth	Bi	3067.7
Zinc	Zn	3345.9
Silver	Ag	3382.8
Nickel	Ni	3414.7

Cu 2961 was used as a variable internal standard to help even out the effects of the fluctuation in the spark-gap distance which had to be adjusted manually.

The remarkable state of preservation of the artifacts allowed the use of a simple high-voltage spark spectrographic analysis technique. The tarnished surface selected for the burn could be lightly sandpapered to clean it of accumulated grime, since the artifacts were not corroded. A test was then carried out on an artifact to determine whether there was much variation of composition at the surface. One of the mace-heads which had been sawn in half for metallurgical examination was subjected to twenty-four detailed analyses, with burns made on both the outside surface as well as on the fresh saw-cut. The results of this examination were then compared with those obtained from four selected standard samples, on which the relative deviations had been determined for the elements sought. The variations from burn to burn on the cut specimen fell within the limit set by the examination of the standard samples.

The overall precision of the analytical results was determined by taking the results of duplicate burns and calculating the relative deviation of the % difference from the mean for each element. These are As – 8.5; Sb – 6.9; Ag – 10.2; Bi – 9.0; Pb 12.0; Ni – 4.7. The limits

TABLE

Specimen Number	As %	Sb %	Ag %	Bi %	Pb %	Ni %
Naḥal Mishmar						
mace-heads						
61–300	4.10	0.250	0.111	0.013	0.080	0.310
61–108	8.60	0.400	0.164	0.016	0.053	0.690
61–131	9.20	0.865	0.144	0.010	0.256	0.218
61–133	7.40	0.705	0.228	0.015	0.101	0.475
61–226	6.90	0.599	0.160	0.025	0.072	0.840
61–231	7.20	0.400	0.108	0.009	0.185	0.605
61–252	1.90	0.098	0.052	0.012	0.091	0.630
61–278	6.50	0.204	0.007	0.001	–	1.350
61–311	6.60	0.580	0.081	0.020	0.320	0.590
61–351	3.50	0.178	0.123	0.001	0.034	0.170
61–426	<1.90	0.025	0.022	0.001	0.054	0.159
standards						
61–2	2.80	0.193	0.077	0.017	0.660	0.282
61–18	3.10	0.390	0.161	0.010	0.215	0.114
61–35	9.60	0.139	0.052	0.002	0.050	>3.00
61–40	<1.90	0.093	0.077	0.003	2.370	0.120
61–48	7.80	0.583	0.206	0.019	2.370	0.120
61–52	–	–	–	–	–	–
61–58	<1.90	0.110	0.047	0.030	–	0.109
61–65	8.00	0.525	0.121	0.005	0.150	0.215
61–86	4.70	0.560	0.138	0.011	0.730	0.198
61–104	–	–	–	–	–	0.098
61–121	11.90	0.609	0.210	0.024	0.039	1.220
tools						
61–135	–	–	0.026	–	–	–
61–141	–	–	–	–	–	–
61–142	–	–	tr.	–	–	0.119
61–144	–	–	–	–	–	–
61–147	1.92	tr.	0.010	–	–	–
61–148	–	–	0.042	–	–	1.90
61–149	–	–	–	–	–	–
61–150	–	–	0.021	–	–	–
Naḥal Ṣe'elim						
mace-head	4.60	0.280	0.112	0.010	0.085	0.340
axe	tr.	0.006	0.028	0.003	–	0.500
Tell Abu Matar						
standard	>12.00	0.715	0.258	0.042	tr.	0.048
Limits of Detection	1.90	0.005	0.005	0.001	0.030	0.010

a dash – = element not detected

tr.   = trace only

of detection were: As, 1.9%; Sb, .005%; Ag, .005%; Bi, .001%; Pb, .003%; Ni, .010%.

The table on p. 237 shows the results of all the analyses. The results of the trace element analyses of the copper arsenic alloy ornaments are graphically presented on logarithmic scales in Figs. 1–6.

The tools, with the exception of No. 166 (Reg. No. 61–147), which because of its polished surface is considered to be an ornament, are all copper with only silver and, sometimes, nickel, such as can be found in native copper. These copper tools seem to be the products of a different technology; it may be that there were two kinds of workshops — one for secular and one for ritual objects. It may be that native copper was used and that the tools were forged into shape. If, on the other hand, they were cast, it may mean that the toolmakers had not had experience of the hardening effect which the addition of arsenic would impart and that the tools pre-date the ornaments.

There is one standard made of pure copper, No. 80 (Reg. No. 61–52). This specimen is not as well finished as the others. No attempt has been made to polish it; this may well be due to the fact that the casting went awry. The molten copper does not seem to have reached the top of the mould before it solidified and a ragged bottom, instead of the flanged bottom, resulted.

In this case the craftsman knew of the casting process but used pure copper which did not wet the mould as well as an arsenical copper melt would have done. It may be that he used the pure metal of other older tools which were kept as a supply of copper. Alternatively he experimented with the green copper carbonate ores found in the Naḥal Aravah at Punon or further south near the Gulf of Eilat. He certainly did not use the nodular copper sulphide ore of the Nubian sandstones. These nodules were shown to contain zinc by Slatkine (1961, p. 294); and slags from Timna and Naḥal Aravah analysed by the author were also found to contain a fair proportion of zinc. It is therefore certain that neither the other analysed objects nor the tools were manufactured from the local copper sulphide ore which contains zinc. They could have been made from the local copper carbonate ores with an admixture of arsenic or arsenic-sulphide ore. However, this seems unlikely, as it would mean that the local copper-sulphide ore had been deliberately rejected, although the trace-element association points to the use of other sulphide ores.

We can now consider how and from what raw material the other objects are made. It must be immediately apparent from the shape and twisted horns on some of them that even at this very early date a cire-perdue process was used to cast the standards. One of the mace-heads had a clay core which also points to casting. This advanced method of manufacture was possible at this early date because the craftsmen used an arsenical copper melt. It may well have been the first step in the process which later produced the ubiquitous tin-bronzes.

The results of the trace-element analyses of the ornaments show that an arsenical copper melt produced from sulphide ores was used, and the evidence for this is now presented. Fig. 1 consists of histograms showing the relative frequencies of the amounts of arsenic, silver, nickel and lead, in the ritual objects from Naḥal Mishmar, Beersheba and Naḥal Ṣe'elim. The first three histograms show a family relationship, and we can conclude that all the articles were manufactured by the same rough process and from the same raw material. The lead-content is more variable and this is probably due to accidental admixture of lead or lead ore to the individual melts.

Figs. 2, 3 and 5 show that there are more or less direct relationships between the amounts of arsenic, antimony, silver and bismuth contained in the artifacts. This can only be accounted for by the fact that copper arsenides such as algodonite (for list of minerals and their formulae see below) and domeykite, together with the silver and nickel arsenides, were used as part of the raw material. The variability in the amounts of these

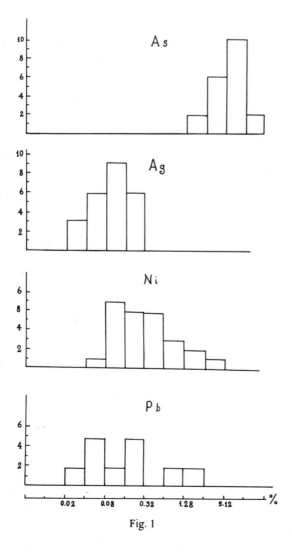

Fig. 1

elements as seen in the histograms may be due to a haphazard admixture of another ore such as enargite or tennantite or even chalcopyrite. The antimony content could be accounted for by isomorphous replacement of As by Sb in tennantite or by an admixture of tetrahedrite, bournonite or stibnite. Furthermore such arsenide-antimonide deposits rarely carry tin or zinc.

Figure 4 shows that there is no connection between arsenic and the nickel content. This may be due to one or other of several factors, such as occasional admixture of gersdorffite or pentlandite or bad sorting of ores.

Fig. 6 shows that there is no relationship between the amounts of silver and lead contained in the alloy. The occasional fairly large amounts of lead may be due to an admixture of scraps of metallic lead from the workshop. Metallic lead was in use and several of the artifacts have casting defects repaired with lead. A qualitative analysis showed this lead to have the expected impurities — silver and bismuth. Addition of a grey metallic mineral may have led to occasional mistakes when the grey metallic galena, lead sulphide ore, or the very similar gersdorffite, a nickel sulpharsenate, was added. Such mistaken additions offer the best explanation for the occasional higher lead and nickel content in the artifacts of this hoard.

From Dana's Textbook of Mineralogy (1932, p. 390), amongst others, we learn that the major sources of copper are those which contain the copper sulphide ores, chalcopyrite, chalcocite and bornite as well as other copper and iron-bearing sulphide minerals. From the descriptive mineralogical part of the book we can also cull the thirty or so copper, nickel, lead, arsenic, zinc and tin minerals which between them account for the bulk of the trace elements found in ancient copper-alloy artifacts. With the exception of the tin and zinc minerals, these are often very similar in appearance, intergrown, and there may be substitution of one metal by another in the actual crystals.

These minerals may be divided into three groups, according to their appearance. There are those that are brightly coloured, those that have a metallic lustre and the third group which is vitreous in appearance. The more important of these are listed below. In many cases certain combinations of these ore minerals are found together. These combinations are due to the physicochemical conditions under which the ore deposits are emplaced. Here it suffices to say that high hydrothermal copper deposits which carry sphalerite, the zinc sulphide mineral, do not usually contain arsenical copper sulphides, these being found in hydrothermal veins intruded at lower temperatures (Goldschmidt, 1954, p. 181).

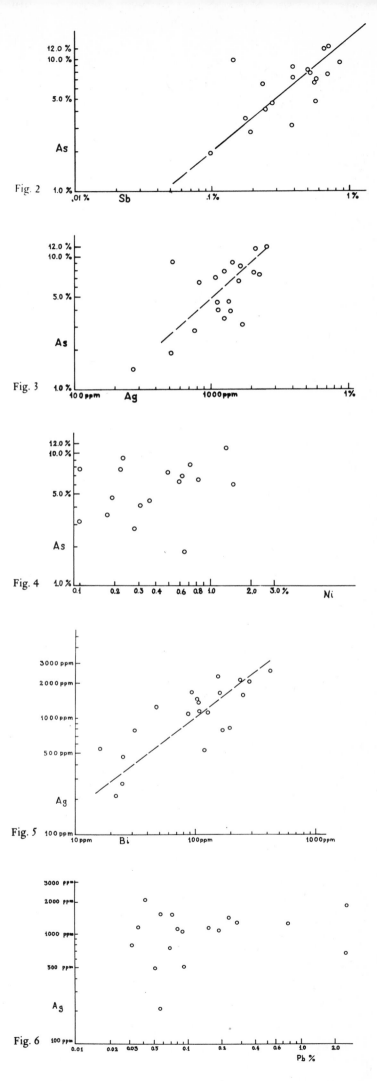

The commonly occurring brightly coloured ore-minerals are:

Malachite $CuCO_3 Cu(OH)_2$, green
Azurite $2CuCO_3 Cu(OH)_2$, blue
Realgar AsS, red
Orpiment As_2S_3, yellow

Copper oxide CuO sometimes occurs as a reddish earthy ore.

The minerals with a metallic lustre, as distinct from the native metals gold, silver, copper, arsenic and bismuth, include most of the sulphide minerals. These can further be divided into two groups, those with a yellowish and those with a greyish metallic lustre.

The yellowish metallic appearance is common to the following ore minerals:

Chalcopyrite	$Cu_2 S.Fe_2 S_3$
Bornite	$5 Cu_2 S.Fe_2 S_3$
Pyrite	$Fe S_2$
Pentlandite	$(Fe Ni)S$

The more important tin-white, steel-grey to black minerals with metallic lustre are:

Chalcocite	$Cu_2 S$
Enargite	$3 Cu_2 S.As_2 S$
Tennantite	$3 Cu S As_2 S_3$
Tetrahedrite	$3 Cu S Sb_2 S_3$
Bournonite	$2 Pb S. Cu_2 S. Sb_2 S_3$
Galena	$Pb S$
Arsenopyrite	$Fe S_2 Fe As_2$
Cobaltite	$Co S_2 Co As_2$
Gersdorffite	$Ni S_2 Ni As_2$
Stibnite	$Sb_2 S_3$
Bismuthite	$Bi_2 S_3$
Argentite	$Ag S$
Domeykite	$Cu_3 As$
Algodonite	$Cu_6 As$

Lastly we have a few important ore minerals which are vitreous in appearance. These are:

Sphalerite	$Zn_2 S$
Cassiterite	$Sn O_2$
Calamine	$Zn OH_2.SiO_3$
Smithsonite	$Zn CO_3$
Cerrusite	$Pb CO_3$

With these descriptions in mind we can formulate a new hypothesis for the development of metallurgy in the Middle East.

The earliest copper artifacts at Çatal Hüyük occur in level IX soon after 6500 B.C.E. (Mellaart, 1964, p. 111). These may be presumed to be native copper. Then in levels VII and VI, more precisely dated at 6200 and about 5800 B.C.E. respectively, we find lead beads and azurite, the bright blue copper carbonate, used in burial rites. This indicates that at Çatal Hüyük, the metallic lustre of galena and/or lead, and the vivid colour of azurite, were attracting the attention of the population. Now it needed only the chance discovery of the yellow copper sulphide ores with their metallic lustre before these too were treated the same way as the galena and the first molten copper was produced. It cannot have taken long before it was discovered that both the pretty green or blue copper carbonates merely formed a veneer on the weathered outcrops of sulphide ore bodies.

The trace element association in the objects of the Naḥal Mishmar hoard shows that the craftsmen had learned to use sulphide ores, which needed roasting before smelting. As against the date of about 1500 B.C.E. assumed by Forbes (1955, p. 575), Wertime (1964, p. 1260) proposes an earlier date of 3000 B.C.E. for copper sulphide ore smelting in association with the oxide and carbonate ores, but implies that the reduction of sulphide ores came later, possibly around 2000 B.C.E. at Ergani in Central Anatolia. However, he also thinks that galena, the lead sulphide ore, may have been used to produce lead at an unknown earlier date. This is indeed the case, because the objects discussed here actually have casting defects repaired with fairly pure lead.

If we postulate that at the start sulphide and oxide or carbonate ore were roasted and smelted together, then it is possible that the other bright pigments, orpiment and realgar, were also used. This could account for the relatively high arsenic content of artifacts such as the ones discussed here. On the other hand our craftsmen may have chanced on an ore-body containing mostly enargite, a sulpharsenate of copper, or the arsenates domeykite and algodonite, and such deposits are known to exist in Azerbaijan (Grigoryan, 1962, p. 388). It is also likely that an ordinary copper sulphide ore, with an addition of arsenopyrite, produced the arsenical copper alloy. However, it must have become apparent relatively early that the fumes produced from arsenical melts were deadly in effect and efforts must have been made to find another metalliferous ore to mix into the copper melt. That the practice of using arsenical copper melts was continued into the Early and Middle Bronze Age in the Caucasus is shown by the analyses of Selimkhanov (1962, p. 77). The analyses quoted by Moorey (1964, p. 72) show that besides arsenic other metals such as lead, tin and perhaps zinc came to be used at later dates in Luristan from between the second half of the third to the middle of the first millennium B.C.E.

Once the discovery was made that such additions not only lowered the temperature of the melt but also that it became more free-flowing, it is understandable that different additions were made in places where one or other of the familiar minerals was absent. Only at a later date did the vitreous crystalline metallic ores such as cassiterite, the tin oxide, and still later, calamine, the zinc ore, become known as possible additives to the copper sulphide ores.

In conclusion it may be said that the Naḥal Mishmar hoard is the earliest dated collection of objects made by the cire-perdue method. It is certain that the craftsmen used an arsenical copper melt made from sulphide ores, which lacked zinc as a trace element. They therefore could not have used the copper ores from Sinai, Israel, Syria or Cyprus (Bear, *personal commun.*), which do contain zinc, and where arsenical ores are unknown. The most likely source of the ore is Armenia or Azerbaijan where there are known deposits of arsenical copper ores and where these continued in use in the Bronze Age, when Anatolian craftsmen were already using tin-bronzes.

Finally I would like to thank Mr. P. Bar-Adon and Prof. Y.K. Bentor in Israel and Messrs. W. Ambrose and I. Glover from Canberra for their comments and criticism.

BIBLIOGRAPHY

Aharoni, Y.   1961   The Expedition to the Judean Desert, 1960, *IEJ* 11, p. 14.

Bear, L.   1963   Director Geological Survey, Cyprus: unpublished analyses of the Cyprus ores.

Dana, E.S.   1932   *A Textbook of Mineralogy*, Revd. W.E. Ford, 4th ed., New York.

Forbes, R.J.   1954   Extracting, Smelting and Alloying in Singer, C., Holmyard, E.J., Hall, A.R., eds., *A History of Technology*, p. 575, Oxford.

Goldschmidt, V.M.   1954   *Geochemistry*, Ed. A. Muir, Oxford.

Grigoryan, G.O.   1962   *Geochemistry U.S.R.R*, English transl., No. 4, p. 388.

Lucas, A., and   1962   *Ancient Egyptian Materials and Industries*,
Harris, J.R.   4th ed., p. 223, London.

Mellaart, J.   1964   Excavations at Çatal Hüyük, 3rd Preliminary Report, 1963, *Anatolian Studies*, 14, p. 111.

Moorey, P.R.S.   1964   An interim report on some analyses of Luristan Bronzes, *Archaeometry*, 7, p. 75.

Perrot, J.   1955   The excavations at Tell Abu Matar near Beersheva III, *IEJ* 5, p. 172, Fig. 20.

Selimkhanov, I.R.   1962   Spectral Analysis of Metallic Articles from Archaeological Monuments of the Caucasus U.S.S.R. *Proceedings Prehistoric Society*, 28, p. 68.

Slatkine, A.   1961   Nodules Cuprifères du Neguev Méridional (Israel), *Bull. Res. Council Israel*, 10G, p. 294.

Wertime, T.A.   1964   Man's first encounter with metallurgy, *Science*, 146, No. 3649, p. 1260.